# Microsoft SharePoint 2013: Planning for Adoption and Governance

Geoff Evelyn

Published with the authorization of Microsoft Corporation by:
O'Reilly Media, Inc.
1005 Gravenstein Highway North
Sebastopol, California 95472



ISBN: 978-0-7356-7164-5

1 2 3 4 5 6 7 8 9 LSI 8 7 6 5 4 3

Printed and bound in the United States of America.

Microsoft Press books are available through booksellers and distributors worldwide. If you need support related to this book, email Microsoft Press Book Support at *mspinput@microsoft.com*. Please tell us what you think of this book at *http://www.microsoft.com/learning/booksurvey*.



**Acquisitions & Developmental Editor:** Kenyon Brown

**Production Editor:** Christopher Hearse

**Editorial Production:** S4Carlisle Publishing Services

**Technical Reviewer:** William Pitts

**Indexer:** Ellen Troutman Zaig

**Cover Design:** Twist Creative • Seattle

**Cover Composition:** Ellie Volckhausen

**Illustrator:** S4Carlisle Publishing Services

# Contents at a glance

# Contents

# Introduction

Microsoft SharePoint is a strategic business platform that allows people to connect seamlessly with each other in terms of centralized content management. Furthermore, as a collaborative tool, SharePoint can be used by anyone, and can be installed and configured very quickly.

The simplicity of provisioning SharePoint in this way, however, leads to issues where a business does not have the opportunity to define a SharePoint strategy, because it might not be aware there are practical and structured techniques for building, managing, and delivering SharePoint solutions. This lack of information is also compounded because SharePoint may have been provisioned through an IT project, with little to no business interaction. In IT projects, service delivery is not often seen as a priority. This often leads to issues concerning ownership, which can negatively affect User Adoption. Therefore, without the business taking ownership of the SharePoint solutions, the result is usually failures with regards to User Adoption, Governance, training, and communications.

## Service delivery encompasses User Adoption and Governance

Successful SharePoint service delivery means understanding, defining, and maintaining business ownership of SharePoint solutions. Through service delivery processes, you will be able to do the following:

- Define the content of services clearly
- Define the roles and responsibilities of customers (those who pay for the services), users, and service providers clearly
- Set expectations of service quality, availability, and timeliness
- Sustain User Adoption and Governance

In my years spent working in SharePoint service delivery, I have witnessed and been a part of SharePoint delivery successes and failures. Some of these failures were due to the business not being able to convince their audience of the value of SharePoint solutions; others were due to User Adoption or training strategies not being included as part of providing a SharePoint solution.

The success of any SharePoint solution relies on a successful User Adoption strategy. User Adoption involves a cultural shift because there may be changes to the processes and procedures that people use when a new SharePoint solution is being provided. And those changes are supposed to improve user productivity and increase return on investment (ROI), or there would be no point in providing the SharePoint solution. However, User Adoption is not simply a technical transition from one system or process into a new system or process. The success of User Adoption is measured by the ability of the users being able to use the replacement comfortably. The replacement system must be governed and supported, meaning that User Adoption, Governance, and support must be sustained throughout the lifetime of the replacement (which is called a *SharePoint solution* in this book).

Successful User Adoption requires a sequenced set of events to work; for example, the creation of a delivery program that encompasses the creation of a SharePoint solution and will include various projects to create a service delivery model: Governance, policy, User Adoption, training, administration, and licensing. Therefore, a phased approach is required.

User Adoption is the key to ROI with SharePoint. Achieving results requires an approach for gaining executive sponsorship and user buy-in. Strong User Adoption goes beyond traditional change management, and you should never underestimate the impact that User Adoption can have on any SharePoint solutions provided.

Essentially, in order for User Adoption to work, you need to consider how SharePoint is going to be provided to the customers. While these are covered in detail in the book, here is a summary of the required points:

- **Carry out customer intelligence.** You must truly define the customer base. Identify the SharePoint sponsor, the stakeholders, and the user audience. Identity what they need and expect from the SharePoint delivery team. Ensure that you can provide a way to measure how the delivery team is doing in meeting customer requirements.
- **Value your SharePoint support services.** The key to delivering great service is people, not the organization. Some SharePoint support services are delivered by empowering their support team to be proactive and be flexible.
- **Understand how customers think.** Part of a method in sustaining User Adoption is to test for the emotional elements of the user experience concerning using SharePoint. Proactively surveying users means plugging into their experiences and resolving issues before the relationship between the customer and those providing the solution to the customer breaks down.
- **Ensure that your SharePoint sponsor believes in SharePoint service delivery.** If the SharePoint sponsor does not believe in service excellence, it won't happen.

The SharePoint sponsor needs to take service delivery seriously.

- **Ensure that User Adoption strategy is aligned with SharePoint support.** SharePoint support excellence is a function of how the organization is designed. Its key elements shape the user experience, and its effectiveness influences the success of User Adoption. This is particularly obvious in the area of customer complaints. How are complaints handled? Are they treated as a priority and sorted according to urgency, or are they chucked in a pile, to be dealt with as and when possible?
- **Make a concrete link to the bottom line.** Good SharePoint service delivery ensures that users who have a great experience are more likely to continue to use SharePoint and more likely to recommend SharePoint to others.
- **Improve services continually.** Sustained User Adoption and Governance come from managing training models, which in turn drives user continuous improvement. Do not settle for a set level of service, even if you think it's good. Even if users are satisfied with service, maybe it could still be improved.
- **Understand that the future will be different.** Technology is changing the way that service is delivered all the time. Failing to grasp the opportunities and threats presented by this inevitability could lead to failure.
- **Learn from your mistakes.** Everybody makes mistakes, but winners learn from them. Advocate a willingness to change and develop your service delivery strategies based on feedback from your users.
- **Make things easier for customers.** Continually use communication channels and User Adoption tactics to identify agile, flexible solutions. Create structured delivery plans so that you do not present unclear pricing, long delivery times, insufficient information, and poor support and service.

## Governance provides business ownership

In my last book, *Managing and Implementing Microsoft SharePoint 2010 Projects,* I devoted a chapter to Governance, and it dealt with what methods should be applied to the development, control, and steering of SharePoint so that the platform appears to information workers to be fully managed and has a coherent service strategy.

**More Info** For more information concerning *Managing and Implementing Microsoft SharePoint 2010 Projects*, visit *http://aka.ms/SP2010Projects/details*.

Over the years, SharePoint Governance has focused on how to manage the SharePoint environment. From a User Adoption perspective, this is critical. Governance underpins the most atomic elements of any business through the creation, management, and enforcement of business rules and policies. Capturing and standardizing the most fundamental of such rules—definitions and their relationships—are necessary for supporting the complex operations of any business. As such, standardization of business rules is a core element of the automated infrastructure of any enterprise. Businesses are challenged with quantifying the ROI of such endeavors in order to make sound, risk-aware business decisions. By using key business experts to understand the concrete benefits of Governance, the organization can understand the costs, benefits, and risks of business rule standardization and has made sound decisions on how to implement the standardization effort.

This book focuses on platform Governance, which defines the rules helping SharePoint solutions scale and grow. This Governance model includes not only the physical makeup of SharePoint and technical management; it includes all facets of SharePoint configuration management, the delivery of SharePoint to meet business performance objectives, and the lifecycle of the SharePoint environment, site, or component.

As discussed in depth in this book, this kind of Governance requires a shift from the perception that IT is responsible for deciding how to make business productivity more efficient. Platform Governance requires the combined strengths of the business and IT to determine the business decisions concerning the administration of SharePoint, a statement of what SharePoint will be used for, and policies concerning service areas of the SharePoint platform.

## Who this book is for

Writing a book detailing how to deliver a SharePoint solution is definitely not easy, and I chose not to go into any detail on any particular solution. This is because there are many levels of delivery, ranging from "I only want an evaluation done" to "I want a full-featured SharePoint 2013 presence." The book is aimed at those wishing to deliver any SharePoint solution, whether it is specific site solution or a complete farm solution. Therefore, this book will:

- Be a source of information that will help you implement a SharePoint presence for your organization
- Be a source of forms, procedures that will help your SharePoint project meet and exceed customer expectations and requirements
- Help you create a SharePoint delivery plan
- Help you create a Governance-aligned User Adoption strategy
- Help you create training and communication plans

## What this book is not for

This book is not a technical guide to building SharePoint On-Premise environments or Office 365–hosted environments. This book is not a cookbook of development/third-party recipes. Furthermore, this book does not provide step-by-step instructions on how to install or complete tasks by using SharePoint 2013 or provide an in-depth coverage or analysis of the new functions. For that level of detail, consult the following books:

- *Microsoft SharePoint 2013 Plain & Simple,* by Johnathan Lightfoot, Michelle Lopez, and Scott Metker, which is aimed at users who are new to SharePoint.
- *Microsoft SharePoint 2013 Step by Step,* by Olga Londer and Penelope Coventry, which is aimed at new and intermediate SharePoint users.
- *Microsoft SharePoint 2013 Inside Out,* by Darvish Shadravan, Penelope Coventry, Tom Resing, and Christine Wheeler, which is aimed at intermediate and advanced power users (who are also referred to as *citizens* or *consumer developers*). This book is also aimed at project managers, business analysts, and small-business technicians.
- *Microsoft SharePoint 2013 App Development,* by Scot Hillier and Ted Pattison, which is aimed at professional developers.
- *Microsoft SharePoint 2013: Designing and Architecting Solutions,* by Shannon Bray, Miguel Wood, and Patrick Curran, which is aimed at IT architects.

## Assumptions about you

At the risk of trying to be all things to all people, I have aimed this book at anybody who is involved with providing SharePoint solutions to users. This book is for those who wish to create a SharePoint delivery program that will encompass User Adoption and Governance, for the delivery manager wishing to deliver a SharePoint solution, for the business analyst who needs to understand adoption tactics, for an organization in need of understanding what it takes to get SharePoint solutions, for those who are considering a career move into SharePoint, and for those potential and existing SharePoint sponsors who wonder what it means to deliver SharePoint solutions.

However, this is not a book aimed at the technologist. That said, there are some SharePoint 2013 concepts discussed in this book that will be useful to the technical audience. Knowledge of the SharePoint 2013 concepts in this book will help you understand and apply practical techniques, to help you build (or be part of) a cohesive, repeatable, and measurable SharePoint delivery program. Knowledge of SharePoint, while useful, is not a prerequisite; however, be aware that in order to deliver a SharePoint solution, you should know something about SharePoint concepts, some of which are described in this book, or you understand the required skill sets to deliver successful SharePoint solutions (also described in this book).

## Organization of this book

This book is intended as a practical guide. The content is largely gleaned from my own experience of many years in IT and SharePoint. A large bulk has come from service delivery in IT and web-based systems, working in support capacities, defining service delivery, User Adoption tactics, and more.

### Chapter 1: Aligning organizational goals and requirements

In any organization, workers represent the biggest line-item expense and the most valuable asset. Therefore, providing SharePoint to meet their collaborative challenges and ensuring productivity in using the platform ultimately affect an organization's profitability. This is because worker productivity and potential is measured against the successful delivery of whatever SharePoint solution that is going to be put in place. Aligning organizational goals and requirements for delivering SharePoint solutions is vital. Without doing this, you will not be able to quantify the value that SharePoint brings, and you will not be able to bridge the gap between technology and the business. Understanding your goals and requirements allows you to obtain better insight and perspectives, which will help you and the business to make decisions confidently. This then allows the business to take full advantage of the investment. This chapter will help you learn how to use goal alignment methods, figure out measurable benefits, and create goals. You will also learn about creating a performance review facility using SharePoint.

## Chapter 2: Defining the SharePoint solution scope

This chapter explains the steps needed to set up a SharePoint delivery program and how to ensure that you can control the implementation of SharePoint solutions (which are listed as delivery items in the program). Setting up a SharePoint delivery program sets boundaries (called *scopes*) and includes initial investigations of what the delivery will achieve, who is going to do what, the schedule, controls, and managing your SharePoint team and stakeholders in an output known as a *business case*. You will learn how to create a learning and knowledge experience, create the delivery plan, and ensure that quality is defined and measurable for the SharePoint solution.

## Chapter 3: Planning SharePoint solution delivery

SharePoint solution delivery is a combination of providing the solution to meet user requirements and ensuring that users can adopt those solutions. This chapter covers the basics of planning solution delivery through plan formation, managing the outputs, and engaging sponsors and stakeholders. You will learn how to set up a SharePoint delivery team, prepare the delivery program plans, create controls, and engage the SharePoint sponsor and stakeholders.

## Chapter 4: Preparing SharePoint solution User Adoption

SharePoint User Adoption is all about perception, which involves the ability to map relevant business needs to SharePoint tools, the development of SharePoint champions, communication planning, training, and engaging sponsors and key stakeholders. User Adoption is not about features and technical components. User Adoption is the most critical factor in attaining SharePoint user ROI. It only occurs when SharePoint solutions are delivered in harmony with supporting organizational and behavioral change programs. This chapter will help you learn how to build SharePoint User Adoption strategies and get support from the SharePoint sponsor. You will learn how to build communication plans, create SharePoint sponsors, and standardize business needs. This chapter also goes into detail on the importance of solution ownership, training, SharePoint 2013 social networking features, how to extract value from SharePoint solution delivery, and Bring Your Own Device (BYOD) considerations.

## Chapter 5: Planning SharePoint Governance

SharePoint Governance is not a hardware, software, or human resource solution. It is an organizational strategy and methodology for documenting and implementing business rules and policies. It is the act of enforcing the use of policies. By enforcing policies, standards are created, and they are designed to protect the integrity of the SharePoint solution and platform. Governance brings cross-functional teams together to identify data issues that affect the company or organization. This chapter will help you address crucial areas of platform Governance and to use practical techniques to bring Governance to your SharePoint solution delivery program and the SharePoint platform. You will learn how to create a Governance committee and a SharePoint service model. You will learn practical techniques in creating a platform Governance model for SharePoint. Also covered are the requirements for creating rules, policies, and the training model, and how to use web analytics and auditing. You will also understand some considerations for consumerization and learn how to build a SharePoint Statement of Operations.

## Chapter 6: SharePoint delivery program considerations

Once a delivery program has been formed to deliver a SharePoint solution, it is important to ensure that key areas concerning SharePoint delivery are understood. Change management is vital because understanding that will help you deliver a solution meeting the required objectives on time and on budget. Managing information and search strategies are the two most important facets of SharePoint, and they must be addressed, as they relate directly to User Adoption and Governance. This chapter helps you understand the implications of provisioning SharePoint in geographically split locations. You will understand the importance of managing change, the importance of information architecture, search, key SharePoint 2013 concepts, and what makes up a SharePoint platform deployment document that describes the SharePoint platform.

## Chapter 7: Organizing SharePoint delivery resources

The road to SharePoint success is defined by the people who envision the design, those who create the design blueprint, and those who build the platform based on that blueprint. All of this needs to run like clockwork to meet schedules and budgets. All SharePoint delivery programs are significant undertakings that will require skilled people and material resources to be a success. The kind of solution that you are going to deliver will invariably dictate the kind of resources needed. This chapter describes those resources and their roles, so you can associate them with your delivery program. Topics include an overview of the delivery team so you can understand their roles and the importance of creating the terms of reference for team members.

## Chapter 8: Building a SharePoint service delivery model

There is nothing like a smoothly running SharePoint support environment. A high-quality support SharePoint environment helps foster great User Adoption and SharePoint champions. The key concept for sustained User Adoption and Governance comes from customer experience of the service, whose sole objective is to sustain customer satisfaction. That takes place in two ways: on a reactive basis, by solving user problems with provisioned SharePoint solutions; or on a proactive basis, by identifying better ways to improve customer experience. This chapter describes the importance of service delivery, how to create a SharePoint support service, and impacts on service delivery from compliance, legal, and cloud issues. The chapter also describes the importance of resiliency and availability of SharePoint solutions and their effects on service delivery.

## Chapter 9: Controlling the delivery program

SharePoint service delivery is not reliant on any particular traditional project planning methodology. That said, the SharePoint delivery manager must have an understanding of planning and control and be able to use SharePoint technical judgment. Controlling the delivery program requires good communication, both within the delivery team and across the organization. This chapter describes key areas of schedule planning, including report delivery and managing costs. In addition, the chapter describes risk and issue management, which is crucial to mitigating the impact of any problems.

## Chapter 10: SharePoint customization impacting User Adoption

Delivery of SharePoint solutions includes the understanding of the levels of customization. Technology commoditization is the rule of today's provision of apps to SharePoint 2013. This is the ability of third-party products to be packaged to allow users to deploy ready-made functionality into SharePoint easily, and to do this without developer or administrator interaction. This chapter focuses on the best practices surrounding the processes concerning the delivery of apps, when to decide customization is required, the various developer options, User Adoption impact, Governance impact, and finally the key to sustaining SharePoint support and training and documentation for any customizations. You will learn how to consider when SharePoint should and should not be customized, what kind of resources are required, what the User Adoption and Governance impacts are likely to be, and the documentation required.

### Chapter 11: Managing workshops and closing the delivery program

Workshops are extremely useful to any SharePoint delivery program. They act as an instructive process to guarantee SharePoint services. You need to have workshops to ask what the SharePoint sponsor and stakeholders need, and to understand the nature of the business to which the solution will be delivered. This chapter describes what constitutes project closure, who does it, and how it is communicated. The chapter also describes what should be done as the project is closed to ensure a handover of the SharePoint solution to the client.

### Chapter 12: Maintaining the solution

You must ensure that User Adoption, Governance, and support service strategies are sustained throughout the lifetime of the SharePoint solution. This chapter will help you understand how to do this. User Adoption is about changing user behavior, Governance is about enforcing business policies and rules, and support is about ensuring excellent service delivery to users and helping maintain user productivity. Therefore, the skills and methods used are not wholly technical or wholly business-oriented. They require a combination of skills and knowledge of how best to apply methods and use the practical techniques described.

## Acknowledgments

There are so many to individuals and groups to thank and praise: First and foremost, my greatest thanks go to my partner, Kaye, and my two daughters, Fifi and Skye; I am utterly blessed to have you in my life. The inspiration for this book came from them, and their support through the long evenings of writing was truly awesome! Thanks to Kenyon Brown and Kathryn Duggan, who did a fantastic job getting the book to production, Bill Pitts for his technical review, and Christopher Hearse in production. In addition, there are loads of people at O'Reilly behind the scenes involved, so many thanks to them also. Writing a book is never an easy task, and a good number of topics covered in this book would not have seen the light of day had it not been for technical aid and advice. Writing a SharePoint book requires a mass of information, and I have been privileged to network with and then build my knowledge to pen great SharePoint details. My thanks go to the SharePoint MVP group and the SharePoint product team, with too many members to mention them all individually (but I am no less grateful to all of you for that), and very special thanks to Ian McNeice, Duncan Hartwig, Matthais Mitze, and program members of the Institute of Analysts and Programmers and the Institute for Managing Information Systems.

## Support and feedback

The following sections provide information on errata, book support, feedback, and contact information.

### Errata

We've made every effort to ensure the accuracy of this book. Any errors that have been reported since this book was published are listed on our Microsoft Press site at oreilly.com:

*http://aka.ms/SP2013AdoptGov/errata*

If you find an error that is not already listed, you can report it to us through the same page.

If you need additional support, email Microsoft Press Book Support at mspinput@microsoft.com.

Please note that product support for Microsoft software is not offered through the addresses above.

### We want to hear from you

At Microsoft Press, your satisfaction is our top priority, and your feedback our most valuable asset. Please tell us what you think of this book at:

*http://www.microsoft.com/learning/booksurvey*

The survey is short, and we read every one of your comments and ideas. Thanks in advance for your input!

### Stay in touch

Let's keep the conversation going! We're on Twitter: *http://twitter.com/MicrosoftPress.*

CHAPTER 1

# Aligning organizational goals and requirements

In this chapter:



Aligning organizational goals and requirements for delivering Microsoft SharePoint solutions is vital. Without doing this, you will not be able to quantify the value that SharePoint brings, and you will not be able to bridge the gap between technology and the business. Understanding your goals and requirements allows you to obtain better insight and perspectives, which will help you and the business to make confident decisions. This then allows the business to take full advantage of the investment.

## Understanding SharePoint goals and requirements

To begin to understand the nature of goal and requirement alignment, you need to understand conceptually how SharePoint is perceived by the business.

If you are responsible for managing a release of SharePoint into an organization, you may well be asked, "What is SharePoint?"

You could respond with: "SharePoint gives people the ability to create and manage data."

However, those who already have SharePoint working in their organization may well describe SharePoint as it relates to what they are doing with it. For example, they may say something like, "SharePoint provides a document management platform," "SharePoint allows us to store and share our stuff," or even "SharePoint provides several applications in our organization."

The problem is the question itself. Instead of asking what SharePoint is, the more important questions are "How can SharePoint solve the information management problem?" or "How can SharePoint solve our collaborative challenges?" If those questions were answered, the objectives of those who are using or contemplating using SharePoint will be exposed, and in turn so will SharePoint's value, return on investment (ROI), and productivity gains.

Through investigating client SharePoint objectives, those first answers can extend further into goals and highlights the value that SharePoint brings.

So, what are those values and goals? And once you are aware of them, how do you expose SharePoint benefits from those values and goals? You start by stating clearly how the benefits that SharePoint brings relate to organizational aspirations for staff information productivity, and then translate those aspirations from goals and values into a business strategy for SharePoint delivery. By doing this, you are seeking to address the organization's collaborative and information management challenges. And as you investigate these challenges further, more goals are realized—brought about, for example, through surveys and workshops with departmental and functional business stakeholders.

You will need to be careful when exposing business goals, because you need to ensure that the related SharePoint benefits are aligned with and provide support for an organization's business strategy. This is critical to business success. The way language is used in stating and implementing the business strategy is very important because information workers need to understand benefits and relate them to their own goals.

Overuse of jargon in any business strategy has the potential to leave people unsure as to why they should use SharePoint at all. Corporate-speak like *out of the box, transformation, tip of the sword,* and *change agent,* interspersed with management terms such as *de-risking, de-leveraging,* and *re-regulating,* leave people feeling, at best, cold and cynical or, at worst, bewildered. The language needs to be focused on collaborative goals (such as "I need to store my stuff and make it accessible"), the goals need to be communicated and recorded, and the feature sets of SharePoint need to be aligned with those goals.

So, to understand the goals, you need to simplify the terminology, without using jargon, in a language that can be understood by all. This is because to implement SharePoint is to implement change, and that change needs to dovetail into a constantly evolving organization.

**Note** A strategy stating what the workforce should be doing with SharePoint is not enough to ensure the workforce to achieve their goals. Another requirement in a SharePoint implementation and planning process is the development of awareness, learning, and support. These elements allow individuals to ensure that they understand how their productivity goals can be achieved. Those goals can then be aligned with the features of SharePoint along with the strategic direction being applied to SharePoint.

Fundamental to the implementation of SharePoint solution delivery is the understanding of the processes needed to ensure User Adoption and Governance. This is not a technical knowledge requirement. SharePoint is a business platform, not a technology provided through an IT project. Those responsible for delivering SharePoint to information workers need to understand concepts concerning setting goals and the communication and recording of benefits. This is true regardless of SharePoint version or product type. This chapter details Goal Alignment, including how to identify SharePoint benefits to meet goals, measurement methods to test the objectives, and how to factor in demand, price, and costs. This is a vital step in establishing a successful SharePoint provision, leading to Governance, policy, and realizing User Adoption.

## Using Goal Alignment methods

Before explaining the purpose of SharePoint Goal Alignment, I would like to describe a situation that relates to how I managed to create it.

The example I'm describing comes from the days of SharePoint 2003. I was on the team whose task was to implement SharePoint 2003 in a large organization with a 5,000+ user base spread over 20 locations. In those days, sending paper over modems (faxing) was part and parcel of the communication landscape. The sponsor (management) was insistent that the platform get implemented as quickly as possible. I was eager to engage and get some traction from the related stakeholders (all 10 of them). So, as part of implementation planning process, I needed to communicate the organization's intention of applying SharePoint to those stakeholders.

Unfortunately for me, the decision to take on SharePoint had not been communicated to the stakeholders by the sponsor. Therefore, there was little to no awareness of a corporate intention to implement the platform. To ensure that all stakeholders were on board, I quickly created workshops aiming to describe a strategic direction, explaining features geared in that direction, and "splitting" the strategic direction into manageable chunks.

Workshops provide a great method of gathering information concerning what the stakeholders wish to achieve. They will give you chances to map those requirements to the sponsors' vision of the platform. This should be an iterative process of goal setting and stakeholder management.

The reality is that the process of setting goals in SharePoint is quite similar to how any goals (even personal goals) are set. The only differences are the types of goals and the organization. SharePoint goals are related to solving collaborative and information challenges within that organization; for example, identifying problems with managing documents and choosing what tools are being used to solve those problems. Solving information challenges using SharePoint solutions will improve both staff productivity and morale.

Here are some examples of key challenges that require a goal, many of which you may recognize:

- "I want to be able to organize content; the problems I have are when I want to find a status report, I spend so much time trying to locate it. I search my desktop, network folder, documents folder, USB stick, and eventually find it in email."
- "I want to be able to find content; the problem I have is that often the report I want to locate is not the right one, and I don't know who wrote the report, or even when I do find the report, I have problems trying to find out who owns the report!"
- "I want to be able to store content; the problem I have is that the report I want to store needs to be classified; the report I want to store needs to be secured; the report I want to store needs to be approved."
- "I want to be able to access my report from home; the report needs to be available from another country."
- "I want to be able to email my report."

The goal with each of these challenges is to address each troublesome process with a solution that provides a productivity benefit to the client. You need to make sure that each solution aligns with the client's aspirations concerning staff productivity and management of information. You will find that some of these challenges overlap; however, the purpose of Goal Alignment is to connect all the benefits exposed from the solutions of each challenge to organizational goals and aspirations.

In setting personal goals, for example, the process of alignment is the same. Regardless of whether your goal is to earn a university degree, get a better job, start a business, buy a home, or lose weight, the process is actually not that different from aligning goals in SharePoint. For SharePoint goals, very much like personal goals, are set to be consistent with an individual's or organization's values. You establish the true identity and standards of benefits related to those goals, which leads to Governance. You then set service delivery standards, which through management inspires motivation, improves productivity, and realizes ROI.

Although the process of investigating and realizing goals is pretty much standard, the actual goals in each organization will be different in terms of how they will be achieved. SharePoint is simply a tool to solve information and collaborative challenges. To do this, you will require assistance to identify the goals and help people adopt SharePoint.

**Note** Deploying SharePoint technology is not going to solve the business problem by itself. Behavioral changes need to accompany it. It is just one part of a SharePoint delivery program that also includes communication and training. Both are key aspects of User Adoption. In Chapter 4, "Preparing SharePoint Solution User Adoption," you will learn how to use methods aimed at getting users excited about using the SharePoint solution. Doing this builds the required momentum to drive the kind of change that leads to success.

In adopting SharePoint, organizations will need to (and want to) set ambitious goals. However, one of the main problems faced by organizations is not in setting these goals, but cascading them to information workers. You will need to guide information workers so that they are able to translate and internalize the organization's goals as their own. Remember that if you do this well, motivation will increase and User Adoption will be easier to attain because information workers will have higher clarity, confidence, and conviction about achieving organizational goals and objectives.

Goal Alignment stems from the executive level and trickles down to the information workers. You must include the following in this process:

- Translate organization goals into their personal goals and objectives.
- Ensure that all participants experience higher confidence and conviction about achieving organization objectives.
- Strive to make everyone achieve greater clarity about the business's goals and each person's contribution toward making that happen.
- Get information workers to take ownership in creating and building on their current competence to achieve organizational goals.
- Formulate practical action plans to achieve business results.
- Strive to achieve a higher level of motivation, trust, and loyalty toward the team, management, and organization.

Goal Alignment is an iterative process. I had to map requirements at a high level for the platform, and then refine them as I continued to work on the more detailed aspect of each goal. I urge you to use these methods when you're trying to understand what the client and stakeholders require. This will also help you with the following:

- Making decisions based on the strategic direction of SharePoint
- Resolving disagreements between stakeholders concerning the organizational goals of SharePoint

Goal Alignment is vital before, during, and after SharePoint implementation because the success of SharePoint depends on users understanding the platform and their ability to use the SharePoint solution being implemented.

Therefore, if every person has a very clear understanding of how his or her specific role in the use of SharePoint helps achieve the business mission, vision values, and goals, it almost instantly gives that individual a sense of purpose that is really powerful. Having a SharePoint solution that meets user requirements empowers users and provides measured productivity gains. Individuals will get the sense that they are contributing to something bigger than themselves. The tasks they achieve using SharePoint solutions will help the company grow, succeed, and improve productivity, profitability, and performance.

## Creating measurable benefits

In order to prove the viability of implementing a SharePoint solution, you need to show that when the users employ the solution, benefits result that can be measured.

**More Info** The key benefits of SharePoint 2013 are defined by Microsoft as "share," "organize," "discover," and "build." These terms are described further in Table 4-7 in Chapter 4. They are also described at *http://sharepoint.microsoft.com/en-us/preview/sharepoint-benefits.aspx.*

You should never communicate SharePoint benefits as just a collection of statements that can be perceived as not being related to the evolving nature of the business. You must clarify each SharePoint benefit with stakeholders, and then record each goal that relates to that benefit. This means that the client and those who are implementing SharePoint fully understand the outcome, which can be measured. This information is recorded in the SharePoint business plan. The SharePoint business plan describes what SharePoint is in non-technical terms, as well as how the implementation of the platform will meet the business objectives.

Obtaining benefits is the sole reason for undertaking any SharePoint solution program. If there are no benefits, then there should be no program. It is for this reason that the role of SharePoint Sponsor is vital. The SharePoint sponsor will help you identify the benefits and together you will be able to glue those to SharePoint features which will make up the SharePoint solution.

*Scenario 1: Fabrikam is a sales company that's been using SharePoint for one year. Most of the company's workers believe that they are competent SharePoint users. They include a small team made up of business members who own certain key sites covering functional areas of the company. This group is known as the stewards of the day-to-day SharePoint business management. One of the business members of this team wishes to propose a new piece of metadata to store information, but she wants it to be made globally available. The benefit of this piece is discussed at length, and an investigation ascertains that there would be great demand for it. A proposal is written explaining more about the new metadata, the business process under which it would be used, adoption planning, and any mitigated risks. A testing platform is provided with the new functionality in place, and the business members (with additional support from staff members) test and write a report on the business process to accompany the use of the new metadata and the choice of which sites they initially appear in. Finally, the business proposal, along with the benefits and drivers are demonstrated, agreed upon, and then released to production.*

This scenario gives a clear indication that business benefits and drivers were realized, and more important, agreed to as a legitimate requirement. Note that I have not included things like whether the solution can be supported or "managed." These are important, of course, but first you need to investigate and identify the benefits that the new metadata would add. There are conditions to this which will define other benefits related to support, resource management, and more. Investigating the requirement will deliver the true value of the solution, and therefore whether effort and resource is warranted in its delivery.

**Important** If there is a rush to provide a SharePoint solution without first developing a plan, then there is no point in providing that solution.

## Ensuring that a SharePoint delivery program is legitimate

To be legitimate, the SharePoint delivery program must achieve at least one of the following objectives:

- Maintain or increase profitable revenue to the business, now or in the future
- Maintain or reduce the operating costs of the business, now or in the future
- Maintain or reduce the amount of money tied up within the business, now or in the future
- Support or provide a solution to a necessary or externally imposed constraint

In short, benefits are about making more money, using existing resources and assets more efficiently, and staying in business. The preceding scenario's benefits show that it meets at least the fourth condition. Drivers are frequently defined by words such as *growth, efficiency, protection,* and *demand,* which reflect the company focus at any point in time.

Note that the first three conditions relate to the net cash flow into the business. Money is without question the key measure of commercial performance, and it includes measurement of revenue, out-payments to contractors, and other elements of running the organization. There are costs to implementing anything in SharePoint, including the fact that extra support of a new internally provided solution using built-in SharePoint features is required, or an extra cost in using external development in terms of customizing SharePoint.

The fourth condition in the previous list is often referred to as a "must-do" project. Nevertheless, it is essential that you fully record financials to determine the lowest cost, highest value, and approach to fulfilling the need. This cost can be placed in the context of the organization as a whole to determine whether the affected part of the organization or the entire organization can afford the change.

## Understanding tangible and intangible benefits

Benefits fall into two categories:

- **Tangible** This type of benefit can be stated in quantitative terms.
- **Intangible** This type of benefit should be stated in detail as much as possible, but it usually cannot be expressed in concrete terms.

Whenever possible, you should ensure that benefits are tangible and clearly articulated. Tangible benefits may be either measured in financial or in non-financial terms.

Financial benefits describe the organizational objectives in terms of the following:

- Revenue
- Contribution
- Profit enhancement
- Savings in operating costs or working capital

Non-financial benefits describe the value added to the organization that is directly attributable to the project, but they cannot be described in financial terms.

As previously stated, you should ensure that benefits are as tangible and measurable as possible. Here are some examples of the types of measurements you can include:

- **Operational Performance Measures,** such as using monitoring statistics to identify search, tagging, and rating patterns. Benefits include knowledge of document management trends, sharing of content, and connecting with people.
- **Process Performance Measures,** such as the creation of a workflow solution to enhance and/or replace business processes.
- **Customer Satisfaction Measures,** such as a company-wide survey created with SharePoint, communication exercises using, for example, the SharePoint 2013 Community Site Template, the creation of training facilities using SharePoint, and the delivery of educational classroom-based training for Microsoft Office 365 in a college or university.
- **Key Performance Indicators (KPIs),** such as the delivery of SharePoint and/or PerformancePoint KPIs to show goal-based information harvested from various locations and data sources to dashboards in one site.

You should query why the organization should spend resources addressing any particular measure or indicator. If a proposed SharePoint solution will not help achieve any of the four conditions listed in the "Ensuring that a SharePoint delivery program is legitimate" section earlier in this chapter, you should seriously consider dropping the project. On the other hand, if the delivery program is legitimate, then for each tangible benefit, you should increase the service quality in SharePoint, which in turn could help a company retain and/or increase the number of internal and/or external customers and financial benefits. Also, increasing service quality may help the organization meet its license obligations, for example. There needs to be a justification for any assumptions, even if the calculation of financial effect is somewhat tenuous.

## Measuring SharePoint benefits

Quantitative benefits involving cost can be measured at the corporate level by the relevant SharePoint sponsors, but they cannot always be measured directly for individual SharePoint solutions in a SharePoint project. However, there are other ways to measure these benefits, including the surrogate measurement and higher-level measurement methods described next.

### Surrogate measurement

You use a surrogate measurement in situations where it will not always be possible to measure value in the implementation of a SharePoint solution. Consider using an alternative measure that has a known relationship to profit. Revenue and margin may be such measures; and even measures such as numbers of customers, churn, and percent utilization. When trying to measure the business benefit of a site, as given previously in Scenario 1, and when the ideal metrics really are too difficult to collect, you should find a surrogate measurement that will give an approximation. For example, if you cannot directly measure the business value delivered from the use of a SharePoint site, you can at least survey the customers for their perceptions of the site. Using a SharePoint survey component is perfect for this, as you can then also ask questions directly about the components being delivered on the site.

### Higher-level measurement

A higher-level measurement should be used when it is not always possible to relate an increase in demand for a SharePoint service, particularly if there is a planned or recent enhancement to that service. For example, in a case where an existing SharePoint environment uses a key third-party component that needs to be upgraded, and there is a requirement to identify the increase in demand.

In such cases, you should consider tying the SharePoint delivery program to a higher-level business program, where the benefits can be measured. An example where one would measure at a higher level is whether an enhancement to a product is tracked at product level, rather than by individual sites and initiatives. Those would be included in the project plan whose objective is to enhance that service. The following quote is an example of a statement coming from the use of a higher-level measurement method.

> *SharePoint projects are coming in at approximately 50 percent of the overall cost of traditional enterprise content management (ECM) systems . . . SharePoint's benefits go beyond the cost savings associated with reducing software licenses.*
>
> *Russell Stalters, director, Information and Data Management at British Petroleum*

## Setting conditions for SharePoint delivery program satisfaction

Even if you have difficulties with the measurement methods described previously, you should ensure that every SharePoint delivery program you undertake has a recognizable method for demonstrating whether it has been a success and met stakeholder goals. Conditions for satisfaction are used to supplement benefits measures. To create these conditions, you should use the S.M.A.R.T. method, as described in the "Creating SharePoint S.M.A.R.T. goals" section later in this chapter.

## Forecasting User Adoption benefits

To guarantee, increase, and prove User Adoption benefits, you should prepare an initial estimate of the benefits (and costs). You do this because you need to provide a proposal for a SharePoint solution to give the relevant stakeholders reasons why they should use the solution. In the following stage, called Feasibility and Definition, the estimates should be turned into firm forecasts and be agreed to by the Project Sponsor.

**Note** The business case for SharePoint should address savings and risk mitigation. They should also explain the benefits of the product's rich functionality and its broad user support. These are distinct selling points for SharePoint.

Forecasts serve two purposes:

- They enable evaluation of a SharePoint project against other projects or proposed investments, and allow proposed changes to the project to be assessed.
- They provide information against which the post-launch performance of the project can be measured.

The overall financial benefit to an organization wishing to deliver a SharePoint solution is the product of demand and price, minus the costs. This is the basis for justifying any solution, whether they relate to the development of components to address SharePoint functionality, the addition of a second server to an existing SharePoint farm, or an improvement to a built-in SharePoint feature in SharePoint. It is important that you keep in mind the overall picture (client vision and strategy) to make sure that no projects get created that merely suboptimize a part of the business, creating little overall benefit. To help you understand this further, examine the following scenario.

*Scenario 2: Fabrikam has now implemented SharePoint. One department was used as an early adopter, and it has already begun using a SharePoint site. It now wishes to display dashboards on its site and has requested the use of PerformancePoint and Microsoft Access. However, other key departments in the organization have some SharePoint knowledge and still need to be trained; they are relatively new to SharePoint. Also, Fabrikam SharePoint support services do not have good knowledge of PerformancePoint and Microsoft Access SharePoint features.*

In this scenario, one would argue that there would be little point in delivering PerformancePoint and Access services because the overall demand could decrease, but costs to support could be higher, and the user-base count required to achieve organizational productivity (which is to increase User Adoption of SharePoint across the organization) may never be realized. The scenario has not given any justification for PerformancePoint or Access services. It could be that the implementation of such services will decrease costs and increase productivity. Although the implementation of PerformancePoint and Access services may not be costly from a technical perspective, the impact on support, training, and User Adoption could be significant. Wise judgment is needed to ensure that priorities are service delivery (support, management) and User Adoption; however, if the requirements are to be fulfilled, it is also important to deal with the impacts and risks of service delivery.

That said, bear in mind that dashboards are a fundamental component of any performance management solution. You should consider using PerformancePoint Services, which provides a set of tools and services for building highly interactive dashboard experiences that can help organizations of all sizes monitor and analyze their performance.

**More Info** For more information concerning PerformancePoint 2013, visit *http://msdn.microsoft.com/en-us/library/ee559635%28v=office.15%29.aspx*. For information about PerformancePoint 2010, visit *http://msdn.microsoft.com/en-us/sql10r2byfbi-trainingcourse_sql10r2byfbi08_unit.aspx*.

## Estimating demand for your SharePoint solution

To gauge User Adoption for any SharePoint service, you make estimates of the demand for that service. Quantitative measures are essential for analyzing opportunities to use SharePoint, whether they are on-premises or off-premises using SharePoint Online in Office 365. Quantitative measures include marketing, training, sizing the infrastructure needed, and assessing resource needs.

In the context of identifying business benefits for SharePoint, demand is simply based on volume. To determine this, you must answer such questions as how many individuals will be using the solution? What will the performance hit on the SharePoint infrastructure be? What is the demand on the level of support required to manage the solution?

Every SharePoint solution goes through an initial investigation to identify the demand for the service. This needs to be done in broad terms only. Where possible, focus on people's experience with similar products. Consider the demand statement in the following scenario.

*Scenario 3: Fabrikam wishes to replace its document management system (DMS) with SharePoint. There is an understanding that at least half the organization accesses the current DMS directly on a day-to-day basis; the others perceive the service as the core tool for managing data.*

To gauge demand in this scenario, a feasibility study would be based on techniques such as the following:

- **Expert opinion** There may be current users of the current DMS who have good working knowledge of its effectiveness, performance, support, and other features. Those people would be interviewed. In addition, SharePoint technical experts are asked their opinions about any integration and/or migration possibilities between DMS and SharePoint.

- **Panels** Key stakeholders in the organization are surveyed to identify problems with the current DMS.
- **Market research** Information is provided about the SharePoint document management capability, including newsworthy information concerning DMS and its use in other companies, and whether those companies have adopted SharePoint (and the reasons behind that decision).
- **Pilot studies** SharePoint test environments are created to allow those involved to try SharePoint document management features under guidance and observation.
- **Competitor experience** Investigations are carried out to identify whether there are any products other than SharePoint whose required functionality is more effective in terms of support. In addition, the issue of whether their support for SharePoint integration is available and supportable by the organization is explored.

**Tip** Panels are extremely useful in brainstorming, even forum meetings. Both are suitable for low-risk projects. These panels must be made of representatives of those who will use the solution and those representing the SharePoint platform.

Estimating demand for your SharePoint solution is a significant task. You should identify people to help you do this, and the SharePoint sponsor can advise you on the kind of resources available to you.

There are many examples where you need to estimate demand for a SharePoint solution including the following:

- The organization has little relevant experience and needs further assistance (such as organizations that require a structured delivery approach).
- The SharePoint project seeks to obtain competitive advantage through differentiation or innovation. This is particularly true for organizations that want to use Office 365 SharePoint as a public website.
- There are rapidly changing market circumstances. This means that solutions created need to adapt easily. In addition, there needs to be flexible design capabilities in the product.
- You need a second opinion to check assumptions. As pointed out earlier, the importance of getting assistance to implement any SharePoint solution cannot be understated. Getting confirmation from experts in the field is vitally important and is extremely useful to back up a business case.
- You need help to achieve a consensus where stakeholders disagree. Chapter 2, "Defining the SharePoint solution scope," details a number of methods you can use to engage the

stakeholders. Also, you need to ensure that all stakeholders understand the nature of the client's vision of and aspirations for SharePoint.

- You want to promote SharePoint. Doing research concerning the key benefits of SharePoint generically, and then applying those benefits to organizational and information workers goals, are key ingredients in designing any solution. Again, this requires help from experienced SharePoint users.

Once the basic demand is understood, you should model the solution to determine the size of the platform infrastructure required to support the solution. For example, there is no point in releasing a solution on the organization's SharePoint production platform if information workers are dealing with webpages that take five minutes to display because the solution is hogging SharePoint infrastructure resources. The following scenario gives an example of what happens if you do not model the solutions infrastructure requirements.

*Scenario 4: Fabrikam requires a business process workflow that will inform specific individuals when to check sales details on a SharePoint site. After investigation, a solution is created by a third-party company on its platform. Fabrikam has little experience in SharePoint platform management; the firm has only a production environment available, and there's no way to test the solution. The third-party organization suggests testing with its equipment, but the infrastructure it uses is better than Fabrikam's, and the test group is only a fraction of the number of information workers that will use the solution. A test is performed that successfully meets the requirement, and the solution is released to production, whereupon there are immediate problems. Fabrikam's entire SharePoint platform performance falls precipitously, information workers complain of being inundated by emails from the new solution, and the information workers originally assigned to use the product find the solution far too slow.*

You can guess what happened to the solution after that, including the impact both from a User Adoption perspective and a risk management perspective. The rule of thumb when gauging demand is to model the solution on the actual infrastructure, with the actual information workers.

## Pricing

All SharePoint solutions cost money regardless of configuration. In terms of ensuring that the program is legitimate, pricing must be considered, and the organization made fully aware of all the costs required to deliver the program.

For a short-duration program that is well understood and where competitor reaction will not affect prices, you should use price projections—the more you do this, the more experience you will gain. You must make sure that your pricing projections take account of the following:

- **Commercial objectives** The overall SharePoint strategy should relate to the needs of the solution. Commercial objectives could relate to organizational positioning; for example, if the organization has global offices, then you need to identify alternatives for SharePoint provision in those offices. Doing so will increase costs like infrastructure and support, but it also improves performance and regional resilience.

- **On-premises versus off-premises** SharePoint On-Premise costs include licensing and any additional costs concerning support, installation, and maintenance. SharePoint Off-Premise (also known as SharePoint Online, part of Office 365) is where SharePoint is provisioned; SharePoint needs a simple configuration, and the cost for support is vastly reduced. This is further discussed in the "Features" section of Chapter 2, and in the "Understand On-Premise and Off-Premise" section of Chapter 8, "Building a SharePoint service delivery model."
- **Pricing strategy** This fully depends on the scope of the SharePoint environment, its type, and the solutions that are in place or are going to be in place. Adding third-party solutions could charge on a server-by-server basis (for example, software provided is charged per web front-end server). Other third-party solutions charge on a rolling scale based on the number of customers using the SharePoint farm.
- **Customer charging policy** To claw back costs and charges for storage, SharePoint features like quota can help. Note that in the early stages of SharePoint On-Premise in an organization, there is no sense in charging customers for SharePoint; however, charging for site use could work for existing SharePoint farms where platform Governance is being further developed. Quota can help enhance platform Governance even further. For example, you could investigate charging per gigabyte for using SharePoint online in Office 365.

**More Info** For more information about SharePoint pricing and licensing details, visit *http://sharepoint.microsoft.com/en-us/buy/Pages/Licensing-Details.aspx*. For Office 365 pricing details, visit *http://www.microsoft.com/en-us/office365/compare-plans.aspx*.

## Estimating costs

When figuring out what a solution costs, you must include any cost that increases as a direct result of the resources required to deliver the SharePoint solution, including the following:

- **Service delivery costs** SharePoint support services cost money. People will use the SharePoint solution only if the service provided is considered to be "good." That means that SharePoint needs to be managed, which will require money and resources. Those costs will increase based on the complexity of the SharePoint environment, combined with the skill sets of those who manage the platform. Those costs will require justification. The support provision will need to be measured to ascertain the value of the service being provided.
- **Operational costs** These are infrastructure-related, material costs. An On-Premise SharePoint platform costs money because that environment is made of servers. These costs also include software, licensing, and annual support. In addition, there could be costs associated with storage (for example, where disk storage is charged back to the business unit based on the quota applied to their SharePoint sites).

Justifying these costs is vital. Higher costs will ensue if there is little Governance applied to SharePoint, as will costs for wasting staff time if, for example, the platform performance is slow or has not been adequately configured (for Search, for example). There is no point whatsoever in choosing a cheap option for SharePoint adoption if there will be a detrimental impact to the ongoing support of that SharePoint provision.

## Creating SharePoint S.M.A.R.T. goals

To align individual and company goals, you should consider using the S.M.A.R.T. methodology. S.M.A.R.T. goal setting is a very effective method of producing peak-level performance by motivating and increasing stakeholder engagement; which in turn increases User Adoption. S.M.A.R.T. (the name is derived from the initial letters of each of the following points) is a widely recognized process with these characteristics:

- **Specific** The specific goals should address the five Ws (Who, What, Where, Why, and When).
- **Measurable** Technologies play a tremendous role in helping define the progress of goal execution, and they need to be able to establish concrete criteria for establishing the exact proportion of a goal that has been realized.
- **Attainable** Realistic goals motivate the SharePoint team, as well as anyone using the solutions created by the SharePoint team. Overly ambitious goals on the other hand, do the opposite.
- **Relevant** Goals must be relevant. They must have clarity of definition to be accepted and understood by all participants.
- **Time-Based** Goals must have a clear, objective time frame.

Specifically, you ensure that goals are specific and measurable, and make sure they are compatible. For example, when creating a SharePoint solution that is going to be used across an organization, you would compare information and collaborative goals from each of the relevant functions in the organization for compatibility and alignment. For example, sales goals should be compatible with operations, finance with HR, quality assurance with manufacturing, and so on. To carry this out, you could use results from user requirements investigations gathered for each function, then compare goals to identify ones align. From there, you focus on those goals, identifying what SharePoint tools, components, and features are relevant. Note that the organization will continue to move rapidly, so ensure that the goals you are collecting are at a sufficiently high level so that alterations in the way the function operates do not affect the goals.

Goals must be unambiguous and articulated clearly. They must state exactly what needs to be achieved, and in what time frame.

Here's an example of a badly written goal:

*"I am going to try to deliver SharePoint search."*

It is badly written for the following reasons:

- It's not specific.
- It's not measurable.

- It's not time-bound.
- There is no indication that someone is going to deliver SharePoint Search by a specific date.
- There is no way of telling whether or when the goal is going to be achieved.

Now, here is an example of a well-written goal:

> *"I am going to optimize SharePoint Search by providing a Query Rules solution to enable Promoted Results by the end of December."*

It includes all the attributes of a S.M.A.R.T. goal:

- The goal is specific. It relates to a facet of Search.
- The goal is measurable. Either it can be achieved or it can't.
- That goal can be agreed to by the relevant stakeholder(s).
- The goal is realistic. Providing Search includes a vast number of facets—Promoted Results is just one of those.
- The goal is time-bound. Promoted Results will be provided by the end of December.

**Note** Query Rules is a feature in SharePoint 2013 that allows you to manage search keywords, which enables Search Result promotion. For more information on this, go to *http://technet.microsoft.com/en-us/library/jj219620.aspx*.

You must make sure that the goals that the SharePoint solution is aimed at are clear and unambiguous. Poorly written goals use indefinite words like *try, could, should, possibly, hope, attempt, probably, might,* and *maybe*.

Here is a real-life example of a goal statement by a client. His company had SharePoint deployed but was experiencing problems with getting people to use it:

> *"We hope that SharePoint will probably be used a lot more by the end of the year..."*

I pointed out to the client that this goal was not specific enough because it did not detail what to do to accomplish it. Instead of saying "by the end of the year," which is not a time-bound statement, I suggested that they pick a date.

**Tip** Creating SharePoint solution goals can be daunting. To help you with this, consider using or becoming a SharePoint business strategist. Morgan and Wolfe is a unique global Microsoft partner that specializes in SharePoint business strategy using the Sequenced And Logical Enterprise Methodology (SALEM™) process. The company has consulted with and advised numerous global corporations, providing leadership. The SALEM process helps organizations define strategy and organizational goals for SharePoint adoption, including instruction on associated technologies. Visit *http://thesharepointstrategist.com/* for more information.

## Understanding Goal Alignment and the importance of User Adoption

Goal Alignment and User Adoption are bound together. Using SharePoint can meet whatever collaborative challenges are based on user requirements; however, you must ensure that whatever objective that needs to be met has "value." In Chapter 4, you will learn how to apply Value Management methods to give a measurement of SharePoint "value."

The following scenario focuses on how SharePoint can help you achieve Goal Alignment.

*Scenario 5: Fabrikam is a sales company dealing in coffee products and is already using several SharePoint solutions. It is currently using SharePoint 2010, planning to improve its main internal publishing portals, and to include numerous features like FAST Search, with a possibility of extending Governance methodologies by implementing specific products. There is a question of whether there is value to go down this route, when the release of SharePoint 2013 is imminent. Is it better to simply upgrade to the newest version rather than trying to improve the existing SharePoint 2010 platform?*

The organization is already using SharePoint 2010. This means that its information workers are probably a combination of people who are used to using SharePoint 2010 and users who are new to the platform. In addition, the company wants to improve its current platform and add more functionality.

Fabrikam's goals are pretty clear: increase the productivity of the current platform by exposing users to more features. Crucially though, they also want to look at Governance, which still requires work.

Since User Adoption of SharePoint is crucial, the answer to this would be to approach any upgrade as a separated program. Two key reasons for this are as follows:

- User Adoption means "business change," and therefore it creates a cultural shift.
- Training and Governance in the current version would ease the transition into SharePoint 2013.

Hence, for this example, Goal Alignment is based on helping the User Adoption plan focus on training and orientation, because that effort will help with the next major project planning into implementing SharePoint 2013.

## Understanding the importance of a performance review site

To design, build, and deliver operations (and management), the SharePoint solution needs skilled individuals representing technical, stakeholder, coordination, and management interests. This team would be spearheaded by a business sponsor and stakeholder group. A SharePoint-savvy project manager will be assigned, who could be a SCRUM master, a service delivery director, or a program manager. Documentation control and management of any deliverables are extremely important. Everything needs to be centrally stored, secured, and accessible to the delivery team.

There is no better place to create repositories to store this information than SharePoint. This is a good way to introduce the business members of the SharePoint solution delivery team to SharePoint. Crucially, this also allows key stakeholders to understand the concept of using SharePoint, even if all they are doing is accessing the information from a link. You should indicate the following to business members of the delivery team when showing them SharePoint:

- SharePoint 2010 includes the ability for repositories to be created and managed, such as project tasks, an issue tracking list, and a task list. In addition, there are workflows that can be configured to work with those components.
- SharePoint 2013 includes all SharePoint 2010 features, and much more functionality concerning project management sites. SharePoint 2013 also has several new features, such as Review Workflows for managing project proposals and Project Web App connectivity. The Project Web App provides lists that include Project Issues, Project Risks, and Project Deliverables.

**Tip** The Project Web App also synchronizes with Microsoft Project 2013. For more information about Project 2013 and SharePoint integration, visit *http://technet.microsoft.com/en-us/sharepoint/fp123606.aspx.*

## Summary

This chapter focuses on the preliminary work that you need to do to develop a program that implements SharePoint solutions. Key points include:

- Goal Alignment is crucial to ensure that corporate goals dovetail into information worker goals and vice versa.
- SharePoint business benefits should be measured against a known baseline.
- Make SharePoint business benefits tangible wherever possible.
- Place those SharePoint business benefits into the wider organizational context.
- Identify unwanted side effects from your SharePoint projects. Optimizing one part of the organization for implementing SharePoint solutions may not be best for the company as a whole.

The establishment of these goals and organizational alignment sets the stage for determining the scope of the SharePoint solution, as described in subsequent chapters. You will also learn about the process of establishing scopes for delivery of solutions, and the various features of SharePoint 2010, SharePoint 2013, and Office 365.

CHAPTER 2

# Defining the SharePoint solution scope

In this chapter:



This chapter explains the steps needed to set up a Microsoft SharePoint delivery program, and how to ensure that you can control the implementation of SharePoint solutions (which are listed as delivery items in the program). Setting up a SharePoint delivery program sets boundaries (called *scopes*) and includes initial investigations of what the delivery will achieve, who is going to do what, the schedule, controls, and managing your SharePoint team and stakeholders into an output known as a *business case.*

In Chapter 1, "Aligning organizational goals and requirements," you learned how to use methods of obtaining goals and how best to align them to organizational aspirations. This chapter continues with those areas, and will teach you how to form a delivery mechanism to provide a solution that matches those goals.

**Note** This chapter refers repeatedly to the term *solution*. In the context of this book, this word specifically means a *SharePoint solution.* A SharePoint solution is a set of SharePoint tools and components that meets a business objective and is listed in the delivery program.

## Creating a learning and knowledge experience

Implementation of a SharePoint solution comes from a vision of the business sponsor, is realized as a set of objectives to meet each stated goal, and then is investigated, designed, controlled, reviewed, agreed upon, and delivered. All the information collected needs to be recorded. You should therefore construct a SharePoint *business case* to hold details of the goals and objectives. All goals must be translated and designed through investigating SharePoint services and available features and mapping them to user requirements stated in the business case. That design makes up the SharePoint solution.

So why should you build a business case? The process of building a business case creates User Adoption and leads to Governance. Any SharePoint solution, whether implemented into an on-premise SharePoint or into a SharePoint Online instance (through Microsoft Office 365) should follow a standard process of implementation. This process involves people such as the business sponsor, the business stakeholders, the support teams, and information workers. And continual review of the progress and communication between the business stakeholders and technical teams is vital.

> *In producing SharePoint solutions, people want one or more of three things out of its implementation. They want the SharePoint solution to be better, cheaper, or faster . . . If you can tick two of those requirements, the business case sells itself.*
>
> *Duncan Hartwig, information architect, AFREN*

The importance of creating scopes and plans of action for releasing any SharePoint solution cannot be underestimated. When you agree to the scope for the delivery of any SharePoint solution, you are creating a maintenance plan, which protects the integrity of the relevant SharePoint environment and provides the basis for platform Governance. To comprehend this fully, you need to understand how solutions get into SharePoint. For all SharePoint versions before the present one, in order to make solutions available to the business, the process was largely managed by IT support—the solution would be made available to IT support staff, and they would then install it in the relevant location. Although this may sound cumbersome, I think this process is useful because it has an element of *Platform Governance*. IT support managed the deployment of the solution to the SharePoint environment, dealt with the relevant issues, and controlled the release of the solution.

SharePoint 2013 has numerous built-in features that give users the capability to get, install, and use *apps* (which are preconfigured and purpose-built applications). (Interestingly, the term *apps* is also used to refer to SharePoint 2013 document libraries and lists.) As well as apps being provided as part of SharePoint 2013, third-party apps are available from an online public SharePoint store (called the Office Store). From the Office Store, users can learn more about apps in the store (and read reviews), acquire (or buy) them, and start using them right away. The Office Store is available at *http://officepreview.microsoft.com/en-us/store/*.

These apps load immediately; there's no need for IT support or SharePoint support to preload them. All the user needs to do is sign in with a Microsoft account, and the apps will be there. To control the ability of users to download apps, administrators can restrict access to the Office Store and create an organizational Internal App Catalog. Users can choose which app to install and work with, and they even have the choice of when to upgrade apps when a developer makes a change.

From a business standpoint, one may think that the availability of apps from the Office Store improves user productivity because of the simplicity of releasing them into a SharePoint site. You must stress that the process of obtaining or creating an app to release starts with a business requirement.

To get to a point of releasing a SharePoint solution into a SharePoint environment, creating a scope of work to release is important and beneficial. You will find that by doing this, everyone connected with delivering the solution gains knowledge and experience. This enhances related business processes and ensures that the solution's implementation process is followed.

The delivery of the solution, from start to finish, has a number of scopes of work because it details the affected services and the features, objectives, and budget (thought of in terms of both time and money) to achieve the objectives.

There is an argument that the client simply does not know what it wants and does not have the time to get involved in building business cases, scopes, and deliverables. In the new world of "technology commodization," where Software as a Service (SaaS) is more apparent (particularly for Office 365), if there is something already built and available, why not simply deploy the ready-made solution? The answer to that question is simple. Policies of the organization concerning all technologies (of which SharePoint is one) would come into play. Security policies dictated by the organization concerning Internet access in deploying apps from the Office Store (to cite just one example) may affect delivery. In short, all aspects of the solution in terms of the delivery covering the testing, User Adoption, Governance, and support become very relevant. In addition, there is no measure of quality in going down that route, and therefore, it's difficult to determine the value, vision, Governance, or return on investment (ROI).

### What Is SaaS?

*SaaS (Software as a Service)* is method used to provide software. The most common characteristic of software provided in this fashion is remote access. Microsoft Office products (such as Office 365) can be accessed anywhere an Internet connection exists. This situation, where a user's device functions for software and information access, is known as *cloud computing*. For users, there's no software to install, and there's less worry that their computer will be insufficient to run the program. The supply chain of the software being made available and supported on the device is mostly bypassed. To find out more about Office 365 provided as SaaS, go to this page: *http://technet.microsoft.com/en-us/cloud/gg697163*.

Due to the various choices available when considering the scope of the SharePoint solution that is going to be delivered, having a structured SharePoint solution delivery program is important. As you go about constructing a SharePoint solution delivery program, consider it a rewarding learning and knowledge experience that comes through involvement and input from business and technology parties who together make a SharePoint delivery team. The business party (including the SharePoint sponsor and business stakeholders) gets to learn about SharePoint, and the SharePoint delivery team (mainly technical personnel) gets to learn about the business and their aims. Through this collaboration, the delivery scope can determine, among other things, the environment and the model under which the solution will be supplied (for example, by using the SaaS model described previously), including an understanding of the organization's problems and why the SharePoint solution is required. The relevant action tasks become part of the delivery scopes.

Traditionally, delivery program scopes have been seen as "alien" to a SharePoint delivery program, because in the past, SharePoint had been delivered purely as an IT project. This is because the IT focus is the installation and deployment of a software application. User Adoption delivery, communication, training, and even user testing of those applications was seen as an afterthought or was left for "someone else to sort out." This perception is changing. Throughout the years of SharePoint provision (from SharePoint 2003, to SharePoint 2007, to SharePoint 2010, and now SharePoint 2013), there has been an increasing need to ensure that SharePoint solution delivery shifts from being purely technological to being business-focused. This is due to the following recent developments:

- A total of 49 percent of all SharePoint clients have no SharePoint strategy, according to the *AIIM Report* released in summer 2010.
- The value of purely IT-led SharePoint solutions cannot be measured by the business.
- IT has deployed SharePoint predominantly as a glorified file share.
- Workers are now more mobile. They are finding more ways to access information from virtually any location.
- Workers require more effective methods to allow them to search, organize, and store information.
- Workers are more in tune with technology products and generally have ideas on what products they would like to use.
- Businesses have had to move faster in terms of their technology requirements.
- Workers are becoming faster at learning new products.

Regarding the last two points, the increase in computing power and the "consumerization" of products that can access online content has been astonishing. To give an example, in 1986, the most powerful supercomputer in the world was the famous Cray2, available for roughly $22 million at that time. In early 2011, Apple released the iPad2 tablet computer, which has about two-thirds of Cray2's performance, but costs only $500. This means that, in 25 years, the price has gone down by a factor of 44,000, so yesterday's supercomputer is tomorrow's tablet computer.

Because workers are becoming more technologically aware, they have access to electronic devices that allow them to collaborate. This has created increasing strains on those responsible for governing access to content in organizations. Administrators and developers, who were considered the sole providers and caretakers of computer environments and technology in the past, are now expected to act more as systems analysts, working with the business to ensure that their goals are aligned with what they are delivering and existing in the background of an ever-increasing myriad of connectable network devices. This is a challenging time for technical workers because the complexity of governing information has increased (for more information, see the "Bring your own device considerations" section of Chapter 4, "Preparing SharePoint Solution User Adoption"). This means that there has an increase in the maintenance of their IT engineering practices in terms of using and understanding network-aware devices, along with trying to keep pace with the skill set of the typical information worker, who is already using these very devices. Organizations are increasingly facing the need to provide audits relating to their business processes, and to prove that those processes are secure and compliant. This is particularly evident in fields related to document and records management. More business processes are being computerized, and information workers are closer to those business processes. IT and the business must work closely to scope what solutions will be created and what solutions will be available, as well as to come to a common understanding concerning their support and availability. Doing so prevents uncomfortable feelings about relevant plans to implement SharePoint solutions and increases User Adoption of SharePoint starting at the right time. And this means developing a scope to cover the intended solution.

When you start creating scope, start from a basic perspective. The scope will expand to cover the relevant facets: delivery, time scale, and so on. There will be areas that are out of scope. To address this issue, provide the opportunity for the solution to scale out so that those areas out of scope can be addressed in future delivery programs. Apply control to govern what is in scope versus what's out of scope, so that the scope does not blossom out of control—a phenomenon known as *scope creep*. Scope creep typically takes place when a delivery program grows in scale and complexity and more individuals get involved. It also occurs as the details of the delivery are presented to the individuals who requested the solution, who then say, "Can you also make it do this or that?"

Consider the following scenario, which is a good example of SharePoint scope creep.

*Scenario 1: Blue Yonder Airlines is a private jet charter management company. Several years ago, it added business jets to its fleet. Blue Yonder required a bigger hangar, so it decided to build one. After getting the required environmental approvals and using just the right touch with the airport authorities, the company purchased and demolished an older and smaller hangar, and the new hangar has been rising in its place over the past year. It will house two business jet aircraft. SharePoint has been suggested as a method of recording progress, centralizing, and sharing material. A delivery manager is set to implement SharePoint. When asked if he needed help, he declined, saying, "Everything is under control." The delivery manager then chose a number of individuals to act as stakeholders in the SharePoint delivery program, based on the assumption that they had the relevant clout and knowledge about aircraft hangars. After he learned that these individuals actually did not have the required knowledge, the delivery manager had to find different stakeholders who had prior SharePoint experience and knowledge. More people got involved, and they suggested that SharePoint also help them with their collaborative issues. More and more time is being spent to collate information on other stakeholder issues; the hangar is still being built; and no solutions are being created to handle information concerning the hangar itself. The hangar has 60 days left to completion, even though there's still a mountain of information concerning the hangar build progress that has not even been classified correctly, and very little has been done concerning creating a SharePoint solution. It also turns out the delivery manager simply had no clue about SharePoint—he just assumed the people he initially brought on board had SharePoint features known. Finally, an emergency meeting is called.*

Through reading this scenario, poor communication was a major reason for the poor execution of the delivery program. The delivery manager understood neither the business nor SharePoint. The purpose of the delivery manager is to define clear communication, ensure that details are defined, engage the right people, and control the outputs by applying a strict scope. Simply delegating everything without follow-up will fail.

> *Seek First to Understand, Then to Be Understood*
>
> *Stephen Covey, Author of* The 7 Habits of Highly Effective People

What Covey means here is that you should listen intently and take time to understand what the business sponsor requires. That will enable you to determine how to convey opinions, plans, and goals; and from that, extract the values.

## Knowing your SharePoint features

Much has changed with SharePoint, both technically and strategically, from the days of SharePoint 2003 Portal Server. In the past, implementation of a platform was based on the division of what are classified as core tools, application tools, and suites of software. These products, delivered mainly by IT, rarely included the User Adoption tasks that would get users involved in the delivery. The reasons for this included the following:

- An assumption that the members of staff already knew the basics of the software or that they could simply "fend for themselves"
- A lack of resources and/or impetus to provide a training program
- A blasé view that successful adoption of a product is measured by the number of help articles and manuals related to the product that are posted by IT support
- An assumption that SharePoint solutions, once deployed, are self-explanatory, requiring little to no training or awareness communication

Alignment of the software with business goals was purely technical in nature. There were no proactive measures to train staff—only knee-jerk reactions to complaints that users did not understand the product. An example of not understanding the business in terms of implementing SharePoint is the following statement, made by a delivery manager who had just had SharePoint deployed and had run into problems because his staff was not using SharePoint:

> *". . . as for SharePoint, I say train them after that application is released. Giving them SharePoint is no different from giving them Office—they will work it out."*

In other words, there's a complete lack of policies and Governance concerning how information workers in this organization would use SharePoint. User Adoption planning exists in a vacuum. The delivery manager seems to have a laissez-faire approach to training, which means there's no stakeholder management, motivation, or control, even to the point of suggesting that the rollout of such an important product central to the organization is trivial. The following quote illustrates what happens if that approach is taken:

> *"In the absence of clearly defined goals, we become strangely loyal to performing daily trivia until ultimately we become enslaved by it...."*
>
> *Robert Heinlein, US science fiction author (1907–1988)*

Relating this quote to the preceding example is simple. If User Adoption is not important, then any roadmap for the platform is unimportant and, therefore, information worker goals are unimportant. This thinking continues until at last, the very reason why the organization is using the platform comes into question.

So why should you care about SharePoint features? You need to know SharePoint features so the software can help you marry up the aspects of planning and design to deliver the solution, and reevaluate the model of support needed to manage the solution going forward. When users begin using the platform, the level of support requirements will be increased. Because the product is software, most users will assume that they should contact IT support staff if they run into problems. This behavior needs to be changed. With SharePoint, support starts with content. Business users are accountable for the data and its disposition. That accountability cannot be the responsibility of the IT staff; they look after the platform and its infrastructure; they are not accountable for the data created by the business. More information concerning the way that SharePoint support is provided to underpin data accountability and support is covered in Chapter 6, "Confirming Readiness for Delivery to the Organization."

As mentioned earlier, information workers who require SharePoint solutions will request it in a language that may not be understood by those who are supposed to provide those solutions, unless they know SharePoint features. SharePoint 2013 enhances the workload experiences by enabling new scenarios that can engage and work with the information worker. Table 2-1 describes the features that have been added to SharePoint 2013.

**TABLE 2-1** New Features in SharePoint 2013

| SharePoint 2013 Feature | Description |
|---|---|
| Application Store | Gives site owners the ability to plant applications into their sites. |
| Better Web Content Management | Variations and Content Translation, Search Engine optimization, cross site publishing, video and embedding, image renditions, clean URLs, and metadata navigation |
| Discovery Center—Records Management | This is a new site type designed for managing discovery cases and holds. It establishes a site through which discovery cases can be accessed to conduct searches, place content on hold, and export content. |
| Microsoft Exchange Server integration | The integration of Microsoft Exchange Server and SharePoint provides a single view of team folders in SharePoint. |
| Mobile Device support | There are two more views added to the mobile view facility in SharePoint. |

| SharePoint 2013 Feature | Description |
|---|---|
| Office Web Apps | These are deployed as a separate farm, not from the deployed SharePoint server, as in the past. |
| Request Management | Provides better administrative management by evaluating rules against requests and identifying what actions to take. |
| Retention policies for Records Management | Compliance levels have been extended. Policies include the retention of policy for sites and mailboxes associated with the site; closure and expiration |
| Sharing | Content from any Microsoft Office 2013 application content can be published directly to the SharePoint site. |
| Saving files direct to Skydrive | In SharePoint 2013, Microsoft has made working with offline information far easier. Previously, organizations had an ability to use SharePoint Workspace or Groove for working offline. In SharePoint 2013, SharePoint Workspace and Groove are no longer available. Synchronization features have been introduced that allows users to take content offline, work on that content offline, and then have that content automatically synchronize when connected back to their SharePoint site. This becomes the default location for saving documents from Microsoft Office 2013. |
| Social Features | Micro Blogs, Activity Feeds, Community Sites, Following, Likes, and Reputations |
| Themes | Built-in themes |
| Web Analytics included | The Web Analytics was a feature in SharePoint 2010 but has been replaced by Analytics processing and is a component of the Search Service. |

**More Info** For more information about what's been changed since SharePoint 2010, visit *http://technet.microsoft.com/en-us/library/ff607742%28v=office.15%29.aspx* and read the article "Changes from SharePoint 2010 to SharePoint 2013 Preview." This article describes the features in SharePoint 2010 that have been deprecated or removed from SharePoint 2013 Preview. Deprecated features are included in SharePoint 2013 Preview for compatibility with previous product versions. These features will be removed in the next major release of SharePoint.

Understanding needs and current business collaboration issues and how they map to SharePoint features is extremely important to anyone concerned with delivering a SharePoint solution, whether on-premises, cloud-based, or through Office 365.

And, because SharePoint is now fully integrated with Office tools, the understanding needs to extend beyond SharePoint to those tools (both the Office client desktop suite and Office Web App through SharePoint). Investigating how users work with these tools and finding ways to improve productivity through using them with SharePoint are very beneficial ways to encourage User Adoption.

The organization's technical makeup does the following:

- Helps determine what features should be used in SharePoint
- Galvanizes the business sponsor of the bigger picture, including service delivery, disaster recovery, and business continuity measures

So how do you get to understand these SharePoint features? There are two kinds of SharePoint (relating to SharePoint 2010 and SharePoint 2013):

- **On-Premise** SharePoint that is provided on an organization's premises and in its infrastructure, technically managed by internal staff.
- **Off-Premise** (through SharePoint Online, part of Office 365). This is an online secure offering of the Office suite that includes SharePoint 2013.

Further information concerning various SharePoint offerings, including a description and links to helpful websites, is given in the Appendix titled "SharePoint Offerings."

Deciding whether to use On-Premise or SharePoint Online depends on the level of control, cost, and other factors. SharePoint Online is provided as part of a cloud-based product. Also, understanding the cloud is not an easy task. If you ask any number of SharePoint Administrators, you are likely to get as many answers. And there are many types of clouds (such as application clouds, infrastructure clouds, and private clouds), and many services offer different cloud options.

Factors affecting decisions concerning using On Premise versus Off-Premise can be very complex, and the biases toward not using SharePoint Online are raised as objections toward all Off-Premise providers rather than a single one in particular. Compliance and security fears tend to be at the top of the list of objections to hosting and transitioning to the cloud. Other fears include the possible use of company data in the cloud for advertising purposes (which is against the security policies of many organizations).

Microsoft provides Software as a Service (SaaS), Platform as a Service (PaaS), and Infrastructure as a Service (IaaS) cloud options. SaaS, as described previously, relates to the delivery of applications, such as Microsoft Office Products, Microsoft Exchange Server, Microsoft Lync, SharePoint 2013, and Office 365. PaaS covers development, service hosting, and management in the cloud. Windows Azure and SQL Azure are products in this arena. IaaS means that the infrastructure is all provided. SharePoint 2013 Online includes the ability to harvest apps from an online marketplace directly, thus following the SaaS model.

However, describing PaaS, IaaS, and SaaS to the business is probably not the best way to explain what a cloud is. I suggest that you explain it without jargon, saying something like this:

> *"Cloud computing is a model for enabling on-demand network access to a shared pool of configurable computing resources."*

So, should you use cloud services (Off-Premise) or On-Premise? Key reasons associated with using On-Premise versus the cloud are based on a perceived benefit, which is the ability to offload IT to a company that provides cloud environments.

Here are some potential business benefits of using the cloud:

- **Reduction and streamlining of IT costs** Cost reductions include SharePoint servers, infrastructure, training of technical teams, connecting external teams, and support.
- **Saving money** Configuration management of a SharePoint environment requires monitoring, updating, and troubleshooting. In a cloud provision, all of which is handled by the hosting service.
- **Disaster recovery and business continuity** Data replication is handled by the hosting service, presumably resulting in less down time.

The question, however, is this: "What kind of organizations will allow their SharePoint environments to be managed by a hosting party?" Large organizations with traditional IT departments that have to handle much more than SharePoint most likely will choose an internally supplied, managed SharePoint environment, simply because that provides more control. In addition, technical services that are already provided on-premises will certainly influence decisions to put other technical services in the cloud.

On-premises and cloud features need to be associated with Governance goals that the organization has, such as security policies and/or geographical rules concerning data. Therefore, simply having access to a list of the key features in SharePoint is not enough. Knowing how to ensure the value extracted from the most viable SharePoint features that most closely meet the client requirements is vitally important. Understanding those requirements and mapping them to SharePoint features requires the right skill set.

## Engaging the right people

If you hire the right people and establish clear user requirements, you will succeed in delivering the intended SharePoint solution. You will need to engage the right people to aid you on your quest to create and be comfortable with your SharePoint delivery scope. Remember that the sponsor and stakeholders need to be kept interested in your solution; having a drinks get-together when the solution has been delivered is not enough. To do this, consider that there needs to be involvement, progress updates, and acknowledgment of their expertise. You will need to be able to show off SharePoint and, above all, communicate to the entire delivery team on a regular basis.

If this does not happen, the delivery program is doomed to fail, simply because the sponsor and stakeholders will completely lose interest or because no one feels anticipation or joy about the delivery solutions program. On the other hand, successful SharePoint delivery programs come about because the sponsor and the relevant stakeholders become interested and feel as if they are part of the SharePoint delivery team. In addition, some stakeholders become SharePoint champions and use their enthusiasm to coach others into SharePoint.

Here are some tips for you to ensure that you bring the right people to your SharePoint delivery program and ensure that the scope of the solution stays on track. The following applies to both the sponsor and the stakeholders.

- You should involve your team in the process and give them the opportunity to take part in it. This means soliciting opinions from the sponsor and stakeholders, giving them the chance to advocate and help select alternatives and make decisions. Continually ask for their feedback and encourage them to communicate their ideas and concerns (and, if you are fortunate, their compliments) to you.
- You should give context to each milestone reached in the delivery program. In progress reports and meetings, be sure to state how all milestones and accomplishes fit into the overall goal. For example, there is simply no point in saying, "We completed building the SharePoint site." Explain the key features that the site now holds, what specific solutions have now been made available, some key benefits, the advantages to the organization now that the site is available, and any issues or trade-offs that had to be made to optimize the site.
- You should not give the delivery team any surprises! While the delivery program is under way and the solution is being crafted, changes will always come up. For example, features may change, or there may be a new organizational implementation of a business process that affects the solution. A task may take longer to complete. I have been in meetings where the sponsor has become infuriated because the cost to alter a feature, which was originally well within budget, had escalated unacceptably. Other examples include stakeholders losing interest because they did not receive SharePoint Office 365 training in a timely manner. Therefore, there should be no surprises to the sponsor or stakeholders. Tell them as changes are being considered. Tell them why the changes are being addressed. Never, ever, force the sponsor to find out changes for themselves!
- You should give credit to the sponsor, the stakeholders, or both concerning the effects of the SharePoint solution on the organization. You should record the feedback in the closure reports and explain how their expertise is reflected in the design of the solution.
- You should continually show the stakeholders and sponsor the solution as it takes shape. This point is vital, as there are so many advantages relating to User Adoption, service delivery, training, and so on. You should ensure that the schedule is designed so that there are points along the way where you can demonstrate the solution. For example, in the delivery of a SharePoint site with numerous features, you could set milestones so that at each one you could demonstrate progress. In addition, use other methods to showcase the solution, such as displaying screenshots, prototypes, or cases where the solution has already been used.
- You should communicate to the delivery team often; do not simply rely on progress reports. You should use other methods to communicate progress, issues, changes, relevant information, and other important data. There are many ways to do this, including email, flyers, and announcements using social media programs such as Twitter, Yammer, and Lync.

**More Info** More information concerning managing the delivery program is available in Chapter 9 "Controlling the delivery program". This includes practical techniques for managing the schedule, communication, and providing progress reports.

Make sure that the people who work on the delivery program are focused on its success. Therefore, gaining and then maintaining interest and buy-in is critical to a successful delivery program because it creates User Adoption, no matter what SharePoint solution is being created.

To create the delivery program scope, you will need to gather the SharePoint user requirements. This process involves asking questions about what the solution was going to do, designing the solution on paper and through prototyping, and then going through a cycle of the user carrying out successive trials of the solution. The key is making sure that there are always concrete goals to be achieved so that there is little scope creep.

Believe it or not, I got things wrong the first few times I tried to do this. I didn't focus on the customer, only on the technical features that would exceed expectations, but I found that supporting these exciting new features would take longer to learn, and were harder to support and maintain, so they weren't worth doing.

While my experience increased, I realized that one of the keys to getting the solution right was to understand the abilities of the platform so that I could craft and fine-tune the solution to match user requirements closely. Each time, I sought agreement on how well the solution was matching the goals.

Doing this well takes time. You have to adapt and focus demands on your time as a SharePoint worker, wearing various hats, from analyst to administrator to developer to architect. The most important task is to convert user requirements into SharePoint solutions. This means having the ability to use the softer skills rather than technical ones. In other words, having good technical acumen is not enough. You need to have good social interaction and be knowledgeable and eager.

Asking questions is not enough; you also have to demonstrate those answers in SharePoint, which means knowing what feature provides the best fit and considering ongoing support, management, resiliency, and other factors. Attempting to identify functionality that is available from within the platform is best. This will help because you will not have to customize SharePoint unduly, which would only lead to further development to meet a particular requirement, costing money and eventually decreasing value.

## Tying analysis to SharePoint features

Before you can ask the right questions to those who require the SharePoint solution to be designed and implemented, you must structure those questions. For example, if your delivery program is focused on providing a SharePoint environment, then the questions that need to be asked would be business-oriented (to find out what the business wants to use SharePoint for), technical (the resources available for delivering SharePoint), and budgetary (how much funding is there available to deliver). In addition, you may want to look at the question of service delivery (how SharePoint will be managed). As another example, if your delivery is a SharePoint solution to be provided through Office 365 using SharePoint 2013, then the questions would again be business-oriented (to find out what the business wants to use the solution for) and strategic (to find out whether the solution is cross-functional or meets a specific requirement, and where does that sit in the overall strategy).

Examine the following scenario's "top-level" SharePoint requirement for Fabrikam, which defines the business-related goals related to User Adoption.

*Scenario 2: Fabrikam needs help delivering SharePoint to its global organization in 10 countries and will need advice about creating a strategy, planning, and obtaining resources to install and then train their staff.*

In addition to the business goals in this scenario, you should consider that there are ongoing service delivery goals. There will be, for example, the cost of training and service support questions to get answers to, since they would relate directly to how much funding should be provided to cover ongoing support and maintenance. In addition, there are technical questions relating to how integrated the solution is with the SharePoint 2013 online provision. Consider the following scenario, which requires the implementation of a custom SharePoint solution.

*Scenario 3: Fabrikam needs to add a component allowing automatic markup of documents. From initial investigations, a third-party component has been identified. The objective is to obtain a trial of the component so that it can be tested by business stakeholders to ascertain whether it meets their goals.*

So, this is an easy case of getting the software, installing it in SharePoint, and letting people test it—right? No. Again, there are problems with cost, service support, funding for ongoing support, and maintenance questions that must be addressed. The issues of obtaining a third-party component (even if that component has already been tested elsewhere) will be virtually no different from delivering a solution using built-in SharePoint features (however, the questions concerning support of built-in features may be easier to answer).

For you to deliver anything for SharePoint requires getting the information that ensures that whatever is delivered meets stated objectives and fits into the overall SharePoint strategy. The art of doing this includes translating business aspirations, setting goals, and dealing with any problems that come up. The following quote encapsulates my thoughts:

> *Building art is a synthesis of life in materialised form. We should try to bring in under the same hat not a splintered way of thinking, but all in harmony together.*
>
> *Alvar Aalto, architect*

Fostering harmony and combined thinking requires people with the relevant skills, including knowledge of the SharePoint interface, benefits, and key features. Additional skills include business process modeling, mapping requirements, and guiding teams.

The complexity of the SharePoint delivery will largely define the kinds of skills required. For example, if the task was to deliver a new SharePoint environment and assist in its release in a large organization, both knowledge of SharePoint and business analysis skills may be required. But if the task is to deliver new functionality to an existing SharePoint farm or to build a new site for a business unit then there is no reason why a SharePoint-savvy business stakeholder could not be resourced. What is important is to use common sense to critically identify who is needed, and not to overthink the situation. I have witnessed failures of delivery where the cost of implementing a SharePoint solution was a fraction of the cost of consultants brought in to engineer it, and there was no engagement with any business users, or even any effort to develop their skills to support the solution themselves. Note that I am not arguing that the use of consultants is good or bad here (in many cases, they are absolutely necessary if experience is required in the implementation of a particular SharePoint solution). The point is that work should be done to ensure that the right people are chosen and that the right level of engagement is introduced, using a mix of technical and business roles. For example, it is not a bad idea is to use someone with good SharePoint user skills (meaning that this person knows how the features are implemented, their advantages and disadvantages, and so on) to back up the business analyst. The SharePoint expert will be able to advise how to balance, refine, gauge, allow, and even resist at times the requirements coming from the business analysis results.

Two types of people will need to be questioned: Those who will be using the solution on a day-to-day basis, often referred to as *information workers;* and the content leaders, who are responsible for the function, business unit, or section related to each set of information workers. Neither group of people needs to know SharePoint, but they do need to have two attributes—knowing how their current content is managed (information workers), and being responsible for making decisions on that content (content leaders).

The size of the organization and its structure will determine whether to speak with content leaders and information workers for each relevant business unit, or just content leaders. In all cases, ensure that the SharePoint sponsor is aware of who will be interrogated, as they will have a much better idea, both operationally and politically. Do not make the mistake of using the SharePoint sponsor to solely dictate what solutions will be released or implemented. They may have a tendency to want a "quick win" and to attempt to advocate a top-down approach. While this may be considered useful, it may detract from the process of getting traction from the majority of business users, especially if they are new to SharePoint. Here's an example:

*Scenario 4: Fabrikam has employed a SharePoint solutions architect to guide the company in its SharePoint implementation. The business sponsor is an enthusiastic SharePoint user and has a SharePoint site. Because the business sponsor has her own SharePoint site, she wants solutions to be implemented from the top down. This means that SharePoint features will be provided generally without business user agreement, or even input. The business sponsor reasons that users will simply use what is provided and do not have the time to help with a decision-making process.*

So, this example means that after the solution is implemented and users have been trained, there may well be an uphill struggle to get users to employ the technology. Why? Because the users have not been involved in the design of the solution, and because they do not gain any value from its implementation—meaning that the goals defined by the business sponsor do not meet or align with the goals of the users. What then results is a great possibility that the solution will be used by only a fraction of the intended users, or even worse, that the solution will not be used at all, resulting in a low ROI.

Users need to be involved in the delivery of the solution. This means that you must communicate with and involve them; they need to at least be made aware of an attempt to improve their productivity through the implementation of a SharePoint solution. That is a key step to ensuring User Adoption.

Using sound judgment, identify the user base and ascertain the best way of communicating intentions and awareness. This could simply entail the use of emails, flyers, meetings, and workshops. Through this process, gathering of responses in terms of feedback is useful to make valuable decisions and solves the issue of users not utilizing the technology.

As already stated, use your best judgment when communicating the solution to users; take into consideration the scope of the solution, the size of the user base involved, and the stakeholders (both technical and business). For example, if the delivery is a new SharePoint environment, then setting up kickoff meetings followed by workshop sessions to learn user requirements is vital. In addition, scheduling those meetings and workshops sessions and communicating the reason and the importance of the sessions are important. As the delivery manager, you should ensure that all meetings and session workshops are scheduled with the business analyst and the relevant users. The communication related to these meetings should state the reasons for them and thank the relevant users for their time.

**Note** For the rest of this section, I am assuming that a role called *business analyst* will have the function of gathering user requirements. The business analysts should record responses relevant to these questions and collate them in the way that is most effective at carrying out analysis on the results and communicating those results to all concerned.

One strategy for recording the responses is through a survey; however, experience has shown that face-to-face contact is good if the organization and/or the target user base is small. Another strategy is to have the responses recorded with, say, a portable tape recorder, since it's quite possible that in the delivery of the answers from the client that you will get information that might sound trivial but actually is critical to how content is managed in a particular business unit.

**Tip** Read the book called *Gamestorming: A Playbook for Innovators, Rulebreakers, and Changemakers* (O'Reilly, 2010). It includes exercises to help the business analyst uncover business difficulties, goals, and user requirements, and it is very useful if you want to facilitate a structured process of group collaboration toward innovation, problem solving, and general brainstorming.

All questions should be generalized, include as little jargon as possible, and be non-technical (although the business analyst may still need to use some technical terms when explaining SharePoint terminology). The questions should not address any specific features. Pertinent questions should be grouped into sections, and each section could relate to workshops. You can combine these in order to ensure immediate progression. Hence, combining workshops and compressing them into shorter time periods could be done. One should bear in mind that compression places a far higher level of information overload on the client audience and requires them to be available for a longer period, focus more and input more. Holding shorter workshops, but more of them, often has a more positive effect on clients in stressful environments, although concentrated workshop sessions work best where availability of stakeholders is a problem. Above all, the purpose of these sessions is to ensure that users have a chance to prepare and collate relevant information and their thoughts. You should run the sessions in the following order:

1. Review the user objectives.
2. Review the solutions' structure, taxonomy, and user roles.
3. Review content and metadata.
4. Review required SharePoint solution features.

**Note** In order to gather user requirements correctly, you must to have the right people to help you design the solution. They must be fluent in SharePoint technologies from a business perspective and have expert knowledge of the product. They will ensure that you match the right process with the right SharePoint technology to make the solution a success. In addition, do not fall into the trap of assuming that users will get their solution after all the requirements have been gathered. Business goals can change rapidly, and the impetus to get a solution available will outweigh the need to gather every iota of information.

Every organization is different (particularly related to security and operational policies), and undoubtedly, the solution will be different and will focus on particular goals. However, the process of gathering user requirements is the same, as users answer questions not just about what they want, but why they want the solution, when they want it, and the particular features that need to be enabled.

**Tip** In the case of an organizational implementation of SharePoint, consider utilizing the skills of a SharePoint strategy partner. Doing this requires serious consideration and a review of prospective partners' offerings. Morgan and Wolfe, a global Microsoft partner, structures the delivery of SharePoint into modules and workshops. There are a number of Gartner reports that describe the offerings of key partners. More information is available at *http://www.microsoft.com/en-us/news/itanalyst/default.aspx*.

**Note** The brevity of investigation in each session depends on the delivery practices, the culture, and, in most cases, the kind of solution being provided. Common sense is required so that the solution is not overengineered and made overcomplicated by attempting to capture too much detail. Some organizations will require written business proposals on any SharePoint solution delivery program; others will allow the implementation of such tools with very little to no record, and often say, "We will document it later after it is working." I would suggest advising the business sponsor that requires the solution to be implemented to follow an approach where, at the very least, key areas are recorded.

For example, here is a scenario involving an organization that requires a SharePoint solution to be implemented, and therefore, a user requirements document must be created.

*Scenario 5: Fourth Coffee is an organization specializing in the production of coffee across the world. Their employees are new SharePoint users, and they use a central portal for corporate news. One goal is to expand SharePoint into other departments. The top priority lies with several project teams, which are responsible for coordinating material resources and interface with a number of other key departments, including supply, accounting, and finance. Fourth Coffee requires a solution where it can manage each project team's collaborative data centrally.*

## Building the user requirements document

The following are sections of the user requirements document that should be completed as part of the business case document. Use the headings for each of the sections, and fill in those sections using the points given.

### Section 1—User Objectives

In the first section, concerning user objectives, you should concentrate on gathering the aspirations, strategy, and key deliverables that the solution will deliver to the sales team. This is the starting point, and a key component of realizing the current status of the business unit and its goals. The information here fits directly into the Sales SharePoint Team Site business case and helps detail why the solution is required.

### Section 2—Structure and Taxonomy

In the second section, which concerns the structure of the solution, you will need to indicate the taxonomy and framework of the Sales site, so the site is located and arranged in such a way that people can understand how the site maps back to the organization framework. You should also describe, from a basic perspective, how information on this site is laid out and where that information can be located.

#### What is taxonomy?

*Taxonomy* is the practice and science of classification. In SharePoint, the resulting catalog is used to provide a conceptual framework for information retrieval. The development of a good taxonomy takes into account the importance of separating elements of a group (taxon) into subgroups (taxa) that are mutually exclusive, unambiguous, and, taken together, include all possibilities. In practice, a good taxonomy should be simple, easy to remember, and easy to use. One of the best-known taxonomies is the one devised by the Swedish scientist Carl Linnaeus, whose classification for biology is still widely used (with modifications). In SharePoint site design, taxonomies are often created to describe categories and subcategories of organization type and/or organization services (for example, human resources, legal, communications, and so on).

## Section 3—Content and Metadata

In the third section, concerning the content of the solution, you will expand on section 2 and will explain the structure of the content in terms of which repositories (that is, Document Libraries and Lists) would be provided, and how the information in those repositories would be classified. This section should be repeated for each repository.

### What is metadata?

*Metadata* is a hierarchical collection of managed terms that can be defined and then used as attributes for items in SharePoint 2013. Metadata can in fact be used to create site navigation, which for dynamic content sites in SharePoint 2013 is a very powerful feature. Examples of this in use are product sites displaying items from a catalog, which then offer navigation features based on what users are searching for on the site. This means being able to build navigation around specific rules without having to modify site components or structure. For more information about metadata in SharePoint 2013, visit *http://msdn.microsoft.com/en-us/library/jj163942(v=office.15).aspx#SP15_WhatsNewSiteDevelopment_MetadataAndNavigation*.

## Section 4—Search and Audience

The fourth section describes who will consume the content being delivered by the solution, and the search functionality required to locate that content.

When asking questions concerning search requirements, you need to work very closely with the stakeholders so that they have a basic understanding concerning SharePoint Search capabilities. This area requires answers concerning the capacity requirements of Search. This will provide the basis for determining things like user response times, user concurrency, and asynchronous tasks, which are key characteristics in the design of SharePoint search in reference to the SharePoint sales site for Fourth Coffee. Gathering user requirements concerning audiences is useful as well. The sales site may require that certain kinds of users see different content, or that, if the sales site is global and split geographically, that those in different regions see different data that is applicable to that audience. Again, this needs to be documented because it will directly affect the search configuration for the SharePoint site, and will affect higher-up strategies where that audience may also be required.

## Section 5—Features

In the fifth section, you must indicate the features that will be provided to meet the solution requirements. The Fourth Coffee sales site will require things like dashboards, reports, and even specific applications. There may be requirements to use specific services to enable those SharePoint features, such as the SharePoint 2013 Access Services functionality.

To help you understand these features better, Table 2-2 describes some of the key services of SharePoint 2013.

**TABLE 2-2** Services in SharePoint 2010 and SharePoint 2013

| Service | Description |
|---|---|
| Excel Services | Excel Services enables information workers to show the Excel file on a webpage. Those accessing the webpage do not need to have Excel installed.<br>Some features include:<br>■ Global settings for managing workbooks (for example, security, load balancing, session management, memory thresholds, caches, and external data connections)<br>■ Management of SharePoint repositories to trust for Excel Services<br>■ An extensive list of trusted data providers for connecting to your data, plus the ability to add your own trusted data provider<br>■ Trusted data connection libraries, which allow you to define which data connection libraries in your farm are trusted by Excel Services<br>■ The ability to add your own user-defined function assemblies<br>A great overview of this is provided at *http://technet.microsoft.com/en-us/library/ee424405.aspx.*<br>SharePoint 2013 includes additional features related to developer functionality in creating Excel Interactive Views related to Excel Services. The key additional functionality lies in the business intelligence integration that now exists between Excel 2013 and SharePoint 2013, particularly as it relates to the creation of scorecards, reports, and dashboards—all of which can be brought into Excel and which then can be easily displayed as dashboards and other functionalities in SharePoint 2013 sites. For more information, visit *http://technet.microsoft.com/en-us/library/jj219751(v=office.15).aspx.*<br>Another excellent feature is PivotTable. There is a wealth of information about this feature (including what it is and how to use it as well as a description of analysis services) at *http://blogs.msdn.com/b/analysisservices/archive/2012/08/02/verifying-the-excel-services-configuration-for-powerpivot-in-sharepoint-2013.aspx.* |
| Access Services | Access Services provides features to publish a Microsoft Access 2010 web database to a SharePoint site. When an Access web database is published, a site is created to host the web database, plus it moves all of the database objects and data to a SharePoint list on that site.<br>Note that while the Access client is not needed to use the published web database, the Access client is required to make any changes to the database structure. In addition, a user account is required to use the web database. Anonymous access is not supported.<br>For more information about Access 2010, visit *http://technet.microsoft.com/en-us/library/ee748653.aspx.*<br>Access Services in SharePoint 2013 has been enhanced. To begin with, the application created through Access Services is stored in Microsoft SQL Server 2012 as a specific database relevant to the application. Access Services is also available with Office 365.<br>For more information concerning Access Services enhancements in SharePoint 2013, visit *http://msdn.microsoft.com/en-us/library/fp179914(v=office.15).aspx.* |
| InfoPath Forms Services | InfoPath Forms Services is a feature that allows individuals to complete forms using the web browser. Forms can be managed in a central location and can be used to streamline business processes. InfoPath 2013 provides integration with other Office programs and servers, which helps improve the way that you collect, organize, and manage data.<br>For more information concerning InfoPath Forms Services, visit *http://technet.microsoft.com/en-us/library/cc262498(v=office.14).aspx.* |
| User Profile Service | The User Profile Service application stores information about users in a central location; social computing features use this information to enable productive interactions so that users can collaborate efficiently. My Sites can be provisioned to enable social computing features such as social tagging and newsfeeds through the User Profile Service, as well as the creation and distribution of user profiles across multiple sites and farms.<br>For more information concerning the User Profile Service application in SharePoint 2013, visit *http://technet.microsoft.com/en-us/library/ee662538(v=office.15).aspx.* |

| Service | Description |
| --- | --- |
| Search Services | SharePoint provides an enterprise search functionality, which needs to index content so it is available for users to search.<br>SharePoint 2013 Search has been enhanced for greater redundancy and scalability. New features in the user interface include Result Types, Display Templates, improved Search Navigation, and Refinement. Query Suggestions have been improved, and Thumbnail Previews are now available (which previously had been available only through Fast Search Server)<br>For more information about these features and functions, visit *http://technet.microsoft.com/en-us/sharepoint/fp123606.aspx*.<br>You might also be interested in reading the article "SharePoint 2013—Search Service Application," at *http://social.technet.microsoft.com/wiki/contents/articles/12403.sharepoint-2013-search-service-application.aspx*. |
| Business Connectivity Services | Business Connectivity Services provides solutions that connect and empower people by integrating external data with SharePoint collaboration and workflow processes. It integrates closely with Office, allowing external data to be read into SharePoint repositories, and allowing data created within SharePoint to be written to external data sources.<br>SharePoint Business Connectivity Services provides features to harvest external data into SharePoint 2013 and Office 2013 through the cloud and on-premises configurations.<br>For more information concerning Business Connectivity Services in SharePoint 2013, visit *http://msdn.microsoft.com/en-us/library/jj163782(v=office.15).aspx*. |
| PerformancePoint Services | Dashboards are vitally important for any performance solution. PerformancePoint Services provides a set of tools can build dashboard solutions to allow organizations to monitor and analyze performance. Custom reports, filters, tabular data sources, and scorecard transforms can be created using PerformancePoint Services.<br>For an introduction to SharePoint 2013 PerformancePoint Services, visit *http://msdn.microsoft.com/en-us/library/ee559635(v=office.15).aspx*. |
| Content Management | The Content Management feature in SharePoint Server 2013 provides new and improved features for web content management that simplify how you design publishing sites and enhance the authoring and publishing processes of your organization. SharePoint Server 2013 also has the following new features that use the power of search to surface dynamic web content on publishing sites:<br>■ The ability to copy information directly from Microsoft Word and to harvest HTML content in SharePoint 2013 automatically<br>■ Thumbnails for video content<br>■ Improved embedding of dynamic content from other sites<br>■ Content redirection based on language setting on browsers<br>■ Catalog-based repositories that can be used on one or more publishing site collections<br>■ Managed navigation using *term sets*, which can then be used to represent product categories (for example, Cameras, Audio, and Computers)<br>■ Category pages to aggregate content that meets criteria from a catalog<br>■ Content Search Web Part, which enables you to search catalogs using Category Pages and Managed Navigation<br>■ Analytics, which provides methods to analyze content in the search index<br>■ SharePoint Branding using various design tools, like Adobe Dreamweaver and Microsoft Expression Web<br>■ Device Channels, which allows a single publishing site to be rendered in multiple ways (for example, targeting different devices)<br>For more information, visit *http://technet.microsoft.com/en-us/library/jj219688(v=office.15).aspx*. |

| Service | Description |
|---|---|
| Translation Services | Although SharePoint 2010 supported building multilingual websites using Variations, if there was a requirement to translate content to other languages, that had to be carried out manually.<br>Now SharePoint 2013 introduces Translation Services, which support translating content into other languages. In SharePoint 2013, content can be translated automatically using Translation Services in the cloud, exported to a package, sent over to a Translation Agency, and, once translated, imported back into SharePoint. For more information on how to configure Translation Services, visit *http://technet.microsoft.com/en-us/library/jj553772(v=office.15).aspx.* |
| Workflow Services | Workflow has been redesigned in SharePoint 2013, and the engine itself has been radically improved. The workflow engine from SharePoint 2010 is installed in SharePoint 2013; however, going forward, there is the additional option to use the new workflow engine running under Windows Azure.<br>For more information, visit *http://msdn.microsoft.com/en-us/library/jj163177(v=office.15).aspx#SP15Whatsnewinworflow_Newwfactions.*<br>Workflows are now closer to business requirements and can still be constructed using SharePoint Designer and Microsoft Visual Studio. In SharePoint 2013, there is a new service called the Workflow Manager.<br>More information concerning the Workflow Manager service, as well as improvements to workflow design in SharePoint 2013, can be found in this article: *http://technet.microsoft.com/en-us/library/jj219638.aspx.* |
| Work Management Service | The Work Management Service application provides the functionality to aggregate tasks to a central location. The service allows users to aggregate and synchronize tasks between multiple environments, such as Microsoft Project Server, Microsoft Exchange Server, and SharePoint. For example:<br>■ Users can view and track their to-do lists and tasks.<br>■ Tasks can be cached to a user's personal site.<br>■ Tasks can be aggregated from Exchange Server, Project Server, and SharePoint.<br>■ The service is based on a Provider model so that other systems can be integrated in the future.<br>■ This is a My Site feature, and therefore allows users to get a centralized statement of their tasks regardless of what system those tasks reside in.<br>To watch a video that describes the functionality in more detail, visit *http://www.bing.com/videos/watch/video/walkthrough-sharepoint-2013-features-in-the-work-management-service-application/10t98eisc?cpkey=df3d9a1e-1de6-47fb-8489-011aafcddd01%7C%7C%7C%7C.* |
| Mobile Services | Organizations will make substantial investments in mobile devices for their workforce. Related to bring your own device (BYOD) policies being adopted and the technical challenges faced by those requiring access to SharePoint resources through their mobile devices, SharePoint 2013 has been enhanced, providing a better mobile device user experience through new and enhanced mobile features. Notable features include contemporary views of SharePoint. HTML5 view support, and a user interface compatible with most mobile devices. Other features include:<br>■ Device channels provide the ability to display SharePoint content directly, without having to duplicate content to suit the mobile device.<br>■ Touch support is available on tablets.<br>■ Push notification meaning alerts set on repositories now get to mobile devices.<br>■ PerformancePoint and Excel Services on IPads are now supported,<br>■ Geolocation field type support, which allows maps to be harvested from SharePoint lists.<br>For more information, visit *http://technet.microsoft.com/en-us/library/fp161351(v=office.15).aspx.* |

## Differences in planning On-Premise versus SharePoint Online solutions

This section describes some potential issues that may help you determine the scope of the SharePoint delivery in terms of whether the solution requires an on-premises SharePoint or an off-premises SharePoint (that is, SharePoint Online) environment.

Due to the vast number of SharePoint solution types, you should use common sense to not only quantify the technical issues and risks, but also to cover business-related issues, like support, training, business continuity, and disaster recovery concerns. For example, there is little point in creating a SharePoint farm for the organization if you are going to have difficulty supporting the users. Likewise, it would not be wise to implement a glossy-looking app that provides a dashboard on your Office 365 site if users need to connect their enterprise tools to it and encounter problems. No matter what the environment, the key aspect is the ability to apply Platform Governance (control of the environment's availability and integrity); consider the following potential issues:

- **Enterprise tools need to be made available to the business.** This depends not only on the complexity of the solution, but how it will be supported. Remember that if an online solution fails, the problem needs to be resolved as quickly as it would if there were an internal dedicated team to handle it. Consider also that guaranteed uptime percentages are usually quite high with cloud hosting providers. Weigh that factor against the cost of an internal team to support the solution. Another related point is that the provider of the enterprise tool needs to be available to provide support. Suppose that you start using a cloud-based app, but then the company that wrote the app goes out of business. This leaves your organization with no support for that app.

- **Web Services created in-house don't scale well.** A typical issue concerning the On-Premise feature is that Web Services that have been created using in-house developers or external consultants simply do not scale with the evolving changes to the SharePoint platform or integrated components. In addition, there is extra cost and complexity in ensuring that they are supported, and even more cost to bring those resources back to ensure that the Web Services stay scaled. In some cases, there could be resultant down time if Web Services fail, costing the organization more in lost productivity. Be mindful of this if the solution entails the creation of Web Services to be installed on the SharePoint servers.

- **The cost of some providers may scare people.** This factor concerns the providers of custom solutions for On-Premise SharePoint and off-premises SharePoint Online. If the requirement is to build a custom solution using external providers, their time and resources will cost money. In the case of On-Premise SharePoint, there will most likely be a license cost based on server count or user count. For SharePoint Online, there will most likely be a license cost based on just user count. In both cases, though, there will be additional support costs (for example, maintenance costs) to consider.

- **Third-party customized tools may not scale correctly.** For On-Premise SharePoint, the investigation of a third-party tool may include performance tests against existing enterprise applications, and there may be assistance from technical teams supporting the infrastructure and those enterprise applications. For SharePoint Online, there may be difficulty in confirming performance because performance is unquantified. Users could be accessing off-premises, from any number of devices and from any location, where they would have difficulty in measuring connection performance to the customized tool. In addition, customized tools may work only with a specific number of components. Here is an example:

*Scenario 6: Fabrikam has an Office 365 site for a product team so it can share content with external partners. The site has a number of solutions (apps) in place, including a customized app that surfaces information from a connected data source from the partner, and uses a component deployed to the individual's browser to provide that connectivity. This component is third-party. When the solution was released, users appeared to have no issues with it. A month later, a new release of one of the solutions was released to the site. However, this solution automatically upgraded the third-party component. This then caused a detrimental effect on the customized app, resulting in a hurried fix and downtime for the product team and partners.*

- **Office tools need to be compatible with off-premises use.** You should ensure that the version of Office being used on-premises is the same as the Office version being used off-premises (including Office Web Apps). This is not altogether a technical issue. For example, if users are using Office 2007 on-premises and wish to collaborate using Office 365 and SharePoint 2013 online, they will face compatibility issues.

> **More Info** For more information about Office, Windows, Mac, and browser compatibility with Office 365, read the article "Software requirements for Office 365" at *http://onlinehelp.microsoft.com/en-us/office365-enterprises/ff652534.aspx.*

- **Remote accessibility issues.** Office 365 provides SharePoint Online, remote access to Microsoft products that enable them to access and share documents; make real-time contact via instant messaging, video calling, live web conferencing, and online meetings; and manage and access email, calendar, and contacts, all via a remote Internet connection from any location and on any device. While benefits include ease of use, improved collaboration, security, and reliability, you should also ensure that another benefit to users is remote access at any time and from any device. This may be difficult to measure and guarantee, simply because of the connectivity being an Internet connection that the organization will not be able to control. Remote access to off-premises locations includes the management site of SharePoint Online, which will be subject to the same kind of access policy rules as On-Premise SharePoint. For example, who is responsible for granting and policing access to content? If the organization has internal IT support staff, they may defer that to them; however, in organizations where self-governance is set, this may in fact be the task of the members of the relevant business units. For On-Premise SharePoint, the organization will employ remote access systems for their users (for example, Zen Desktop or Citrix). In this case, the issues concerning compatibility of software arise to ensure that the products they use on their desktops are the same through the remote access systems provided.

**More Info** More information concerning the support implications is available in Chapter 8 "Building a SharePoint service delivery model", section "Understand On-Premise versus Off-Premise"

There will undoubtedly be other differences, which will be brought to light during the initial investigations. With each of these decisions, concerning the options to choose will influence the support, maintenance, and costs.

## What makes a SharePoint delivery program successful?

The most vexing question faced by organizations is how to predict and measure the success of investments in the implementation of a SharePoint solution. A significant portion of an organization's capital and operating expenditure could be consumed by a SharePoint delivery program. Therefore, ensuring delivery of return on the ROI of this expenditure is vital.

Many businesses still have no effective technique for predicting and ensuring the success of SharePoint, and that is because businesses generally do not think about what would constitute success before they begin.

The success of SharePoint delivery rests on a combination of the following related activities: delivering on time, adhering to the budget, having the required features and components in place, and reaching the desired quality standard. All these elements need to be measurable (profit margin, user productivity, decrease in avoided costs, reduced time required to train new employees, and so on).

Here are 10 guidelines to help you attain success factors for SharePoint solutions.

- **Choose the collaboration tools that match the business goals.** You must keep the business goal in mind when choosing a solution; make sure that even implementing a generic solution may not address the real collaboration issues in the organization. The most transformative behaviors are revealed by targeting technology selection to respond to the real problem. To make the greatest impact, look for the simplest fix.
- **Learn from consumer-oriented social networking.** You should not implement solutions that require users to negotiate unintuitive web interfaces, cumbersome navigation, and technical terms. Users will avoid those types of solutions. Use easy-to-use technology, as that will pose fewer barriers to adoption.
- **Ensure that the solution can be integrated with other systems.** The value of users being able to access everything from one place drives the next requirement: make sure that collaboration is embedded into the rest of the information infrastructure.
- **Put someone in charge of making change happen.** Even if the solution has been chosen, there is no guarantee of success. With no oversight and no one person assigned for collaboration initiatives related to the solution, there is no systemic opportunity to improve habits. There will not be any sustained success resulting from a grass-roots, technology-led

initiative. Make sure that you get the right delivery manager and sponsor in place to guarantee the success of the SharePoint solution.

- **Reward members of staff for changing the way they work, and then use the enthusiasm of early adopters.** Potential users will always have in the back of their minds, "What's in it for me?" You should identify SharePoint champions and call on them to tout the software to less enthusiastic colleagues and help them discover how to collaborate more effectively using the solution. SharePoint champions naturally understand the business and are already immersed in collaborative tools. Do not force tools on staff; rather, let them discover the benefits gradually and learn from one another.

- **Migrate the right content from existing systems.** Prepopulation of content can go a long way toward encouraging participation. An empty SharePoint site is not going to inspire much interest. That said, content migration and consolidation require a lot of effort. You can help alleviate this by centralizing information fragmented across many different technology platforms and locations into SharePoint repositories, and configuring searches to target areas of content that will not be moved into SharePoint repositories. That way, individuals using SharePoint sites can still locate that data. Note that managing redundant information requires careful consideration and a lot of manual labor. There are content migration tools available, but data owners must be identified and involved in the process.

- **Help users find the content and expertise available.** Management of content and Governance of the solution, once implemented, are both crucial. Proliferation of content is a major risk; indexing strategies for Search are required to ensure suitable performance and accessibility. For example, a product on Amazon is considered more trustworthy if it is rated highly; the same principle can and needs to be applied to SharePoint Search, especially when it comes to finding specific information on a topic.

- **Be aware of hidden costs.** Organizations can be easily persuaded to invest in SharePoint solutions by the fact that the latest generation of web-based collaboration tools comes with a low initial price. Purchase and installation of these tools is just a small part of the total cost, however. The practical reality is that the solution requires a certain level of infrastructure to run, has a price tag that depends on the number of users and servers involved (and in most cases has an annual recurrent cost), and may even need extra modules of functionality before it can behave as a complete solution. Other costs relate to the development of unified taxonomies, metadata, and retention policies. Ongoing training and support also carries a price; ensure that the organization can roll out a solution with minimal follow-up cost. You must ensure that the solution is intuitive and user-friendly, reducing the need for further consultation.

- **Address security concerns.** All SharePoint delivery focused on collaboration and User Adoption can be undermined by security-savvy staff made more aware by security issues by news reports concerning loss of laptops and universal serial bus (USB) sticks. In fact, this has a detrimental effect, causing the blockage of collaborative tasks between partners and the organization. You must ensure that SharePoint solutions be configured to enforce agreed security measures. Consider the following example.

*Scenario 7: Fabrikam implemented a SharePoint solution for a construction group to allow the group to share drawings, specifications, and other documents, both internally and with suppliers and builders. The company made sure that only particular groups had access to particular documents or functions. Third parties were not able to view all internal documentation.*

- **Eliminate duplicate tools.** Remove redundant or duplicate tools; otherwise, SharePoint solutions will remain fragmented as staff continue to use multiple systems or old ways of working and bypass the delivered solution. Redundant tools not only cost organizations in terms of operation, management, and maintenance, but they can also do the opposite of what is required.

## Creating a SharePoint solution delivery plan

In order to deliver a SharePoint solution—whether it is a SharePoint environment of servers, a SharePoint collection of sites, a single site, or an app—you need to follow a process that includes the following steps:

1. Define what the solution is, who is going to deliver it, and how it is going to be delivered.
2. Create and engage a team to help design and deliver the solution.
3. Create a plan that includes a schedule of tasks and assignments.
4. Establish controls to manage the delivery program.
5. Engage the sponsor and stakeholders as part of the delivery team.

The purpose of setting up the delivery of a SharePoint solution is to state formally the business drivers, scope, and objectives. That plan then becomes the roadmap for solution delivery. Building a successful roadmap involves three areas: people, process, and technology. People are those who are required to state the goals and aspirations of the solution, as well as those who can design and build it. Business processes represent the way people capture information, organize and store it, and, ultimately, use it to make decisions. The technology functions include all system components that make up the SharePoint solution. However, even the best technologies and logical business processes will fail if the user community does not readily adopt them. The goals of the roadmap are to help the business users understand their needs and how SharePoint will help them achieve their goals. In developing the roadmap, information needs to be captured. The following topics need to be addressed, documented, and agreed to:

- Why is the solution being delivered?
- What will the solution deliver?
- When will the solution be delivered?
- How will the solution be delivered?
- Who will be involved?

- How much will the delivery cost, and what are the benefits?
- How will success be measured?

You will need to gather this information in a document called the *business case,* which, along with the associated plans, provide a starting point (called the *baseline*) which all subsequent decisions will be hinged upon and against which delivery performance can be measured. Table 2-3 describes what goes into a SharePoint delivery business case.

**TABLE 2-3** SharePoint Delivery Business Case Contents

| Area | Title | Description |
|---|---|---|
| Summary | Background | Gives a description of the history leading up to the business requirement and goals. Explains the situation in terms of how the requirement came about (for example, as a result of a strategy study, as a result of findings from another delivery). Refers to other associated initiatives, business plans and programs, or conclusions from other studies. |
| | Business Objectives | Describe why the delivery of the solution is going to be carried out. What business objectives will it satisfy? How does the SharePoint solution support the business strategy? How does the SharePoint solution meet requirements and goals? |
| | Benefits | Describe the benefits that the business hopes to achieve once the delivery of the solution is complete. Include a statement on what else will be accomplished; for example, say what new possibilities will be created (operationally, commercially, or for new delivery programs). Define metrics and benchmarks here so that they can be compared to revised metrics and benchmarks after the solution has been delivered. |
| | Conditions of Satisfaction | Describe the minimum conditions of satisfaction required in order to declare the delivery program a success (for example, the achievement of key stakeholders signing off on the solution). Define the method for measuring and confirming the achievement of each condition and the date by when it will be achieved. Use Value Management techniques to query objectives rigorously.<br>For more information, visit *http://www.sharepointgeoff.com/managing-value-for-sharepoint-solutions.* |
| The functionality | Development Definition | Describes in one paragraph what the delivery will produce overall. For example:<br>*"A product-based portal; search results will expose products for sale, and these will be displayed using dynamically created pages using navigational taxonomy."*<br>**Note:** SharePoint 2013 provides features allowing developers to create portals based on managed navigation and dynamic pages. The Term Store now carries navigational taxonomy, meaning that top-level navigational links can be used to provide content based on what has been exposed through search results. For example, search results can expose results where they are tied to centrally managed navigational taxonomy, which means that dynamic pages can be delivered quickly.<br>For more information, visit *http://msdn.microsoft.com/en-us/library/jj163978(v=office.15).aspx.* |
| | Scope, Impacts, and Interdependencies | State the tasks necessary to meet the business objectives. List the high-level tasks that must be undertaken, the boundaries, the impacts on current operations, the business functions that will be affected, any aspects that are specifically excluded, and key interdependencies with delivery programs. |

| Area | Title | Description |
|---|---|---|
| | Deliverables | List the major deliverables that are needed to create the output described previously. Deliverables may take two forms:<br>■ **Final deliverable,** which is to be handed over by the delivery team to the users when the solution is implemented<br>■ **Intermediate deliverable,** which is to be produced during the course of the delivery for review<br>For each deliverable, summarize:<br>■ The format and content in which the deliverable is to be produced<br>■ The named individual accountable for the production of the deliverable and the target date for completion<br>■ The named individual accountable for reviewing and signing off on the deliverable |
| The business context | Risks | Describe the significant risks that may potentially jeopardize success.<br>Actions that will be taken at the outset to reduce the likelihood of each risk occurring<br>Actions or contingency plans that may be implemented should any risk happen.<br>State any events which, if they occur, will lead to consideration of the delivery program being terminated prematurely. |
| The approach | Solution Implementation Approach | ■ **Shar ePoint vision:** Work with senior managers to align the SharePoint vision with business goals.<br>■ **Governance:** What is needed to allow all departments or parties to help define and implement the SharePoint system?<br>■ **Determine desired features:** What functionality is needed?<br>■ **Prioritize features:** Determine the complexity and importance of each feature.<br>■ **Technology gap analysis:** Understand and document what technologies are needed for the overall solution.<br>■ **Roadmap**: Define in text and chart format what will happen over the next 18-24 months. |

## Adding quality to your delivered SharePoint solution

Excellence in SharePoint solution delivery is a key quality indicator and driver. Particularly due to the emergence of SaaS, which encompasses the cloud offerings of SharePoint online through Office 365, and the abilities of SharePoint 2013 to use the Office 365 Marketplace, your SharePoint sponsor and stakeholders will be eager to measure the quality of any SharePoint solution. In addition to the technical quality (a performance measure) that needs to be investigated before a solution is implemented, they will want to factor in quality measures to identify the overall ROI against the implemented solution.

Due to the vast number of solution deliveries that could be related to SharePoint, there can be no single opinion of what the word *quality* means, but a number of main approaches can be discerned, as follows:

- The solution meets its purpose (meeting organizational objectives).
- The solution aligns inputs, processes, outputs, and outcomes (meaning that the solution meets the relevant business goals and organizational strategic goals).

- The solution meets or exceeds customer expectations.
- The solution produces emotional, passionate commitment on the part of the users (User Adoption).
- The solution fits into the platform Governance provided by the organization.
- The solution either reduces costs, increases revenue, increases profit margins, or decreases avoided costs.

A delivery manager who was responsible for deploying a SharePoint solution was asked, "How do you make sure the SharePoint solution is good enough?" His response was, "Survey the users."

Although this response may answer some questions concerning quality from the perspective of SharePoint support service, more work still needs to be done to measure quality. Equally as important is whether the solution meets all the business requirements, is supportable and maintainable, and has business rules that govern its use.

*Scenario 7: Fabrikam is using SharePoint 2013. The sales business unit has indicated a requirement to add a module that helps in its Customer Retainment application, which is a document library that uses special workflows. That business unit prefers a top-down approach of implementation by immediately purchasing the application from the marketplace; the application is immediately deployed into the Sales site and appears to work as required. However, no investigation was carried out to ascertain the cost of support, the annual recurrent cost, or the maintenance cost to the existing SharePoint team.*

In this scenario, there is no approach to determining quality, so the result is that support will be difficult to manage and the solutions value difficult to justify. The Governance, adoption, value, goal alignment (vision), and ROI of the solution were never investigated or defined. This section suggests a method of ensuring quality in the delivery of a SharePoint solution; namely, examining each of the areas that, combined with the others, defines the quality of a SharePoint solution: Governance, User Adoption, Value, Vision, and ROI.

## Governance

A SharePoint solution is designed to meet a business objective, and that solution must be sustainable. This means that from a service delivery perspective, the solution can be supported and managed, and that data integrity through the use of the solution is maintained. The fundamental concern is that the users are comfortable with using the solution and that they consider the service provision of that solution to be of a high quality.

Any SharePoint solution needs to conform to Governance, which is realized through business rules and policies, to ensure that the integrity and configuration management of SharePoint is maintained. Historically, it has been suggested that SharePoint solution Governance relates to the SharePoint platform itself, giving organizations a false belief that SharePoint Governance can be defined solely through the use of technical tools.

In Chapters 4, 5, and 6, the importance of information workers being part of the Governance process is covered in detail. Governance comes from the realization of policies, standards, procedures, support, and training—and only users can supply that.

## Adoption

For the adoption of a SharePoint solution to take place, information workers are involved. If their productivity and proficiency have been increased and optimized using the solution, then it can be considered successful.

However, information workers are not the only people to consider when it comes to measuring quality in adoption of a SharePoint solution. The effectiveness of the solution concerning the level of support available for it is also measured. This indicates whether the solution can be merged into the support that is provided with all other tools.

Other ways to measure the quality of User Adoption is related to the cost of materials for online training and support. For example, if the quality of documentation of a solution is higher and training materials more varied, these factors increase the likelihood that the solution will be adopted. Examples of this could be where solution documentation is provided on a centralized SharePoint site, or even using the SharePoint Productivity Hub (when available for SharePoint 2013).

**Note** The SharePoint Productivity Hub was developed for SharePoint 2010. The Hub is a SharePoint Server collection site that serves as a learning community and is fully customizable. It provides a central place for your training efforts and includes training content about Microsoft's core products. Microsoft also provides ongoing and updated content packs. Currently, this product is not yet available for SharePoint 2013. More information about the Productivity Hub is located at *http://www.microsoft.com/en-gb/download/details.aspx?id=28178#overview.*

Getting users involved in an implemented SharePoint solution as it evolves helps User Adoption. Aligned with communication and training, this leads to the development of consistent and engaging learning content developed by users. Users could get involved in the creation and delivery of e-Learning titles, blended courses, and context-sensitive, in-application support solutions.

This leads to cost efficiencies in the creation of documentation, classroom materials, online training, and support content, as well as the centralization of support content.

## Value

The value of the SharePoint solution lies not just in the cost of the solution; it is the value that is applied to the organization where the solution has been implemented. The value of it is based on the functionality, maintainability, documentation, clarity (user acceptance), and successful tests. Of course, an app that has been obtained and written by a sole developer with little documentation and is untested will not be anywhere near as valuable as an app that has been tested, has committed users, and has an organization and support behind it.

### Vision

Having an implemented SharePoint solution that meets the user requirements, organizational goals, and vision is a major win. Those solutions are aligned with organizational strategy.

*Scenario 8: Fabrikam needed a SharePoint solution that allowed the organization to have a centralized and searchable people finder. This was seen as one of the strategic aims related to its SharePoint search strategy. To proceed, several investigations were carried out to identify and create the relevant architecture and engage with assigned stakeholders. Through this exercise, the company was able to measure and implement the delivery of the solution, which was seen as a great success, and it is still one of the favorite and most-used apps on the Fabrikam SharePoint site.*

### ROI

Organizations are therefore now seeing how important a strategy is for delivering and managing SharePoint which is seen as their enterprise content management system. Creating a strategy and associating that with a platform roadmap is vital; businesses are more reliant on and interested in computerized business processes to increase ROI. Additionally, and not surprisingly, organizations are now requesting sustainability, not simply a delivery of SharePoint.

To gauge ROI, you need to measure the time and cost of the existing process and then compare that to the time and costs of implementing a SharePoint solution. These considerations will include the resources required to provide the solution, like people costs. Other costs include time for investigation, user testing, rejections of solutions, and then reinvestigating new ones. The marker of quality concerning ROI is whether there is a marked productivity improvement from the user base. However, this criterion is intangible and needs to be measured using review methods.

**More Info** In Chapter 4, in the section "Extracting value from SharePoint solution implementations," I discuss methods of determining and managing value, which in turn helps gauge ROI; namely, value management (selecting the solution that provides best value for money) and value engineering (optimizing the value for money delivered by a chosen solution).

## Summary

The key to ensuring the success of any SharePoint solution delivery is communication and matching the goals and aspirations of the business to the features of SharePoint. If you do this properly, it will ensure the success of the implementation, resulting in a high level of User Adoption, which in turn leads to policy creation and governance.

This chapter discussed the creation of a business case that attempts to capture what needs to be achieved (the scope), including all decision making concerning the solution to be implemented, the kind of questions that need to be answered, and some areas of interest concerning the relevant features of the current SharePoint platform that needs to be considered and appraised. Also discussed in this chapter was the process of building an action plan to deliver the solution, and the quality indicators to determine whether the implementation of the solution has been a success.

Chapter 3, "Planning SharePoint solution delivery," describes how to build the delivery program itself, including the creation of the team, preparing the action plan, setting the controls, and engaging the stakeholders.

CHAPTER 3

# Planning SharePoint solution delivery

In this chapter:



Microsoft SharePoint 2013 provides an incredible number of benefits that can empower business users, enabling them to collaborate; tag, rate, and publish content; and track tasks. Even with all this technical capability, none of it will be meaningful to users unless there are plans set to design, implement, and communicate training to users. SharePoint solution delivery is a combination of providing the solution to meet user requirements, and then ensuring that users can adopt those solutions. This chapter covers the basics of planning solution delivery through plan formation, managing outputs, and engaging sponsors and stakeholders.

Providing a SharePoint solution is not something that can be achieved by one person. You will need to build a solution delivery team to design and implement the solution. The structure of the delivery team very much depends on the solution scope, the solution's complexity (technical implementation and business User Adoption), and how the solution fits into the SharePoint environment (including the support and maintenance of that solution going forward). The kind of human resources required for implementing the solution to an on-premises SharePoint environment will be different from off-premises SharePoint. SharePoint Online, through Microsoft Office 365 off-premises solutions, is implemented in a Software as a Solution (SaaS) environment. This represents a shift from traditional on-premises software solutions.

With SharePoint on-premises, solution implementations usually involve internal technical staff being involved because they govern the internal SharePoint platform under which the solution would operate. There would be technical and security-related policies concerning how any solution is deployed. This also relates even to SharePoint off-premises environments that are Platform as a Service (PAAS), where the environment is available in the cloud but still managed by a SharePoint team.

Delivery of SharePoint to an organization is based on meeting the organization's information and collaborative challenges. Here are several actions that will be requested:

- Creation of a SharePoint Farm
- Creation of a Web Service
- Implementation of an off-the-shelf app (including customization)
- Implementation of an off-the-shelf app (not including customization)
- Implementation of an SharePoint built-in app
- Implementation of a third-party tool (to provide extra functionality to SharePoint)

No single person can deliver any of these solutions. Implementation of SharePoint is not simply a technical installation—it requires business and technical teams to work together. Therefore, a team that offers various types of people skills will be required to help implement and support the solution. Chapter 7, "Organizing the Delivery Team," describes the roles required to deliver a SharePoint solution delivery program. In Chapter 8, "Building a SharePoint service delivery model," the "Build in support to aid service delivery" section provides more information on the roles required to support the solution.

Therefore, to analyze, design, build, test, and deliver a SharePoint delivery program, you will need to put together a SharePoint delivery team. Let's now examine in greater detail how to do this.

## Setting up a SharePoint delivery team

As previously stated, SharePoint solutions are limited only by the imagination of their creators. They can be designed and implemented using SharePoint on-premises or off-premises. However, the construction of the delivery teams differs depending on the desired result. Regardless of the kind of solution implemented, there are support requirements to consider, which then increase the team size required (because this may include internal teams, external teams, or both). Consider using external providers who can help build your SharePoint delivery team. Table 3-1 describes the types of providers and their offerings.

**TABLE 3-1** Types of services to deliver and support SharePoint solutions

| Offering Type | Description |
|---|---|
| Consulting services | Paid on the basis of what you want them to tell you. Examples include strategy, development, configuration, and auditing. |
| Professional services | Paid on the basis of what you want them to do. Examples include SharePoint training, installation, and support. |
| Managed services | Paid to manage entire environments. Examples include back-end monitoring to resolution of Office 365 environments, back-end administration on-premises SharePoint, Administration, and so on. |
| Outsourcing services | Paid to operate specific parts of the environment. Examples include third-party solutions that are integrated into SharePoint. |

Organizations may simply want guidance or perspectives concerning SharePoint or best practices and may be looking for consulting services as well. Others may want to apply a consultant's expertise to specific objectives, and that is where consulting blends into professional services. Extending the train of thought even further, where the organization wants very limited involvement and is looking for a vendor to own and provide the full service, managed or outsourcing services typically are engaged.

The reason that these concepts are important lies in the way that they relate to the proximity of the solution to the organization. If, for example, the organization is just procuring an off-the-shelf solution, for example, then they typically would need basic support and training services. On the other hand, if an Office 365 environment is being provided as a managed service, the organization would ask the vendor to manage the entire environment from a support perspective and have very little involvement with the product itself.

The size and complexity of the solution being delivered will also identity the size and skill sets required to deliver the solution. A solution could be as simple as implementing a Microsoft Access packaged app solution from the Office Store, or as complex as delivering customized apps or full-blown SharePoint environments.

**Note** Consider using consulting services to help you deliver the solution. No one is a SharePoint superhero; do not expect your IT teams to have all the answers.

There are three types of SharePoint solution delivery teams:

- **Short-term** This kind of delivery team is established only for the duration of the delivery. This could be a consulting service, or members of an existing SharePoint team (where the solution delivery is non-complex).
- **Cross-functional** This kind of delivery team provides necessary skill mixes. For example, in the delivery of an on-premises SharePoint farm, resources may be required from other parts

of the organization, which are responsible for support parts of the technical infrastructure. Examples of this include Microsoft SQL Server teams, network teams, and platform-building teams. Also, you should consider that in most deliveries, individuals are required to represent the business to provide guidance on user requirements; they are also part of the delivery team because they provide skills relevant to understanding and defining business requirements. Most delivery teams for SharePoint are cross-functional.

- **Frequently part-time** This kind of delivery includes members who are fulfilling line and delivery tasks.

Bearing this in mind, it is essential that from the very start you fill the key delivery roles (business sponsor, and delivery manager). See Figure 3-1 for an example of hierarchy of roles.

**Note** You do not have to use the job titles "business sponsor" and "delivery manager," so long as the roles are fully understood across the delivery team.

Many of the team members are likely to be part-time or have other daily duties to attend to, so get their line manager to agree what their commitment is and how changes to that commitment should be handled. The line managers may wish to, or be asked to, undertake a quality assurance role (as described in the "Adding quality to your delivered SharePoint solution" section in Chapter 2, "Defining the SharePoint solution scope"). If so, this must be agreed upon.

For each team member, you should write a Terms of Reference agreement describing the responsibilities of the role and ensure that each team member signs it. Once this is done, summarize those roles in the SharePoint solution's business case.

**Note** For delivery teams where there is cross-functionality, there may be a requirement to create a Terms of Reference document confirming exactly what their role is in helping shape and deliver a SharePoint solution. Taking those previous examples, building a SharePoint farm on-premises and requiring consulting services will require a terms of reference summary for that team, and terms of reference for internal interfacing teams, and for specific areas where individuals need to collate user requirements (for example, business analysts).

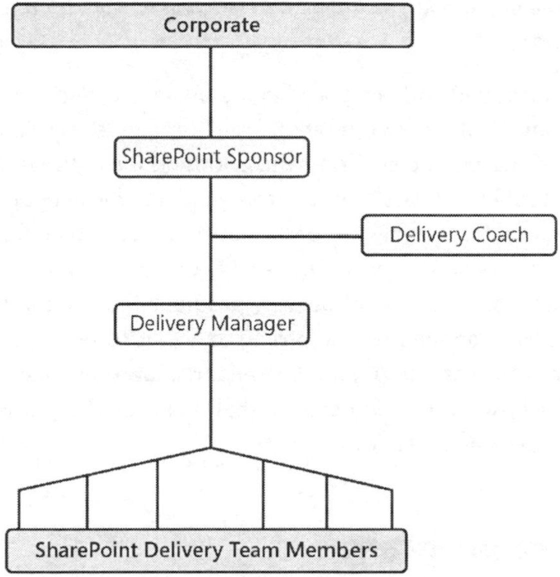


**FIGURE 3-1** A typical SharePoint delivery team's roles and hierarchy.

When a SharePoint team is working well together, they have complementary skills and are committed to delivering a SharePoint quality solution and user experience. You should aim to build a delivery team that has an environment of openness and trust because this creates a solid communication base. Doing this right when you set up the delivery program is ideal. Even if you are clear on what needs to be done, you should allow some time for the team to understand and contribute, because that will lead to greater commitment and better results. You do not want a delivery team starting as in the following scenario:

*Scenario 1: Fabrikam uses On-Premise SharePoint for basic collaborative services. Its HR department had a request to enhance the People directory, housed in a third-party system. The department wanted to use SharePoint social features and decided to use the skills and tagging features, as well as the SharePoint profile builder. For this to happen, the third-party system would need to be integrated into SharePoint. A delivery manager was selected to deliver the enhanced People directory in SharePoint through integrating the third-party system. The delivery manager, who had a good understanding of the existing directory, drew up a plan of action. However, in that plan, he did not check with the HR team. His reasoning was that the implementation would be faster using a consultancy. The delivery manager assumed that the consultancy would know intuitively what had to be done, and he stated that he did not want "too many long, drawn-out discussions and workshops." The delivery manager requested that the consultancy start building prototypes for a new People directory to replace the third-party system. Unfortunately, when the consultancy staff met with HR to demonstrate one of the prototypes, they faced a hostile reception, which resulted in backtracking and chaos. There were many angry exchanges, and the delivery manager was blamed for inadequately communicating his intentions to HR. He was also blamed for the failure to construct the delivery team and not keeping all parties informed concerning the delivery plan. Finally, Fabrikam executives intervened and replaced the manager with another individual from the same department, who better understood the business requirements. Replacing this manager cost time and money, including him needing to work hard to rebuild confidence and trust with the HR department.*

SharePoint solution building can be highly charged and fast paced in the beginning, and eventually, it will become part of the organization's standard operations. The delivery team will form and then form again as more SharePoint solutions join the environment. Choosing the right people for your delivery team is a vital element of an evolving SharePoint environment, and those people need to be willing to be part of the team. That said, willingness to participate in a SharePoint delivery team does not guarantee SharePoint solution implementation success; ability to function within the team is also vital. When people are thrown into a SharePoint delivery program, those without experience will flounder and will need assistance. Plan the team according to how focused each person is, and ensure that managers also focus on promoting good SharePoint knowledge building of their team members. This creates strong delivery successes, and creates SharePoint champions, who then can further promote and showcase their skills and creations.

## Preparing a SharePoint delivery program

You will need to prepare a SharePoint delivery program so that you can do the following:

- Map user requirements to SharePoint features and capabilities correctly.
- Set, agree on, and prioritize solution delivery.
- Identify materials requirement and resources (for example, SharePoint infrastructure, connected teams).
- Staff your SharePoint delivery team appropriately (covered in the previous section, "Setting up a SharePoint delivery team")
- Train the delivery team so that all its members can understand the key features of SharePoint that will be implemented.

A SharePoint delivery program requires a delivery scope, a sponsor, and a method to measure progress and success.

- **Creating and managing the delivery scope.** This topic is described further in Chapter 2. The scope is where activities are specified, prioritized, and scheduled.
- **Assigning accountability** SharePoint solution delivery can be as simple as adding features to a site, or as complex as creating a new SharePoint environment. Either way, you should assign an owner for each activity who will be accountable for its completion.
- **Monitoring progress** In addition to assigning accountability, you will need to assign people to roles that monitor progress and ensure that that progress reports are given to the SharePoint sponsor and stakeholders. The delivery plan provides a baseline against the progress of key activities on the plan.

## Building the SharePoint delivery plan

A core aspect of the SharePoint delivery program is planning. *Planning* describes the work required to implement the SharePoint solution. You should prepare two sets of plans. The first is the *Detail Plan,* which includes the delivery schedule. The *delivery schedule* is a progress bar chart used by the delivery manager and team members to control their day-to-day work. The second plan is an *Outline Plan,* which is a management summary used to present the overall progress of the delivery to the SharePoint sponsor and other interested parties. This should show the stages, milestones, and other important activities needed for an overview.

**Tip** Always consider risk when developing your plans. For each stream of work, ask this question: "What are the risks of taking this approach?" If a significant risk is found, consider how the approach can be changed to avoid or reduce the risk.

The Detail Plan manages the business case and all associated documentation concerning the implementation of the SharePoint solution. It is a complete record of the delivery program, which describes the implementation of the solution, including the User Adoption planning. The Detail Plan includes four segments:

- **Envision** This segment includes performing the initial investigations, creating the business case, confirming the success criteria, and stating the high-level milestones for progress reporting.
- **Plan** This segment includes creating the team, building technical and user (business) requirements, confirming the design of the solution, and determining a User Adoption strategy (communications and training).
- **User Adoption** This segment includes the provision of communications, training, and education. It also includes the testing and validation tasks carried out by the users.
- **Build** This segment includes the tasks necessary to build and then operate (deliver and provide service for) the solution.

**Note** The User Adoption and Build segments are closely connected. For example, the Build segment includes tasks relating to the creation of test platforms, prototyping, and solution implementation, which will include testing. These must be validated by the users. Relevant User Adoption tasks, including testing, usage, training, and service delivery, comprise a very important area. User adoption planning is described in Chapter 4, "Preparing SharePoint solution User Adoption."

There is another segment, Closure, which relates to the official completion of the delivery and is validated by the success criteria detailed in the Envision segment. This segment is discussed in more detail in Chapter 11, "Managing workshops and closing the delivery program."

Figure 3-2 shows the format of the SharePoint delivery Detail Plan, including some high-level tasks. The dotted arrow lines show how the segments are connected. As stated, a key aspect of the Detail

Plan is the delivery schedule, which lists the work required to implement the solution and when it must be completed. You should lay out the Detail Plan and work closely with the needed delivery team members (including the sponsor and stakeholders) to map the relevant tasks to the solution and record them in a Gantt chart. Ensure that each task is assigned to one or more team members. The Detail Plan forms the basis for progress reporting and gets recorded in the Outline Plan.

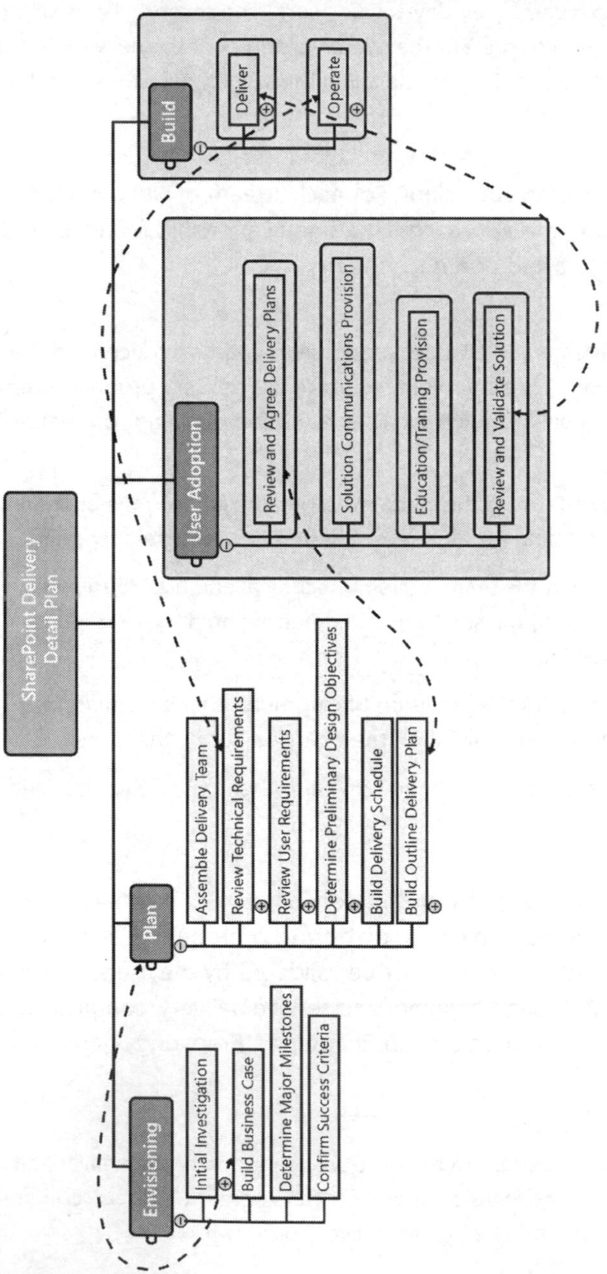


**FIGURE 3-2** Format of a SharePoint Delivery Detail Plan.

**More Info** A fuller and expandable version of this map can be found at *http://www.sharepointgeoff.com/articles-2/sharepoint-delivery-detail-plan.*

You should ensure that there is a place to centralize the business case, delivery plans, and other documentation such as user requirements, issue logs, and risk logs. Use SharePoint to accomplish this. The delivery team could use a SharePoint site as a central location for all its activities; the site also acts as a showcase to sponsors and stakeholders, and of course, it also can be used to record delivery progress.

Taking this idea further, here is a scenario depicting the implementation of an app to a SharePoint site:

*Scenario 2: Fabrikam wants to implement an app into its SharePoint environment. The company has enlisted a delivery manager, who has created a small team to help deliver the solution. The delivery manager wants to use a SharePoint site to contain the Detail Plan, so he would have a central place to manage high-level tasks in the delivery schedule. The SharePoint site also would be used to keep related documents and contact details for the team. The tasks stored in the site would be assigned to team members, as is any relevant documentation to be managed.*

Figures 3-3 and 3-4 depict an example of how Fabrikam could have used SharePoint components to help manage the delivery program as described in Scenario 2. Figure 3-3 shows an example of a SharePoint 2013 site using the built-in Deliverables app, and it also illustrates the Detail Plan relevant to implementation of a SharePoint solution.

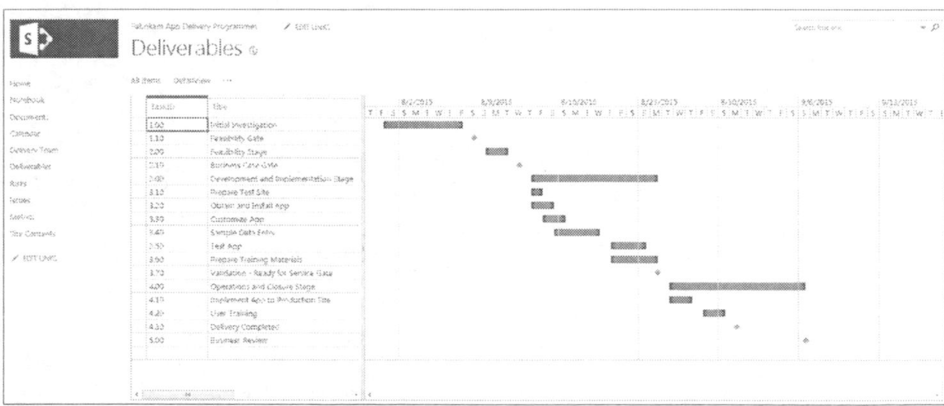


**FIGURE 3-3** The Deliverables app in SharePoint.

Figure 3-4 shows the Detail Plan as a task list. Note that two extra columns have been added: an Accountability column, which shows the contact accountable to the task; and the Related Document column, which is bound to content stored in a documents library, showing the title of the document related to the task. Figure 3-5 shows the contacts list, which is bound to the task list as the Accountability column.

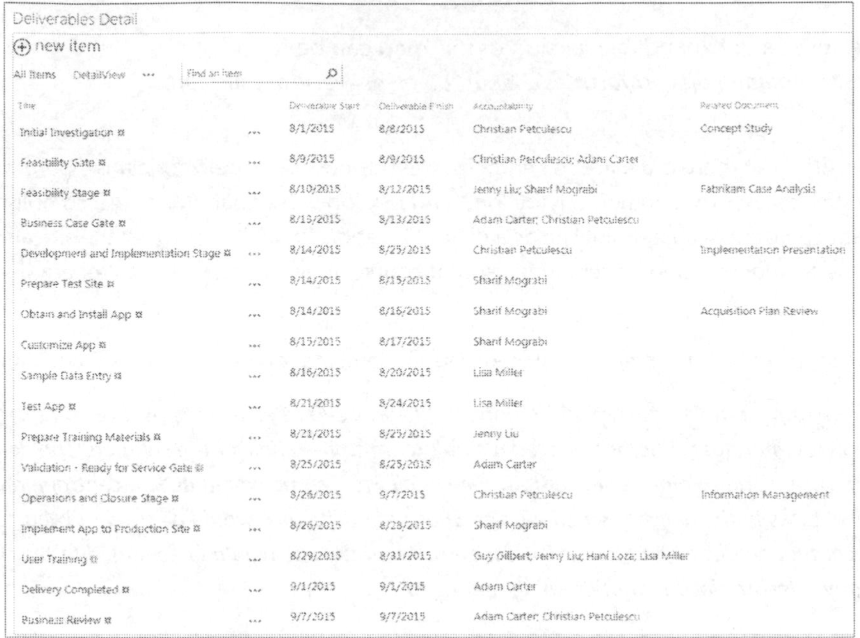

Deliverables Detail

new item

All Items | DetailView | ... | Find an item

| Title | Deliverable Start | Deliverable Finish | Accountability | Related Document |
|---|---|---|---|---|
| Initial Investigation | 8/1/2015 | 8/8/2015 | Christian Petculescu | Concept Study |
| Feasibility Gate | 8/9/2015 | 8/9/2015 | Christian Petculescu; Adam Carter | |
| Feasibility Stage | 8/10/2015 | 8/12/2015 | Jenny Liu; Sharif Mograbi | Fabrikam Case Analysis |
| Business Case Gate | 8/13/2015 | 8/13/2015 | Adam Carter; Christian Petculescu | |
| Development and Implementation Stage | 8/14/2015 | 8/25/2015 | Christian Petculescu | Implementation Presentation |
| Prepare Test Site | 8/14/2015 | 8/15/2015 | Sharif Mograbi | |
| Obtain and Install App | 8/14/2015 | 8/16/2015 | Sharif Mograbi | Acquisition Plan Review |
| Customize App | 8/15/2015 | 8/17/2015 | Sharif Mograbi | |
| Sample Data Entry | 8/16/2015 | 8/20/2015 | Lisa Miller | |
| Test App | 8/21/2015 | 8/24/2015 | Lisa Miller | |
| Prepare Training Materials | 8/21/2015 | 8/25/2015 | Jenny Liu | |
| Validation - Ready for Service Gate | 8/25/2015 | 8/25/2015 | Adam Carter | |
| Operations and Closure Stage | 8/26/2015 | 9/7/2015 | Christian Petculescu | Information Management |
| Implement App to Production Site | 8/26/2015 | 8/28/2015 | Sharif Mograbi | |
| User Training | 8/29/2015 | 8/31/2015 | Guy Gilbert; Jenny Liu; Hani Loza; Lisa Miller | |
| Delivery Completed | 9/1/2015 | 9/1/2015 | Adam Carter | |
| Business Review | 9/7/2015 | 9/7/2015 | Adam Carter; Christian Petculescu | |

**FIGURE 3-4** An example of a high-level task list from the Deliverables component in SharePoint.

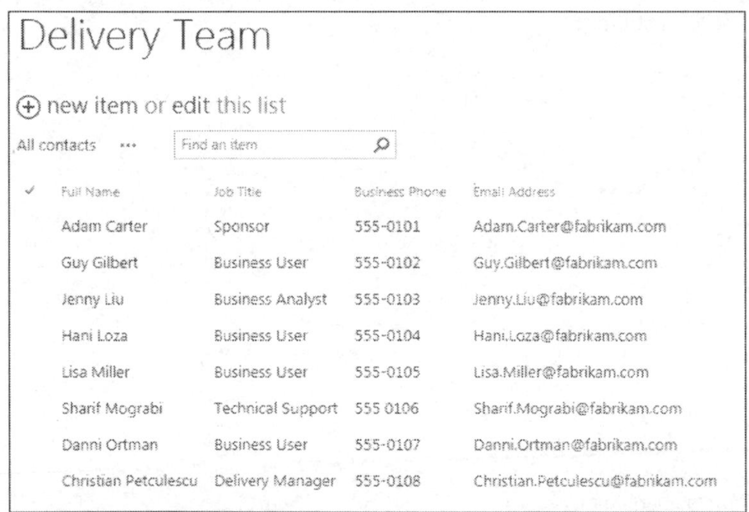

Delivery Team

new item or edit this list

All contacts | ... | Find an item

| Full Name | Job Title | Business Phone | Email Address |
|---|---|---|---|
| Adam Carter | Sponsor | 555-0101 | Adam.Carter@fabrikam.com |
| Guy Gilbert | Business User | 555-0102 | Guy.Gilbert@fabrikam.com |
| Jenny Liu | Business Analyst | 555-0103 | Jenny.Liu@fabrikam.com |
| Hani Loza | Business User | 555-0104 | Hani.Loza@fabrikam.com |
| Lisa Miller | Business User | 555-0105 | Lisa.Miller@fabrikam.com |
| Sharif Mograbi | Technical Support | 555 0106 | Sharif.Mograbi@fabrikam.com |
| Danni Ortman | Business User | 555-0107 | Danni.Ortman@fabrikam.com |
| Christian Petculescu | Delivery Manager | 555-0108 | Christian.Petculescu@fabrikam.com |

**FIGURE 3-5** A sample delivery team list has been created using the Contacts app in SharePoint.

Using SharePoint to build the delivery plan, contacts, and documents is a great way to help ensure that information is centralized. There are other benefits, too, particularly in aiding early User Adoption to business members who have access to the site and implementing solution apps for SharePoint sites. For example, the solution app could be deployed to a subsite of the delivery team's SharePoint site and demonstrated there, and then the results could be captured to a list that can aid the business review at the closure of the delivery program.

As previously described, the solution delivery schedule is required to identify the tasks to be achieved, including information about those tasks (for example, who will be doing those tasks and the time frame in which they should be completed).

**Note** The delivery schedule is a high-level set of tasks structured by break points. Each break point represents a place where the relevant set of tasks can be reviewed and progress updated.

**See Also** More information concerning building the detail and outline schedule is in Chapter 9 "Controlling the delivery program", section "Create a delivery schedule."

As already has been pointed out, each task in the delivery schedule must contain a set of associated information. The details of delivery plan structure are given in Table 3-2. When you're building the delivery program schedule from the Detail Plan, perform a review of work required. Some parts of the delivery program will form *Work Packages* in their own right. For example, an element of the Detail Plan could be to configure Search. This could have a number of subtasks, like obtaining service accounts, defining the scopes, and identifying crawl rules.

**TABLE 3-2** Structure of a Delivery Plan

| Items to include in the Delivery Plan | Description |
|---|---|
| Stages | Stages represent the natural high-level break points in the program life cycle. Examples include Initial Investigation, Feasibility, Development, Implementation, Operation, and Closure. |
| Work Packages | Work Packages represent the clusters of work within each Stage, focused on a key deliverable. For example, one Work Package could be the customization of a SharePoint app to meet user requirements. Another could be the testing of that app by selected business users (who are also part of the delivery team). |
| Activities | Activities are the individual components of work within the Work Packages that must be undertaken to complete the project. Each Activity should be defined in terms of its start and end dates and the name of the individual accountable for its completion. |
| Accountability | A single, specific person should be accountable for every Activity and Work Package in the delivery program. |

| Items to include in the Delivery Plan | Description |
|---|---|
| Milestones | Milestones are significant events (often representing gates at the start of a Stage) that should be used to monitor progress as a summary. |
| Deliverables | Each of the key Deliverables defined in the program should be shown in the plan (indicated in the business case). |
| Reviews | Include Reviews at key points throughout the program when progress and performance can be evaluated. This is particularly important for the Validation portion of the program, where the solution has been made available to the business users for testing. |
| Interdependencies | All inputs from (and outputs to) other programs must be explicitly shown. This is very important for cross-related programs. For example, in the implementation of a SharePoint farm, there could be related programs of work from various work streams; there could be one centralized delivery schedule with all work streams connected to that schedule. |
| Costs | Using the delivery program, include Costs for materials and resources against each Work Package. At the end of each Review, outline the costs for delivering the Stage as part of the outline plan that summarizes progress. |

# Defining controls to manage SharePoint solution delivery

As the SharePoint solution delivery program is being designed, build in controls that manage communication and authorization. Without mechanisms to ensure that there are reviews, reporting, authorization for changes, and managing documentation, there will be miscommunication and misalignment with goals. The result in many cases would be that the solution program gets dropped or withheld indefinitely, or it runs into a cycle of noncompletion (because the scope has not been reviewed and then confirmed, for example).

Therefore, once the delivery program has been defined and a schedule set, you must ensure that other organizational aspects of the program are addressed. These areas should be detailed in the SharePoint business case, as discussed next.

## Ascertaining progress reporting needs

You must periodically update the sponsor (and members of the delivery team, as necessary) on the progress of the SharePoint solution implementation. To do this, you should first agree with the sponsor how reporting should be performed and the mechanisms used to do so. For example, you could use the delivery schedule in SharePoint to send out email notifications when a particular task is completed. There are other methods of progress reporting as well. You could summarize progress on a page on the SharePoint site and have that available for viewing, or provide a report based on a template that is provided from a Reports document library. For the purpose of standardization, choose one method of progress reporting. The key is to attempt to centralize reporting and to make things as easy as possible for those who need to access the progress reports. The last thing you need is the sponsor not reading the progress reports or assuming things about the delivery, which could well happen if progress reporting has not been defined or agreed upon. Once agreement has been reached, record the reporting requirements in the Outline Plan.

As delivery manager, you are responsible for controlling the delivery and taking the necessary actions to ensure that the solution is delivered to the expected outputs (that is, the business requirements). This means guiding and coordinating team tasks. You should make sure that the delivery team meets regularly to check the progress of the relevant tasks and to forecast other tasks to be performed in the future. You should also assess the issues that arise and mitigate any risks of tasks not completing on schedule. In my experience, the best way to assess issues and collate progress reports quickly is to request a brief progress or checkpoint report from each of the team members. You can gather this detail by recording the details in a SharePoint task list, which can then be linked back to the Deliverables app (previously shown in Figure 3-3).

By using the SharePoint tasks list, reporting progress can be captured for each task (see the Task list app example in Figure 3-4). That could then be used to add detail to a weekly report. Alternatives to this approach include creating a SharePoint custom list that holds the reports. Figure 3-6 shows an example where the SharePoint Task list app has been connected to the Deliverables app so that further detail of a high-level task can be captured, and progress of the related task recorded.

**More Info** More information concerning progress reporting is in Chapter 9 "Controlling the delivery program", section "Create Schedule Reports"

## Identifying who can authorize changes

Typically, the only individual who can make changes to a solution delivery program is the SharePoint sponsor. However, the SharePoint sponsor could choose another individual close to the delivery program to authorize changes on his or her behalf. You must ensure that the details of how to contact those who can authorize changes is recorded. When changes come—and they will—make sure that they are critically reviewed to ensure that they do not affect the delivery scope. Whether there is a change in scope or not, there may be further ripple effects down the line; alterations may require further review to ascertain any risks, issues, and dependencies. For example, if the task is to build a SharePoint site that houses a customized app, and then it is expanded to include building another app, this change needs to be scheduled and resourced, and any issues concerning support, maintenance, and training need to be considered as well. Therefore, reviewing each change and seeking approval for it is vital. The impact of getting a solution delivery wrong due to lack of getting approval or failing to record the reasons why the approval was required could lead to User Adoption issues, both during and after delivery.

## Keeping the stakeholders informed

Good communication leads to User Adoption, as does keeping the users informed and enthusiastic about the implementation of a SharePoint solution. There will invariably be changes concerning the SharePoint solution as it is being designed, built, and implemented. Changes in requirements can be rapid and unpredictable—even the organization can change focus and priorities, which can affect the progress (or even the need) for a project. You should have regular points of review to ensure that what is being provided continually meets user requirements. The reviews need to be formal since they involve making and recording decisions. These reviews should be built into the delivery schedule, and those attending should include both delivery team members who are accountable for the relevant tasks leading up to the review and the stakeholders.

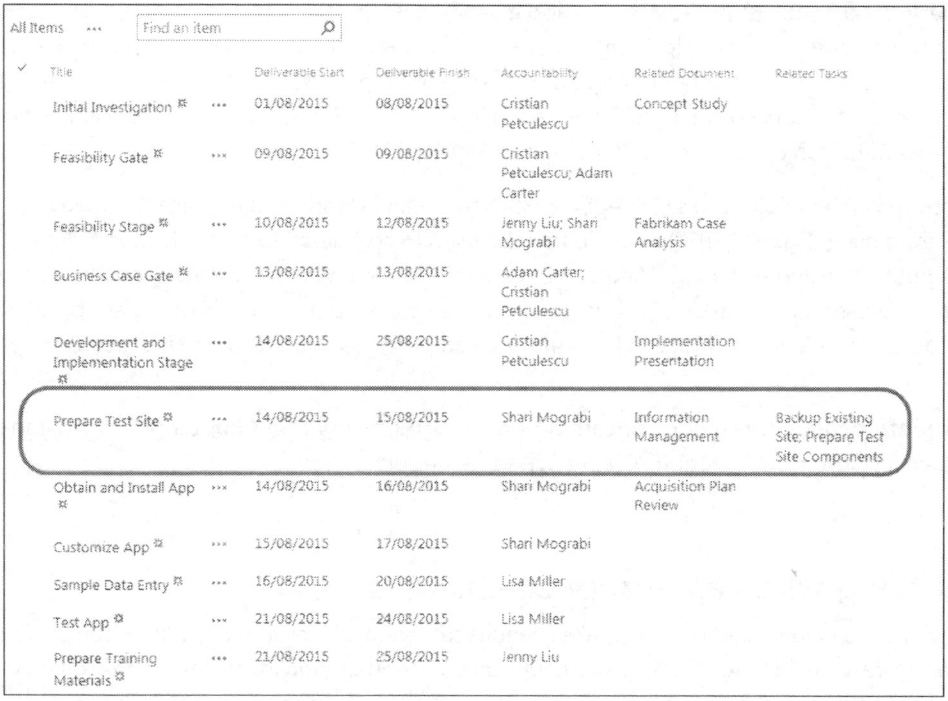

All Items ... Find an item

| Title | Deliverable Start | Deliverable Finish | Accountability | Related Document | Related Tasks |
|---|---|---|---|---|---|
| Initial Investigation | 01/08/2015 | 08/08/2015 | Cristian Petculescu | Concept Study | |
| Feasibility Gate | 09/08/2015 | 09/08/2015 | Cristian Petculescu; Adam Carter | | |
| Feasibility Stage | 10/08/2015 | 12/08/2015 | Jenny Liu; Shari Mograbi | Fabrikam Case Analysis | |
| Business Case Gate | 13/08/2015 | 13/08/2015 | Adam Carter; Cristian Petculescu | | |
| Development and Implementation Stage | 14/08/2015 | 25/08/2015 | Cristian Petculescu | Implementation Presentation | |
| Prepare Test Site | 14/08/2015 | 15/08/2015 | Shari Mograbi | Information Management | Backup Existing Site; Prepare Test Site Components |
| Obtain and Install App | 14/08/2015 | 16/08/2015 | Shari Mograbi | Acquisition Plan Review | |
| Customize App | 15/08/2015 | 17/08/2015 | Shari Mograbi | | |
| Sample Data Entry | 16/08/2015 | 20/08/2015 | Lisa Miller | | |
| Test App | 21/08/2015 | 24/08/2015 | Lisa Miller | | |
| Prepare Training Materials | 21/08/2015 | 25/08/2015 | Jenny Liu | | |

**FIGURE 3-6** An example of a Task List app connected to the Deliverables app in SharePoint.

## Documenting your SharePoint implementation

There will be a lot of documentation as you work on your SharePoint solution. You will need to centralize all of it because each SharePoint solution is a historical (and auditable) event in the evolution of the software's use in the organization. Creating a structured method of recording the schedule, maintaining tasks, and monitoring progress, costs, issues, and risks (and in fact, any communication concerning the delivery of a SharePoint solution) is vital. For example, if a change is required to a solution one year after it has been implemented, then having the original documentation of the implementation of that solution is crucial. Do not simply rely on placing a copy of the solution into an inventory as a record of implementation. SharePoint gets updated, sites receive new content and design, technology evolves, and business requirements change. That means you have to know not only what solutions have been deployed, but also how those solutions where implemented and who was involved in doing that. As previously mentioned in this chapter, consider creating a SharePoint site as a delivery program site to store and manage everything.

There will be a lot of documentation as you work on your SharePoint solution. You will need to centralize all of it because each SharePoint solution is a historical (and auditable) event in the evolution of the software's use in the organization. Creating a structured method of recording the schedule, maintaining tasks, and monitoring progress, costs, issues, and risks (and in fact, any communication concerning the delivery of a SharePoint solution) is vital. For example, if a change is required to a solution one year after it has been implemented, then having the original documentation concerning the implementation of that solution is crucial. Do not simply rely on placing a copy of the solution in an inventory as a record of implementation. SharePoint gets updated, sites receive new content and design, technology evolves, and business requirements change. That means that you have to know not only what solutions have been deployed, but also how those solutions were implemented and who was involved in doing that. As previously mentioned in this chapter, consider creating a SharePoint site as a delivery program site to store and manage everything.

Here is a case in point from a SharePoint consultant:

> I worked with a financial corporation in America that had *many* employees and documentation for over 1,000 apps housed in the World Trade Center when it was destroyed on 9/11. They lost all their people and all *that* documentation on that one day. It cost them millions of dollars to migrate the apps to SharePoint because they had not originally stored configuration records about the apps.
>
> *–Bill Pitts, director, Portals and Collaboration, Salient6, Inc.*

## Establishing controls for SharePoint solution delivery

The path to implementing a SharePoint solution successfully is based on the structure and management of the controls applied to delivering that solution. All too often, SharePoint solution delivery programs fail because no control was established from the very beginning. If no control is assigned to the program, then any policies oriented to the solution after its implementation will fail. You can use the checklist in Table 3-3 to ensure that the solutions delivery plan has controls in place.

**TABLE 3-3** Controls checklist for SharePoint solution delivery

| Control | Description |
|---|---|
| Create a mechanism to capture delivery program content. | Places the various SharePoint 2013 repositories, such as the Document Libraries app and the Task List app, in a central site, which will be for the sole use of the delivery team. |
| Set up progress reporting formats (applications and templates) and reporting lines (a list of those who should receive the reports). | Uses SharePoint lists to record reports. Provides easy access to those who need to receive the reports. |
| Create a mechanism to capture and mitigate risks that could affect the ability to deliver the solution. | Creates a SharePoint list to record risks. Customizes the list to include risk mitigation information and status. |
| Create a mechanism to capture and manage issues to resolution. | Creates a SharePoint list to record issues. Using the issue-tracking app in SharePoint 2013 allows you to customize the list to include references to delivery program content (among other elements). |

| Control | Description |
| --- | --- |
| Create a mechanism to capture changes to any aspect of the delivery program, including approval processes. | Creates a SharePoint list to record changes. Customizes the list to refer to delivery program content. Uses built-in workflow functionality so that approval of changes can be managed. |

**Tip** SharePoint 2013 has several built-in apps that allow you to capture and manage tasks, changes, contacts, risks, issues, and schedules. Built-in workflows allow the approval of content in those lists. In addition, SharePoint 2013 includes a feature called Project Web App Connectivity, which provides the lists required within a project site for integration with Project Web App, including issues, risks, and deliverables. Project Web App Connectivity is available in Office 365. However, for On-Premise SharePoint, Project Server 2013 is a prerequisite. For more information, visit *http://office.microsoft.com/en-us/project-server-help/whats-new-in-project-web-app-for-microsoft-project-server-2013-HA102848108.aspx* and *http://technet.microsoft.com/en-us/library/cc303399.aspx*.

## Engaging your sponsor and stakeholders

As already mentioned in previous chapters, stakeholders are those affected by the delivery program. A SharePoint sponsor is a manager or executive who acts as a visionary. He or she is advised by the delivery manager of the SharePoint delivery program and can articulate how the SharePoint can meet the solution requirements. Both are stakeholders, as they are both on the delivery team. However, there are also people who take no direct part in the delivery program as team members, but whose activities will be changed in some way as a result.

When releasing SharePoint as a solution, where the implementation of the platform into an organization is required, the number of individuals affected could be significant. Therefore, you must identify stakeholders and their *power* (that is, are they decision makers, influencers, or require consent?), so that they can be enrolled in the delivery program at an early stage. This is done to ensure that stakeholder power does not cause the delivery to fail later. You should always have a backup plan in case your stakeholders use their power to undermine your delivery plans.

*Scenario 3: Fabrikam is implementing a SharePoint solution that is a system to automate its sales process by automatically emailing documents marked as Sales. Following an investigation, the suggested procedure is to provide an extra option in all document libraries that is a component of the SharePoint solution. The functionality will be implemented as a new button in a SharePoint document library. Heading the delivery team is a SharePoint-savvy business manager who believes in a top-down approach and wields significant power in determining the shape of the solution. Believing that the only users are from the Sales department, he communicates with that department directly. Some weeks later, the solution is deployed across the entire company and into all SharePoint document libraries and all sites. Calls come streaming into the IT help desk from confused and dissatisfied users. The callers are asking questions like, "What is this button in my library?" "Why were we not informed about all this?" "How do I use this new doohickey?" and "My library is much slower—is it because of this new button?" As a result, the solution is removed, pending further investigation. The solution has yet to be implemented because the time frame to deploy the solution has passed, and the business has moved on to other challenges.*

This scenario describes a typical problem when you implement a solution without taking stakeholder power and identification into account. If stakeholders are not involved in the development of the solution, the outcome can be disastrous, resulting in wasted effort, time, and money.

The delivery manager and the SharePoint sponsor must ensure that all stakeholders are adequately briefed on the solution being implemented. Care must be taken concerning the level of communication provided. Too much data will drown them, but not enough will mean that users will not give the delivery the level of priority that the delivery program team wants.

Enrolling stakeholders, and keeping them engaged, are taxing but essential tasks. You accomplish them by both a formal communication plan and by "enrolling behavior" on behalf of all the delivery team on a planned and opportunistic basis.

Stakeholders make up a vital part of the User Adoption process. By encouraging stakeholders to become "SharePoint champions," they become warriors on behalf of the cause, helping users come to grips with new SharePoint solutions and, in turn, helping SharePoint evolve. They also are critical to the creation of policies related to platform Governance of solutions that have been implemented going forward.

Stakeholders need to be identified as part of the initial investigation into building the business case. There are three kinds of stakeholders:

- Those who have a positive attitude toward the delivery program
- Those who have a negative attitude toward the delivery program
- Those who are not committed one way or the other

For each stakeholder or group of stakeholders, consider the following questions:

- Do they play a decision-making role in the delivery program?
- Can they exert influence (positive or negative)?
- Is their consent required for the delivery program to succeed?

**Tip** Build a stakeholder map (described in Figure 3-7 later in this chapter) to help you gauge who is positive, negative, and noncommittal.

Now consider the following scenario:

*Scenario 4: Fabrikam needs to implement a SharePoint solution that will affect the entire organization. The SharePoint sponsor says that contact should be made with the customer director, who manages a team responsible for the areas of the company most affected by the new solution. His consent will be required to gain access to his team members. The team members are potential users of the new SharePoint solution. The chief executive has informed the SharePoint sponsor that two additional people, Phil and Jim, could be used to influence the customer director's consent and act as SharePoint champions. After further investigation, the delivery manager discovers that Phil works with the customer director, Jim is a key member of the engineering team under the engineering director, and that a significant number of potential stakeholders are involved. Therefore, the delivery manager and SharePoint sponsor create a Stakeholder influence map, which is updated some more after discussions with each of the potential stakeholders.*

The diagram in Figure 3-7 shows the connections between the identified stakeholders and identifies who is a decision maker, an influencer, someone whose consent is required, or those who must be targeted for User Adoption planning. The plus and minus signs, zeroes, and exclamation points shown with each stakeholder indicate whether that person is positive, negative, or noncommittal, or whose attitude is unknown. In Figure 3-7, which shows an example SharePoint delivery stakeholder map, Phil is indicated as a "feed" to the customer director, and Jim is indicated as a "feed" to the engineering employees.

You should consider a stakeholder map a useful way to help build an initial business case; the map adds clarity to stakeholder communication, attitudes, and approval levels. However, stakeholders are not identified only so you can find out whether they will consent to or are positive about the delivery. Consider that point when engaging with stakeholders: either you will require information from them or they need to be influenced with respect to the delivery of the solution, and they might need a demonstration of how SharePoint would solve their information and management challenges.

Based on the type of communication that the stakeholders require, choose wisely the medium, timing, and the kind of consent required. Also, ensure that all stakeholder information is recorded in the plan, and tied to the relevant milestones concerning the release of the SharePoint solution.

In the "Building the SharePoint delivery plan" section earlier in this chapter, I suggested a method of using SharePoint to record and manage the delivery plan for the solution which was to construct a site whose sole purpose was to manage and communicate the delivery of the solution and progress. If you have such a site, consider providing the stakeholders with access to it. This will give team collaboration a major boost because that is where anything to do with the delivery program is located, including all reports and decision-making documentation.

Because SharePoint solution delivery is scheduled into segments (see the "Preparing a SharePoint delivery program" section earlier in this chapter), consider assigning decision-making stakeholders to the sign-off of the relevant gate at the end of each stage. As stated earlier, consent of stakeholders is not the only thing required—you also need to get their approval of a solution that will meet their (and their relevant users') needs.

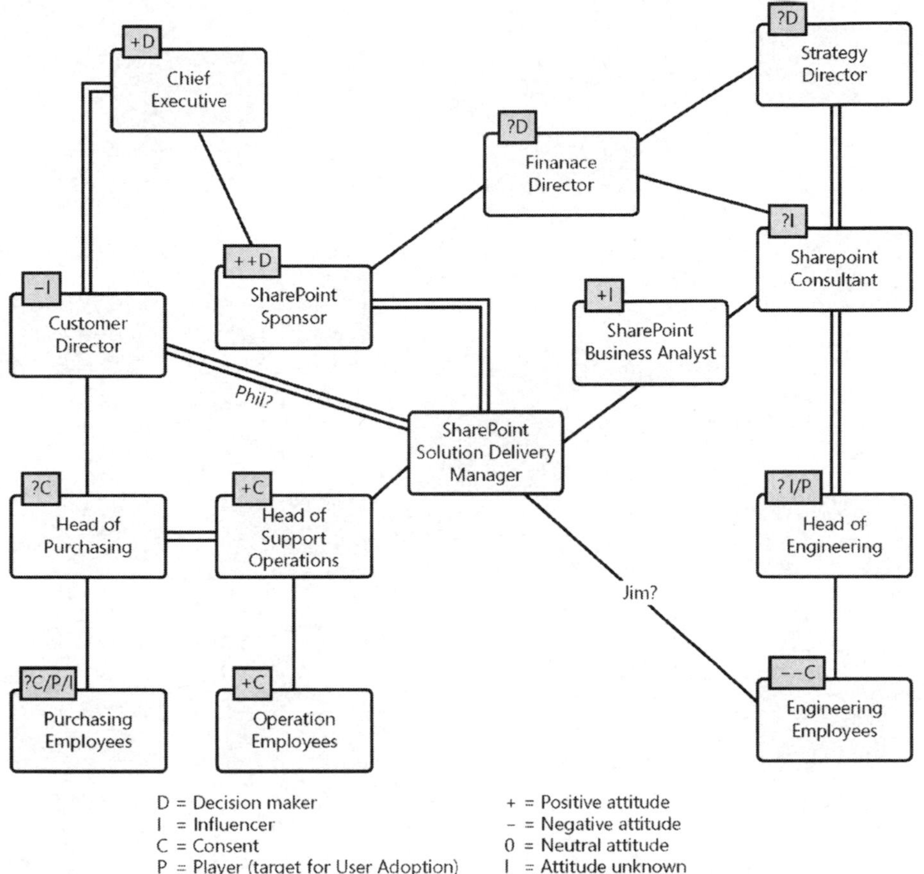


**FIGURE 3-7** An example of a SharePoint delivery stakeholder map.

## Summary

This chapter described how you can build a SharePoint delivery program, which entails setting up the delivery team, creating a delivery plan, and managing the stakeholders. The creation of this program is vital, as it details exactly how a solution will be implemented and contains success criteria that are crucial to User Adoption. The complexity of the program relates directly to a combination of elements: reach of the solution across the organization, number of stakeholders involved, importance to the organization as a whole, and the culture of the organization where the solution is going to be delivered.

The next chapter develops the discussion of the delivery program further. The text delves into what is required to prepare User Adoption and looks at methods to engage the SharePoint audience. Other topics covered include building cases for SharePoint solutions with user input in mind, ensuring that there are ongoing, two-way communications between those responsible for supporting SharePoint and business users engaged in using the solutions provided, and building training models to get users comfortable with using the implemented solutions.

CHAPTER 4

# Preparing SharePoint solution User Adoption

In this chapter:



Microsoft SharePoint has been designed to provide a platform and framework that can be used for many different types of functions in an organization. The limits of what SharePoint can do are dictated only by the creativity and imagination of the users. The key objective of using SharePoint is to improve the efficiency and decision-making ability of those users by empowering them to create and manage online content.

This includes the ability for users to further develop and customize SharePoint to meet ongoing business information challenges. Your purpose in providing relevant SharePoint features is to match business requirements and to enable information workers to be more productive by solving their collaborative challenges. If information workers are to succeed, they need to be guided. They need to be made aware of the benefits SharePoint provides and be shown how to carry out relevant tasks with the software. To do this, you need to build a SharePoint User Adoption strategy.

SharePoint User Adoption is all about *perception*, which involves the ability to map relevant business needs to SharePoint tools, the creation of SharePoint champions, communication planning, training, and engaging sponsors and key stakeholders. User Adoption is not about features and technical components; it is the most critical factor in attaining SharePoint user return on investment (ROI). SharePoint User Adoption occurs only when SharePoint solutions are delivered in harmony with supporting organizational and behavioral change programs.

**Tip** Users will not accept a SharePoint solution if it lacks the essential features that they require, or where the implemented solution is of poor quality, or when there has been a failure in addressing information and management collaboration challenges through the implementation of a SharePoint solution. If the SharePoint solution solves problems that users have with managing information, then they are more likely to use the solution.

Even having the best SharePoint solution, with lots of sophisticated features, analytics, integration, and other benefits, will not add any value whatsoever unless people use it. The key result of using the solution must be productivity gains.

To identify productivity gains, there are numerous factors to consider, like ease of use, support, incentives, and training. There are various maturity model frameworks to understand, such as knowing where users are in a particular area and then helping them move one level up in the maturity framework. From a practical viewpoint, a delivered User Adoption plan helps set the following in motion:

- Create SharePoint champions who can then train their peers using the same training models.
- Showcase SharePoint solutions across the SharePoint landscape.
- Develop training plans that allow people to become knowledgeable in the use of SharePoint tools.
- Build the business culture into your SharePoint delivery program.

## Building SharePoint User Adoption strategies

You need to start building a User Adoption strategy the instant you get confirmation that a SharePoint solution will be implemented. This is because the strategy is the most important aspect of users' ability to use the solution and will give rise to their requirements for training and support.

You will need to complete the following tasks to build a SharePoint User Adoption strategy:

- Review the business culture and mission (that is, objectives and vision), as discussed in Chapter 1, "Aligning organizational goals and requirements," and Chapter 2, "Defining the SharePoint solution scope."
- Identify the kinds of users you will be dealing with in the strategy.
- Develop a communication plan.
- Build a training plan.

Training is a crucial aspect of a change management initiative and is part of a SharePoint solution delivery program. Don't be fooled into thinking that once the solution is ready for use, you can simply instruct people to "use it." That will assume that users already know how the solution will work, when in fact, they will not have a clue as to how the solution will benefit the organization or other users. And that assumption that users will simply "use it" probably means that you did not involve users in the design or implementation of the solution. The result of that is slow (or even nonexistent) user buy-in. In other words, the solution will be ignored, perceived to be pointless, or misunderstood. Users may even try to interfere with the solution's implementation because they were not involved (or were not allowed to play a role) in its development.

Here is an example that shows the importance of involving users. I was involved in a delivery of SharePoint to a large business function. I needed to assess various team skills to gauge their training requirements, and to accomplish this, I held a number of meetings with team managers. One team manager stated that his team was "computer savvy," added that "they will pick it up in no time," and finished by stating, "They will have no choice but to use it."

This example works only if users are "power users" who were accustomed to working with SharePoint. Unfortunately, that was not the case: when I asked the users, "How do you save your content on SharePoint?" I just received blank looks in response.

Therefore, the key to planning User Adoption strategy is understanding the business culture and building accurate user personas for each delivery program. That comes from knowing the mission, objectives, vision, and strategies that have been created through your SharePoint delivery plan. Remember, one of the key aspects of building a delivery plan for SharePoint is capturing the company's mission, because it is that mission that further relates how the company perceives itself, its customers, and importantly, how SharePoint can be part of aiding that mission's success. Here's an example of a mission statement:

*The Contoso Coffee Shop's mission is threefold, with each of the following parts being as integral to our success as the next:*

- ***Product Mission*** *Provide customers the finest quality beverages in the most efficient time*
- ***Community Mission*** *Provide community support through customer involvement*
- ***Economic Mission*** *Operate and grow at a profitable rate through making sound economic decisions*

In this mission statement, there are phrases where SharePoint could assumed to be of value and benefit (for example, evaluating *finest quality beverages* by surveying customers, fostering *community support* through discussion boards, making *economic decisions* through performance indicators). Hence, studying the mission statement is useful because it communicates to staff how SharePoint could meet requirements and helps them adopt SharePoint for their information management needs. In addition, you should get as much information as possible concerning the business culture from your engagement with the various SharePoint sponsors. Understanding the business culture is crucial, as this shows how users interact, influence each other, and work together.

**Tip** Another important thing to factor in is whether the customer uses a quality management system such as Six Sigma or Lean, so you can map SharePoint solutions to the syntax and semantics of the quality management system.

**More Info** Six Sigma is a set of tools and strategies for process improvement originally developed by Motorola in 1985. For more information read this article: *http://en.wikipedia.org/wiki/Six_Sigma*

**More Info** The Lean management process looks at understanding customer value and focusing customer key processes to continuously increase value. For more information on Lean Management read this article: *http://www.lean.org/whatslean*

You will need to gain SharePoint sponsor buy-in. This is vital to successful User Adoption because without it, there will not be a stable learning program. You will need to investigate and understand user skill sets and needs—not addressing this is a primary reason why User Adoption fails. You must not guess or assume the level of user ability to understand the SharePoint solution provided. To have a successful User Adoption program, you need to understand what motivates people to use the software, what their competence is, how related SharePoint solutions are to their daily work lives, and how user skill sets can evolve.

Understanding your audience is another important aspect of building a SharePoint User Adoption strategy. You need to get detailed information about the users who will be trained, so you can identify their training requirements and tailor the User Adoption planning to them. You do this because those users can make all the difference to the success of a SharePoint solution that they will have to use. If they are not factored into your User Adoption strategy, then you will find very quickly that they will become "pessimistic influencers," or "laggards," as I call them. Users will be resistant to change where they have not had any input in what they are being asked to adopt. In other words, they will grumble and groan about the SharePoint solution (in some cases without even attempting to use it), or they will come across hurdles that could have been overcome had they been trained in the first place. Identify the kind of people they are, in terms of how receptive they are to the new solution, and look at the scale of the solution implementation. All users will fit into a User Adoption strategy that takes place right from the start.

There are five kinds of user adopters:

- Innovators
- Early adopters
- Early majority adopters
- Late majority adopters
- Laggards

Each type of adopter will treat the solution differently. Therefore, to guarantee cohesion in the use of the SharePoint solution being provided, you need to know what kinds of strategies to apply to each of them. Table 4-1 lists the traits of each of these adopters and strategies when working with them. You should take this table to workshops with potential users of the SharePoint solution and list the names of individuals next to the type of adopter each person is. Then you need to meet with your SharePoint sponsor and show him or her the list of user assignment types that you compiled during the workshops.

**TABLE 4-1** Types of User Adopters

| Type of Adopter | Traits | Strategy |
| --- | --- | --- |
| Innovators | ■ Adventurous<br>■ Take risks<br>■ Like to play (that is, try any SharePoint feature without understanding its purpose)<br>■ Do not mind failing<br>■ Are often referred to as "geeks" | ■ Identify them quickly<br>■ Do not involve them immediately.<br>■ Give access to Sandbox environments.<br>■ Involve them in the design of the solution.<br>■ Evangelize best practices. |
| Early adopters | ■ Command respect from their peers<br>■ Are cautious<br>■ Appreciate guidance | ■ Identify them early.<br>■ Capture business requirements.<br>■ Identify SharePoint champions.<br>■ Make them early adopters.<br>■ Meet with them continually to identity successes, problems, and failures.<br>■ Initially guide and train them, so they can eventually become more independent.<br>■ Work with them to build business rules and policies concerning SharePoint solution use. |
| Early majority adopters | ■ Slower in the adoption process<br>■ Above-average social status<br>■ Contact with early adopters<br>■ Seldom hold decision-making positions in SharePoint solutions | ■ Apply same strategy as early adopters.<br>■ Create success stories for late majority adopters.<br>■ Plan regular meetings to identify issues.<br>■ Communicate solutions to early adopters.<br>■ Teach them to become more independent.<br>■ Build policies of governance to manage and guide.<br>■ Be patient; build on their strengths and expose and address their weaknesses through training and communication. |
| Late majority adopters | Not part of original solutions implementation; introduced by attrition | ■ Build bridges between early and late majority adopters.<br>■ Formalize decisions concerning modifications through policies. |
| Laggards | ■ Do not like change<br>■ Strive to use traditional methods<br>■ Fear the replacement solution | ■ Involve them, but do not force them to use the solution.<br>■ May need top-down delivery support from the SharePoint sponsor.<br>■ Ignore resistance (but keep records of it) |

Identify where the users are within these categories and find out which ones can apply pressure to other adopters. This will take time, but it's vitally important and extremely beneficial.

*Scenario 1: Fabrikam is a $2 billion energy-generation company that needs to implement a SharePoint platform that would be used by hundreds of employees in power plants throughout the country. Maintenance is one of the highest costs for power plants, so the new system would provide significant financial benefits. Many of the plants used manual processes, so a switch to SharePoint represents a major change. The sponsor recognizes that there is a risk of user rejection, and she needs help developing a User Adoption strategy.*

Although your scenario may not be as complex as this one in terms of implementing a SharePoint solution, bear in mind that the process of creating a strategy encompassing the interviewing of users and building a communications and training plan should be consistent and in line with the organization's expectations. You will need aid in the form of trainers and business analysts (for more about this, see Chapter 7, "Organizing the Delivery Team"). As service delivery manager, it is important for you to know whether these resources will be required and that there is sufficient budget to fund them.

*Scenario 2: Fabrikam is a manufacturing company that plans a significant upgrade to a SharePoint site by including a cost estimating app. The estimating app would provide an essential link between the company and its customers. Fabrikam is concerned that if customers do not quickly accept the new app, or if they do not learn to use it correctly, there might be serious financial consequences. In addition, Fabrikam assumed that its information workers would lack the expertise required to use the app. A change initiative was required that would include a User Adoption strategy, training activities specific to particular audiences, design activities to support the app rollout, and a provision for various training elements like courses and Computer-Based Training (CBT) products.*

In this solution, the training plan needs to be in line with different types of user adopters and their roles. A strategy must be formulated for dealing with the kind of adopters that will emerge during this project. A key aspect of this strategy is *communication*. User Adoption requires communicating awareness of the solution, creating ways in which users can be trained, and developing guides. Therefore, the User Adoption strategy is a full investigation whose output is a collection of documents spelling out the strategy required to get the users on board with the solution. These documents include a Communication Plan, a training schedule, and training guides. Here's a closer look at what needs to be in these documents:

- **Communication Plan** This plan summarizes the SharePoint solution, sells the benefits of its use, and indicates the modes of communication available to those who are intended to use the solution. When building the Communication Plan, ensure that you promote the awareness of the solution to the audience—this is the only chance you have to really sell the solution to them, in terms of what benefits it will bring to them and its value to the organization. In larger organizations, where there is a communications team, use their skills and expertise (including the fact that they will have direct access to marketing teams), and ask them to send consistent, recognizable, and standard messages to others about the solution. In the "Developing Communication Plans" section later in this chapter, you will learn the format of the Communication Plan and how to build one.
- **Training schedule** The training schedule comes from a Communication Planning *Messages Framework*, and the *Channels* and *Tactics* defined in the Communication Plan. This schedule

describes the training time frame, who will be carrying out the training, and the Channel and Tactic to be used. This area is as complex as the kind of SharePoint solution being implemented. For example, if a SharePoint platform is being delivered, you must include Microsoft Office tools because users will be using Office to manage SharePoint content. Hence, the schedule needs to be tailored to the specific needs of the organization. The details of the schedule in terms of the time frame is relevant to those being trained, and therefore, you should consider the kind of training being provided and the available resources.

- **Training guides** There are three guides, covering the needs of the user, the manager of the solution, and those who will be supporting the technical aspects of the solution. The training guides focus attention on the solution's flexibility to the users, communicating the solution's context, and, of course, educating users. They are written with no technical jargon and aimed at those who will be using the provided solution.
- **Manager guide** This guide covers the aspects of the solution that require more knowledge than users. For example, consider a SharePoint site as a provided solution.
- **User guide** This guide covers how to use Document Libraries, add items to lists, and other activities. You may consider splitting this into two sections: one for the users, and the other for the owners of that site, which will cover administrative aspects of the site (for example, setting permissions, managing site settings, configuring site functionality).
- **Technical guide** This guide is an operations guide that is provided as part of the handoff to the technical team marking the implementation of the solution. That documentation is necessary to support the solution and its relevant infrastructure.

Before you begin the creation of your User Adoption strategy, the most important aspect is SharePoint sponsor support, which will be discussed next.

## Getting support from your SharePoint sponsor

The essence of SharePoint business sponsorship revolves around the other person. It's not about what the sponsor accomplishes, but rather what others achieve through the use of SharePoint, provided through meeting the user requirements, agreed to by the SharePoint sponsor. Moreover, a SharePoint sponsor does not dictate what happens on SharePoint using unilateral action; there is a requirement to connect with other business users who are going to use the platform. Therefore, the SharePoint sponsor's job is more than simply anticipating and navigating change, or even defining it. Rather, they need to deliver this change by linking the organization's information purpose (its reason for using SharePoint solutions) to people longing to be part of an information framework bigger than themselves.

A SharePoint sponsor requires help, and not simply from a SharePoint "guru." Implementing SharePoint is dynamic, and for users moving from an older system to using SharePoint, it can be seen as cataclysmic. The bridge between desire and outcome means empowering users and then helping them empower themselves. To help achieve this, you should create SharePoint champions who understand how SharePoint meets the sponsor vision, so they can assist other users to focus on their SharePoint goals. This would in turn lead to the development of successful policies, further aiding Governance of the platform.

Choosing the right level of sponsorship is important. This depends on the culture of the organization and the type of SharePoint solutions that are going to be put in place. Table 4-2 shows three scenarios and describes the solution for each and the kind of sponsorship needed from the business.

**TABLE 4-2** SharePoint solutions and sponsors

| Scenario | Solution | Sponsor |
| --- | --- | --- |
| We need a platform to hold our documents to ensure that users use SharePoint to store their documents, and to move away from using shared folders. | Save links to specific SharePoint Document Libraries in parts of the existed shared folders, and then make these parts read only. | Line manager and user champions. |
| We need a platform to allow employees to have communities with open sharing features, including noteboards. | Create centralized and specific discussion boards and blog sites. Provide training and play-area sites. | Corporate sponsorship and inspiration (get them to walk the talk and use some of the tools like discussion boards, articles in blog sites, and so on). This is a significant cultural change that requires leadership to encourage new methods of collaboration. |
| We need to be able to create solutions on our team sites on our own. | This is more self-service-oriented, with case-by-case solution delivery. | Individuals identified from the relevant unit, who are keen to use SharePoint tools, and who could be turned into SharePoint champions. They could provide low-key support, including coaching members of their team. |

As you can see from these scenarios, gaining SharePoint sponsor support is not done through the efforts of only one individual; several people are vital to User Adoption. To gain sponsor support, you need to manage the sponsors; to do that, you need to understand how to best provide solutions to them and their users. Business culture is crucial. I have found that understanding the sponsor aids in understanding the business culture. After all, sponsors are also going to adopt the platform, and they can be powerful ambassadors for you. Look at the following quotes and try to match them with the adopters listed in Table 4-1. This exercise is quite useful, as it will indicate the work required to keep the SharePoint sponsors aligned to the solution being delivered.

*"There is no right and no wrong."*

This message is quite common, and arguably very useful. SharePoint solutions are limited only by their creativity; therefore, each solution could be directly tailored to meet specific business requirements. And the specific requirements can be simple or complex. For example, take a Document Library in SharePoint. A SharePoint solution could require a Document Library with no version control, or one with check-in abilities. To some, this may be the wrong approach—however, if that Document Library requires connection to a third-party product that continually writes data into that Document Library, then using version control might not be the right thing to do, especially if the files being written are large and do not require auditing.

Another example could be if a SharePoint form in a list repository needs to capture information from an external data source. Alternatives could include developing a customized app that sits as a web part on the Edit Form page, which feeds data into the form; implementing a third-party solution that completely replaces the SharePoint Edit Form, which hooks directly into the data source; or using a configured External Content Type to map into the external data source, using that as a feeder to the column in the SharePoint Edit Form. The point I am making is that there is no right or wrong decision here; each could be suitable depending on the business objective. However, value must be attached to each decision. Each of these examples has disadvantages and advantages, along with implications concerning risk, cost, ROI, and service delivery. You must ensure that you investigate, discuss, test, and agree on an approach with your SharePoint sponsor. I use a process called Value Management and Value Engineering, which is covered in the "Value Management and Value Engineering" section later in this chapter.

*"Just put out solution xyz—we will deal with the problems as they arise."*

When you hear someone say this, you need to understand a couple of points. First, are there some solutions that could be put in place to ensure that if a problem arises, the issue can be resolved quickly? Remember that when implementing a SharePoint solution, you must provide adequate support for that solution. Creating a model to provide support is definitely required before releasing a solution, as the business expectation will be that if any problem can be dealt with expeditiously. In addition, communication and training comes back into play here; you should ensure that SharePoint sponsors are aware that simply deploying a solution requires effective communication, as this is key to making a transition into using a SharePoint solution.

*"I want this done my way . . ."*

*"It will be a top-down approach."*

A top-down approach works if the solution's reach is global (for example, a delivery of SharePoint to an entire organization); the Communication and Training Plans are going to be a major aspect of the approach; the sponsor has a high level of credibility and trust with the relevant users. However, also note that driving User Adoption does not have to be from top-level branches (particularly if the solution is for a department, business unit, or individual site owner). Based on the terms "done my way" and "top-down approach" in these statements, you should immediately examine the implications of the solution on organization culture because that will affect a top-down approach. Also, one could assume that the solution being placed would not need user awareness, which could be an issue in terms of User Adoption. If the top-down approach method is simply to tell users, "Go start using this solution," without giving them information about the benefits in using the solution as well as training them how to best use the solution, then the top-down approach will fail because users have not bought into the solution.

*Chapter 3, "Planning SharePoint solution delivery," describes the work required to identify sponsor and stakeholder influence in more detail. You can use the mapping exercise in the "Engaging your sponsor and stakeholders" section of that chapter to identify who will be most affected by the top-down approach and see if there will be any bottlenecks.*

*"The scope can be changed the way I see fit."*

Although your SharePoint sponsors do not need to understand the details of developing a SharePoint solution, you must ensure that they are clear on the process of delivering it. This is accomplished through the creation of the delivery plan, which includes details of what will and what will not be delivered. Without this understanding, whatever you do in delivering the SharePoint solution is vulnerable to unplanned changes at the behest of the sponsor, with no traceability. And if you do not manage or account for changes in the solution, the sponsor can easily start playing "priority bingo" (that is, choose any priority at random, without making any judgments). The sponsor will simply assume that changing the scope will have no impact on the schedule, and understand less and less about the goals. This then affects your ability to control the amount of time delivery takes (which would have also been agreed to if there was a delivery plan).

*"Users are not using SharePoint the way I want them to. Why is this?"*

This comment could relate to a host of reasons related to a common issue. The SharePoint solution has been implemented, or this could be an existing implementation. Yet, if the method of implementation does not include user engagement, the reasons relate to miscommunication, lack of training, lack of trust in the sponsor, or the business culture has not been factored into the types of users who are going to use (or are using) the SharePoint solution. So if you hear your sponsor saying something like this, that sponsor will be at odds with the delivery of the solution because users are doing one or more of the following:

- Using features that were included but not trained on
- Making mistakes related to the use of the solution
- Using a solution that seems to do a better job of helping them in their tasks
- Not using the solution due to not being involved
- Not using the solution due to a lack of credibility and trust
- Not using the solution because no one has told them how important the solution is to the organization and to them

The solutions to these issues are covered by dealing with the last three statements, as they all relate to successful User Adoption. You should aid the sponsor in building a communication and training plan. You should focus on the core users and run workshops and demonstrations so you can instill the vision and benefits of using the SharePoint solution as communicated by the sponsor.

*"I am not sure what I want, but I will know it when I see it."*

This comment means that the delivery strategy is not clear or is undefined in terms of what business requirements the SharePoint solution is intended to solve. The wrong response to this is to automatically build all kinds of solutions into the production process in the hope that the sponsor will pick one (or generally a combination), and then attempt to glue those disparate components together. Doing this wastes time that should have been spent identifying the relevant business requirements and then mapping them against the actual components in SharePoint—or, if those components do not exist, identifying alternatives. Those making these statements as SharePoint sponsors tend to be innovators, which can be dangerous, especially if that same sponsor leads the entire SharePoint environment and is supposed to be able to make informed and strategic decisions as to how SharePoint will solve information challenges and meet the organizational vision.

*"I am not sure how to store stuff, so I want to see all the options."*

I am including this comment because it shows why it is so important to guide the sponsor through the concepts of managing information (read the "Understanding the importance of Information Architecture" section in Chapter 6, "SharePoint delivery program considerations," to find out more about Information Architecture and building a good Information Architecture strategy), as opposed to looking at the technology first, then going through a process of trial and error to find something that fits. If the sponsor needs to see all the options, what you should *not* do is immediately run a 10-hour workshop, going through every possible option and configuration of a Document Library. That kind of focus on one detail is a complete waste and will probably confuse and increase the number of questions (and probably complaints) you hear. What you should not do is assume that SharePoint is a "nirvana" that will bring the sponsor to a utopia of document management collaboration. What you should do is explain some of the concepts of document management (creation, storage, workflow, retention, and archive) and have those concepts related to business challenges currently faced in the organization.

*"Why can't the XYZ feature show me everything it can do so I can pick and choose?"*

This comment relates to the previous one in the sense that it expresses a requirement to see all options. Here, the sponsor, faced with an implemented SharePoint solution, now wishes to see all the features related to the solution so they can "pick and choose" the components to use. This request is normal; however, what you should do is again identify what the business requirement is and prioritize the related key aspects of the SharePoint solution to the sponsor. Showing every aspect of a particular feature is time-consuming and likely to cause a lot of confusion (not to mention probably useless).

These example statements are only a sample of what I've heard from various SharePoint sponsors; there are lots more. The point here is that the sponsor needs help in the delivery of a successful SharePoint solution. To help facilitate and increase User Adoption, and to ensure a smooth implementation of a SharePoint solution, SharePoint sponsor support is required. You should tell them that they need to make the point to other people that a SharePoint solution is about much more than just software. They need to communicate that the solution is an ongoing strategic initiative that is supposed to live well beyond its implementation. The SharePoint sponsor needs to remind users of the organization's vision and commit to providing users with updates concerning implementation, listen and respond to suggestions and feedback, and back any relevant training program.

## Sparking excitement in your potential users

*"A journey of a thousand miles begins with a single step."*

*Lao-tzu*

You must always be on the lookout for ways to quickly improve user productivity and solve information challenges using SharePoint, as these will introduce methods to get more users using the platform. Introducing new methods not only increases usage of the SharePoint solution, it also strengthens service delivery of SharePoint. For SharePoint support, a quick win brings confidence and increases visibility to your SharePoint sponsors. It also demonstrates that SharePoint support is making progress. In particular, in a SharePoint delivery program, this helps you hit key milestones. Table 4-3 describes a number of scenarios where the solution is a quick win and is likely to be seen as an immediate benefit.

**TABLE 4-3** Quick Win Scenarios and Solutions

| Scenario | Solution |
|---|---|
| The IT help desk sends out "Did You Know" emails to all staff on a biweekly basis. These emails include information on features in software that individuals could use, for example. When users were asked about these emails, they said that they generally ignore them because either (a) they did not use the relevant software, or (b) that they had so many emails it was difficult to remember the information. Also, when asked if they might refer to these in the future, the answer was yes, but then they would have difficulty locating the information, and in the end, they would have to ask IT. | Set up an email-enabled Document Library. The IT help desk could continue to send the emails and would forward a copy to the email address assigned to the Document Library. Those items could be indexed by SharePoint Enterprise Search so that subsequent requests for aid could be located quickly. |
| New users joining the organization need to know the purpose of the various business units while using SharePoint. | If you have an existing site list available to your users, create a Description column in which you can provide a statement concerning each site premise and the top two names of the individuals responsible for each site. If you do not have an existing site list, you should make one, as that leads to improving search capabilities, training, and User Adoption. |
| You need to enable users to find sites and at the same time enhance search capabilities of SharePoint | Enable Search Keywords against the sites. You could also use the description as a Promoted Result for the SharePoint site. |

Remember that building custom SharePoint solutions is limited only by your creativity; however, always try to solve real business information challenges. Always look for new, but simple (in terms of implementation) methods to improve user productivity using SharePoint built-in features, and a combination of regularly used tools: for example, Office and Windows. Make sure that whether you or your sponsors come up with ideas, that you assign them to themes of your evolving SharePoint environment. Table 4-4 shows a list of common themes of a SharePoint environment. Use this as a guide to identify solutions that are simple to implement and provide training materials for. Table 4-5 describes a few scenarios that combine tools such as Office, SharePoint, Windows 7, and Windows 8.

**TABLE 4-4** SharePoint Themes for Quick Wins

| Theme | Description |
|---|---|
| Information Publishing | A centralized single source for content sharing and collaboration, including content life cycle and business process management. |
| Search | A consistent search experience for all employees to be able to find electronic content with minimum fuss. The content management platform must have an extremely powerful Search service. |

| Theme | Description |
|---|---|
| People Search and User Profiles | People Search is an aspect of the Search feature that provides a mechanism for individuals to be located from content stored in their attributes (for example, last name, cost code, department, and so on). The sum of the attributes per user is called a User Profile, which shows information about an individual in the organization. |
| Knowledge Base | The processes, methods, tools, and systems provided to allow information workers and other SharePoint users to engage and learn how to use the platform and features. |

**TABLE 4-5** Scenarios with Quick Implementations Related to Office, SharePoint, Windows 7, and Windows 8

| Scenario | Solution | More Reading |
|---|---|---|
| A business unit using Microsoft Word is continually researching and investigating information to build its content. It stores content in various sites in the SharePoint environment and regularly accesses Internet-based partner sites. There have been comments that there is a significant amount of time spent locating information, particularly in having to swop between the Internet browser and SharePoint. | This relates to Information Publishing, Search, and People Search. Use the Microsoft Research feature, which could be set to search part of or all the SharePoint environment from within the Office product. | For more information on the Research feature in Word, read the article at *http://blogs.technet.com/cfs-file.ashx/__key/communityserver-blogs-components-weblog-files/00-00-00-84-45/3487.Microsoft-Word-Research-_2D00_-Providing-SharePoint-Search-features-from-within-Microsoft-Office-2010-and-2013.pdf*. |
| Users in an organization are used to finding resources using Windows. They use the Search feature in Windows Explorer to locate information on their shared drives. They use the People Search feature to locate individuals. You need to find a solution that allows them to find information without having to visit a SharePoint site directly. | Use the Windows Explorer Search option and the People Search option available from the Search SharePoint site, which provides SharePoint search at the Windows level. | For more information on the Windows Explorer Search and People Search connectivity feature in SharePoint 2013, read the article at *https://www.nothingbutsharepoint.com/sites/eusp/Pages/sharepoint-2010-search-locations-in-windows-7.aspx*. |
| You have a thriving SharePoint environment used by many key functions in an organization: Technology, Legal, Finance, and Accounting are just some of the business units represented. There have been various calls for users within these departments to create articles that describe how to use systems and processes within their relevant features. You need to centralize this activity so that there is a single source of knowledge in the organization. | Use the SharePoint Productivity Hub to create blogs for the relevant business units, and get them to use the Blogging feature of Word. Note that you can also link this to the social aspects of SharePoint 2013 Community sites. Use the blogging template from Word 2013 to post blogs into a SharePoint blog site. Or use the Community Portal Template, which will allow the positing of discussions that can then have comments associated with them. | For information about Community sites and portals, read the article "Overview of communities in SharePoint 2013" at *http://technet.microsoft.com/en-us/library/jj219805.aspx*. |

Always look for simple methods of providing productivity, and start small. Doing this means the following:

- The amount of work required is justified and can be linked to "business as usual."
- Solutions can be tried and then released into production very quickly.

- Communication and training is minimal, the sponsors and stakeholders are manageable, and the training can be provided in the quickest methods possible (for example, blogs in a centralized training site).

Idea gathering does not just come from your creativity as a SharePoint worker. Use business workers, especially those individuals marked as SharePoint champions. Regularly have workshops and demonstrations to not only showcase SharePoint and solutions as the platform grows, but also gather feedback from attendees. Amalgamate those, identify quick wins, and quickly provide them in a user acceptance test (UAT) environment to demonstrate them to key users and push them into production.

## Developing Communication Plans

Before, during, and after the implementation of your SharePoint solution, you need to start communicating to the relevant users, at least in announcing the SharePoint solution. To do this, you need to develop Communication Plans for your SharePoint solution. This allows you to translate big-picture ideas and goals of the solution into manageable and effective communication. When you have created a Communication Plan, you will be able to explain clearly why the delivery of the solution matters and make a case for support of all kinds (help, ideas generation, and so on), including communicating on a regular basis with key stakeholders. The Communication Plan can be used not just for informing business users; you can use facets of the plan to help the technical teams responsible for supporting and maintaining SharePoint to be better prepared to deliver services. Using Communication Planning, you can inform all kinds of users using a standard, unambiguous message. The point is that the communication drives home the point that the SharePoint solution matters to the organization. Communication Planning is a key aspect of User Adoption, relates to how the provision of training and assistance to users will take place, identifies clearly what the perception of the solution, and states how you will steer that perception and the tactics used.

Communication Planning is not a single event; it must be a sustained effort. Many SharePoint implementations fail because of a lack of sustained communication and public relation exercises targeted at audiences. Failures include not taking advantage of using some basic techniques, such as collecting email addresses, sending out mass emails, posting news and information, providing materials for download, and other activities. Failures also include simply installing the solution and not involving any audiences or even communicating with them other than stating, "The solution is live, so use it." Other failures relate to an underestimation of the solution's importance. Because SharePoint is being implemented as an IT project, communication with users is seen as a "luxury." With technology playing such a leading role in our world, fundamentally being used to drive communication efforts, email, websites, eBooks, online surveys, online videos, and other technologies are all easily available. Yet organizations fail to understand or identify what technologies can be used (or should be used), or do not attempt to go down any communication routes, fearing cost and time required. And yet the value of the solution can be measured best by users' perception of it, and only a Communication Plan can give you information about that.

In essence, Communication Planning helps you understand and identify the communication objectives and tools and ensure that they make sense, given the organization's goals, budget, and culture. This section will help you understand the aspects of the Communication Plan, what you need to do to build one, and the actions that need to be carried out once the Communication Plan is ready.

There are two types of communication in an organization: strategic and tactical. Strategic Communication Planning covers much more than a SharePoint delivery program. Strategic communication deals with developing programs and processes that support the organization's mission and strategic direction, of which SharePoint is an important information and collaboration aspect. Strategic communications consist of providing institutionalized and corporate communications to strengthen goals such as business cost reduction, marketing, and operational effectiveness. It is perceived as a master plan. The details of strategic Communication Planning are beyond the scope of this discussion, but if you would like to know more about how tactical planning lends itself to strategic communications, read the article "Redefining the Role of Communication and Winning Support from Leadership," by Chris Gay, available at *http://www.roico.com/comm_article_actionplan.html.*

Tactical Communications Planning is related to meeting User Adoption goals, requires a more practical and productive approach, and is more likely to produce results and momentum.

The remainder of this section will help you understand how to build a Communication Plan for SharePoint delivery based on using tactical communications planning techniques.

Before you start building a Communication Plan, you should do the following:

- **Ensure that you have a storage place to collect facts, statistics, and other data.** Create a SharePoint site that includes your Communication Plan and links it to your SharePoint delivery plan.
- **Prepare a frequently asked questions (FAQ) document outlining common queries and answers.** Consider the basic queries that individuals will have concerning the SharePoint solution and write them down, including the answers. Request feedback and bolster the relevant FAQs. Note that a wiki page in SharePoint can be very effective in building FAQs.
- **Create a template or use the organization's provided templates.** You should ensure that a common message uses a standardized and common format. Users will be able to recognize the messages quicker and will relate them to the SharePoint solution immediately. Be mindful of whether you should use your own template or the ones provided by the organization. For example, if you are putting SharePoint into an organization that is new to communication exercises concerning software User Adoption and that does not have a culture where a central bank of communication templates is provided, then you should create a template, get approval for its use, and then use it. However, if the organization has a central communication team, you must ensure that you follow its processes and use its supplied templates.
- **Develop a relationship with each audience.** Communications Planning is not just saying, "Hey, we have a new SharePoint offering, take a look at it." It is an ongoing event intrinsically linked to training. It can even be measured to confirm SharePoint solution value and ROI. Your audiences are crucial, and they can vary considerably. If you have not already identified those audiences, you should immediately do so, introduce yourself and the delivery program, and

state your intention to involve them in the User Adoption plans (which, of course, will include the Communication Plans).

- **Create a list of categorized contacts.** You will need a bank of contacts who should receive key messages about the solution. These could be relevant SharePoint sponsors, influencers, and SharePoint champions that you have worked with during the delivery of the SharePoint solution. They could also be audience members who need to be informed about the SharePoint solution. You could build a SharePoint site with a list of contacts that are then categorized by the SharePoint solution. As more solutions are delivered, indicate the relevant contacts next to each one.
- **Maintain a wish list.** While SharePoint grows, and the more users become engaged with it, you will get queries from them asking whether SharePoint can solve a particular issue, and requests for aid will increase. Generally, SharePoint can meet all business information requirements; however, while recording those requirements, you should also create and maintain a wish list. These can be as simple or as complex as needed. The key is to ensure that the wish list is grouped into themes, as in Table 4-4. The wish list should be in a common, accessible, and prominent location, and linked to a discussion thread so that users can describe and discuss those wish list items further.
- **Create a SharePoint site for media communications and regularly update the communications site.** You should be proactive in making sure that there are regular updates to the communications site. Such a site would harvest persuasive content (such as multichannel marketing, lead generation, and customer self-service). This shows the visitors to the site that you are passionate about the SharePoint solutions and value keeping all users updated.
- **Ensure that you have a clearly defined message framework.** A message framework will help you ensure that you communicate the correct information to the people who need to see that information, using a standard, concise process. The message framework is a key aspect of the Communication Plan and is further described next.

Figure 4-1 shows a format of a SharePoint tactical Communication Plan. The plan has three sections: Background and Context, Effective Messages, and Message Delivery. The Background and Context section sets the scene so that audiences understand what SharePoint is, the solution being implemented, and the organization's vision of the benefits that the solution will provide. The Effective Messages section is a list of messages that should be used in any method of communicating to the audiences what benefits, attributes, and features are important to them. Message Delivery indicates what methods of communication will be used, technological or otherwise.

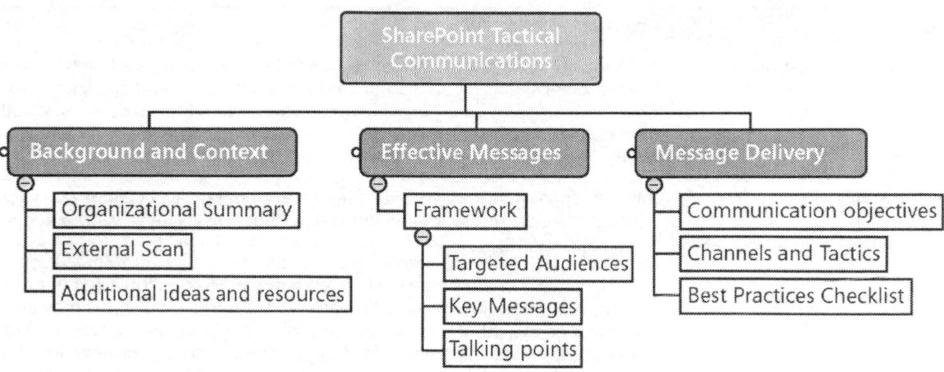


**FIGURE 4-1** Format of a SharePoint tactical Communication Plan.

You should take time to develop a model following this guide so that you are able to create a standard approach to communicating information about any SharePoint delivery program. Try to keep the SharePoint Communication Plan simple and easy to follow. It is not uncommon to see a SharePoint Communication Plan laid out on one page. You will see that the headings do not just relate to communicating the aspects of the solution to audiences, but also lend to the development of policies that are a core aspect of SharePoint Governance. Like managing SharePoint Governance, SharePoint Communication Plans do not have an end; they are completed when the SharePoint platform no longer exists in the organization. So long as you are providing SharePoint solutions, there is always a requirement to communicate those initiatives using Communication Plans. And the higher up the chain that the SharePoint solution being implemented is, the more detailed the Communication Plan needs to be. For example, you should consider building a Communication Plan against each of the SharePoint themes for quick wins that were previously described in Table 4-4, especially if the delivery program is a full implementation of SharePoint.

Table 4-6 takes the SharePoint tactical Communication Plan format depicted in Figure 4-1 and suggests actions for each of the headings. You can use this as a guide to building your own Communication Plans.

**TABLE 4-6** Format of a SharePoint Tactical Communication Plan

| Heading | Action |
|---|---|
| Background and Context | An upper-level section, Background and Context sets the scene for the SharePoint solution being delivered or an aspect of that delivery program. |
| Organizational Summary | A standard statement explaining to the reader what SharePoint is; the organization's history, purpose, reach, and commitment; and why SharePoint has been (or is going to be) implemented. |
| External Scan | Address and document areas related to the provision of the SharePoint solution where you do not already have information. Basically, this provides further background information. For example, evaluating the benefits against the cost, ease of delivery, how the solution relates to the sponsor's mission, and the general impact on staff required to implement the solution.<br>To do this, consider surveying (using the Survey feature of your central SharePoint sites), particularly asking about service delivery—specifically, perception on what the delivery team is going to provide, what the delivery team does well, and what kind of information would be useful. Results of these surveys should be indicated or referenced in this section. |

| Heading | Action |
|---|---|
| Additional ideas and resources | You should indicate here a list of key ideas taken from any wish lists, discussions, and workshops, which could come under consideration and are related to the SharePoint solution being provided. You should also list any sources, whether they are people who are instrumental in providing those ideas, locations of any surveys, and wish lists that can be referred to. |
| Effective Messages | This is an upper-level heading. Building a message framework allows you to create the most effective messages and then relate those messages to various audiences. |
| Framework | You should create a list of effective messages in this section, or refer to each of them depending on how many messages needs to be communicated (for example, you may have a specific message for each part of the roadmap). The messages framework gives a list of messages surrounding the SharePoint solution, which then includes positioning (statement of the organizational mission statement and/or philosophy that ties into the solution), taglines (keywords or phrases that make the solution unique), and a statement of the solution's purpose. Then this is split by the audiences, benefits, attributes. and features. |
| Targeted Audiences | In this section, you should list the Targeted Audiences and their purpose in relationship to the solution being implemented. The "Engaging your sponsor and stakeholders" section of Chapter 3 includes a map to help you identify the types of audiences that you will need to communicate the SharePoint solution to. Your audiences can also be standardized based on their functional location in the organization; for example, sponsor, business manager, information worker, technical and development, and security. It is vital that you include this section. Targeted Audiences is there to ensure that a "message" is designed so that it is meaningful to that audience. For example, you would not send messages about the technical features of the SharePoint server administration to your SharePoint sponsor, who is the chief information officer (CIO) of the organization, as she would not benefit from hearing that message. |
| Key Messages | In this section, you should list five key messages related and tailored to your SharePoint solution. These should be simple, single sentences, and not overexplained. Here is an example of a key message: "SharePoint allows individuals in an organization to easily create and manage their own collaborative websites." This kind of message is direct, unambiguous, and positive. Creating key messages is very useful in providing the audiences with consistent and standard information concerning the SharePoint solution and what it means to users. |
| Talking Points | Talking points are meant to give people a quick and easy way of staying on track—not wandering off topic or saying something completely different from what somebody else in the same organization is saying. Use your research from your External Scan to pull in data and examples. Offer concise highlights of outcomes, or cite research that creates the need for the solution to be implemented. Talking points are extremely useful for marketing the solution and at the same time recording the history of successes (and failures). You should ensure that relevant talking points are recorded here and that they are not communicated outside the organization. Because the Communication Plan is a working document, you can add talking points to the document, either individually or as a separate list (a great way would be a SharePoint list with items referring to the related SharePoint solution), then referenced back to this section. Here are some examples of talking points:<br>■ "Fabrikam opened up the SharePoint solution to offshore drilling functions. As a result, and after one month of initial training, there was a significant increase in use by the drilling administrators. This has resulted in a significant lift in information management productivity because drilling reports are now centralized and accessible from single locations instead of relying on email."<br>■ "The Fabrikam SharePoint information team ran a competition for two months to find the most innovative SharePoint site in their company. The Commercial business unit won and was awarded a night at the opera courtesy of the company."<br>■ "Fabrikam Investments has implemented a SharePoint workflow solution that has increased reporting productivity by decreasing the time taken to obtain approvals. This will save the organization over $20,000 per year." |

| Heading | Action |
| --- | --- |
| Message Delivery | This upper-level section is where you focus on creating objectives that allow you to prioritize tactics and create schedules to send out messages of crafted communication resources (for example, email, blogs, articles, videos, flyers, workshops, and so on). |
| Communication objectives | This subsection is where you need to state what you wish to accomplish through the creation of the message framework, which details the vision, and the kinds of messages that should go to the audiences and who the audiences are. Line up the objective with the channels and ensure that they connect back to the message framework. |
| Channels and Tactics | This subsection refers to the method or the route that you will use to deliver your messages about the solution. Examples include anything from media outlets to online media.<br>These tactics are required because your users will want the information quickly, their attention span will not be what you expect, and yet interaction from those audiences targeted is expected. Your tactics will include investigating the best ways to create the messages. For example, you may need to create messages that include presentations of SharePoint to the sponsors, or post video for information workers to understand how to use the SharePoint solution. You will also need to devise case studies so that business unit managers can decide whether to adopt the solution for their requirements, and so on. This is based on the audiences you have defined and the external scan taken to identify what kind of information they wish to see. Gather the relevant resources and document which resources relate to which message, pointing each message to the location of the resource. This means that channels of communication are located in one place. This is where SharePoint 2013 comes in handy. Remember earlier that I said you should create a central SharePoint communications site to house your Communication Plans. Therefore, using that, you could also centralize the materials (videos, articles, publications, flyers, newsletters, and email messages) into your SharePoint communications site in Document Libraries. The usefulness of doing this is that they become searchable and easy to access and maintain. Tactics can also be recorded using a SharePoint calendar, connected to the resources used for communication as mentioned.<br>Note that SharePoint 2013 includes captioning of content, and this is very useful for video content, as it allows the user to play a video without having to open the document directly from SharePoint 2013. |
| Best Practices Checklist | This subsection lists the tasks associated with the key channels and tactics that will be used, and indicates any special requirements for communicating the messages. These may be references to an overall communication policy that the organization uses, names of business units responsible for approving communications, or both. |

Once you have completed the Communication Plan, you are ready to detail the communication objectives as follows:

- You will be able to make a clear statement about what you wish to accomplish.
- You will be able to clarify the specifics of the SharePoint solution.
- For each of the audiences, you will be able to define measurable objectives for the communication efforts, and each will bring about a change event. The change event gives user perception, which drives User Adoption training.

**Note** Knowing your target market (audience) will focus your communications on those who will value and use your SharePoint solutions. "Audiences" are types of people whom you can clearly define by common characteristics, such as what issues they care about and how they access information. Identifying your audiences points you to specific content for your message and to the best method for delivering your message. For example, the messaging content is used to describe your organization in terms of what's important to a particular group. Understanding your target audience's behavioral patterns points you to the communications channels and tactics to use to deliver your message. Knowing your audience helps you to deliver your message in ways that reach the audience and capture their attention.

Your SharePoint Communication Plan relates to information security, particularly how the communication channels and tactics are handled. (For example, if you are building a new SharePoint presence that is going to be a public website, the last thing you would do is announce to your competitors before building it that it will have particular features that are better than theirs.) There will be policies that state how public relations work within the organization and how secure any communications should be.

When delivering a SharePoint solution, ensure that information and communication policies have been set and adhered to. For example, even though the organization has a responsibility to provide the platform, each user is responsible for using that platform in an acceptable manner and in accordance with the relevant legislation. This is why the Communication Plan should always include the security team in the organization, so that information relevant to the benefits and features is available to them.

*Key policies concerning Governance, such as the Communications Policy and Information Policy, are discussed further in Chapter 5, "Planning SharePoint Governance."*

Creating a SharePoint Communication Plan is part of successfully delivering a SharePoint solution that the organization will use. The construction of the Communication Plan begins when your User Adoption planning does. Make sure that you have people to help you build the plan. This is particularly important not only if the solution being deployed is going to affect the organization, but also if the organization's culture requires a formal communication release. This section described the reasons why a Communication Plan is important, as well as the format and actions required to build and then execute the Communication Plans. Execution of the Communication Plan, however, is not a single event. Each message that you collect has an associated channel and tactic, and each tactic is carried out on a particular calendar date. For each tactic completed, ensure that you gather feedback and address the Communication Plan continually. Run regular communication reviews as part of the delivery program reviews to identify any issues or risks. Include your SharePoint sponsors in any key messages and continually keep them up to date with the Communication Plan.

**More Info** Communication Plans also are mentioned in the SharePoint User Adoption guide. Although this was written for SharePoint 2010, the example sheets in that document could be useful in SharePoint 2013. Download it from *http://sharepoint.microsoft.com/iusesharepoint/landing.aspx.*

A SharePoint Communication Message Framework is available for download at *http://www.sharepointgeoff.com/sharepoint-communication-message-framework*. Use this to record decisions against identified communication channels. This resource is very useful to target training, further adoption tactics, general communication concerning SharePoint, Governance, etc.

## Creating SharePoint champions

Using SharePoint, organizations aim to use every asset they have as effectively as possible. To do this, you need to invest time and resources to make sure that users are fully utilizing the functions made available to them, especially the capabilities that can help them be more productive and meet their objectives.

As indicated earlier, gaining support from your SharePoint sponsor or sponsors is vital at the start. However, you will not be able to get individuals to embrace the solution without their buy-in and support. You will need help to do this.

Enlisting aid from the business is a great way to build best practices and policies in the use of SharePoint and addressing User Adoption. This assistance comes from information workers who are SharePoint evangelists—aka *SharePoint champions.*

A SharePoint champion is a great intermediary who is a business individual situated between information workers and IT support staff. A SharePoint champion is provided with specific training, education on solving basic issues, and information on SharePoint best practices in reference to the SharePoint solutions provided to their peers. By creating a SharePoint champion, you are in fact reducing the load on IT support because basic problems are resolved faster. The existence of SharePoint champions will drive User Adoption, reduce support costs, and bring organizations closer to achieving the goals that drove their investment in SharePoint.

A SharePoint champion understands how the organization operates, what kind of information challenges are prevalent in their respective functions, and key problems experienced by their peers. They are not gurus in SharePoint, nor are they technical experts. Rather, they are prepared to discuss, propose, and help make decisions concerning the future of SharePoint solutions.

- SharePoint champions are representative members of the organization who see the advantage of using SharePoint and help find ways to use the software in new and advanced ways. These people understand business operations, are not technical experts as such, and are certainly not SharePoint technical gurus.

- They come from various parts of the organization. It's great to have a group of information workers from different areas of the company who take on the mantle of SharePoint champion.
- They are aware of the overall organizational strategy, business unit strategy, and purpose, and are eager to support and evangelize SharePoint best practices from a business perspective.
- They are recommended by their line managers to be a SharePoint champion. This is an important step because it shows that their line manager backs SharePoint initiatives.
- They will benefit from increased SharePoint knowledge and help provide this knowledge to their peers.
- They are enthusiastic and want to learn about the SharePoint solution and associated technologies.

As SharePoint evolves, so will SharePoint champions. They will increasingly act as key SharePoint information workers. They will assist in SharePoint support because they can serve as initial points of contact with other users. They will become an important resource in the development of SharePoint content management best practices and Governance. To keep your SharePoint champions motivated, they need to feel as if they are part of a fun team. A great method is to create a "Champion Badge," which they can proudly wear. Another great method is to ask members of the executive board to publicly state how important the champions are to the organization.

Gamification is a great way to manage innovation. It consists of applying game design to non-game applications to make them more fun and engaging. You should consider using gamification methods to identify and create sustainable motivation in your SharePoint champions. For more information on this technique, read the article at *http://www.gamification.org/wiki/Gamification_of_Work*, and watch the video at *http://www.youtube.com/watch?v=u6XAPnuFjJc&list=PL39BF9545D740ECFF&index=11&feature=plpp_video*.

Here's a recap as to why the User Adoption strategy and the Communications and Training Plan are important:

- **User Adoption Strategy** This will help you identify early adopters of the SharePoint solution through workshops, presentations, and discussions. In these forums, you will be able to state your intention of building a group of SharePoint champions. Then further investigate whether the individuals who are interested in being SharePoint champions would bring value to the group. Be sure to include your SharePoint sponsor in your inquiries.
- **Communication Plan and Training Plan** Your Communication Plans will include Channels and Tactics. Use your Communication Plan to inform information workers of a SharePoint champion group. Use your training workshops and courses to further identify SharePoint champions.

All methods involve communication. Also, ensure that you keep your SharePoint champions up to date with SharePoint features and how they can solve business information challenges, particularly in the following areas:

- Administration of content
- Management of users, including what roles users should have and how to secure information

- Management of repositories and sites
- Basic branding and customization of repositories
- Basic understanding of user profile information and My Sites areas concerning tagging, notes, and organization charts
- Design and enhance common business processes
- Help train other employees using SharePoint using the Training model

Managing SharePoint champions is a continual event that requires that they meet regularly to confer with each other, bring up points of interest, discuss business issues that require a SharePoint solution (and that are linked to the overall strategy), and review and propose changes to relevant SharePoint policies. Consider also setting up a centralized site for SharePoint champions, which should include training materials, information concerning enterprise tools that they can access, and links to policies concerning Governance, Acceptable Use, and Statements of Operations. Ensure that you have the necessary time and resources to allocate to such a group. Once the group is established, consider having the group elect a member as its leader, ensuring that this person continues managing the centralized site and the group. Keeping this leader in place could be difficult, given that "SharePoint champion" is not these people's formal job description; however, the importance of having such a group cannot be underestimated.

**Tip** Consider using the Community Portal Template available in SharePoint 2013, which allows a SharePoint champion forum to be created. For more information, read the article at *http://www.sharepoint911.com/blogs/laura/Lists/Posts/Post.aspx?ID=184*.

*Scenario 3: Tailspin Toys is a boxed game seller employing 500 people. The company has just acquired Fabrikam, a retail store that sells stationery, children's games, toys, and sporting goods. They are going to implement a SharePoint solution that will revolutionize the receipt or order process through invoicing, stock control, and sales ledgers. A delivery team is formed to coordinate the implementation. The staff members who are responsible for the stock control have not been introduced to SharePoint, whereas the invoicing team at Tailspin Toys has been using SharePoint for some time. Fabrikam executives have stressed that communications and training are key, and that any notion of providing manuals is "simply not enough." (The last time a system was implemented, employees were not given any training and were just told to "read the manual." Needless to say, that didn't work very well.) The stock team is cautious as a result, and there may be resistance unless they are directly involved in training. The SharePoint delivery team holds workshops and demonstrations of SharePoint for the stock team, but as a step to add comfort to the stock team, they asked key people within the invoicing team, known as "SharePoint champions," to act as a friendly face and lead demonstrations on the invoicing SharePoint solution. After several demonstrations, members of the stock team have become enthusiastic by listening to Tailspin Toys staff talk about their use of SharePoint. The delivery team then worked closely with the invoicing team of Fabrikam, and through cooperation with Tailspin Toys, created full, focused, and directed SharePoint training, identifying SharePoint champions from the stock team. The SharePoint solution is now successfully implemented, including new business rules concerning its use.*

This scenario spells out how crucial it is to have SharePoint champions. Note that User Adoption in SharePoint is not automatic. The successful development and implementation of User Adoption in SharePoint requires the intersection of several goals, improvements to business processes, user requirements, and motivation. SharePoint champions can be a very useful in helping you reach those goals because SharePoint champions can generate enthusiasm and quell anxiety associated with change. Before and after the SharePoint solution is implemented, it is essential that time and help is provided so users can adapt to the change in their procedures caused by using the new SharePoint solution. Using a combination of SharePoint champions, training, and communications will aid users in adopting the SharePoint solution.

## Standardizing business needs

As SharePoint grows in an organization, success stories relating to how SharePoint solved business and information challenges will emerge. These success stories should be investigated and showcased on a continual basis. Success stories will be communicated by, and through, your SharePoint champions, sponsors, and adopters. By reusing successful SharePoint solutions, existing business rules will be met, and Governance of those solutions will be easier to define.

One of the key reasons why User Adoption fails is that you have failed to manage evolving business needs through the use of implementing and reimplementing SharePoint solutions. Throughout this book, I have used the term *solution*. I do this because the generic approach to implementing anything in SharePoint is that you need to solve a business requirement or need. To further explain why I use *solution*, here's a typical question that I get asked, followed by my typical answer:

*Question: "What is the purpose of SharePoint?"*

*Answer: "SharePoint allows individuals to create, manage, and share content in an online platform."*

To users concerned with content management (creating, storing, retaining, archiving, sharing, and workflow management), that is a SharePoint solution.

Microsoft identifies the key drivers for providing SharePoint solutions as *Organize, Build, Discover,* and *Manage*. Table 4-7 describes the main features of each of these drivers.

**TABLE 4-7** Key Business Drivers

| Driver | Description |
| --- | --- |
| Organize | Classify information and store it centrally.<br>Create, store, retain, archive, and share information. |
| Build | Develop reuseable apps.<br>Develop repositories to organize content. |
| Discover | Archive, retain, label, and search content. |
| Manage | Share, audit, and process content. |

As you deliver SharePoint solutions, you will find that those solutions can and should be reused. Reasons for this include the fact that that organizations, with respect to IT, aim to justify ROI and obtain value at minimum cost, as follows:

- Integrate and unify their eclectic technologies.
- Align technologies closer to business strategies and priorities.
- Be seen as a more agile service provider.
- Remove costly older or outdated applications.
- Reduce the total cost of ownership.
- Reduce administrative overhead.
- Provide true value for money.
- Extract greater business value from existing systems and licenses.
- Be seen as current in terms of technology thought leadership.
- Cope with ad-hoc business requirements without spending more resources.
- Harness the possibilities of cloud technologies.

We then consider these aims with reference to the following business and information challenges:

- Business-critical data stuck in siloed systems
- Business users with no direct access to vital data
- Inefficient processes among disconnected teams
- Different vertical applications used by different teams

By aligning those issues with organizational aims, reuse of successful SharePoint solutions increases User Adoption. In addition, the following key features of SharePoint 2013 are available to deal with the above-mentioned challenges:

- SharePoint 2013 includes features to connect with line of business (LOB) systems, allowing integration features to connect systems and centralize collaboration activities.
- SharePoint 2013 can harvest business-critical data in siloes and provide that data securely.
- SharePoint 2013 provides cross-functional collaboration and workflow with LOB data.

**More Info** Further reading concerning LOB connectivity can be found in the article "Overview of Business Connectivity Services in SharePoint 2013," at *http://technet.microsoft.com/en-us/library/ee661740.aspx*.

**Note** SharePoint is also available through Office 365 (also known as SharePoint Online or SharePoint Off-Premise), which allows organizations to run SharePoint in the cloud. Benefits include faster delivery of new features and updates, reduction of the storage footprint, and improvements to scalability and performance.

*Scenario 4: Fabrikam requires a very rapid method of collecting information from its various partners. Although it runs a SharePoint environment in-house, the firm does not want to invoke costs from the IT department or disrupt its SharePoint environment. Its current users are aware of SharePoint. The company decides to use a SharePoint 2013 online site provided through Office 365, so it creates a SharePoint site and then shares that site with the various partners. The ownership of the site is set to specific business individuals.*

Creating standardized approaches to solving business needs provides benefits related to ongoing service delivery. Support becomes more stabilized because more individuals can easily adopt a solution that has been reused. Training becomes standardized, and the cost of implementation is less. In addition, various solutions become part of the everyday user tasks, and ROI increases. The value of the solution also increases, and the vision of individuals creating and managing their own content is reinforced.

## Building collaborative ownership

One part of the User Adoption strategy is to create a service delivery model that allows the business to take control of the SharePoint solution in such a way that it can manage that solution and train users using a standard training model. Creating the service delivery model allows the business rules to further take hold. There are key reasons for this—one specifically pertaining to the fact that SharePoint is a business-driven and -managed platform. Crucial to delivery of a SharePoint solution is the ability to ensure that the business can not only use the solution, but manage the use of it going forward. This is ownership; and ownership of any SharePoint solution lives and thrives in the business. Ownership also means that there will be others who will collaborate to create more content and refine existing content in whatever lifecycle that content happens to be in. Collaboration is the art of humans combining to create products to enrich others. The following quote explains this well.

> *The concept of collaborative use and "ownership" of resources has been with us since time began. Indeed collaboration is one of the hallmarks of human society and may be a fundamental part of our nature. . . . Humans have been collaboratively creating and owning knowledge for as long as we've been able to communicate, and such knowledge forms the basis of our ability to function as societies today in more or less every field of endeavor one cares to examine.*
>
> *Rishab Aiyer Ghosh,* Collaborative Ownership and the Digital Economy

You will immediately identify ownership even before the delivery program takes hold. The SharePoint sponsor, whose support will be required, clearly owns the vision and the top-level business requirements. Further refinements are then obtained through involvement with key stakeholders, influences, information workers, and the audiences in your Communication Plans. The success of defining ownership is directly related to User Adoption. If the delivery program is run as an IT project, then it is likely that the language used to provide that solution will be IT-specific. This will most likely confuse the business users, which will discourage the business from owning the SharePoint solution. Instead, any decisions concerning its use will remain with IT, and that will lead to a serious flaw in how users adopt SharePoint.

So you will need to ascertain ownership of the solution and build that into the User Adoption strategy. This needs to be detailed against the kind of the solution being implemented. If the SharePoint solution is a SharePoint 2013 site provided through Office 365, or an on-premises SharePoint 2013 site, then the ownership is specific. The ownership could pertain to management of the site, content repositories on that site, a SharePoint app that has been implemented on that site, or even specific content in a repository on that site.

If the solution is an Office 365 tenant that includes the SharePoint Online site, then the ownership of the site could also include the administrative aspects of the Office 365 tenant: Users, SharePoint Sites, Exchange, and Lync.

**Note** Although you can initially define who has ownership at the start of the delivery program for the relevant parts of the solution (and the solution as a whole), this will change over time. You will not be the person refining or even reviewing the ownership—the business does that. You should, therefore, help the business define the initial rules and policies, so this then allows the business to assign, manage, and refine ownership. Because it is those owners who manage the SharePoint solutions, those solutions evolve. This process is irrespective of the kind of solution and extends from the site all the way down to the content in Document Libraries, lists, pages, workflows—in fact, any content.

The key is that ownership relates to policies and rules, and it revolves around a solution that has been constructed and implemented. Those policies and rules have been agreed to and are managed by relevant owners. And that can succeed only when the solution fixes a business problem. After all, if you are not trying to fix a business problem, then why adopt SharePoint?

When implementing a SharePoint solution, new users will be unaware of the business standards and best practices when using SharePoint. The last thing you want to do is simply leave users to their own devices. You, the SharePoint sponsor, and the SharePoint champions therefore should agree on a number of top-level business rules and collaborative ownership rules.

Collaborative ownership shows up in the use of the new community site features in SharePoint. These features provide forum-based experiences in SharePoint, which means that users can create and manage discussions across the company, seek assistance, and share content ideas. Ownership comes from the creation of business rules and policies concerning the management of the community functionality, which can be present in a site. A good example is a member of the HR department using community features to launch discussions concerning a staff development form.

Typically, the HR department would have to be responsible for owning the collaboration and the content that is potentially going to be shared, and audit the communication with those who should be participating in the collaborative exercise. Again, the point you need to consider is that there are many features of SharePoint. Be aware of the ownership of the features being delivered, not from a technical perspective (for example, security), but from a business ownership viewpoint, particularly business rules associated with collaborative engagement on content, irrespective of those who own that content.

As previously mentioned, collaborative ownership relates to everything about SharePoint content management, and even goes beyond that, into the management of the platform itself from SharePoint support and associated teams. Ownership is related to a roadmap of information services, of which SharePoint could be one (as SharePoint integrates with other enterprise systems), showing the connection between business services and who the key stakeholders (that is, the owners) are for each service. From a User Adoption strategy perspective, there needs to be some top-level statements that prove to users that the platform is service-managed. You would create some basic rules concerning its use.

SharePoint 2013 makes collaborative ownership even more important because of the improvements to My Site (as discussed in the "Social networking in SharePoint 2013" section later in this chapter). There is a SharePoint 2013 feature within each user's Newsfeed page (also discussed in the same section), which is called Share. This option allows users to share the content with a site, group, or individuals they happen to be "following." Although this feature does have a benefit in that it allows individuals to connect with each other, there is an element of responsibility needed to ascertain who "owns" what, what is being shared, and whether that content should, in fact, be shared. So, business rules need to be defined for informing users not only about those "social" features, but also about the ramifications of potentially sharing confidential content with the wrong audience.

**Note** An example of Collaborative Ownership is given in the article "SharePoint Collaborative Ownership" at *http://www.sharepointgeoff.com/sharepoint-collaborative-ownership/* . This could be applied to SharePoint, whether the platform is SharePoint On-Premise or SharePoint Online. Consider these as starting points, and use the table format to create a table of business rules and policy statements. These should be posted in a centralized location, accessible to all, and linked to in training information for anyone who may be in the position of having to understand collaborative ownership.

## Understanding the importance of training

Training is a change management initiative that is crucial to the successful delivery of a SharePoint solution. You cannot instill a need to use a SharePoint solution unless users get a reinforcement of new skills relevant to that solution. When users receive training, they will feel more confident that they will be able to use the SharePoint solution to carry out their tasks.

As you have read in this chapter up to now, delivery of a SharePoint solution comes from a delivery program that is business-led, not IT-led. In IT projects, rarely is there a budget for training or business User Adoption; instead, SharePoint solutions are released in the hope that people will just "pick it up." Although it is possible to make technology easy to use, there are as many different users as the day is long. What may seem easy and intuitive to some may be difficult and incomprehensible to others. People sell their time to work and get money, so introducing new technology and making people's work harder (at least for a while) is not a route to success unless they are assisted through the transition.

Therefore, as part of the delivery program, you have a responsibility to ensure that every user who will use your SharePoint solution is able to perform their roles to an acceptable standard. If users are well informed through communication and training, they will be reassured that they have the adequate skills for the tasks at hand. Transitioning them to using the SharePoint solution is easier. Training, like Governance, is a continual road and must be sustained. Training is not a one-time event and will require continual monitoring, review, and enhancement. As users become more sophisticated in their use of the SharePoint solution, so will the requirements for relevant training.

Training in SharePoint is of the utmost importance for the success of User Adoption, and it deserves a detailed look into creating, managing, and delivering SharePoint Training. The "Creating the SharePoint Training Model" section of Chapter 5 goes into detail about the creation and management of the training program.

## Social networking in SharePoint 2013

SharePoint 2013 enables users to share information about themselves and their work easily. This sharing of information encourages collaboration, builds and promotes expertise, and targets relevant content to the people who need to view it. You can tailor content to each user in the organization and create policies to protect individuals' privacy. Users can organize, discover, build, and manage their professional work through collaboration; that's where the social aspect comes in.

To do this, SharePoint social features are built upon a database of properties that integrates data about people in the organization; and the information can be integrated from third-party applications and directory services. Social features are geared to users following, tagging, and mentioning people, content, and sites. This information is displayed on the user's personal page, along with any related aggregated content and relevant information associated with the user's designated audience.

Unfortunately, with the advent of social networking being used to sell and bring people into Internet global groups, naturally one of the very first questions asked is, "What does *social networking* mean?" (I have been asked this question countless times during demonstrations of SharePoint.) If the question was asked three to five years ago, *social networking* would be recognized as writing blogs and using discussion boards and forums available on specific sites.

**More Info** For information about the ways in which organizations can unlock value and productivity through social technologies, read the article "The Social Economy: Unlocking Value and Productivity Through Social Technologies," at *http://www.mckinsey.com/insights/mgi/research/technology_and_innovation/the_social_economy*.

The Oxford Dictionary *(http://oxforddictionaries.com/definition/english/social+network)* defines a *social network* as

1. A network of social interactions and personal relationships
2. A dedicated website or other application which enables users to communicate with each other by posting information, comments, messages, images, etc.

Nowadays, there are hundreds of social networking sites, all aiming to build their own groups, and having various features designed to encourage User Adoption. From an organization's perspective, executives may be confused and bewildered when faced with requests to have a social networking site or features.

No wonder they are confused, not to mention extremely cautious. Looking at the online landscape of social networking platforms, anyone would be confused and concerned about the vast number of choices, all promoting an online service that focuses on facilitating the building of social networks or social relations. This is among people who, for example, share interests, activities, backgrounds, or real-life connections. This has led to consternation, and even amazing comments that "SharePoint is like Facebook" (which is like comparing apples to oranges). This has further led to implementations of social features at Internet social networking sites being installed into SharePoint, in a bid to make SharePoint more acceptable to the user and on the assumption that doing this improves User Adoption of SharePoint.

Before social networking features can be added to a User Adoption plan, the following questions must be answered:

- What is defined as "social" when placed against the culture of the organization?
- How will being "social" improve worker productivity?
- As an individual, what value will being "social" provide?
- How will social networking features be supported?
- How will social networking features be governed?
- How will social networking features be integrated?

To try and answer those questions, this section will further describe what the word *social* means in SharePoint and list the benefits and value using some example customer scenarios. This text will give you a good understanding of planning personalization features, as that is an important aspect of User Adoption concerning information about people and the facilities available to locate them.

In SharePoint, social networking is not a feature-specific component—it's about focusing on getting the work done. In SharePoint, the word *social* is synonymous with *collaboration*—finding better methods of working together and finding easier ways of achieving goals.

**Note** The key point of social networking is to transform information from tacit knowledge to explicit knowledge. The United States and United Kingdom face the loss of 40 to 50 percent of all knowledge workers in the next 10 years as baby boomers retire. If corporations don't concentrate on capturing this tacit knowledge and turning it into explicit knowledge that acts as an IP asset to the organization, they are going to lose a competitive edge.

SharePoint 2013 has a user-centric feature called *Enterprise Social*. That means using new ways of working together by putting people front and center, as follows:

- Allows users to be engaged in conversations to stay informed and make better decisions
- Provides "communities" so that users can gain insight and find answers
- Makes it easier to work as a team and manage your projects

Those ways of working have been applied in SharePoint 2013 user-centric features as follows:

- **MySites** This is the key user interface, providing a simplified and unified navigation for all organization members. You can get more insights into other people by going to other people's profiles, identifying who they know, and expanding your social network.
- **Community Sites** This is a forum provided as a reusable site app that allows people across organizations to create and manage discussions. Community Sites can be categorized and managed by those who own those sites.
- **Newsfeeds** This is a page of activity that shows newsfeeds of activity and allows users to post comments, replies, pictures, and links. Users can also create keywords that other users can follow and search for. Activities that are displayed in a user's MySite can also be displayed in their individual Microsoft Outlook "notification" emails.
- **Mentions** This allows users to "mention" other users (like using the Twitter @ sign) in posts and replies. Users can also use "Like" features to rate content, "Follow" people, sites, and documents, and tags and customize their newsfeeds.
- **Web Analytics** This is continually running. For example, visit counts will be shown, as well as trending tags in all content.
- **SkyDrive** You can work offline with content and have that synchronized to your MySite.

Therefore, if you want to know how a person can find out more about other people in the organization, there are many ways available from looking at these features. In addition, you would be able to see the people you are following, sites, and tags. You would visit Newsfeeds, so you could "Follow" all the information important to you. You could use Mentions so you could send and pick up messages to other people. All content can be tagged and liked, so you can "Tag" and "Like" the information most important to you. You can also "Follow" sites, and each site has specific members, so you could post messages from your NewsFeed to those members on those sites, and by utilizing "Sharing," you can hold discussions directly with them.

The following scenarios describe situations where including social networking in the SharePoint solution might be beneficial.

*Scenario 5: A user wants to get information on coffee production from specific individuals who may have knowledge on the subject and provide input. She wishes to discuss subjects with those individuals and be able to rate discussion threads for others to see and participate in.*

The Community Site template is a new feature of SharePoint 2013. A *community* is a special type of SharePoint site, where groups of people who work on a specific project, document, or other entity can network. By using a communities site, you will be able to visit a specific community, create a new community, post discussions (if you are a member of the relevant community), and view discussions, hot topics, top contributors, and more. All discussion threads are exposed on the user's NewsFeeds page for easy access.

*Scenario 6: Individuals from multiple teams need to work together on a project. These individuals are currently members of different SharePoint sites where they can access their own task lists. However, they now need a central location where they can see all these task lists combined. Some of their task lists are synchronized using Outlook.*

Each individual's MySite has a Task display that automatically aggregates Tasks from any sites where a Task List is provided and where tasks have been assigned to them. Tasks that have been synchronized from Outlook will also be displayed here. Therefore, the following results:

- Users can track and view their Tasks and To-Dos.
- All tasks are pushed to the individual's personal site.
- Tasks can be aggregated from Microsoft Exchange Server, Microsoft Project Server, and SharePoint 2013.
- Other systems can be integrated in the future.

**Note** To centralize tasks from various sources requires a SharePoint 2013 service application to be delivered. This is called the Work Management service application, and it provides the ability to aggregate tasks to a central location. You can learn more about this application by watching the video "Walkthrough of the SharePoint 2013 Features in the Work Management Service Application" at *http://www.bing.com/videos/watch/video/walkthrough-sharepoint-2013-features-in-the-work-management-service-application/10t98eisc?from=*.

Understanding how social features are to be used is vital, and you need to build a User Adoption strategy that encompasses Enterprise Social. The following five steps will help you build this strategy:

1. Get SharePoint sponsorship to evangelize. Exploit their enthusiasm by getting the sponsors to start using the MySite area. Provide them with the necessary awareness of the social features, including Follow, Tag, Discussion, and so on.
2. Provide a community site and link that back to the relevant SharePoint sites so that individuals from each site can locate other groups.
3. Include social networking features in the Training model.
4. Bring on SharePoint champions to help users understand the social networking features.
5. Set up an Internal User Group (Governance) to define business rules and best practices.

**Important** Thoroughly plan and deliver at a structured and measured pace. Don't go for a "Tell everyone to go there and try things out" approach without sending some kind of communication, running some kind of awareness, and creating a testing group. This will result in people simply not understanding the use of the features and not having the relevant competence. And if that is done without business rules in place, policies and rules concerning the use of the Social Networking features will not be enforced.

In the following two scenarios, the organizations want to implement social networking features as part of their SharePoint solution. The first scenario describes an organization that wants to follow a structured approach.

*Scenario 7: Tailspin Toys is a global manufacturing company with stores in Africa, Germany, and the United States, with 4,000 employees and an annual profit of $20 billion. The main office is the U.S. office. The company has a new SharePoint implementation, and it wants to improve collaboration among the staff, with key aims to get its staff groups to connect with each other, identify skill strengths, and help foster the building of dynamic project teams. The company wants to ensure the credibility of the implementation at the U.S. office before providing it to the Africa and Germany offices.*

Steps to be taken include the following:

1. Obtain executive and HR sponsorship and elect key influencers. Assign a small area of the company to act as early adopters (from the U.S. office). Communicate intention of delivery to the U.S., Africa, and Germany locations.
2. Create basic concepts. Communicate features, train key influencers, identify and appoint SharePoint champions, and run workshops.
3. Design functionality, define key business rules, map into operations, and provide support.
4. Monitor and maintain usage in the U.S. office and broadcast success stories to the Africa and Germany offices. Record all feedback and reviews. Identify channels and tactics for adoption to specific areas of the Africa and Germany offices. Wrap the usage into support provisions.
5. Repeat steps 2 and 3 until all offices are covered and maintained as described in step 4.

The second scenario describes an organization that does not follow this approach.

*Scenario 8: Tailspin Toys has two offices in London, which have been informed about social features in SharePoint by a third-party vendor. The vendor team installs and deploys these social features, writes up a guide, and posts it on the IT team's SharePoint site. Users found out that the technology was available and started trying the features. As a result, part of the technology failed concerning tagging, and all tagging information was lost. The IT team did not have the knowledge to fix the issue, and in response to complaints, stated that there was no Signed License Agreement (SLA) covering support of the social features. The company executives were alarmed to find unwarranted and uncontrolled social connections and were aware of the complaints from staff concerning the lack of SharePoint function. The entire SharePoint platform started being considered useless because of the failure of the tagging features. For two weeks, the tagging issue was investigated by the third-party vendor, but after finding that the original vendor would charge an additional $50,000 to correct the issue, the company decided to stop using the social features altogether. This led to a major downturn in the use of SharePoint altogether.*

Creating a SharePoint social networking strategy is not the same thing as trying the various features and attempting to obtain "Wow!" reactions from a few users. Fancy "bells and whistles" are not sustainable, and neither is a strategy for usage, support, or Governance. Make sure that you involve the right resources at the start, specifically the SharePoint sponsor and representatives from the HR department. Ensure that those resources can evangelize, communicate, and provide advice about best practices in terms of business use. Most important, continually communicate success stories, train adopters, and run workshops.

**More Info** For more information concerning SharePoint 2013 social features, please read the following guides:

"What's New in Social Computing in SharePoint 2013" at *http://technet.microsoft.com/en-us/library/jj219766(v=office.15).*

"Overview of Communities in SharePoint Server 2013" at *http://technet.microsoft.com/`en-us/library/jj219805(v=office.15).*

"Overview of Microblog Features, Feeds, and the Distributed Cache Service in SharePoint Server 2013" at *http://technet.microsoft.com/en-us/library/jj219700(v=office.15).*

"Plan for My Sites in SharePoint Server 2013" at *http://technet.microsoft.com/en-us/library/cc262500(v=office.15).*

## Value Management and Value Engineering

In delivering a SharePoint solution, you need to do the following:

- Ensure that there is a good ROI and can prove that the SharePoint implementation adds benefits and improves productivity.

- Describe the objectives the SharePoint solution will meet, the alternatives addressed, and what alternative has been selected based on its value.

Doing this creates a "SharePoint quality stamp" and proves that SharePoint has been optimized for service delivery. To create the Quality Stamp, you need to define the "value" of the relevant SharePoint solution and use methods that prove value. You need to address SharePoint solution alternatives, and by using "engineering" methods, identify and select which of those provides the most value. From my experience in the field, I've witnessed the results of SharePoint implementations put in place for these (rather dicey) reasons:

- There were licenses to be used and money to be spent.
- There was no alternatives addressed and the product was deployed in a hurry.
- No objectives were defined, so what was put in place did not meet client needs. This is because those doing the implementations did not take the time to perform proper assessments, did not know of any procedure that could help them, or both.

This section will help you understand how to manage the value of SharePoint and address alternatives, while avoiding the above-mentioned pitfalls.

Managing value means optimizing the use of the SharePoint platform and its resources. While much of determining the best solution to go for involves establishing effective decision making and control processes, managing value focuses on selecting the best option. This is irrespective of whether the plan is to build a SharePoint farm, determine the best site taxonomy, or build a site solution for a client to ensure user productivity is at its optimum—in other words, optimizing the solution to deliver value for money. You should take decisions during the early stages of implementation, as this will have the greatest influence on the outcome and will affect the total expenditure and benefits significantly. Do not wait until SharePoint is implemented and then "deal with its value" when things start to fail.

In the following scenario, you will see that being reactive is not managing value.

*Scenario 9: An IT project is created for Fabrikam to implement SharePoint, deploying to a single-server farm in an organization of 15,000 users. No investigation is done to identify usage; users, left to their own devices, start storing content on the site. More users join in. Little management or review from IT to identify usage. Complaints ensue from users; SharePoint's performance is slow. IT does an investigation and finds no backup, degraded performance, with little resiliency and no Governance. In addition, unfactored costs are indicated, due to the increased licensing and infrastructure needed to resolve the issues.*

Managing value is not always just about saving money; managing value ensures the business requirement is met when delivering a SharePoint solution. Consider the following scenario.

*Scenario 10: Client B decides to build a Publishing site to accommodate a team new to SharePoint, whose members are mainly going to share documents.*

Managing value in this regard is more related to User Adoption, as opposed to using relevant features. Be aware of when technical terms appear in requirement statements, and challenge their use when appropriate, as they can cause confusion and other difficulties. For example, to SharePoint technical staff, the word *Publishing* would mean using the Publishing Infrastructure site feature. However, that may provide far too much functionality to meet the request, particularly given the level of documents and team size. Turning on unnecessary features may not necessarily meet the objective and in fact be overkill, which may require more support than necessary.

*Scenario 11: Client C wants to use stored Microsoft Visio diagrams in SharePoint and is asking you whether this is a good idea.*

Managing value is about identifying the best solution and weighing the alternatives. While Visio is great for things like drawing organization charts, its link with SharePoint Designer could hamper the process of deciding the best solution to adopt. While some people will see this as a Governance issue, it is actually more to do with how to position this tool strategically with others. Remember that when faced with questions like these, you still need to go through a Value Management exercise and identify alternatives to Visio depending on what the purpose is and who will be using the tool.

When I advised clients about the methods of obtaining SharePoint solution value by using managing-value methods, one IT manager said, "So why do we need to manage value to implement a SharePoint solution? Can't we just jump in and give the client what they want?" But giving the client "what they want" doesn't mean the client will adopt your solution if the cost for development, purchase, and support is not within their budget. You need to ask yourself the question, "What is the client going to use SharePoint for?" and make sure that whatever you put in place meets the requirements.

Consider the following analogy. A council is asked to provide new swings for children in a local park. Two swings are installed, but without protective bars to keep the children from falling off. After a slew of complaints, they then put special safety bars on the swings, but this then prevents the older children from using the swings. So the council then installs more swings, but this takes up so much space that there is no room for any other amenities, like a place for people to sit. As a result, fewer people use the swings, and attendance at the park itself falls off. Eventually, very few people visit the park each day, and the complaints (and redesigns) continue.

Of course, the obvious question is: "How was the swing solution analyzed?" So let's now apply managing-value thinking. Think of the cost that the council paid to provide the swings. Second, think of whether the swings will be continued to be used and the work and cost to install the safety bars. If you are already thinking of solutions, you are already trying to manage value.

To give the client what it wants in SharePoint, you must go through the process of requirement gathering, usage analysis, and design. Some of this is business design, and the rest is more of a technical nature. However, while doing this, you still need to question requirements, identify alternative solutions, and assess them before agreeing with the client the final framework of the solution you want to put in place.

The technically minded might refer to this practice as "Solutions Architecture"; in reality, it is simply Value Management.

There are two key tools you can use:

- **Value Management** Selecting the solution that provides best value for money
- **Value Engineering** Optimizing the value for money delivered by a chosen solution

Value Management should be used during the Initial Investigation stage to test the business requirements, or at the start of the Feasibility and Definition stage to assess alternative options.

Now, let's look at the question of how to use Value Management and Value Engineering in your SharePoint implementation to ensure that whatever solution you are attempting to put in place represents best value for money and refines the selected solution to optimize value for money.

## Objectives of Value Management

In SharePoint, Value Management is primarily concerned with ensuring that the business needs concerning a delivering solution are clearly defined in terms of value, and that those involved know what is going to be produced to achieve value. The primary objective is to create a common understanding that covers the design problem, identifies the design objectives, and achieves a group consensus about various courses of action.

In the context of implementing a SharePoint service, you may be thinking that I am only talking about developing and implementing a SharePoint solution (i.e., a custom farm solution). No, I'm not talking about the details of taking a solution created by a developer and deploying it to a farm. And I'm also not talking about a specific service application such as Search Services, Visio Services, User Profile, and similar apps. A SharePoint solution is anything that the business requires from SharePoint. That requirement might end up as a business workflow, it might end up as an implementation of Access Services, it might be part of the work of designing a SharePoint site for a department or division, or it may even be the study of what features and components to be included in a new SharePoint farm. Value Management is vital; it must be used when designing anything within the SharePoint platform that will deliver a service.

So, you may be thinking, "Value Management is simply a business process; there's nothing for technical people here." Wrong. Value Management is a journey of discovery where technical know-how meets business requirements. Value Management methods should be used by SharePoint workers, from administrators to developers to architects to program managers. By working with Value Management techniques in SharePoint, this establishes to the delivery team (the technical camp and business camp) that delivering SharePoint solutions is not just a simple, click-done-finish project, and that simply applying a quick design solution at the start is enough.

I was once describing Value Management techniques in a workshop. A SharePoint administrator said, "That's boring. Why can't I just build the thing and think about it later?" So, who do you think he was representing? It wasn't the user, that's for sure.

When someone says, "Hey, let's use SharePoint to solve our problem," her ideas often revolve around preconceived solutions. For example, she may have seen the same solution carried out in another company, and she may assume that SharePoint has some component or feature that meets a business objective.

Whatever the reason, Value Management helps you challenge such preconceptions by questioning and testing the business objectives and then distilling them into a list of key requirements that are independent of any solution. This means SharePoint can be used to confirm whether these key requirements can be met, no matter what the situation.

Also, Value Management is a key part of helping you determine an ROI. Remember the question that was asked earlier in this section: "What are we going to use SharePoint for?" Value Management gives you that answer when it is applied to a specific solution that is going to be designed and delivered. It will inspire confidence that the following is so:

- The business understands and agrees the decisions made to deliver the solution.
- The technical requirements of the components being delivered by SharePoint can meet those requirements.

You should perform the Value Management exercise when creating the SharePoint solution scope (which is covered in detail in Chapter 2). At that stage, you would also know who the key stakeholders are and the delivery date for the project.

Create workshops involving the right individuals at an appropriate level of knowledge and authority. For example, in the design of a specific site, those individuals would be the key users and the SharePoint specialist. In the design of a new SharePoint farm, they would be the key sponsors (such as the SharePoint architect), key members of interfacing technical teams, and the project manager.

It is strongly recommended that a coach be assigned to facilitate each of these workshops. This will help ensure the participants stay focused on the key aspects and to challenge their conclusions. SharePoint delivery teams are discussed in more detail in Chapter 7, "Organizing the Delivery Team."

### Step 1: Structure the objectives

To identify the key objectives of any SharePoint solutions means going through investigations. In my experience, I have found that the best way to go is to set up workshops and act as a kind of project facilitator.

When gathering requirements and making and agreeing on decisions, ensure that you state clearly what the objective is for the solution, and that any ideas, suggestions, or points related to that key objective are captured as secondary and subobjectives.

Secondary and subobjectives are vital in working out the value of the solution. They give weightings on the basis of priority and allow you to evaluate and assess the value of secondary objectives and subobjectives.

Both a site and subsite have a reason or a premise for their existence. The same thing goes for SharePoint objectives: to meet them, you need to complete a number of secondary objectives, which in turn are made up of subobjectives. To explain this even further, here are examples of SharePoint objectives, each with a secondary objective:

- Build a SharePoint Farm that has good availability and good network performance.
- Build a Project Management site that has a Schedules management component.
- Build a Server Automation tool that needs to be audited.

During these workshops, start small and set clear objectives. All ideas making up these objectives need clear guidance (having the right people on board will ensure that this happens). Ideas generated during meetings without facilitation could introduce pitfalls in cost, resiliency, compliance, and storage of the resulting SharePoint solution. Figures 4-2, 4-3, and 4-4 illustrate how important it is to do an investigation to define the system specification fully, so that it meets the objective (and is scalable).

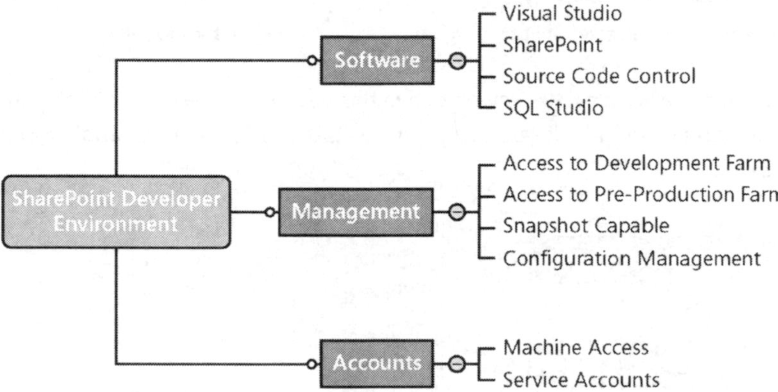


**FIGURE 4-2** SharePoint Developer Environment showing primary and secondary system specification objectives.

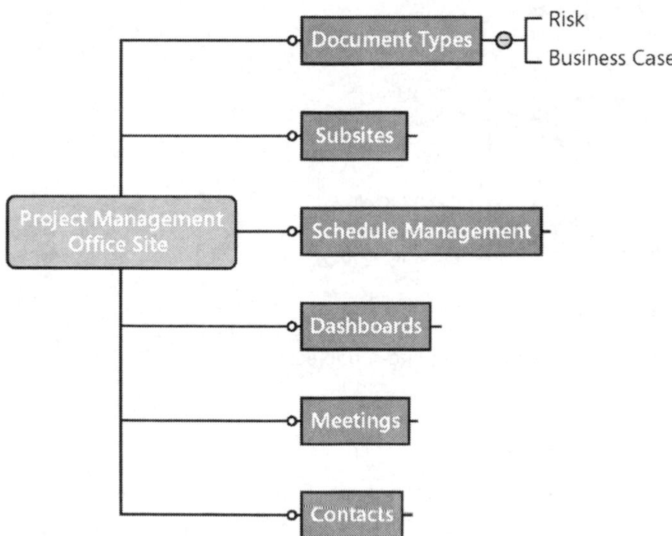


**FIGURE 4-3** A SharePoint Project Management solution objective, split by repository and then by content.

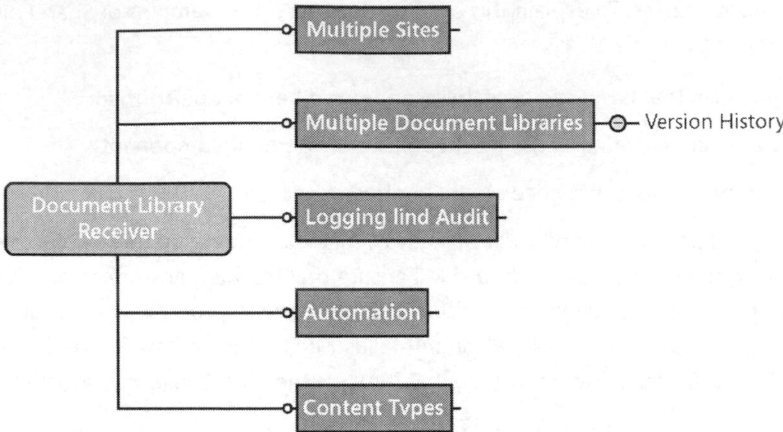


**FIGURE 4-4** Custom Document Library receiver, split by primary objective, and then by subobjectives.

As you can see in these three examples, the key objective has been extracted. From that, you can then expand the secondary objectives and, if necessary, expose subobjectives. An example format of this is depicted in Figure 4-5.

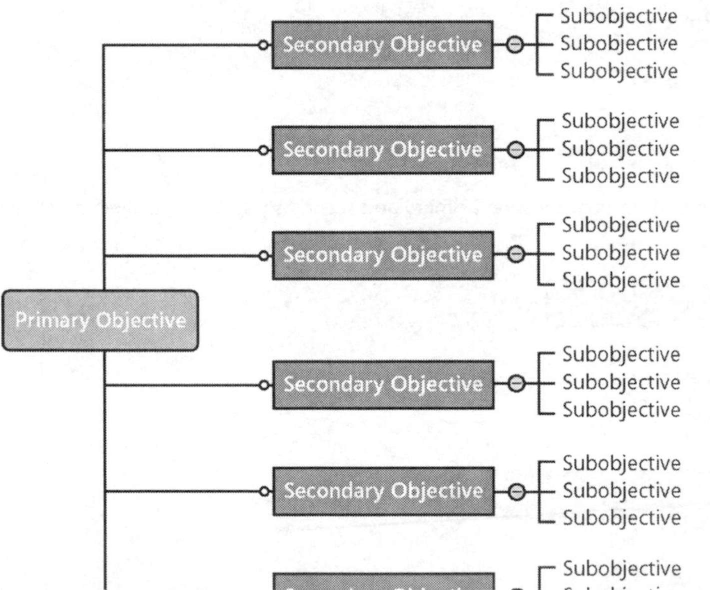


**FIGURE 4-5** A primary objective split into secondary objectives and subobjectives.

## Step 2: Assign importance weightings

Look at the example in Figure 4-3, showing a Project Management Site whose objective is to store content related to a particular project. You should further design the primary objectives, breaking them into secondary objectives and assigning processes and rules to each, as shown as Figure 4-6.

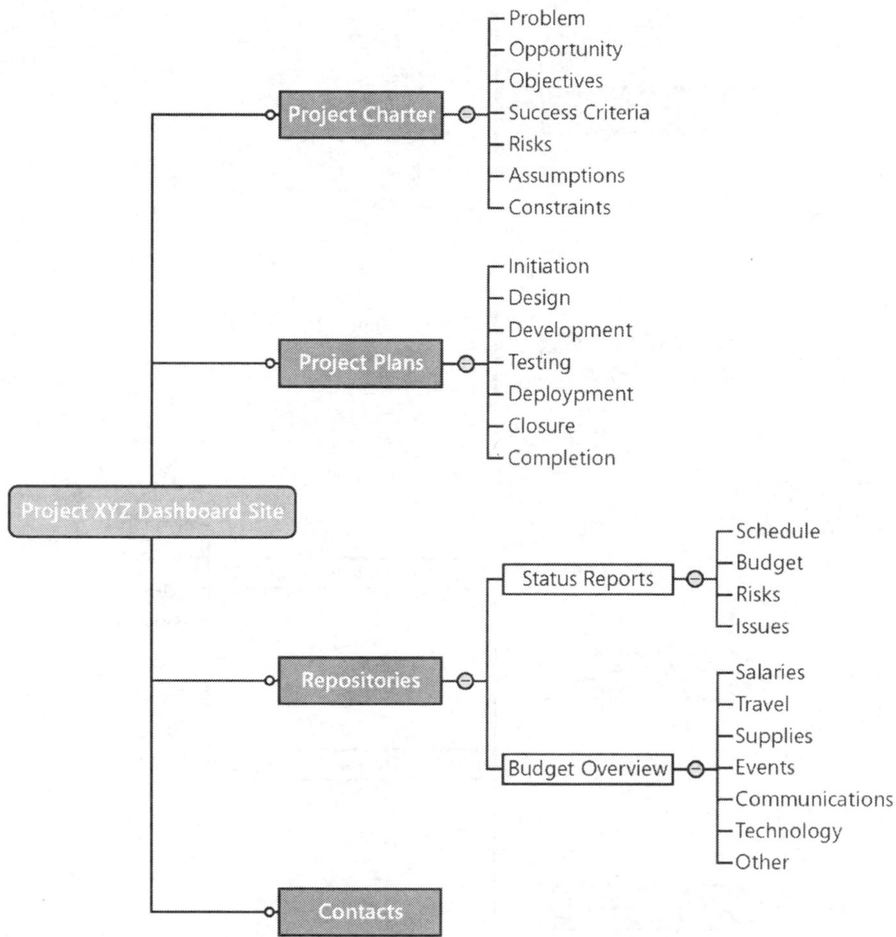


**FIGURE 4-6** A Project Management solution divided into primary and secondary objectives.

Even at this level, you will need to clarify which areas of the site (as shown in Figure 4-6) get more attention than others. For example, Budget Overview may not be important if there is already another central site that is used to record financial information—a decision may have been made to connect and provide that detail without duplicating it to this site. Project Plans may be multiple project plans, and they may even require their own sites, and therefore be of critical importance.

You will need to record each decision and then apply weighting figures (based on relative importance) to each objective. All the subobjectives must add up to 1.0. Again, taking the example shown in Figure 4-6, I have applied weightings to all the objectives (see Figure 4-7).

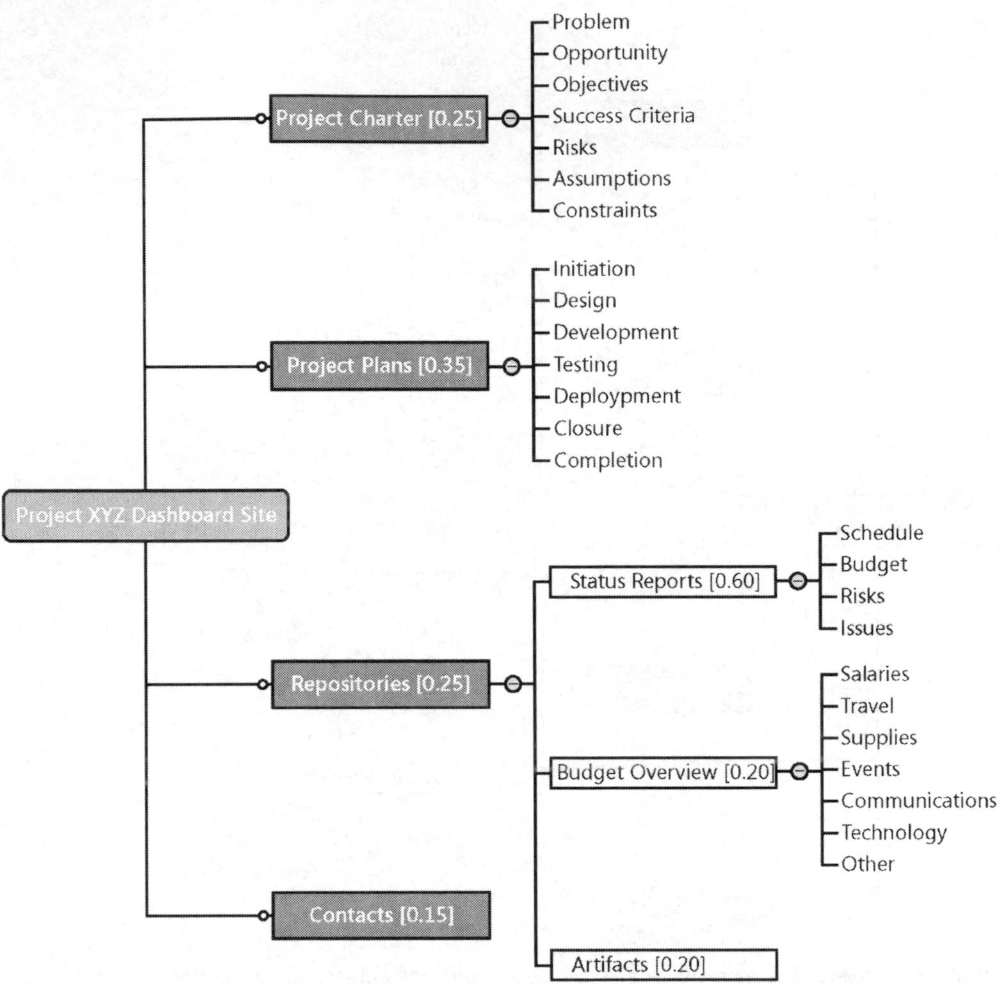


**FIGURE 4-7** Project Management Solution broken by primary and secondary objectives and with weightings applied.

One thing you may have noticed in Figure 4-7 is that Project Artifacts becomes a repository and is more important than Budget Overview. Also, all subobjectives add up to 1.0, as they should.

Applying weightings is a delicate matter that requires business acumen, knowledge of SharePoint, and the initiative of decision makers. Business and technical decisions will also add to or subtract weighting from any objective. Whatever happens, when applying a weighting, remember that these are subject to change due to changes in the business, technology, or both.

## Step 3: Evaluate each option

In step 2, you applied weightings to the objectives. Next, you will need to calculate a utility score. Taking the example from step 2, enter a code for each of the objectives. The first secondary objective is A, followed by B for the next secondary objective, C for the next, and so on. For each subobjective, start with the letter of the secondary objective, followed by the number of that subobjective. For example, if a secondary objective is C, then the first subobjective of that is C1. Figure 4-8 gives an example of coding the objectives. You'll need to do this to create the table to store the utility score and assess value.

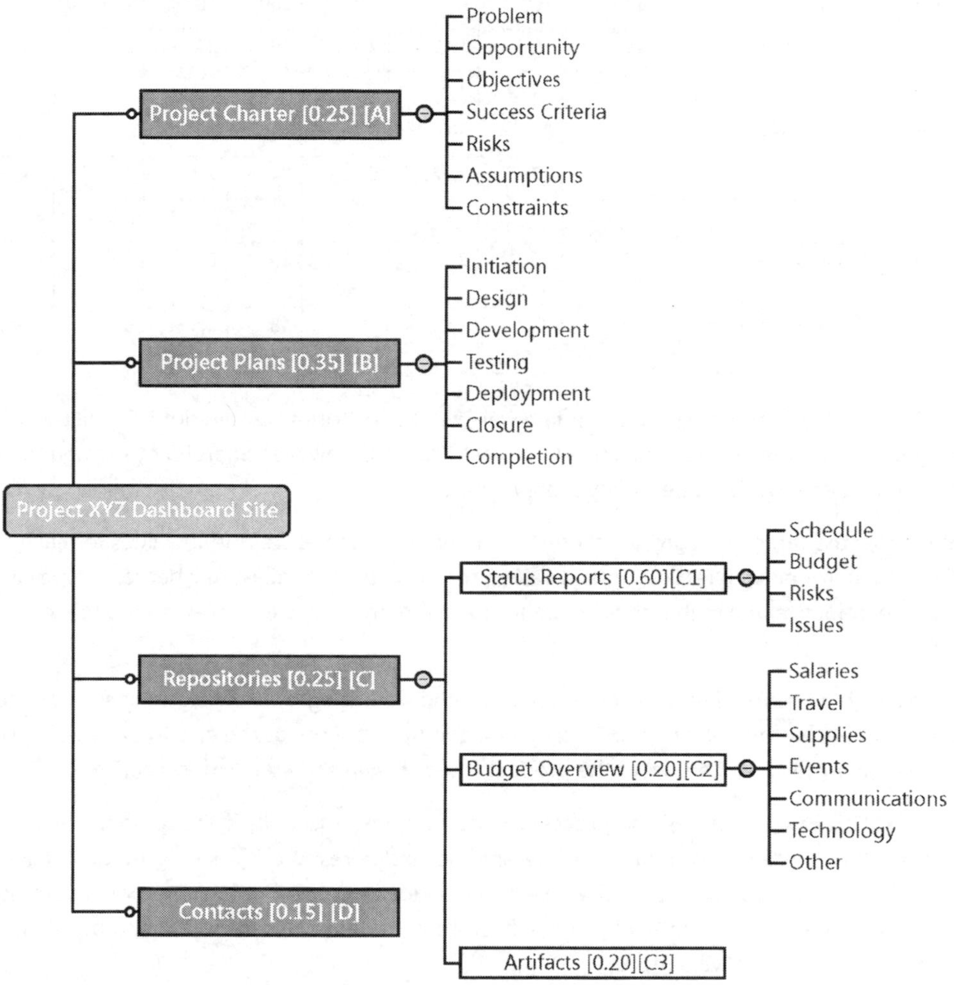


**FIGURE 4-8** The Project Management solution, now coded with a letter for each objective.

Now, investigate each of the alternatives in terms of what technologies can be used to meet the objectives. For example, say that you have selected SharePoint, CMS Product A, and Doc Mgmt Product B to ascertain which of those products will meet the objectives. To aid the recording of that investigation, following the format to build a diagram like Figure 4-8, you would need a table to record weightings, a raw score, and a weighted score for each of the products against the objectives. Construct a table to record this. The format of the table is given in Table 4-8.

**TABLE 4-8** A Project Management Solution Showing Weightings, Raw Score, Weighted Score, and Utility

| Option | Objective | A | B | C | D | D1 | D2 | D3 | Utility |
|---|---|---|---|---|---|---|---|---|---|
| | Importance Weighting | 0.25 | 0.35 | 0.15 | 0.25 | 0.60 | 0.30 | 0.10 | |
| SharePoint | Raw Score | 100 | 100 | 90 | 90 | 100 | 80 | 20 | |
| | Weighted Score | 25 | 35 | 13.5 | 22.5 | 60 | 24 | 2 | 182 |
| | | | | | | | | | |
| CMS Product A | Raw Score | 40 | 90 | 80 | 70 | 100 | 40 | 40 | |
| | Weighted Score | 6.25 | 12.25 | 2.025 | 5.625 | 36 | 7.2 | 0.2 | 69.55 |
| | | | | | | | | | |
| Doc Mgmt Product B | Raw Score | 80 | 80 | 90 | 80 | 80 | 80 | 60 | |
| | Weighted Score | 20 | 28 | 13.5 | 20 | 48 | 24 | 6 | 159.5 |

In Table 4-8, CMS Product A seemed to fare well with Repositories but did not have all the necessary features, especially for objective A (Project Charter). However, SharePoint seemed to cover all the bases and achieves a higher utility score overall.

To construct the table to record the scores, you need to enter the weighting values for each of the objectives. Then, for each objective, enter a value (from 1 to 100) to measure whether the product can meet the objective; the higher the value, the closer the product is to achieving the relevant objective.

For the weighted score of each objective, multiply the weighting by the weighting score. Repeat this process for each of the objectives. Then, finally, add up the score at the end to get a utility score. Again, the higher the value, the closer the product is to achieving the relevant objective.

For some SharePoint solutions, this process can be complex, especially if the solution has a number of objectives. Make sure that you have the relevant knowledge resource, meaning that you have someone who can give you advice on the objective and advice concerning each product's strengths and weaknesses against each of the objectives. It is also extremely important that you be 100 percent honest when making your evaluation.

## Step 4: Assess value

Following the assessment of each objective relevant to the alternatives, you will need to assess the value that each objective brings. You will need to obtain the cost (licenses, support, and infrastructure) and TCO (that is, the total cost of ownership over the life of the asset). This gives a Value measurement of each alternative. Table 4-9 takes the information given in Table 4-8 and includes the Cost and TCO columns expressed in millions of U.S. dollars. In this example, the product will be in place for at least three years.

**TABLE 4-9** The Project Management Solution Figures, with Cost and TCO Added

| Option | Objective | A | B | C | D | D1 | D2 | D3 | Utility | Cost | TCO |
|---|---|---|---|---|---|---|---|---|---|---|---|
| | Importance Weighting | 0.25 | 0.35 | 0.15 | 0.25 | 0.60 | 0.30 | 0.10 | | | |
| SharePoint | Raw Score | 100 | 100 | 90 | 90 | 100 | 80 | 20 | | | |
| | Weighted Score | 25 | 35 | 13.5 | 22.5 | 60 | 24 | 2 | 182 | 5 | 8.20 |
| | | | | | | | | | | | |
| CMS Product A | Raw Score | 40 | 90 | 80 | 70 | 100 | 40 | | | | |
| | Weighted Score | 6.25 | 12.25 | 2.025 | 5.625 | 36 | 7.2 | 0.2 | 69.55 | 4 | 20.0 |
| | | | | | | | | | | | |
| Doc Mgmt Product B | Raw Score | 80 | 80 | 90 | 80 | 80 | 80 | 60 | | | |
| | Weighted Score | 20 | 28 | 13.5 | 20 | 48 | 24 | 6 | 159.5 | 14 | 11.39 |

In this example, SharePoint cost $5 million, versus CMS Product A at $4 million and Doc Mgmt Product B at $14 million, and the TCO over three years is a little more than $8 million for SharePoint. Logically, the selection of SharePoint over the other alternatives is clear, because it meets the relevant objectives for the lowest TCO.

## Step 5: Check sensitivity

The process of scoring and ranking is not always objective. You must assess the sensitivity of scores and check them against the decision-making process, especially those scores that you intuitively believe are misleading. As these are assessed, the results can be used continually as a basis for debate and discussion. Be prepared to redo the exercise as many times are possible so that before you agree on the final solution, you know that all the objectives have been compared with all the possible alternatives.

## Critical success factors

To ensure the success of Value Management, a SharePoint solution must include the following:

- **Senior management support and input** You need to make sure that decision makers attend your workshops to prioritize the objectives.
- **Appropriate level of management** Decisions from the business itself must be made by people who have the appropriate level of authority. Ensure that they are part of the Value Management exercise, which helps ensure that the results are not undermined.

- **Effective facilitation** Make sure you have the right people from the business to provide knowledge, and ensure that you have the right SharePoint Delivery team members to answer queries and to help the business make decisions.
- **Sufficient information available** When you're looking at various options, make sure that you have the right information available that allows you to understand how the product meets requirements.

## Applying Value Engineering to SharePoint solutions

Demonstrating *how* something will be achieved and *why* it is going to be achieved is one of the most compelling ways that a SharePoint specialist can convince the client that a decision to apply a feature, component, or set of processes will help solve a business requirement. Using Value Engineering methods will also show where you can save capital, improve ROI, and have the delivery program demonstrate where decisions have been successful (or even unsuccessful).

Value Engineering is a method used to help clarify the decisions that will address the objectives (see the "Objectives of Value Management" section earlier in this chapter for more information concerning building objectives). These decisions in this process are formatted so they can be understood by the delivery team.

Organizations will want to solve a business or information challenge using SharePoint. Value Engineering methods will help in the following circumstances:

- The organization requires SharePoint to meet a specific business objective, which in turn will make its staff more productive in managing and creating content.
- The organization has a large number of requirements for using SharePoint, so it's difficult to determine what should be done first.
- The organization has a clear set of requirements using SharePoint, but it's difficult to see what feature will provide the best functionality.

For each of these scenarios, you apply Value Engineering to help analyze, record, and prioritize requirements.

The objective of Value Engineering is to refine a selected solution to optimize value for money. This can be achieved by doing the following:

- Removing unnecessary functionality and cost
- Increasing functionality at no extra cost
- Maintaining functionality at lower cost

The most important element of delivering SharePoint solutions is to make decisions. This is true regardless of whether you are an analyst, administrator, architect, or project/program manager. You will continually have to make decisions about user experience, adoption, sustainability, availability, and configuration management of the platform. Value Engineering helps by providing a method to structure these decisions, to set priorities, and thereby determine which alternatives and solutions best optimize your decisions. There are gains for SharePoint sponsors and key stakeholders because there is a historical, audited approach. They will also know the costs (and benefits) associated with each solution. This section will help you understand the methods used, beginning with the FAST method.

FAST stands for Functional Analysis Systems Technique. FAST is used to define the basic functions that are required for the deliverables from the project as a whole or from any part of the delivery program. To use this method, you start by stating what you are trying to achieve and then, by asking a series of "how" questions, you decompose this into increasingly specific statements of functionality.

This method can be used for virtually any objective where you must advise how an objective will be achieved. For example, if the objective is to increase SharePoint User Adoption, one requirement to fulfill that objective would be to provide a Proof of Concept/Sandbox environment where users could try SharePoint's built-in features and, if necessary, any third-party solutions. Value Engineering can be used to decide not only about that approach, but also about what should be used to ensure that approach is a success, by exploring more deeply into the proposal and optimizing solution delivery.

In addition, the technique can be used in reverse where you have been given a set of discreet functions. You list them and against each, ask the question "Why have this element?" You can then derive the relevant diagram, eventually arriving at the basic objective. This technique helps you identify and filter out unnecessary functionality.

An example of the technique used in reverse with SharePoint is when you have to decide which service applications to use in a new SharePoint farm that needs to provide the correct level of services to ensure the performance and availability of the environment. For example, in a SharePoint farm where one application server is used with limited infrastructure performance on that server, one would not enable every service application unless that service application was required (that is, it has a premise). So, if one of the basic objectives was to provide the business with the ability to create dashboard Excel Services, but it also requires every business intelligence (BI) feature, then the objective would be to enable the relevant service. However, by doing this, you would then need to decide on the level of infrastructure required (for example, the requirement of every BI feature being used in Excel Services requires Microsoft SQL Server 2012 SP1, not SQL Server 2008 R2. This increases infrastructure requirements, RAM, and CPU, all to ensure availability and maintain performance, including support requirements.

To help explain and to provide a method of helping you build a decision matrix, I've provided three basic scenarios, which show (without too much detail) the process of mapping out through brainstorming the basic objectives into subobjectives. The basic objective can also be called the *solution;* the subobjectives are known as *elements*. Figures 4-9, 4-10, and 4-11 depict a basic scenario, each with basic objectives then refined into subobjectives.

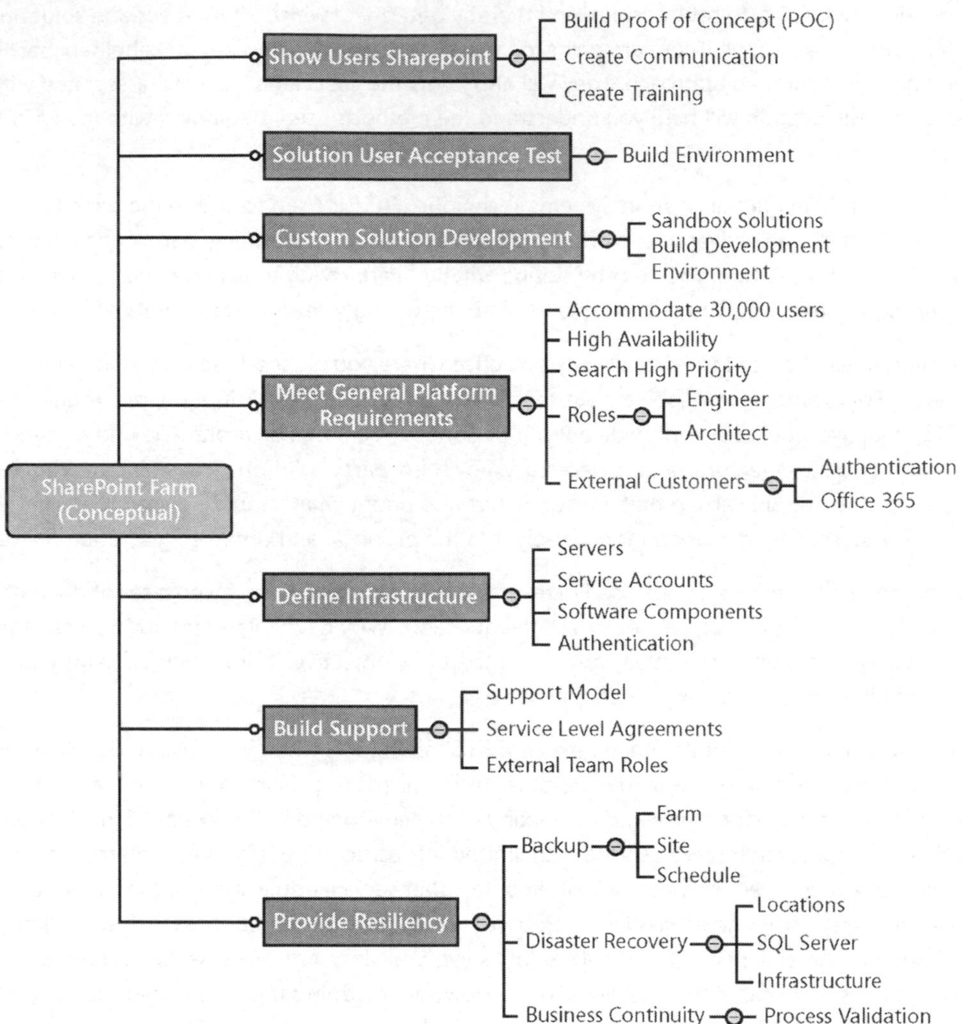


**FIGURE 4-9** Deliver a SharePoint farm which is subject to high-impact usage and a medium-level user count.

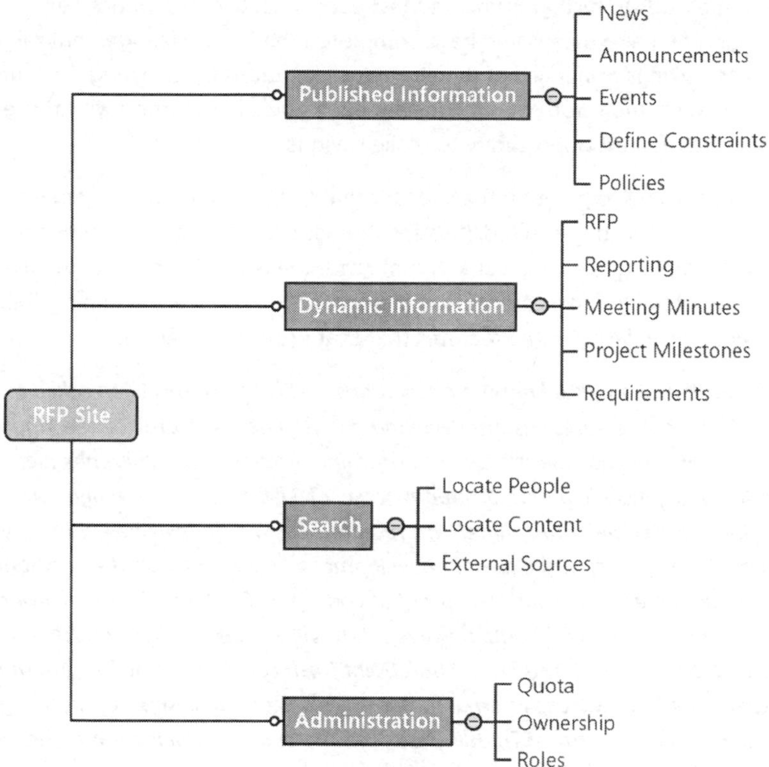


**FIGURE 4-10** Deliver a Request for Proposal (RFP) SharePoint site for the company to manage business cases.

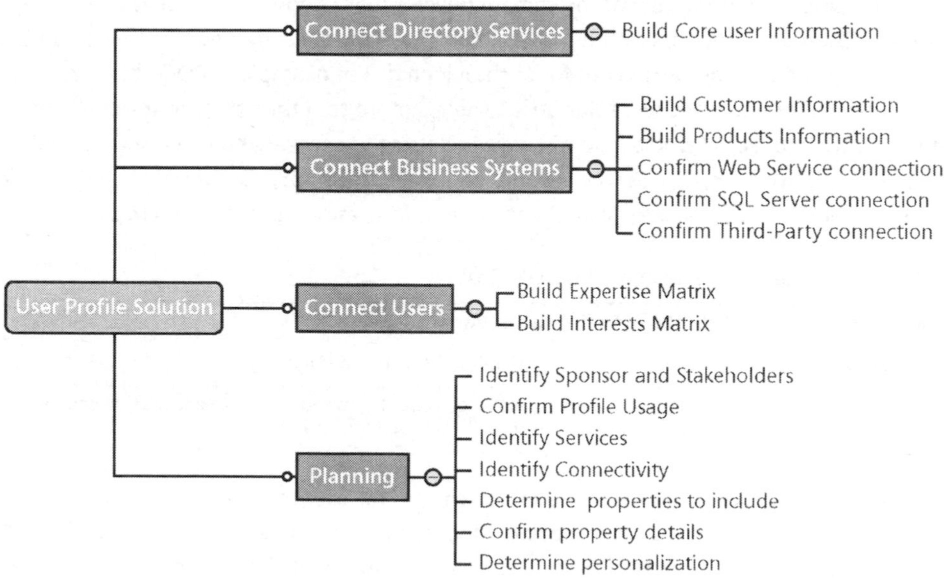


**FIGURE 4-11** Deliver a user profile enhancement to an existing SharePoint 2013 platform.

Use Value Management methods to further refine and test each objective to produce key requirements. Once done (and that also means you have completed the Value Management table), you can identify possible cost savings from each of the alternative solutions by assessing the whole life cost of each element in that solution. You should consider each objective, starting with those with the highest cost and hence, the greatest opportunity to make savings.

This stage is important if you want to prove to the sponsor that the cost burden is commensurate with the solution that has been (or will be) selected. It forms the basis for solutions that may be delivered in the future. For example, in creating a SharePoint farm, the whole life cost can be used to define the next level of costs for specific elements that may need to be created, assuming that the engineering of that SharePoint farm includes the features that that project may adopt.

*Scenario 12: John works for Fabrikam as a SharePoint solutions architect. He has been asked to provide a SharePoint 2013 farm that requires custom development, and needs to provide the whole life cost for a SharePoint farm life. From initial investigations concerning infrastructure, John has identified that there will be a $10,000 outlay, including annual support costs of $2,000. From investigations concerning system life cycles, the lifetime of the SharePoint requirement will be reviewed in three years; therefore, John has calculated the life cost of the custom development (one element in the solution) to be $36,000 ($12,000 × 3). Other objectives include the proof of concept (POC) SharePoint environment, which will cost $5,000 plus licensing costs of $2,000; however, that will not be required for the next two years. John has indicated that as an alternative, a SharePoint farm could be provided without the custom development. Instead, the farm will use internal features. This choice falls short of meeting all the client requirements but is expected to save $20,000 (however, the business will incur a higher cost because it must use other alternatives to address the shortfall of not having the custom development objective completed).*

With this scenario, you would record the custom development and POC objectives and assign costs to these. When doing this, be aware that you need to explore each option further to understand what functionality needs to be carried out for each objective. For example, a POC objective does not just mean "Get a server and put SharePoint on it." There's more to it than that, considering that users may need to be trained. For example, you will have to source the server and use resources outside your direct remit (networking, SQL Server, security etc.). For Office 365, you would have to provide the relevant owner resource, training, SharePoint site administration, features, and more.

**TABLE 4-10** Sample Objectives, Showing Whole Life Cost

| Sample Objective | Whole Life Cost | Comment |
|---|---|---|
| Custom development | 36k | Addition of search features |
| POC | 48k | Not required after two years; also, specification can be modified to increase savings |

Continue adding the core elements to the table. Once done, identify where you can optimize the solution by streamlining objectives, reprioritizing, identifying alternatives (for example in Table 4-10, custom development could be offset by using the built-in features of SharePoint 2013), reducing infrastructure costs by confirming the licenses required, or by using SharePoint Online through Office 365. Use the tips in Table 4-11 as a guideline.

**TABLE 4-11** Tips to Define Value Engineering for SharePoint Solution Objectives

| Tip | Description |
|---|---|
| Carry out detailed element decision making. | Understand the current proposed solution—don't use guesswork—and analyze the solution. Remember that no one is a SharePoint superhero—ask for help if you need it. |
| Brainstorm alternative approaches. | Use the knowledge and expertise of the SharePoint sponsor and delivery team to find alternative solutions that can enhance the solution without increasing cost (or, if the cost is going to increase, make sure that you can justify it). For example, if you are going to build a farm and have separate technical teams, use the knowledge of those teams to help identify alternatives. |
| Assess the most promising options and discard unworkable solutions. | Don't fall into the trap of scope creep, and don't assume that you get better value for money if you add more solutions, even if you're sure the client will like them. Stick to the proposal. |
| Estimate the cost of any alternatives, along with any pros and cons. | Note that building physically separate farms may increase data integrity, but it also could increase admin complexity and license costs. |
| Decide whether to continue with the original proposal. | SharePoint may be limited only by one's creativity, but that doesn't mean you try to reach that goal by all means possible without looking at the bigger picture. Think about topology, structure, Governance, support, and so on. Don't be afraid to indicate to the sponsor that the proposal has become untenable. |
| Investigate objectives fully. | As part of the decision process for the objectives, confirm the viability of alternatives available for delivery. For example, if there is a need to build diagrams to show a business process and have that turned into a workflow in SharePoint, a good alternative is to use Visio Professional 2013, which allows you to publish diagrams that can be viewed in a web browser. |
| Try always providing alternatives using built-in SharePoint components and tools first, before looking at third-party products. | Do not immediately assume that third-party products will provide viable alternatives to SharePoint built-in features. There are further implications; some technical, some platform, and each have different costs. Your SharePoint support needs to be able to provide a valuable service to users. If one of the requirements is not met by the third-party product, discard it for the proposal. You can always pick up that discarded option for another proposal later. |

## Critical success factors

To ensure the success of Value Engineering, the following things must be done:

- Obtain input from the entire delivery team. Do not leave any decision solely for a technical team to make.
- Ensure that those participating have the authority to speak for their domains.
- Use coaches in meetings. Good facilitation pays dividends.
- Have sufficient information at hand.

## The importance of Value Management and Value Engineering in SharePoint solution design

Value Engineering is vital in aiding your decision making so that you can optimize a solution through its objectives, and at the same time measure the cost and resources needed to deliver the solution. Value Management will help you choose how to provide the solution that best meets the objectives. Here's a review of the key points that were covered in this section:

- Find ways to choose from a list of alternatives that could satisfy a SharePoint solution requirement.
- Optimize the solution so that it is the best fit and provides the best support model.
- Test assumptions.
- Assess the implications of any relevant risks.
- Consider delivery aspects.
- Consider the quality criteria and testing.
- Take account of corporate architectures.
- Find out whether the proposed functionality is really needed.
- Determine where the money is spent.
- Identify alternative approaches for high-cost aspects.

**More Info** Value Management and Value Engineering are globally recognized standards. To learn more about this topic, read the article "Function Analysis Systems Technique—The Basics," at *http://www.value-eng.org/pdf_docs/monographs/FAbasics.pdf.*

# Planning for BYOD

BYOD (which you'll recall means "Bring Your Own Device") means that the use of personal mobile devices is allowed in the workplace. There are various reasons why companies are beginning to do this:

- There will be over 1 billion smart phones by 2016, and 350 million of those will be used at work.
- By 2016, a total of 82 percent of the world's online population will be engaging in social networking.
- By 2016, a total of 50 percent of enterprise customers will be actively using cloud services.
- The smart phone outsells the PC, and 49 percent of the smart phones shipped in 2011 are running Google Android.

- Apple sold almost 70 million devices in the first month of 2012.
- Every day, 850,000 Android devices are activated.
- By the end of 2011, 35 billion apps had been downloaded to smart phones.

These devices are many times more powerful than what was used to put a man on the moon. Smart phones are no longer just phones; they are guides, assistants, advisers, and even best friends.

We are living in remarkable times. Never before have we been so connected. Never before have we had the opportunity to share our ideas, thoughts, and feelings with people around the world with such ease and speed. This is all because of the introduction of mobile devices. Organizations have to ensure that individuals using these mobile devices have access to their work data. This presents cultural, security, cost, and support and Governance challenges. Mobile device costs are on the rise because of increases in the number of mobile users. An employee could easily carry more than one mobile device (such as a laptop, smart phone, or tablet) as part of his work. This means that employees today are using these devices in a "blurred" landscape that includes public places (cafes, airports, trains, and so on). When employees bring their personal mobile devices to work and use them to share files or data inside and outside the office, it is difficult for IT to maintain visibility and control. Conversely, it is clear that employees are more productive using personal mobile devices at work. Additionally, the organization where they work even allows mobile devices to access networked services over wireless connections. And even if the organization supplies mobile devices to employees, they will allow personal mobile devices not owned by the company to access services over wireless connections.

With the increasing prevalence of social IT culture and technologies, this increases the pressure on organizations to provide and allow their workers to use mobile devices in the workplace. This means allowing those mobile devices to connect to the roadmap of connected enterprise systems and platforms (of which SharePoint is one). This means providing support for mobile devices, irrespective of location and time zone. While this has been posited as a worrisome trend, providing this kind of open connectivity using mobile devices has been viewed as a major boon for organizations. Benefits include staff retention, ROI in terms of increased worker productivity, increased job satisfaction and motivation (and less stress), and an enhanced image for the organization (that is, it is seen as proactive and progressive in tolerating, encouraging, and sponsoring the use of such devices).

In SharePoint, there are User Adoption challenges with providing a user experience that are no different when you are using mobile devices to access SharePoint. In SharePoint 2010, there was the "mobile view."

**More Info** For more information concerning mobile compatibility, visit *http://technet.microsoft.com/en-us/library/fp161353%28v=office.15%29.aspx* and *http://technet.microsoft.com/en-us/library/jj673030.aspx?*.

In SharePoint 2013, this is not as prevalent because most mobile devices can display SharePoint without having to resort to a mobile view. However, there are technical challenges to overcome with applying this to all mobile devices. In addition, there are business security and management issues. Executives may already have their own rules in response to BYOD, such as the following (ranging from hugely restrictive to permissive):

- Users are not allowed to access SharePoint using mobile devices.
- Don't inform or advise users of any available mobile device use, or even mislead employees about any enterprise platform having such mobile device features or capabilities.
- Allow users to use only specific mobile devices, and advise that those mobile devices not on the list are either not supported or barred altogether.
- Give in. The IT department has far too many other things to do, and any awareness, communication, training, or policy about mobile device use is ignored.
- Embrace change. Build communication, awareness, workshops, training (User Adoption strategy); ensure readiness and police usage.

This section assumes that the organization wishes to embrace mobile device use (the last bullet point in the preceding list). You should consider the following points to fully ensure that User Adoption is factored into your BYOD provision to the organizations users:

- Ensure that the organization defines each mobile provider as a *Trusted Community Asset*. Choose the mobile devices that the company will supply and/or support (meaning that they are trusted). For example, the Windows Smartphone, the Apple iPad and iPhone, and the BlackBerry are all "trusted."
- Define and agree to which apps and services will be available for use by default on mobile devices. You will require aid from executives and the IT department. They will need to make decisions based on the best services offered by these devices in terms of how they fulfill business strategies, meet IT security requirements, fit financial aspects, and can be supported.
- Mobile device usage communication, awareness, and training must be delivered. Use Communication Planning and training, as detailed in this chapter, to help you create channels and tactics.
- Monitor mobile device use. Ensure that users are following the awareness guides being provided, perform periodic reviews, and give users feedback.
- By setting out a User Adoption strategy that includes BYOD, you will foster trust with employees, and those employees will gain a competitive edge through increased productivity, better employee satisfaction, and retention.

*BYOD Governance is covered in Chapter 5.*

## Summary

SharePoint has literally hundreds of features that give it the ability to integrate with hundreds of products and systems. Don't go down the route of attempting to list every one of the features from the start simply because you want to give users a "wow" factor. Presenting far too much glitz, whistles, bells, and technical wizardry with SharePoint solutions will confuse users and/or produce far too many questions to answer and prioritize, wasting their (and your) time and energy. Instead, focus on familiarizing users with the key functionality and nurturing them as the platform grows. Continue enhancing awareness, knowledge, productivity, and sharing. Build Communication Plans and training plans to nurture your User Adoption strategy. Seek to improve productivity by enhancing and helping build business rules. Apply Value Management and Value Engineering methods to ensure the SharePoint solution fits objectives, is measurable, and has an adequate budget.

CHAPTER 5

# Planning SharePoint Governance

In this chapter:



SharePoint Governance adds legitimacy to Microsoft SharePoint solution delivery. It is a road, a path, a journey to a destination that has no end. *Governance* means literally "the act of governing"—it is *not* a form of government.

In Chapter 4, "Preparing SharePoint solution User Adoption," in the "Building collaborative ownership" section, I said that as part of SharePoint solution delivery, the business should take ownership of the SharePoint solution because that aids User Adoption. That ownership acts as a driver for SharePoint Governance, and it does not happen successfully without a certain level of cooperation from business and technical audiences. Members of the business audience cooperate because they have the foresight to apply business controls to a SharePoint solution to ensure that business processes and business rules are applied to SharePoint solutions by policy. Members of the technical audience cooperate because they have the foresight to apply services associated with SharePoint, and help apply rules and policies concerning SharePoint platform configuration management. They ensure the integrity and availability of the solution and the SharePoint platform to the business. It is that combination of foresight from different people that provides a SharePoint solution that can be sustained and governed accordingly.

SharePoint Governance is not a hardware, software, or human resource (HR) solution. It is an organizational strategy and methodology for documenting and implementing business rules and policies. SharePoint Governance is the act of enforcing the use of policies, and by enforcing policies, standards are created that are designed to protect the integrity of the SharePoint solution and platform. SharePoint Governance brings cross-functional teams together to identify data issues affecting the company or organization.

This chapter will help you address crucial areas of platform Governance and to use practical techniques to bring Governance to your SharePoint solution delivery program and the SharePoint platform.

## Creating a Governance committee

SharePoint is a business platform. The business owns SharePoint. In Chapter 3, "Planning SharePoint solution delivery," in the "Engaging your sponsor and stakeholders" section, I explained the purpose of having a sponsor. In order for the SharePoint solution to match directly the way that the business wants the solution to work, the delivery team (which includes the sponsor and stakeholders) has to list the relevant rules under which the solution is owned. This would include the basic rules of operation (through communication and training), and the business process rules concerning management of the solution.

The business process rules of a SharePoint solution give rise to policies that ensure consistency and enable information integrity. For example, people working together to create information need rules of information ownership. Setting the rules concerning the ownership of that information helps ensure that the information is relevant and kept up to date.

Policies aid in service delivery, which in turn enables the business to manage SharePoint by ensuring that SharePoint capabilities (people and platform) and support are linked. For example, if you are running many SharePoint sites as an administrator, and you find you are spending 90 percent of your time managing permissions, then you should consider policies to enable business content owners to take more control of managing permissions. This policy aids support, empowers people to manage their own content, and enhances capability.

Let me repeat the sentence in the first paragraph of this chapter: The business owns SharePoint. You need to make this happen, and you will need help doing that. To do this, start by creating a SharePoint Governance committee. Make the SharePoint sponsor the head, and include decision makers across the business and key members of technical teams providing the SharePoint platform. The Governance committee should be formed during the delivery of the SharePoint solution, generally at the planning of the SharePoint delivery program (described in Chapter 3). The top priority of the Governance committee is creating a SharePoint Statement of Operations (if there is none in place already). That output also is the key aspect of the SharePoint one-stop shop (described in Chapter 7, "Organizing the Delivery Team," in the "Building the SharePoint 2013 one-stop shop" section) and should be reviewed regularly. All solutions get listed in the Statement of Operations.

The SharePoint Governance committee needs to keep its operation simple and understandable, and focus on what really matters. SharePoint Governance outlines the maintenance, administration, and support of the organization's SharePoint environments and helps identify lines of ownership for both business and technical teams. A common understanding of the SharePoint provision is required before the committee team is formed. By doing this, the various members will be able to assign policies properly. One technique you can use is to create a model that describes at a high level how the different site types of SharePoint fit together. This will tell you whether the SharePoint solution being delivered fits into the model and thus into a site type, and then that will tell you what kind of Governance should be applied.

## The model

Figure 5-1 shows a few of the site types that are included in a typical SharePoint platform. As with all things hierarchical, there are a few high-level sites at the top. The number of sites will increase as divisional portals, team sites, project sites, and even personal storage using SkyDrive are added.

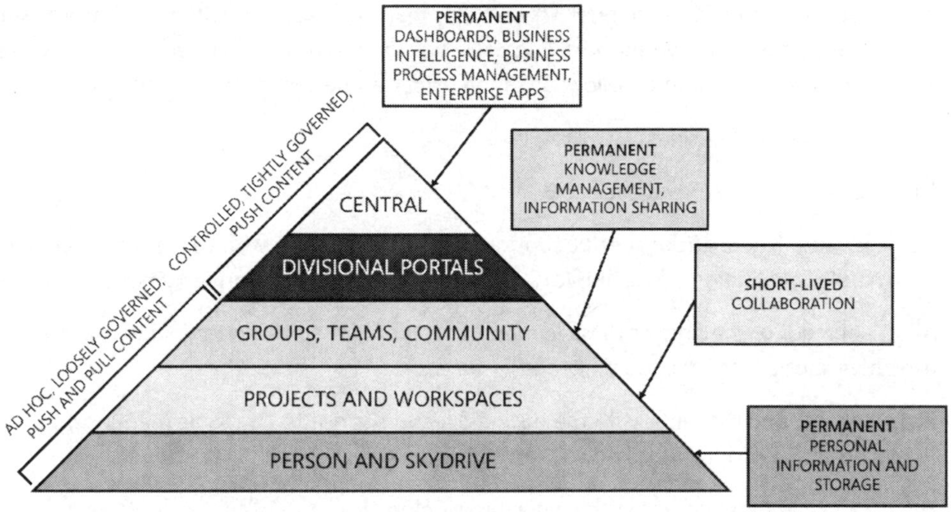


**FIGURE 5-1** A sample SharePoint Governance model.

The important thing to note about this model is that the site and portals at the top consist mostly of published content and usually require tight Governance. As you move down the pyramid, Governance becomes looser, and the purposes are more related to team collaboration than corporate communication.

Also, more temporary or short-lived sites exist in the lower half, and the permanent sites are more prevalent as you move up the pyramid. Sites in the lower half usually need to be provisioned quickly so that people can collaborate efficiently. The sites at the top are visible to many more people and require a bit more planning.

As part of the build of the Governance plan, you should list the key hosts within the segments of the pyramid. This gives the Governance team real data to associate with each of the relevant areas. The SharePoint solution being delivered maps into this pyramid by relating to one or more areas of the pyramid.

## Building a SharePoint Governance committee

You need to assign appropriate individuals in the organization who have defined responsibilities in the Governance committee and appropriate decision-making power. The best approach I've found for building a Governance committee is to start with the lead steward. This individual (you also can have more than one person in this role) should be selected by the SharePoint sponsor, with some input from you. Having the sponsor pick the lead steward ensures that he or she will have a strong incentive to build the team; it also means that the lead steward has exposure to upper management and likely has some clout within the company.

The key part of this is the clout or recognition that the lead steward has inside the company. You'll need that lead steward to leverage that visibility to build the stewardship council.

Your lead steward comes from the business side, has many connections within both the business and technical teams, has executive support, and likely has the leadership to help shape the SharePoint Governance committee. The path to follow, at a high level, can be summarized as follows:

1. Identify the lines of business (LOBs) involved.
2. Find a business leader from each LOB.
3. Find technical leaders from specific supporting technical teams who can provide services to the SharePoint solution (for example, SQL, Active Directory, Networking, Security, and so on).
4. Allot 5 percent of the time of these leaders for SharePoint Governance initiatives. Use executive support as leverage if needed.
5. Have one-on-one meetings with the business leaders (prior to any large meetings) to show the value of the program and how Governance can help them and their teams.
6. Have a kick-off meeting to get the initial buzz going.

The lead steward brings together the business and technical teams and creates a Governance committee made up of members of two groups that are working closely with each other: the strategy team and the tactical team.

As Figure 5-2 shows, the Governance committee brings the strategy team and tactical team together. The tactical team is made up of people whose roles cover site administration, functional owners, portal administration, the development team, and the operations team. Creating a schedule for meetings is vital, and once made, the schedule should be adhered to. You should ensure that the strategy team will meet with the tactical team on at least a quarterly basis. The Governance committee is an extension of the strategy team and tactical team and meets regularly to make the necessary decisions.

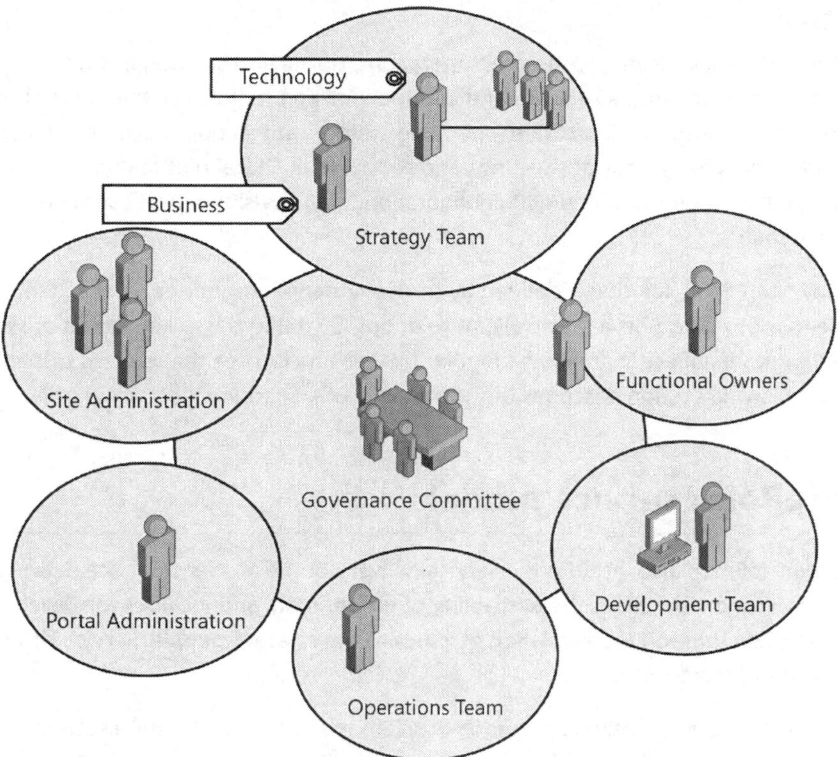


**FIGURE 5-2** The strategy team and tactical team for SharePoint Governance.

The Governance committee is concerned with requests for new high-level sites, customization, and configuration; oversight and scheduling of operational changes; and many other functions. This committee must have representation from all members of the tactical team (site administration, data owners, portal administration, technical, and developers), and also overlaps into the strategy team. This structure provides good representation and communication flow.

## Strategy team

A good strategy team includes a balance of business owners and technology leaders. This team has active involvement from the SharePoint sponsor, executive and financial stakeholders, IT and business leaders, security and compliance officers, development leaders, and information workers.

The strategy team is charged with finding the right balance between technology and the business and between centralized control and decentralized empowerment. They drive deployment from a strategic perspective and provide the overall insight and direction needed by the tactical teams. They are constantly looking for synergies where SharePoint can help the organization operate more effectively or efficiently.

They understand how the business is growing and what areas it could be growing in. In the end, their role is to use SharePoint to improve business processes.

## Tactical team

As the name suggests, a tactical team is focused on operations, portal and site administration, functional ownership of specific sites, and building the framework and features of the portal. The tactical team builds the infrastructure (hardware, operating system, and so on), provides database support and network connectivity, provides security, and supports all SharePoint features. These teams are also responsible for global SharePoint configuration, site provisioning, site administration, and SharePoint maintenance.

Ownership of any SharePoint solution is defined by the Governance committee, which identifies who is accountable for delivering relevant SharePoint solutions. By doing this, a key aspect of service delivery for SharePoint is identified: SharePoint support. This is a crucial area that creates sustainable User Adoption. The following section describes the importance of a SharePoint service model.

# Creating a SharePoint service model

Providing a SharePoint solution also includes the service delivery of the product. Service delivery covers all support information, describes the availability of the solution, and includes top-level information of the solution through the escalation of issues to the relevant people. Service delivery can be both reactive and proactive.

A service that is *reactive* is effectively waiting for a problem to happen, and then resolving the problem. For example, when there is a problem with the solution, requests will be made to correct it. People involved in fixing the problem are in investigation mode. For example, if there is a request to create a document library that also uses the SharePoint Records Management feature, then work must be done to investigate and then deliver the solution.

A service that is proactive continually addresses the solution instead of waiting for a problem to occur. Solutions are always monitored and reviewed, and changes made to ensure that they deal with potential problems.

Service delivery is reactive and proactive, particularly because new tools may be investigated, learned, and adopted, or customized work may need to be carried out. However, to enhance User Adoption, improve customer experience, and enhance Governance, you should ensure that there is a significant emphasis on the service model being *proactive*.

Building a proactive service model needs to take place even before SharePoint is delivered as a platform. If you do not have a service model in place and are already providing a SharePoint solution, then you do not have any method of supporting or controlling the solution and will be in reactive, firefighting mode forever.

A service model provides all customers with information related to the capability of the platform, the people involved in providing that platform, and support procedures. Successful support for SharePoint requires information workers to get involved. Of course, there will always be some kind of technical support made available; but through the delivery of good business rules and policies, it is possible to create a service model where the support of SharePoint solutions can be provided and understood by information workers.

The thinking behind using information workers to aid support is very important, especially in relationship to the Microsoft Office 365 support model, where back-end technical support is provided by Microsoft technicians rather than by the organization. In Office 365, support of SharePoint 2010 is specific to administration; it is not on the back end. On-premise SharePoint requires administrators, engineers, and support administrators to provide services to the SharePoint farm.

Whether the solution is provided for Office 365 or on-premise SharePoint, the reason why you need a service model is the same: to provide the customer with assurance that the solution is supported and information on how it will happen. The question is, where do you start? You start by documenting based on a number of various activities. Table 5-1 describes the activities involved in building a service model for SharePoint.

**TABLE 5-1** Activities to build a service model for SharePoint

| Activity | Description |
| --- | --- |
| Service planning and improvement; capacity and availability | Support the planning and operation of services, including service strategy, availability, capacity, security, disaster recovery, and business continuity planning. Work with the business and service delivery managers to gather information on expected service levels. Support service delivery managers in improving provision of service from suppliers. Seek opportunities to improve service provision and communicate them to service delivery managers. Support service delivery managers in executing initiatives to improve service-level performance. Check all change requests raised to confirm that they fall within the agreed remit of a change request. Support the planning of the capacity and availability of systems. |
| Service operations and service-level management | Support service provision and delivery operations. Support the resolution of incidents and problems. Support the definition of service levels, and document, share, and maintain them. Monitor and track service performance against agreed service levels, and flag issues to service delivery managers. Analyze data and report on the performance of services, including partner performance, and identify issues and trends. Support regular operational performance review meetings with the business to give feedback on performance and discuss continuous improvement opportunities. Identify and help raise and implement changes required to maintain and improve performance and service levels. Create regular and ad hoc reports on service performance. Maintain and update administrative procedures and processes for management control and business communications. Monitor availability and future capacity of systems, providing reports and raising issues to the service delivery manager, and taking corrective action as required. Provide internal and external expert advice, assistance, and guidance in any area associated with the planning, procurement, provision, delivery, maintenance, and effective use of IT systems and their environments. |

| Activity | Description |
|---|---|
| Partner management | Establish effective partnerships with external suppliers and ensure that the client gets great service from its partners. Ensure communication of the agreed quality of service targets and updates to partners. Support the service delivery managers in managing partners effectively. Where appropriate, manage service provider relationships directly, with guidance from the service delivery managers. Raise purchase orders for ongoing services, as per contracts and for agreed change requests. Support the finance team in processing invoices from the service providers. |
| Stakeholder management | Build effective relationships, understanding the business needs and providing effective communication. Build good working relationships across technology and the business to ensure regular communication of service requirements, service changes, service outages, and any service issues. Where the business requires direct regular communication with partners, ensure that there is clarity between the business and the service provider about how this process will work and who the key contacts are. |
| Installation and integration | Create installation, integration, testing, implementation, and decommissioning guides. Ensure removal of SharePoint solutions in accordance with agreed standards and controls. Control operational acceptance integration testing as part of a delivery. Ensure that there is development of implementation plans and schedule implementations as part of the change request process. |

## Creating platform Governance

Platform Governance relates to the technology-focused view. Technology does not exist on its own; it is a subset and facilitator of the business vision.

Human interaction and intervention is vital to managing SharePoint solutions. Do not rely solely on SharePoint tools and features, or on third-party tools. They will mask the true intention, which is for the business to control SharePoint.

The goal of platform Governance is to bridge the gap between the business and technological groups, ensure good return on investment (ROI), and mitigate risks associated with IT projects that affect SharePoint.

Business users know what would make their working lives better, their jobs more efficient, and the business more successful. It is arrogant for IT departments to believe that they truly know best, when in fact, they often do not. It may be that the business is unable to interpret or vocalize its business requirements in terms of a specific technology solution, which is fair because that is the specific job of the IT department. To do this most effectively, there is then an expectation that the IT department comprehensively understands what SharePoint is capable of and what features are best used in which scenarios and what features are best to avoid. Or it was that way a few years ago, anyway.

Today, the plethora of powerful and predefined business cloud services available means that business audiences now have the opportunity of bypassing IT departments and purchasing services directly from cloud vendors that are already fit for purpose, scalable, reliable, and immediately available. The compromise lies in the fact that the cloud solution may meet only 80 percent of ideal business needs or may not be adaptable. This opens up a new area of Governance: platform Governance driven directly through business purchasing for platforms that are not under the direct control of the organization.

Therefore, SharePoint administrators need to embrace a service model that allows them to provide a resilient, available, and supportable SharePoint solution, and communicate the capabilities of that solution to the business. The business then needs to accept those capabilities as rules that will underpin the technical management of the SharePoint solution, allowing the SharePoint solution to evolve as the business does. Platform Governance is the definitive design and rule book as to what SharePoint is to be used for, and it defines the policies that will be used within the various service areas of the SharePoint platform. Platform Governance is there to ensure that the SharePoint platform meets the requirements and scalability of the long-term business program goals that may extend over multiple years, not weeks or months.

First, you need to understand the areas to cover to build SharePoint Platform Governance. To help you do this, answer the following questions, and then use those answers as a basis for the SharePoint Governance committee to build the Statement of Operations:

- **User group management** Have you formed a SharePoint champions group for SharePoint comprising business members who are enthusiastic about touting SharePoint, and have you created rules for this group? This topic is discussed in the "Creating SharePoint champions" section of Chapter 4.
- **Quality management** What will be in place to measure the quality of the provision of SharePoint service delivery? This issue is discussed in the "Measuring SharePoint benefits" section of Chapter 1, "Aligning organizational goals and requirements."
- **Risk management** What will be done to mitigate the risk in the availability of the platform? What business continuity and disaster recovery methods will need to be put into place? Read the article "Managing SharePoint Platform Risk" at *http://www.sharepointgeoff.com/sharepoint-platform-availability-mitigating-the-risks/*.
- **Subcontract technical management** What support arrangements are there for third-party products being integrated with SharePoint? Read the article "Service Delivery—Working in harmony with external SharePoint agencies" at *http://www.sharepointgeoff.com/service-delivery---working-in-harmony-with-external-sharepoint-agencies-2/*.
- **Risk, issues, and change control** What is the configuration management model in place to manage risks and issues? What standards of documentation are there? How is the verification of the solution carried out? What acceptance criteria needs to be in place? Read the article "SharePoint Configuration Management" at *http://www.sharepointgeoff.com/sharepoint-configuration-management/*.

To help drive the building of the Statement of Operations, from a practical perspective, your delivery team needs to ask the following questions:

- Is SharePoint obligatory as a platform?
- What is SharePoint to be used for, and what should it *not* be used for?
- Is it business critical?
- What levels of business continuity are to be supported, and via what operational-level agreement (OLA) or service-level agreement (SLA) levels?
- Is SharePoint a geographically dispersed federated service platform?
- What browsers and devices will be supported?
- What version of Office products can be used?
- Will SharePoint be accessible to external users?
- What level of interface customization will be allowed?
- How much scalable storage will be required?

During this investigation, and as part of building the system specification, more and more platform Governance issues will come into play, such as the policies regarding quotas, devolved administration, central administration, site collections, content databases, federated search, UI design, accessibility and disability compliance access, version control, formats, retention, publication, workflow, access, security, and so on.

Therefore, in terms of SharePoint platform design and build and solution design and build, Governance must take responsibility for raising the required questions and finding the right answers to facilitate program progression. The key is to understand the right questions to ask and when. Organizations that try to manage SharePoint solutions face problems if they do not address several important questions. Consider the following questions as part of defining what the solution is supposed to deliver, how SharePoint will be used, and who will be asked to manage aspects of the solution:

- What services will SharePoint be used to deliver primarily?
- What types of content will SharePoint need to support?
- What policies come into play or define each of the SharePoint business service areas?
- What policies are required to define the use of SharePoint?
- What policies are required to define the contents of SharePoint?
- What services are required to function under change control?
- How will the platform be designed to facilitate scalable service growth?
- In what ways will the SharePoint platform be restricted?

- What security levels are to be applied to the platform and how?
- Who will manage the platform from a farm administration level?
- What service-level agreements are required?
- What will the platform look like from a UI design point of view?

**More Info** Although it is written for SharePoint 2010, there is a good Governance overview article at *http://technet.microsoft.com/en-gb/library/cc263356(v=office.14).aspx;* and Microsoft has provided good Governance tips for determining SharePoint app use in organizations at *http://technet.microsoft.com/en-gb/library/fp161237.aspx.*

Successfully implemented SharePoint Governance planning depends on the culture of the organization because it needs to define the rules applied to the management of SharePoint and the rules applied to content when people work with the platform.

For example, one organization may have an open culture, allowing any user to create sites on the SharePoint production platform, whereas another company may request that users make a helpdesk call to have a site created. Some people will say, "It's better for users to create their own sites on SharePoint," and I would not wholly disagree with that. However, if that type of access to SharePoint is left unchecked, there is no way to control the growth of the SharePoint platform.

Here is a list of areas in SharePoint where, in my view, decisions about data or site management need to be reviewed:

- Can users access information via Web Folder clients? This is the ability to see or access SharePoint via a mapped URL back to your Office client software. For example, company ABC might allow users to map a drive letter to a document library on a SharePoint site and to manage files through the use of Windows Explorer; however, this leads to a misuse of document classification and limits the change behavior.
- Can users create and manage their own websites?
- Is distributed administration provided through technical staff only or through a combination of business and technical staff? The geographical distribution of the company might affect the level of support supplied if the SharePoint implementation follows the regional spread of the company. For example, if you are considering having one administrator responsible for a regionalized SharePoint installation, something is going to slip. How are records and documents described (how is metadata used) to ensure descriptions are consistent across departments, divisions, and agencies?
- Should users be trained on how to administer sites before they need to manage them? Do you need to train the trainers so that a cascade of training can be provided? Check the service delivery and the support model—for example, if your support model includes users as the initial contact of SharePoint support and administration, your training plan must include that as well.

SharePoint delivery needs to be provided as a repeatable mechanism to deliver a SharePoint solution. You need to ensure that a framework is in place, which allows you to then build an inventory of what makes up the SharePoint solution. In terms of providing a full SharePoint platform, the elements described in Table 5-2 must be considered in the framework.

**TABLE 5-2** Elements requiring clarification in a SharePoint Governance framework

| Area | Description | Questions |
|---|---|---|
| SharePoint design | Physical platform, geographical dispersal, platform configuration, disaster recovery, business continuity, location access services and hosted platform, and on-premises SharePoint 2013 farm structure and quality. | What level of SharePoint topology has been defined (server structure)? What are the connectivity, resilience, and performance levels? What is being provided to ensure SharePoint farm integrity [test, development, user acceptance test (UAT), and production farms]? What third-party tools are integrated with SharePoint? |
| Content design and data management | Information structure, navigational structure, UI design, content types, web structure, data retention and archiving, business applications, document management, email management, digital asset management, imaging and capture, web content management, enterprise resource management, digital rights management, electronic records management, and e-Forms | What kinds of sites are being provided? What key features are set to them? What is the taxonomy? What metadata is in place? What framework is in place to structure sites (for example, managed paths, logical separations at the site level, and so on)? |
| Content management | Business administration, support levels, support roles, ownership, security, auditing, compliance | Who will assign users and permissions in SharePoint 2013? Who will create and approve content for sites? Who will approve content to be marked for retention? Who will secure sensitive information? Who will be able to create new sites? Who will be able to publish content to websites? Who will be able to customize sites? What are the quota levels? |
| Content classification | Business usage classifications, organizational metadata | Are there skills available to build taxonomies and metadata? How will classifications be exposed in SharePoint? How will the classification model be tested? Who will be responsible for managing data classification? How will training be applied concerning classification? |
| Search Services | Search engine capability, search optimization, content optimization | What keywords will be associated with content? What search features should be applied? Who will monitor search usage? What optimization techniques for search need to be applied? |
| Content Presentation and Access Services | SharePoint portals, desktop applications | What SharePoint portals are restricted and why? What desktop applications are supported with SharePoint? What priority support is used for SharePoint solutions that require specific desktop applications? |

| Area | Description | Questions |
|---|---|---|
| Process and Collaboration Services | Process Management, Workflow, Collaboration, Business Analytics | What workflow engine will be used? What processes will be automated? How will they be managed and deployed? What usage statistics are required? |
| Content Middleware | Security, Enterprise Application Integration, Content Integration, Taxonomy | What security, privacy, and compliance polices should be adhered to? What enterprise applications should be integrated with SharePoint? What external content should be accessible? |
| Infrastructure and storage | Storage migration, backup and restore, storage location, cloud | What content stored externally should be migrated into SharePoint? What content stored in SharePoint should be archived and when? What backup retention schedules should be in place? What constitutes a restore of content? What content should be structured in separated locations? What external publishing needs to take place in the cloud? What policies should be set for SkyDrive usage? What rules should be applied to SkyDrive file storage? |

The outcome of investigating the elements described in Table 5-2 will be clearly defined policies, which can be communicated, and then users can be trained. This leads to User Adoption. Note that failure to adopt SharePoint is not the fault of the business user when there is a lack of clear guidelines and training provided by the platform owners and the program sponsor. Business rules and policies are vital. Consider the following statements concerning SharePoint solutions provisioning. Each of these statements would need associated business rules and policies:

- SharePoint may fragment into multiple service farms.
- SharePoint may blend with cloud services.
- SharePoint may migrate to the cloud.
- SharePoint will diversify in terms of services.
- SharePoint will scale and expand.
- SharePoint will become mission critical.
- SharePoint will become business critical and require redundancy.
- SharePoint will be asked to integrate with other platforms and information services.
- SharePoint will become the central access point for other information silos.
- SharePoint will offer the primary central search service.
- SharePoint will become customized in terms of look and feel.
- SharePoint will challenge business processes and traditional ways of working.

- SharePoint will push integration with Office, Microsoft Lync, and Microsoft Exchange Server, as well as customer relationship management (CRM) services.
- SharePoint will introduce the subject of third-party services, add-ins, tools, and related technology solutions.
- Some business owners will not interact with SharePoint due to fear or lethargy.
- SharePoint will require a suitable program budget.
- SharePoint will require suitable resources that include more than just developers.
- SharePoint will affect business time and resources (particularly for solution testing).
- SharePoint will potentially require internal administration (that is, not outsourced).
- SharePoint will trigger a large number of new and unplanned business service requests.
- SharePoint will trigger a strategy requirement for social networking (which typically are applied social networking techniques).
- SharePoint will initiate automated processes through electronic workflow.
- SharePoint will frequently trigger a new host of remote access services for business users.

## Creating business rules

Without Governance, there is no policy; and without policy, there is no User Adoption. Governance includes consideration for data that needs to be retained and/or archived. The reasons for this could be a combination of audit, internal policy, legislation, compliance, industry regulation, HR requirements, state law, federal law, local regulations, and data protection.

To identify benefits and drivers for Governance, you must create business rules associated with the use of the SharePoint solution. Business rules establish commonality and help maintain consistency. SharePoint processes that are designed to automate or replace manual business processes require business rules to be operated correctly. There is no point in saying that people should use your SharePoint solution without business rules that state best practices and policy. Business rules affect User Adoption. For example, if you are going to implement records management into an existing SharePoint environment, you would not just start telling users to go into this SharePoint site and upload their content, because your users would get completely confused and not understand the reasons why they should use the site. In the end, this lack of rules would create chaos.

In addition, defining business rules helps foster business continuity for the relevant SharePoint solution. In the event that SharePoint is not available, for example, the business needs a way to continue during SharePoint downtime.

Every SharePoint solution must carry one or more business rules. For example, a particular rule could be the following statement:

> *"All documents requiring approval must be published using SharePoint."*

The reason to create business rules is that all organizations have statements that define or constrain some aspect of the business. Therefore, a business rule is intended to assert business structure or to control or influence the behavior of the business.

Taking that concept a step further, information within the business has many subtypes and components (its architecture, which then creates these entities, known as *metadata*). These subtypes and components relate to managing that information (in other words, the acquiring, producing, packaging, and distribution of that information). Therefore, the information produced may be referenced with various codes, abbreviations, and terms. SharePoint helps by ensuring that they can be managed and located centrally.

**Note** Information Governance includes policies to manage the evolution of the organization classification systems. *Metadata* is the description of physical content (also known as information about information). For example, a SharePoint document library is comprised of columns. Each column holds information about the document. The grouping of metadata is carried out by the information architect at a global level and then regionalized into site administrators at the department, office, and group levels. Collation of this material is key to defining the aspects of search and to content scoping. Metadata is also a crucial aspect of Enterprise Content Management (ECM) and lends itself to the categorization of functional site material. For more information on ECM, there are lots of good articles at *http://blogs.msdn.com/b/ecm/.*

*Scenario 1: Fabrikam is a large manufacturing company with more than 50 locations across the world. They produced more than 500 unique products and have more than 50 stock managing units. They needed a platform to help maintain consistency across all their automated systems. To do this, they gathered the key business rules and carried out analysis against the value that SharePoint would bring. This included documenting the required information architecture. During this analysis, the delivery team identified that several processes could be streamlined. Further analysis of these processes described the components of those processes more fully, and particularly key coding, which could be expanded for use in other business units. After several workshops to further refine these processes were held, policies were created stating the business rules under which these key processes could operate. These rules were then documented and explained as part of the communication and training plans to those using the SharePoint tools surrounded the business process. Those business rules were then expanded and introduced as SharePoint policies guiding the use of the SharePoint solution.*

So, as part of the User Adoption strategy, you must incorporate basic business rules that support the SharePoint solution's use. These business rules should form part of the training and provide configuration management for the solution. As a result, changes to the solution can be tracked, and therefore, impacts to the solution being modified can be identified and agreed upon.

You will need help from the key stakeholders and sponsors relevant to the SharePoint solution. First, you list the business rules under which the SharePoint solution should operate. For example, if the SharePoint solution is a sales ledger site containing workflows to automate invoices, the business rules should be indicated as a diagrammed flowchart that depicts the automated processes provided by the SharePoint solution. This is easier for stakeholders to understand. Present the processes to your stakeholders to get their approval. Critically, check that the business rules do not affect the productivity gain that the solution should be providing. If the business rule diminishes the value of the SharePoint solution in any way, then the solution does not meet the business requirements.

To summarize, here are some key points to keep in mind when you're creating business rules:

- Set rules of engagement.
- Remember that User Adoption will fail unless there are rules that then create policies. There are both internal and external policies, which may be accompanied by compliance and legislation. Consider both business and IT policies.
- Keep the classification scheme (taxonomy) short to be effective.
- Combine email and SharePoint archive for any public-sector FOI solutions.
- Define a clear data retention policy.
- Treat records management as a "business as usual" activity.
- Consider the interactions between external and internal collaborative teams.
- Identify when internal services need to be shared with externals.
- Ensure that a formally structured environment has been created for all visitors.
- Ensure that an unstructured environment has been created for collaboration groups on a by-request basis, and make sure it is not linked to anything else.
- Ensure that linking of internal information is out of the reach of general visitors.
- Identify the relevant supporting and administration requirements and constraints for external visitors.

**Tip** Use the SharePoint one-stop shop as a central repository for business rules and policies concerning SharePoint use. You could create a simple list that gives the title of the policy or rule, along with a description, and attach the relevant policy document to that item. Making the policies central makes finding that content easy, as well as aiding in user training.

## Creating a SharePoint training program

Providing a training program lends to Governance of the solution and is a key aspect of User Adoption and Governance. Training is a way that policies and business rules can be communicated. Through the delivery of training, users can understand the rules concerning the use of the solution. SharePoint support needs a *devolved business administration,* and this can happen only if training is part of any SharePoint delivery program. It should also include awareness of security and the service support model, which will allow owners to help define measurable success criteria for each SharePoint solution service release.

**Note** Devolved business administration means that assigned business users perform basic administration of SharePoint sites. They are normally approved by their line managers and are trained for this purpose. This means that in terms of SharePoint solution delivery, training, support, and User Adoption all benefit, because the business owns the sites, and therefore it also will own any delivered solution to that site.

In this section, you will learn how to create and manage a SharePoint training program. You can use the techniques described here for any SharePoint delivery program (from the provision of a SharePoint platform to the provision of a SharePoint app). The training program needs to be designed so that it is intuitive and needs to be carried out for the following reasons:

- There are legal requirements for staff training.
- Training helps the service support model.
- Without training, User Adoption will fail.

You need to choose the method of training that matches the organization's culture, funding, and resources. Nowadays, old-fashioned IT training methods are no longer valid; they have been replaced by blended learning and e-learning methods to supplement standard IT training techniques. Your training methods should include a combination of traditional classroom training, methods supplemented by multimedia presentations, demonstrations, floor-walking activities (where previously trained users can be on hand to help new users), and user guides (preferably online and accessible and customized for the user).

This section describes what elements are required to put together a training plan, and gives examples of training delivery. The training plan is a document that has the following headings:

- **Summary—organizational** A statement of the SharePoint solution and its purpose. The summary of the training plan can be drawn from the "Background and Context" section of the SharePoint Tactical Communications plan. See Table 4-6 in Chapter 4 to review the headings in the communication plan.
- **Audiences** A table indicating the roles that will require training, as described in Table 5-3. Note that you can use the audiences as defined in the communication plan, as they may relate closer to the solution being implemented.

- **Types of training to be provisioned** A table indicating the types of training that will be provided.

The first things you will need to identify are the different audience types. These audience types are defined relevant to their role and use of the solution. (For more information about audience types, refer to the section "Developing communication plans," in Chapter 4.) Your training plan would be created based on the audiences selected, as summarized in Table 5-3.

**TABLE 5-3** Training user types and roles

| User Type | Role |
|---|---|
| End user desktop | A user who works with Office and Microsoft Outlook and wants to collaborative at different levels dependent on job function |
| End user mobile device | A user who is mobile and who works with Office and Outlook, but also requires access to information offline |
| Information contributor | A user who wants to collaborate using team sites and edit and amend or create information for others or in conjunction with others |
| Team site publisher | A user who wants to collaborate using team sites and edit and create information |
| Team site administrator | A user who has the role of managing a collaborative environment on behalf of the business peers |
| Workflow manager | A user who designs or manages business processes |
| Content administrator | A user who manages content produced by others |
| SharePoint champion | A user who has been tapped to evangelize and help their peers in the use of SharePoint |

Many other roles can and will exist over time, but the information given in this table is important in indicating that although basic training in Office 2013 may suffice at the outset, this will quickly be usurped by more enhanced needs applicable to specific job functions when using SharePoint. Create a table like Table 5-3 that lists the user types. For each type, use the audiences defined in your communication plan to complete the Role column.

The communication plan is also important for helping determine when users will be trained, and an indication of what kind of training they will receive. Be mindful that some users will avoid being trained or try and pick things up themselves (these people are known as *innovators* in the User Adoption individual types). If this is the case, use the methods of dealing with innovators as described in Table 4-1 in Chapter 4. You should stress the importance of the training and ensure that all users be trained and must attend training sessions as set in your training schedule. Training is not an optional exercise for users.

*Scenario 2: Fabrikam is a children's toy manufacturer. A SharePoint platform has been implemented for the company, and as part of that delivery, a communication and training plan was set. Schedules of the training program were sent to users via email, but there was no follow-up to ensure that people participated. As a result, sessions were missed by users who didn't get the message due to technical issues, thought it was unimportant and deleted it, deliberately ignored it, or already had plans and therefore declined the invitation to come to training. This resulted in repeated and delayed training sessions. Luckily, Fabrikam executives strongly supported the SharePoint implementation and forced a top-down approach that "cordially advised" users go to the training sessions.*

Like communication planning, training is provided using channels and tactics. Tactics relate to the type of training being provided (whether it is a human-led training event, or a resource such as Computer-Based-Training materials). Channels cover the best way to provide the type of training (or materials). Table 5-4 lists examples of tactics and the channels that could be used to help you focus your training plan.

**Tip** As SharePoint Delivery manager, when associating the channel (which is a resource) against a tactic, discuss with the SharePoint sponsor whether the resource chosen is adequate, given the available budget, business culture, resource constraints, time scales, and so on.

**TABLE 5-4** SharePoint training tactics and channels

| Tactic | Channel |
|---|---|
| Awareness sessions | SharePoint Helpdesk |
| On-site demonstrations | SharePoint Helpdesk and SharePoint Champions |
| FAQs | SharePoint Helpdesk |
| User guides | SharePoint Helpdesk |
| Introduction to Collaborative Working | SharePoint Helpdesk |
| Intermediate Collaborative Working | SharePoint Helpdesk |
| Advanced Collaborative Working | SharePoint Helpdesk |
| Policies and guidelines | SharePoint Helpdesk/SharePoint Governance |
| Multimedia presentations | Intranet Team/SharePoint Helpdesk |
| SharePoint champions | Direct support to user groups during and after implementations |
| Support services | One-stop shop provision of answers to user questions and advice and guidance on how to use SharePoint |

As you may have noticed, three of the tactics listed in this table are training courses that would be provided by the SharePoint Helpdesk team. In addition, workshops can be part of the training plan (resources and budget permitting). Table 5-5 gives some examples of the types of courses that might be offered as part of this plan. Construct a table in the same format as Table 5-5, listing the training tactics you want to use. In the Channel section, indicate who will be responsible for implementing the tactic.

**TABLE 5-5** Training courses and descriptions

| Course | Description |
| --- | --- |
| Introduction to the Single Information Platform | Awareness presentation (lasting 30 minutes) introducing SharePoint key features on a live platform. |
| Introduction to Collaborative Working | Beginner training for the key Office features in conjunction with Outlook, particularly Tasks, Calendars and Documents, team sites and document libraries, version control, sharing, community sites, and newsfeeds. Takes potentially half a day. |
| Intermediate Collaborative Services | Intermediate-level course using SharePoint services on site, and introducing Communicator services, Excel Services, and different methods of information sharing using Outlook and SharePoint sites. Will include one-to-one sharing, one-to-many sharing, publishing, and an introduction to workflows. Also includes more in-depth use of authoring and version control features. This may be a half-day or one-day course. |
| Advanced Collaborative Services | Aimed at the advanced user, examining business intelligence (BI), focusing on Excel Services, using the full collaborative features of SharePoint services, including temporary workspaces, workflows, acceptance, publishing, creating sub sites, and so on. This should be a one-day course. |

If you are going to run training courses, then you will need supplementary resources for users that will support the training courses. Table 5-6 gives an example of supplementary materials and who is responsible for creating them. Do not expect that after a three-hour training course, attendees will remember the first thing covered in the session (or maybe even the third!). Therefore, provide materials to reinforce their knowledge. Remember the communication plan and match the materials provided to the channels and tactics described in Table 4-6 in Chapter 4.

**TABLE 5-6** SharePoint training supplementary materials and producers

| Material | Produced by |
| --- | --- |
| An Introduction to SharePoint 2013 | SharePoint Helpdesk |
| SharePoint 2013 Team Site Quick Start Guide | SharePoint Helpdesk |
| Microsoft Office 2013 e-learning modules | Online e-learning material from Microsoft |
| Microsoft Outlook 2013 Quick Start Guide | Online e-learning material from Microsoft |
| SharePoint 2013 My Site User Guide | Online e-learning material from Microsoft |
| SharePoint 2013 FAQ and Usage | SharePoint Helpdesk |
| Course Materials for Collaborative Working | SharePoint Helpdesk |

## Training resource requirements

Based on the culture and available resources of the organization, you will need to identify who will provide the training. Table 5-7 indicates the types of training resource and description for each. You should use this information to choose which are mandatory and which are optional, based on the budget, culture, and SharePoint solution being delivered.

**TABLE 5-7** Training resources and descriptions

| Training Resource | Description |
|---|---|
| Training company | This is a professional organization used to assist in resources, coordination, scheduling, and delivery. Typically used in larger firms where there is a significant number of people requiring training and/or when a specific SharePoint solution is being provided and the knowledge of the product is not available internally. |
| Trainer | A skilled instructor who can run sessions for introductory, intermediate, and technical courses. |
| Internal shadow trainer | An individual who has the necessary skill set to allow the organization to cover supplementary course sessions and retain skills in house. |
| Training coordinator | An external training provider or individual(s) within the organization who provision training materials, schedule, quality and delivery assurance, room allocation, training PC allocation, and any other facilitation of training service requirements. |
| Materials creator | An individual who creates training guides, quick-start guides, and any other supporting materials. |
| FAQ coordinator | An individual who creates and publishes training material that support users. |
| Communications coordinator | An individual who uses tactics and channels to communicate information concerning all training materials on a regular basis. |
| SharePoint champion | An individual within the organization who can initially attend training sessions and then train users in their relevant groups. |

## Training plan scheduling

You need to create schedules for the topics relevant to the training plan. Examples of these include the following:

- Schedule for technical administrator training
- Schedule for staff training
- Schedule for SharePoint sessions
- Schedule for site owners to basic collaborative working sessions
- Schedule for site owners to advanced collaborative working sessions
- Briefing sessions

Each topic has its own direction and content, and each schedule should be separated and published as an individual entity. In addition, you may need to schedule the following:

- Open-access (drop-in) scheduled sessions
- Sessions on request to specific audiences
- Demonstrative sessions to key staff
- Demonstrative sessions to other departments on request

## Communication and support

Each schedule should be communicated as soon as possible using the appropriate methods:

- Email to all staff
- Publication via the intranet

It is highly likely that sessions will need to be self-service, with a maximum quota in some areas (for introductory and intermediate SharePoint courses). Once users have been trained, they will require assistance in using their new skills from SharePoint Support and Helpdesk. With the introduction of a new service to the desktop, users will be backed by on-site SharePoint champions. However, it is advised to look at the provision of supplementary skilled staff to assist users if there is a justifiable requirement. For more information concerning SharePoint support, please read Chapter 8, "Building a SharePoint service delivery model."

## Technical training

Support staff and the technical administrators will require specific skill training of a technical nature. These may be direct training courses offered by third-party training organizations, which eventually leads to Microsoft certification. This will include the following:

- Rotational shadow activities
- Supplier- and vendor-specific training
- Technical support documentation
- Technical FAQ creation and upkeep
- Training company technical courses
- Microsoft certifications are available for IT professionals covering SharePoint 2013 at the Microsoft Certified Solutions Engineer (MSCE) level. These cover server installation and configuration. MCSE certification requires you to show continued technical ability in SharePoint 2013 by completing a recertification exam every three years.

**More Info** For more information concerning technical training for SharePoint 2013, visit *http://technet.microsoft.com/en-US/sharepoint/fp123606*. For information on MCSE SharePoint 2013, visit *http://www.microsoft.com/learning/en/us/mcse-sharepoint-certification.aspx*.

## Using web analytics and auditing to provide substance to Governance

SharePoint Web Analytics is a useful tool for Governance and User Adoption because it improves the usability of your SharePoint solution, drives collaboration, boosts ROI, and enhances the overall productivity of SharePoint users. You would use SharePoint Web Analytics to analyze SharePoint content, in order to improve the SharePoint customer experience for owners and visitors.

SharePoint Web Analytics is useful in the following situations:

- You want to get usage data concerning what pages on the sites are viewed.
- You want to know what customers are using as search queries to locate SharePoint content. In this case, analytics results can show you what terms customers are entering in the Search features provided on SharePoint sites. This allows you to optimize the search process so they are able to find the content.

Analytical results will help you to understand what elements of SharePoint sites customers like and dislike, what they interact with, and what they do not. Using analytics allows you to proactively review the ability of the SharePoint sites to improve the customer experience. By doing that, you are creating a consistent and standard method of improving collaboration on the sites, and you are providing raw information concerning site use that is relevant to the business rules in place for that site.

*Scenario 3: The Human Resources department at Fabrikam has a SharePoint site that provides forms for holiday, sickness, leave, job applications, and other HR functions. As a company rule, all sickness forms must be completed and then uploaded into a document library on the Human Resources site. Human Resources needs a monthly report showing all interaction with the forms on the site, particularly those related to sickness, so that they can monitor them and ensure that the rule is being adhered to.*

SharePoint 2013 includes two types of built-in analytics and auditing reports: Popularity and Search Reports and Audit Log Reports. Table 5-8 describes the Popularity and Search Reports, which are popularity trend reports, providing an insight into how and what content has been accessed.

**TABLE 5-8** Popularity and Search Reports

| Report | Description |
|---|---|
| Usage | This report shows historical usage information about the site collection, such as the number of views and unique users. Use this report to identify usage trends and to determine times of high and low activity. |
| Number of Queries | This report shows the number of search queries performed. Use this report to identify search query volume trends and to determine times of high and low search activity. |
| Top Queries by Day/Month | This report shows the most popular search queries. Use it to understand what types of information visitors are seeking. |
| Abandoned Queries by Day | This report shows popular search queries that received low click-throughs. Use this report to identify search queries that might create user dissatisfaction and to improve the discoverability of content. Then, consider using query rules to improve the query's results. |

| Report | Description |
|---|---|
| Abandoned Queries by Month | This report shows popular search queries that received low click-throughs. Use this report to identify search queries that might create user dissatisfaction and to improve the discoverability of content. Then, consider using query rules to improve the query's results. |
| No Result Queries by Day | This report shows popular search queries that returned no results. Use this report to identify search queries that might create user dissatisfaction and to improve the discoverability of content. Then, consider using query rules to improve the query's results. |
| No Result Queries by Month | This report shows popular search queries that returned no results. Use this report to identify search queries that might create user dissatisfaction and to improve the discoverability of content. Then, consider using query rules to improve the query's results. |
| Query Rule Usage by Day | This report shows how often query rules are used, how many dictionary terms they involve, and how often users click their promoted results. Use this report to see how useful your query rules and promoted results are to users. |
| Query Rule Usage by Month | This report shows how often query rules are used, how many dictionary terms they involve, and how often users click their promoted results. Use this report to see how useful your query rules and promoted results are to users. |

**More Info** For more information about Popularity and Search Reports, visit *http://technet.microsoft.com/en-us/library/jj219554.aspx.*

Table 5-9 lists Audit Log Reports that are available in SharePoint 2013. Audit Log Reports allow activity tracking to take place inside all SharePoint sites. These reports can be used by SharePoint owners to determine whether business rules concerning the usage of relevant content are being met. Audit reports cover content management, information management policy, and security and site settings.

**TABLE 5-9** Audit Log Reports

| Report | Description |
|---|---|
| Content viewing | This report shows all events where a user viewed content in this site. |
| Content modifications | This report shows all events that modified content in this site. |
| Deletion | This report shows all events that caused content in this site to be deleted or restored from the Recycle Bin. |
| Content type and list modifications | This report shows all events that modified content types and lists in this site. |
| Policy modifications | This report shows all events related to the creation and use of information management policies on content in this site. |
| Expiration and disposition | This report shows all events related to the expiration and disposition of content in this site. |
| Auditing settings | This report shows all events that change the auditing settings of Microsoft SharePoint Foundation. |
| Security settings | This report shows all events that change the security configuration of SharePoint Foundation. |
| Custom Reports | Run a custom report. |

**More Info** For more information about Audit Log Reports, visit *http://office.microsoft.com/en-us/sharepoint-help/view-audit-log-reports-HA102772739.aspx.*

You can use Audit Log Reports to track the following activities:

- List access
- Library access
- Opening of documents
- Editing items
- Check-in and check-out of documents
- Copying, moving, and deleting items
- Searching
- Editing permissions

SharePoint analytics and audit features aid Governance and improve User Adoption. Consider the following questions, as this will allow you to create Audit Log Reports to suit your needs:

- How many people are using the portal?
- What are most users doing on the portal?
- What is the most popular search?
- Where are users coming from?
- What are customers downloading?

## Understanding IT consumerization Governance

A challenge for platform Governance is the impact of personal device use and how to manage the risks associated with it. IT is now overwhelmed by mobile devices, with employees now using these devices in a "blurred" landscape of their workplace (not just in the office, but in cafes, airports, their homes, and so on). When employees bring their personal mobile devices to work and use them to share files or data inside and outside the office, it is difficult for IT to maintain visibility and control. At the same time, there is evidence indicating that people using such devices for work purposes become more productive.

Increasingly, organizations are supporting a movement called "bring your own device" (commonly referred to as BYOD and the consumerization of IT) and allowing employees to connect the devices that they bring to the workplace to technologies previously restricted to IT personnel. This has been seen as a major boon for companies in terms of retaining staff. For organizations supporting BYOD,

ROIs have been reported concerning increased worker productivity, less stressed personnel, increased job satisfaction, and increased motivation. These successes result in improvement to an organization's image, particularly since it is being seen as proactive in tolerating, encouraging, and even sometimes sponsoring the use of such devices.

In SharePoint, there are more challenges associated with providing an experience that allows users to employ smart devices to access SharePoint as if they were working from a laptop. These challenges are not just technical; there are business security and management issues as well. Organizations have taken a wide variety of stances on BYOD:

- They forbid users from accessing such resources using the devices at all, finding that is affecting User Adoption of products that are mobile aware.
- They don't inform users of any available integration to such devices, or mislead them about the capabilities of these enterprise platforms.
- They allow employees to use only specific devices, and those off the list are either not supported or barred from use.
- They do not police BYOD use in any way, using such excuses as that the IT department has far too many other things to do.
- They embrace change, ensuring readiness, procedures, business rules, and policies.

For organizations adopting SharePoint as their collaborative platform, BYOD needs to be treated with extreme care and caution. For a start, there needs to be a requirement that providers are treated as trusted community assets to the company. In other words, Apple devices such as the iPad and iPhone, as well as Blackberry and certain other smart devices are "trusted," and then you need to consider and specify exactly what applications and services should be made available for use on those devices.

Therefore, to form a BYOD strategy, company leaders must make key decisions based on the best services offered by these devices in terms of how they fulfill business strategies and meet security requirements, given their financial and workforce resources. Once that is achieved, organizations that foster trust with their employees will gain a competitive edge through increased productivity, better employee satisfaction and retention, enhanced customer satisfaction, and a more credible voice because they are taking a position that supports employee needs, not just business needs. In addition, creating these good community relations translates into increased employee giving and volunteerism through the use of social applications and tools that have been integrated.

So defining security for personal devices that users wish to use with SharePoint needs to be balanced with the need to provide a user experience that does not prevent or detrimentally affect their productivity or introduces an unnecessary level of control. The following quote shows how important it is to balance control with the need for people to be productive:

> *"Even though worker capacity and motivation are destroyed when leaders choose power over productivity, it appears that bosses would rather be in control than have the organization work well."*
>
> *Meg Wheatley, writer and management consultant who studies organizational behavior*

Consumerization of IT is an employee-led revolution. It is a blending of personal and business technology use that strikes at the heart of every standardized, built-for-cost enterprise infrastructure. More than ever, information workers are investing their own resources to buy and learn a wide range of popular consumer technologies. *Consumerization* is an increasingly accepted term used to describe the growing tendency for new IT to emerge first in the consumer market, and then spread to business and government.

Fundamentally, this means that things like mobile phones and tablets, which in the past may not have been acceptable for use in business, are now seen as key drivers of staff productivity, particularly for those who work remotely and/or travel (a trend that is also on the rise). Examples of this include companies now actively allowing staff with certain types of mobile devices access to the corporate network. Some have even gone as far as to allow any mobile device to be used (with constraints) to access the wireless network.

So, a company issuing mobile devices to remote employees could be seen as a less cost-effective measure than allowing staff to BYOD (so long as security is in place, risks are mitigated, and the company is fully aware of the services that will be consumed through the use of mobile devices).

Mobile devices are able to consume many resources, each of which presents challenges from a support and security perspective. Figure 5-3 shows some of those services, software, and mobile devices, all of which may affect SharePoint from a customer experience, security, and risk perspective.

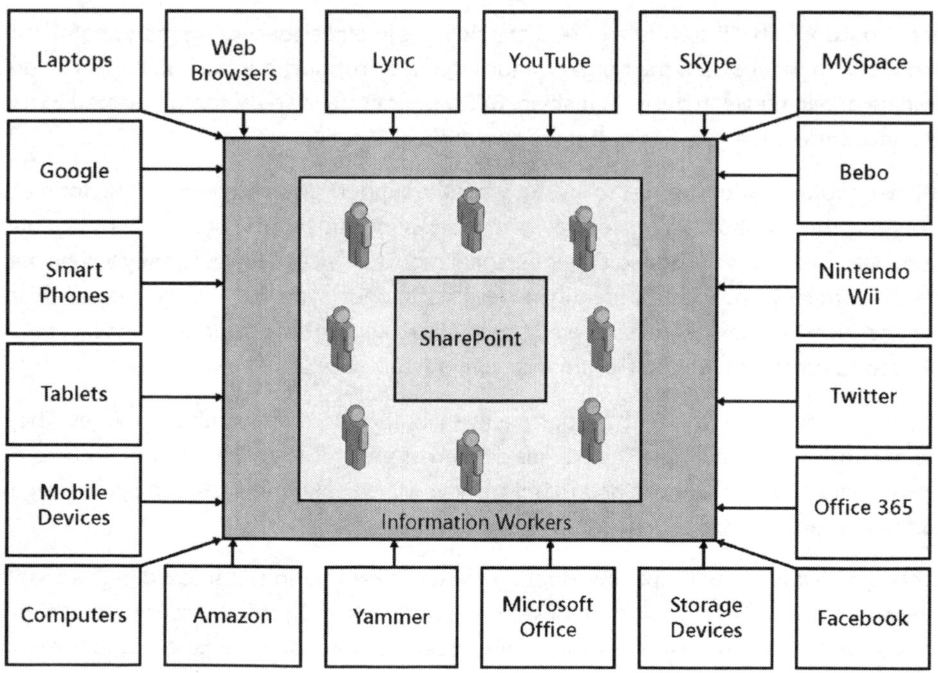


**FIGURE 5-3** Consumerization in relationship to SharePoint.

With 101 million smart phones shipped in 2010 as opposed to 92 million computers shipped that same year, the trend is moving away from the use of computers due to the drive to provide more benefits, features, and performance to mobile devices. Aligned with this is a marked increase in the number of applications available, which will further entice users away from the stand-alone computer.

With desktop computing, security has traditionally been more controlled due to the simple fact that computers are hard to move around, and data is more secure due to the standard devices available to protect it (such as hardwired dongles, network protection, and so on). Laptops are less secure due to intangible issues concerning misappropriation, theft, and loss; and with smaller devices such as tablets and smart phones, security risks increase yet again. Now that personal devices are being allowed to access corporate data remotely, companies and employees face even more security challenges. You should not assume that approaching the subject of BYOD security with users will frighten them. Be careful when addressing security: You must not indicate that security is to be used as a control mechanism or be an excuse to restrict access to mobility. In the past, IT has been known to use these methods to try to curtail the use of mobile devices and to impose control, with IT in the role of the governor and owner of BYOD policies.

If you attempt to do this, then people will attempt to bypass your security restrictions because they will see them as unproductive. People are becoming more tech-savvy, and they will inform their managers and peers what they need to do with the devices. It is the job of Governance to inform those users how they can use those mobile devices to accomplish what they need.

You need to work with HR staff to ensure that a policy is in place concerning the use of mobile devices, and to help them assure their organizations that they support business managers. In doing this, HR will be providing aid in decision making. BYOD policies need to be communicated to users via the Governance committee. The business must own the BYOD policy.

You will need to work with support to lay out what the support arrangements will be for mobile device users. Consumerization of IT gives way to user self-support. Support staff will not be able to control completely what users install on their personal mobile devices. However, they will be able to enforce the company's policies. By identifying levels of support, you will address the capability of support and identify what resources need to be in place. Again, these arrangements must be communicated to users through the Governance committee.

Doing this gives the IT department the perspective that they do not own BYOD policies. They are only there to enforce those policies. This work is defined as proactive service delivery. You are seeking to cover ownership of BYOD support, and therefore, you will be able to measure the effectiveness of enforcing the relevant policies.

BYOD cannot be addressed simply by adopting the technical solutions discussed in this chapter; rather, they are solved with a combination of security awareness and common sense, Governance, and the ability to monitor content use in the environment. Let's take a look at some of these challenges.

## Lost devices

Even if sufficient security is implemented in wireless virtual private networks (VPNs), if a device is lost or stolen, the entire corporate intranet could be threatened if the device isn't protected by passwords and other user-level security measures. For example, an individual could access SharePoint by simply opening the browser whose user credentials had been cached on a mobile device if steps are not taken to address those and related risks.

## Lost IP

Mobile devices use wireless connectivity; therefore, anything that could affect access from that perspective is considered a security issue. For example, here's an email that was sent to the support department from a user who got a virus while using a tablet, and as a result the wireless connection became disabled:

> *"My IP address seems to have been lost. It's currently at 0.0.0.0. I tried to reset the tablet, but it would not connect. I'm running out of ideas, and with a 10-page research paper due tomorrow, I need to figure this out fast. Any help would be appreciated. Thanks."*

This issue, while it might sound arbitrary, could cause serious loss of business use. What if that user were a key employee preparing a business case that required submission to secure funding and had a tight deadline?

## Security breaches

As consumerization continues to become a larger part of daily business operations, the costs related to security will invariably increase, and this could cause serious costs and potentially humiliating issues to a company. Even if the company has security policies, it will face the following challenges:

- The security policies need to adapt to a mobile work environment.
- Decisions need to be made concerning what kind of technology is needed to manage devices and enforce policies.

Indeed, the indirect costs associated with security breaches are often far greater than the direct costs of mitigating damages; beyond costs of data remediation and possible fines for compliance rule violations, security breaches can cost companies their competitive advantage. They can embarrass companies or key people in those companies, creating bad publicity and legal problems. They can cause a loss of customer and partner confidence. Ultimately, security breaches can damage a company's brand and its ability to do business.

In addition, if there is little monitoring in place to identify the nature of a security breach, this could further undermine the ability to provide a service. Therefore, it is important to consider how monitoring tools and auditing can be provided in such a way that self-Governance in data access from business users can be provided.

## Information leaks

Information leaks are a primary concern for mobile devices. The problem is that companies have almost no control over what documents are available on the devices. Mobile devices are a great source of information leakage because they often have inadequate or nonexistent security controls available.

## Patching of mobile devices

Even with corporate accounts, mobile devices are updated at the whim of the mobile carrier, who would usually prefer that you buy a new device with the updated operating system (and extend your contract as well). So let's look at how mobile device use gets supported from a basic perspective.

Support (or the company help desk) sometimes gets neglected when it comes to consumerization, simply because IT support wrongly thought that they did not have time to understand what device is connected, and therefore decided that once the user is successfully connected, that unless rigid monitoring is in place, they will not be able to provide information about what the user is doing on the personal device (remember that the Acceptable User policy must extend to mobile device use).

As more devices get connected via an open wireless system in a corporate network, it's essential that IT support knows about the various SharePoint and business challenges caused by the use of mobile devices as they plan their approach to securing the device on their networks. One example of where this can go horrendously wrong is the provision of a wireless connection to an unprotected device, which could be compromised without any policies in place from IT support to protect the network or even identify the culprit.

## Creating policies for mobile device use

Policies should be defined around mobile devices to help protect sensitive SharePoint content. This can include securing the mobile device by using a PIN or lock and ensuring that you can erase the data on the mobile device remotely. Should you implement any of these policies, be aware that consistent standards for these practices are not in place yet, and that various mobile devices feature different programs and features.

You can educate users about how they can help protect their user credentials. This can include signing out of sites, closing the mobile web browser when they are done. and ensuring that the browser does not enable any option that keeps them signed in, remembers their passwords, or stores *cookies*. This can help prevent others from using their user credentials to log on to a SharePoint site if the mobile device is lost or stolen.

## Getting the users involved

Users need to be comfortable knowing that the data housed on SharePoint is secure and available, and that the platform on which it sits is resilient and performs well. Security of the data is paramount in ensuring a structured and managed SharePoint environment, and this must apply to technical and business users alike. Technical security includes authentication, service application scalability, integration of other data sources, and platform connectivity. Users do not care about the technology or the way the security works, but you must still ensure that security issues concerning how they connect their mobile devices to the corporate network are addressed for the relevant device, and also that security policies are well defined, communicated to users, and enforced on all devices. Security policies must be regularly reviewed, and by getting the user involved in this process, you can do the following:

- Learn what the user wants to do (that is, what applications will be run on the device to access SharePoint)
- Learn where the user wants to visit within SharePoint
- Create more possibilities for guidance, which in turn leads to better Governance

Some company strategies openly advocate the use of personal mobile devices as part of their march to create a better social networking attitude. Do not become a prima donna and attempt to curtail use of devices altogether unless there is a valid security risk that is high enough to invalidate their use (and the client approves of this policy). That said, this requires more time and resources to investigate issues. However, there are tools that can help you, and you should be proactive in investigating their benefits. The following scenario is a good example of why policies need to be created and communicated to users:

*Scenario 4: Fred is an account manager for Fabrikam, a large manufacturing company about to strike a deal that could make it the leader in sports equipment. The company allows any devices to connect to the Fabrikam internal network, and it is deploying SharePoint. Fred goes on his lunch break, and he downloads a new game app onto his mobile device. Unknown to Fred, the new game app has a spyware element. The developer who created the app can use it to collect data from a mobile device, and he does so, gathering information concerning the phone, passwords, and text messages. He then uses all this to create a wider dossier on Fred, by utilizing social networks, logging on to the SharePoint site as Fred, and visiting the MySite space to get further social interactions and contacts. Now that this information has been gathered, the developer identifies that an important sales meeting concerning the company merger is in Fred's diary and his task list on his MySite space. The developer then instructs the phone to record that meeting so he can sell insider information concerning the deal to competitors—and Fred has no idea that any of this is happening.*

The scenario is not a prediction—it's simply a warning, but it's one you need to take seriously. You must set up policies to protect the integrity of company information, but they cannot be enforced unless users are made aware of the security implications in using mobile devices. Consider also that any risks concerning SharePoint data integrity through mobile device use are mitigated. Ensure that users know how to lock their mobile devices with passwords. Because mobile devices use apps, you must also ensure that users stick to official app distribution channels, check the app publisher's reputation, and check the privacy permissions that the app is asking for. Also, consider investing in mobile security and app software. For SharePoint 2013, use the App Management provision.

Although these instructions are not directly related to SharePoint, advising users of these simple steps will protect the integrity of content on SharePoint.

**More Info** For more information about SharePoint policies concerning apps, visit *http://technet.microsoft.com/en-us/library/fp161237.aspx.*

## Building the Statement of Operations

As described in the "Creating a Governance committee" section earlier in this chapter, a SharePoint Statement of Operations acts as the core information resource concerning the SharePoint platform and solution service provision. This document provides a basic outline of SharePoint in the organization, support responsibilities, key policies, escalation of SharePoint issues and outages, service availability, and the makeup of the service. It should be regularly updated, and it is a key output of the Governance committee.

This section will help you understand what makes up the Statement of Operations. You can build this document using the following information to ensure that you include everything that is required. You will also need the help of the Governance committee to modify and edit the Statement of Operations. Use the Governance committee meetings to examine and review the Statement of Operations, and ensure that any major changes are communicated to necessary parties.

The Statement of Operations includes the following:

- **SharePoint hosts on the production farm** Create a list of all the SharePoint hosts, including a description of the host objective and who the owner or owners of the host are.
- **SharePoint platforms** Create a list of the SharePoint platforms (for example, the test, user acceptance, and production platforms). The list should be divided into sections by type. For example, you might have a mixture of SharePoint 2013 and SharePoint 2010 platforms.
- **SharePoint solutions** Create a list of the key enterprise solutions, apps, and third-party products in the SharePoint environment. Each of these should have a one-line description explaining its purpose. This list should then link to more detailed information.
- **Support** Describe how the SharePoint platform is supported, including the location of FAQs and training material. Explain the levels of support available to SharePoint users, as well as a description of the support model (how SharePoint is maintained). For example, some organizations have their technical support teams split into three levels: first-line (people who first receive user calls, logs and escalates), second-line (those who deal with escalated issues and maintain SharePoint sites), and third-line (SharePoint administrators, the architects who maintain and design SharePoint in the organization).
- **Responsibilities** Describe who is responsible for technical site administration (typically, the SharePoint administrator), maintenance, and configuration. Describe who is responsible for business site administration (typically, site owners) and the escalation paths based on certain parts of SharePoint. Business administration specifies the different levels of SharePoint

permissions (Owner, Contributor, Reader, and so on) and who is responsible for what in a SharePoint site.

For example, sites could be configured in such a way as to disallow the creation, renaming, and deletion of team sites within subareas. This then compels that the business process to manage SharePoint sites be followed. Specific members could be granted rights to create sites within the site collections, but this would be managed by second-line support staff and coordinated from third-line design activities.

Another important point is data integrity and the ability to ensure that by defining responsibilities. Therefore, be aware of using Owner in SharePoint sites. Consider that people designated as SharePoint Site Owners are given Owner permissions because they are assumed to know how to set user permissions in a SharePoint team site and why the permissions are being set. This makes them fully responsible for managing the integrity of site content. Therefore, a policy could include that Site Owners set the permissions and approve access to a site. The help desk should never set the rights from a request unless it is absolutely necessary (for example, for a SharePoint site where there is no defined Site Owner manager).

- **Training** Summarize the SharePoint training model, including where users should get training from, how training is requested, and the scope of training provided (for example, contributor, owner, administrator training, and so on).
- **Policies** Management of SharePoint requires the creation of policies that educate users on best practices and following business rules. The Governance committee should draft these initially as documents, and then take the key statement of the relevant policy and inject that into the "Policies" section of the Statement of Operations. Policies allow users to see immediately which policies are in place and how to find out more information. The Governance committee should consider the following policies (not in any particular order):
    - General web policy and security awareness, which describes how the user will manage content securely and what areas of SharePoint are provisioned for secure content
    - Site creation policy, which describes the process by which sites are created and who owns sites (devolved business administration, for example)
    - Content management policy, which describes the style, whether Java, JQUERY, and other web technologies are allowed, and if so, to what extent
    - Publishing policy, which describes the process followed to mark specific content for publishing, describes the schedules and retention periods used, and so on
    - Personal information publication policy, which describes the kind of content that can be managed in personal locations, such as SkyDrive, and the responsibilities that users have to managing personal content
    - Version control policy, which describes what version control processes are in place and what kind of content is defined
    - Auditing policy, which describes the auditing process in place for sites, libraries, and lists

- Team site policy, which describes how team sites will be managed
- Image use policy, which describes what images are allowable on SharePoint sites, copyright management, requests for usage, personal photos on user My Sites, and so on
- Contact list use policy, which describes the kind of information required when storing contact information, applicable privacy policies, and so on
- Alert policy, which describes the use of notification in SharePoint and where alerting can and cannot be used
- Discussion board policy, which describes how discussion boards are to be mentored
- SharePoint site storage size (quota) policy, which describes the storage limits set for new sites, the levels of storage allowed for certain types of sites, the process for requesting quota changes, and so on
- Server hardening policy, which describes what web application authentication is used, what software is installed, the strength guidelines for passwords to service accounts, what network ports are available, what firewalls are in place, what backups are in place, how the server environment is physically secured, and so on
- SharePoint 2013 Branding and Design policy, which describes what design elements of a site can be altered and under what circumstances, what design elements cannot be altered, what logos can be used, and so on
- Data storage policy, which describes how the SharePoint content is stored, what storage devices are allowed by users (for example, USB sticks, portable hard drives), and whether organizational data can be stored on the devices
- Workflow Services policy, which describes the process used to create workflows for users following a sequenced set of events
- Search index policy, which describes what content is and is not searchable, search schedules, what constitutes prohibited search data, and so on
- Metadata and categorization policy, which describes metadata terms that are classified organizational, what content must have metadata set, the basic procedure for classifying content, who owns metadata classifications, and so on
- MySite content update policy, which describes the customizations applied to the My Site page, what security is enforced, and the Terms of Use policy applied
- Site information policy, which describes the compliance requirements with legal, governmental, or internal business processes, what areas of SharePoint have policies to track documents, who has access to documents, and how long documents can be retained
- Access Rights policy, which describes who is responsible for setting site permissions and what the procedure is for setting permissions
- Customization policy, which describes what constitutes SharePoint customization and the policy and rules under which customization could occur

**More Info** Further resources concerning other policies, plans, and documents can be found at *http://www.rharbridge.com/?page_id=726*.

Other areas are relevant to availability, what services are in use, how escalation will be dealt with and any other related documentation that supports the statement of operations. The following areas are covered:

- **Availability** Describe the operating times of the SharePoint environment. List planned outage periods when essential maintenance will occur.
- **Inputs** Describe the key services that SharePoint consumes and relies upon—for example, Active Directory, Exchange Server, SQL Services, Lync, Office, and so on—including the names of the owners of those connected technologies.
- **Escalation** Describe the procedures concerning escalation of SharePoint reported issues and who are part of the chain of escalation.
- **Key links** List links to key processes, procedures, and related documentation.

The Statement of Operations should be made available to all staff in the organization. It needs to be simple, secure, searchable, and scalable. Consider displaying the Statement of Operations as webpages in a central location, and use that as a mechanism to update and review going forward.

**Tip** The following quote is from an MSDN blog article concerning site quota management:

*Set quotas at a level that balances the need to manage storage with increasing numbers of support calls from site owners who are being told their site is out of space. Do the math in your organization by understanding the current and anticipated storage needs for sites and determining how many calls you want to get. Don't set your quota at the expected average site collection size, or you will get support calls for quota increases for half of your sites. Instead, set quota size toward the top end of the acceptable level of storage and consider how much the storage costs versus the support call or the cost of time involved in increasing the quota. Although storage has become very cheap, quotas will encourage users to be responsible with their data. If, for example, you anticipate having 1,000 site collections supporting team collaboration, and you anticipate that site collections will require between 100 MB and 600 MB of storage, evenly distributed across that 500 MB range, then by setting a quota of 550 MB, you can anticipate that 10 percent of the site collections will end up over quota. That means you can expect, over time, approximately 100 support calls requesting "exception" from the policy.*

**More Info** Quota Management is discussed further at *http://www.sharepointgeoff.com/how-do-you-manage-the-size-of-your-sharepoint-sites/*.

## Summary

In SharePoint, you can have Governance, or you can have chaos. If you are not prepared to have Governance in your SharePoint solution, do not start a SharePoint delivery program at all. Platform Governance allows you to ensure that you have resilient, available business roles and policy-driven SharePoint solutions and platforms.

The aims of SharePoint Platform Governance are as follows:

- Galvanize the people and the infrastructure to enforce business rules and policies continually.
- Provide a service model to support SharePoint environments.
- Communicate the need for the business to provide the ability to apply Governance to the areas of SharePoint that matter to the business.

So, be prepared to educate the user base and show the importance of SharePoint Governance. Be evangelistic when talking about the relevant procedures and policies. Set up awareness sessions and restate the reasons and benefits of implementing SharePoint 2013.

Don't be scared to meet all kinds of representatives from the business and describe how Governance can be implemented successfully. Provide encouragement and show appreciation. Some client environments will not have SharePoint Governance; in order for them to implement it, you will need their participation. Consider the client population, and create a program that continuously provides encouragement and support.

Maintaining a positive outlook is key. Having a more positive attitude when working with strategic and tactical teams will make a positive difference to users. Although good people are the foundation, it is also crucial that requirements and goals are adequately articulated, baselined, and understood by those working in Governance. Lack of will, unforeseen personal and corporate agendas, vague business rules, diffused objectives, and above all, poor communication are all contributing factors to Governance failure. Communication is a vital key. Great communication leads to reassuring Governance team members and users who embrace change through business rules and policies. This in turn fosters continued and proactive service delivery.

Technology is not the sole answer to Governance success. What is needed is a cohesive track to run on, and a checklist of tasks so that everything that must be done is done to a sufficient level. Several "fast solutions," including apps, the cloud, and mobility, are growing in popularity, but this will place significant pressure on the Governance committee as it tries to create or improve a Governance methodology. This is especially true if there were no fundamental principles of preparing, creating, and sustaining good Governance already in place.

CHAPTER 6

# SharePoint delivery program considerations

In this chapter:



Once a delivery program has been formed to deliver a Microsoft SharePoint solution, it is important to ensure that key areas concerning SharePoint delivery are understood. Change management is vital because understanding that will help you meet the solution objectives on time and on budget. Managing information and search strategies are the two most important facets of SharePoint, and they must be addressed, as they relate directly to User Adoption and Governance. If the solution needs to be delivered in multiple offices, you will need to understand the implications of using SharePoint in geographically split locations. Finally, you will need to understand what makes up a SharePoint platform deployment document that describes the SharePoint platform.

## Managing change in the SharePoint delivery program

Changes are inevitable facts of SharePoint delivery. However, SharePoint delivery programs will not go exactly as planned. Changes need to be managed so that you do not lose sight of the program's objectives and scope because if they are not managed effectively, you will lose control of the program. Managing change does not mean that you prevent changes from taking place; it means that you should allow only beneficial changes.

*Change,* in the context of a SharePoint delivery program, is any modification to the benefit, scope, time, or cost targets that have previously been approved. This means that there can be a change only if there is an approved standard, or *baseline.* The baseline is provided by the delivery plan, which defines the following:

- The program should state the basis of an investment or change. Delivery programs must demonstrate the return on investment (ROI) or value that the owning organization will achieve by the proposition in the delivery program. Delivery programs must demonstrate how the value or return will be delivered by identifying specific benefits that making the investment or change will bring.
- Scope of work and detail of each deliverable
- Delivery time scale and intermediate milestone dates
- Program cost

Change may result from a number of sources, including the following:

- Changes in business requirements driven by the SharePoint sponsor or other stakeholders
- Changes in the business environment (for example, economics, social factors, and the actions of competitors)
- Problems or opportunities that occur during the course of the program
- Modifications or enhancements identified by the delivery team
- Faults detected by the delivery team or the users. You need to understand how to manage change in the SharePoint delivery program. *Change management* is the process through which changes to a program (to cost, schedule, and/or the scope of benefits) are introduced and evaluated prior to their adoption or rejection. The following is a definition of change management from Wikipedia:

> *Change management is an approach to shifting/transitioning individuals, teams, and organizations from a current state to a desired future state. It is an organizational process aimed at helping change stakeholders to accept and embrace changes in their business environment or individuals in their personal lives. In some project management contexts, change management refers to a project management process wherein changes to a project are formally introduced and approved.*
>
> *Wikipedia (http://en.wikipedia.org/wiki/Change_management)*

**More Info** Another good article that discusses organizational change, process, plans, change management, and business development tips is located at *http://www.businessballs.com/changemanagement.htm.*

*Scope creep* is a phenomenon where a delivery program overruns its agreed time scale and budget due to many extra (often minor) "features" being added in an uncontrolled manner. To prevent this from happening, it is often advisable to bundle a number of small changes together and assess them as a whole, choosing to implement only those that further the program objectives. At the other end of the scale, it is wise to consider delaying the addition of a major change until after the program is completed and introduce it in a secondary phase. Remember, the primary aim of a SharePoint delivery program is to fulfill a stated business requirement. So long as this need is satisfied, fine-tuning, enhancing, or embellishing the outputs is a potential waste of resources.

Inevitably, a time will come when an issue will arise in the SharePoint delivery program that cannot be resolved while keeping the SharePoint delivery program viable. Either a time window will be missed, or costs will be so high that even a marginal cost analysis leads to the conclusion that the program is not worth continuing. In these cases, the impact assessment will recommend terminating the SharePoint delivery program. Such an outcome should be treated as a success, as there is little point in continuing with a SharePoint delivery program that is not viable in business terms.

*Scenario 1: Fabrikam, a manufacturing company with 20 offices around the world, needed to integrate stock records with functions for financial management and resource management. It was already using SharePoint and wanted to add features to enable external systems to integrate. Following detailed building of schedules, plans, and investigation of user requirements, the cost was predicted to be $800,000. However, due to continued changes, the program was stopped after it exceeded its original cost estimates by $500,000. The program, scheduled for implementation in 2007, did achieve partial deployment (12 out of 20 offices had the solution implemented), but rising costs resulted in a decision to cancel the delivery program in 2012. The plan involved the purchase of an add-on, which would then be modified to meet local requirements. Unfortunately, the gap between the local requirements and the functionality of the add-on required modifications that were much greater than envisioned. In the end, the add-on was largely rewritten, which resulted in the massive cost overruns. Similarly, because the design was not a clean sheet, the system as implemented was regarded as difficult to maintain. An audit of the delivery program found a lack of planning and criticized the project managers for failing to do sufficient analysis before making key strategic decisions. (With regard to the business case, the auditor was quoted as saying, "I would say it was more of a concept brief rather than a fully written business case."). Key failures included not developing a solid business case before making key strategic implementation decisions, poor planning, lack of governance and oversight, and attempting to modify a purchased software package beyond the point where it made financial sense.*

As a practical technique to identify whether changes will affect the SharePoint delivery program adversely, you should consider using a benefit, cost, and time model (such as the one shown in Figure 6-1). This will graphically show whether costs of the SharePoint delivery program have exceeded budget, whether the team has the ability to deliver, and/or whether the time to deliver has unduly affected viability.

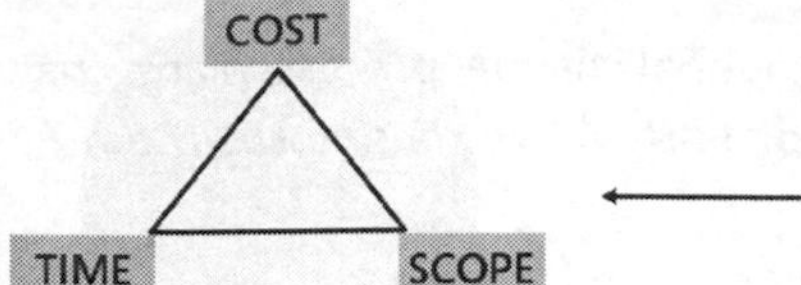


A SharePoint delivery program requires a balance between cost, time and objectives. Together, these should be within the bounds of viability for the program.

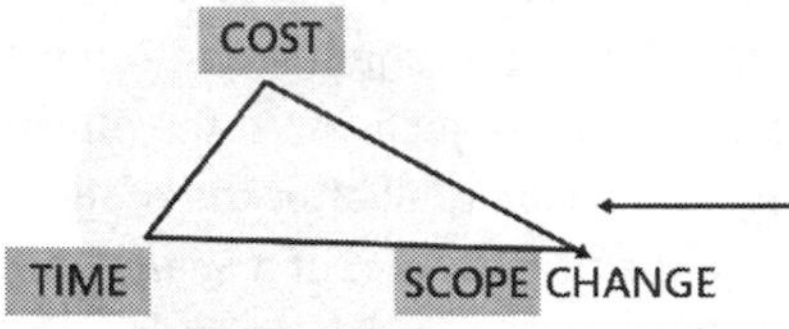


Any change will affect one or more time, cost or objectives and may take the SharePoint delivery program out of bounds of viability. The program must be brought back into balance and the viability checked. If the SharePoint delivery program is still outside the area of viability, the change should be rejected or the program terminated.

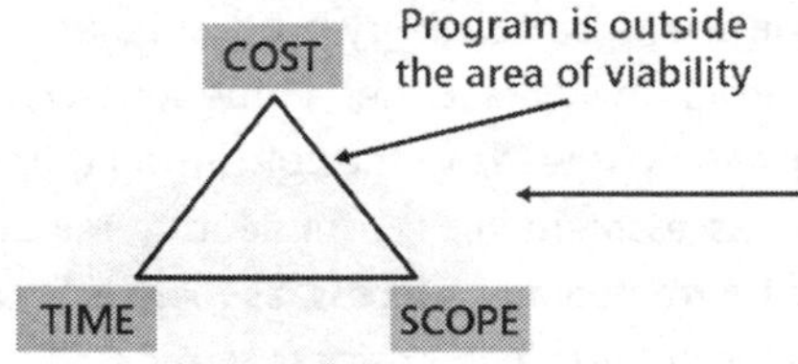


In this case, the bounds of viability has shrunk. The SharePoint delivery program must be changed to bring it back into viability. Alternatively, it should be terminated.

**FIGURE 6-1** Benefit versus cost, time, and scope.

Because of the potential that changes will reduce SharePoint delivery programs to chaos, it is preferable to adopt a formal approach to assessing and authorizing changes right from the start. Use these practical techniques to do this:

- Note the proposed change in a change log.
- Plan each change and assess its impact on the SharePoint delivery program and any interdependent programs.
- If it is within the delivery manager's authority, reject or accept the change proposal.
- If it is outside the delivery manager's authority, refer the decision (with a recommendation) to the SharePoint sponsor or to the appropriate level for a review and decision.

The change proposal may be:

- Accepted for immediate implementation
- Accepted, subject to certain conditions being met
- Accepted, but implementation is deferred to a later stage
- Rejected

Once the decision of what to do with the proposal has been made, the delivery manager should:

- Obtain further financial authorization (if needed)

- Record the outcome in the change log
- If the change was accepted, the delivery manager should do the following:
  - Implement the change
  - Update the delivery program documentation
  - Inform all interested parties about the change
- Inform the originator of the outcome and, if the change was rejected, give the reason.

You should use a change log to record changes in the SharePoint delivery program because this will serve as important historical information and can be used for audit purposes. In addition, this serves as an important resource when the program is being closed (where the business handover is carried and/or the program is terminated). A sample change log is given in Figure 6-2. Use this as a model to create your own change log in the SharePoint site where the delivery plan content is located. The delivery plan site is described in the "Building the SharePoint delivery plan" section in Chapter 3, "Planning SharePoint solution delivery."

| Ref No. | Description | Originator | Date Raised | Impact Assessment By Name | Approval By | Approved Yes/No | Date Approved | Date Authorized | Comments |
|---|---|---|---|---|---|---|---|---|---|
| 1 | Expand scope of tracking system to include all customers | | 06/03/2013 | | | Yes | 08/04/2013 | 08/05/2013 | No impact on time scale. Extra $12k cost required. Funded from contingency |
| 2 | Change process for communicating to customers | | 10/01/2013 | | | | | Not Required | Required as a result of legal and regulatory issues which were not taken into account at the start of the program. Extra $2k cost. Funded from Scope Reserve. |

**FIGURE 6-2** Example of a SharePoint delivery program change log.

For any given change, people can occupy a wide range of roles that will strongly influence their perceptions of the change and their reactions to it. These are roles such as champion, user, developer/builder, watchful observer, obstructionist, and others. As on the stage, some people may occasionally play more than one role. In other cases, the roles are unique. Unless we clearly identify both the players and their roles in any change situation, we risk making decisions and taking action based on generalizations that are not true for some of the key players.

As already discussed in this book up to this point, stakeholders have some interest or stake in the quality of both the change and the change implementation process. The role of the stakeholders is subject to change, especially during a change process that extends over time.

When you are going to implement change, the following steps are critical:

1. Identify what roles stakeholders are occupying in the process.
2. Identify what roles others involved in the process are playing, being careful to recognize when someone is playing multiple roles.
3. Monitor throughout the process whether any roles are changing.
4. Plan the change management process and ensure that the rest of your delivery team is aware of that process. An example of a change management process is shown in Figure 6-3.

**Tip** A Change Request Form is a useful and concise way of documenting changes. It comprises a description of the change with impact assessments. Use this as a connection to the change log.

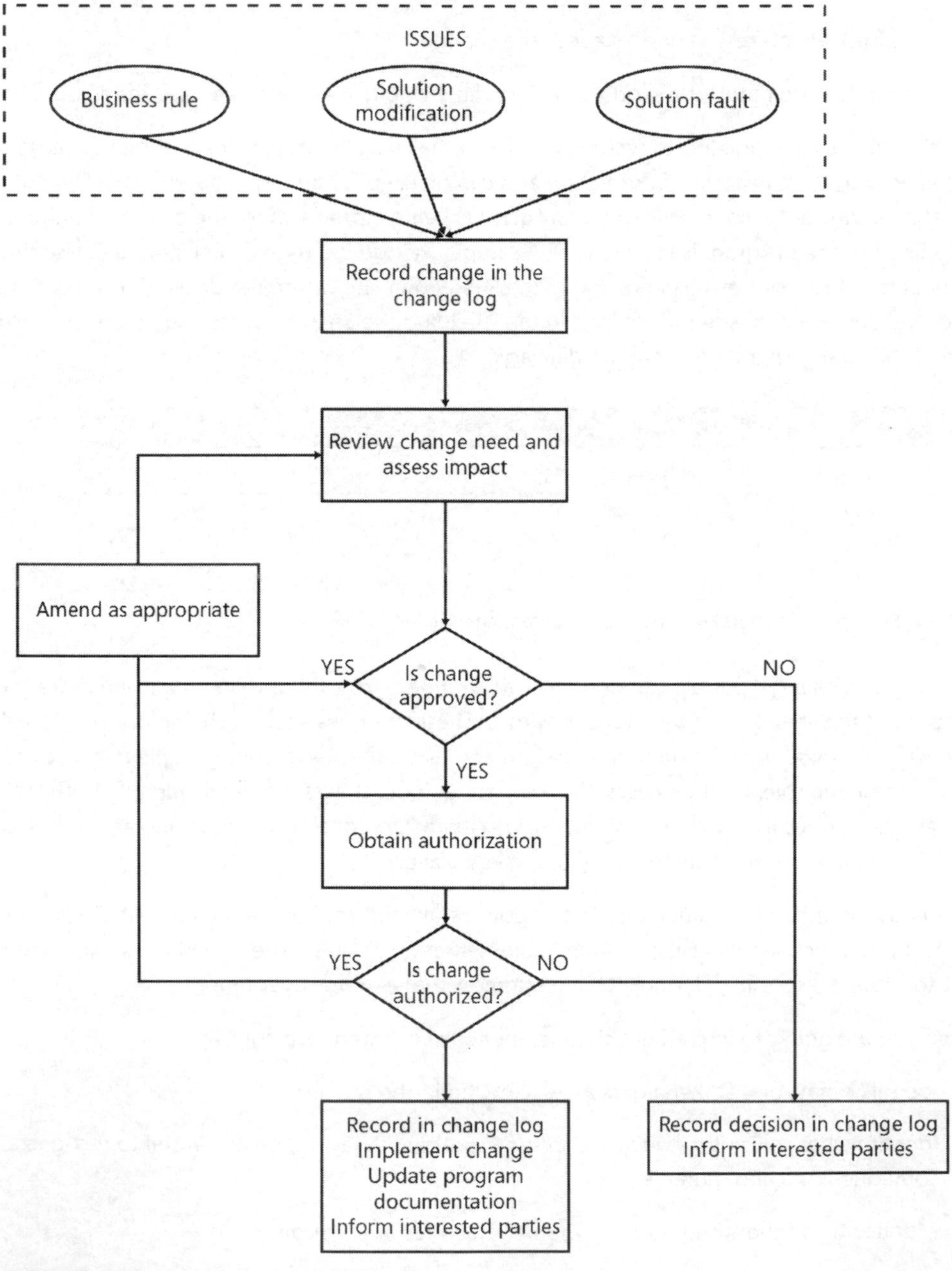

**FIGURE 6-3** A typical SharePoint delivery program change management process.

All proposed changes need to be reviewed and their impact assessed before they are implemented or rejected. A SharePoint delivery program may have several levels for the review and authorization of changes, depending on how serious or far-reaching the change will be. Table 6-1 suggests such levels.

**TABLE 6-1** Suggested levels for the SharePoint delivery program change management decisions

| Impact of Change | Approval Required By |
|---|---|
| No impact on overall scope, schedule, cost, or benefits | Delivery manager |
| Minor impact change affecting scope, schedule, costs, or benefits that can be accommodated without affecting other programs and projects | SharePoint sponsor or designated executive |
| Major impact change affecting scope, objectives, benefits, schedule, or costs that cannot be accommodated within the authority or tolerance delegated to the SharePoint sponsor, or that affects other programs | Designated executives |

Notice that the first two levels of authority lie within the program itself, as the impacts do not affect other programs. Once other programs are affected, it is necessary to have the change reviewed and authorized by designated executives, who can balance the conflicting needs of different programs and sponsors.

The impact levels should be defined and agreed upon when the program is authorized. Confirm this when building your sponsor and stakeholder list. See the "Engaging your sponsor and stakeholders" section in Chapter 3.

## Understanding the importance of information architecture

All SharePoint delivery programs relate to providing the ability for users to manage content online. This means that you will need to have an understanding of information architecture. *Information architecture* is the study of information, organizational structure, information flow, and process flow. Information architecture is important in the design of the solution to ensure that users actually use the solution know-how to navigate through it. Each page needs to have navigation that clearly shows users where they are and gives them a quick way to get to any other section. In addition, information architecture allows the organization to consider the content lifecycle (creation, storage, workflow, retention, and archiving of content). Information architecture requires skill and is best delivered using content strategists, coordinated by the delivery program, and fed back to the solution architect. (These roles are described in more detail in Chapter 7, "Organizing SharePoint delivery resources.")

As previously mentioned, building information architecture requires resources. Most large organizations have documentation plans and methods of managing their data across the organization, such as content retention, archive plans, and other elements. They also tend to have information analysts to manage and coordinate that work. Small and mid-sized organizations generally do not have those resources. Regardless of its size, every organization must meet certain legal and regulatory compliance requirements relating directly to how data is retained over the long term. One example of such a regulation is the Sarbanes-Oxley (SOX) Act of 2002, which established records management and retention requirements. Sections 302, 304, and 409 of this law have the greatest impact in terms of ongoing obligations. Therefore, companies that need to retain content must have a records retention policy that complies with regional and national guidelines.

**Note** If you have a policy that adheres to both regional and national retention policies under SOX (for example), you are only liable to retain the information stipulated within those guidelines, and that information is all that may be used in a lawsuit. So you don't need to worry about trying to save every piece of data. Another plus of having regulations about record retention is a decrease in the overhead cost of storage because you will not be storing superfluous materials. Building a data retention process requires knowledge of information architecture. Understanding information architecture allows you to interpret the distinctions and categorization of information into a coherent structure. Information architecture concerns itself with setting control and compliance to information so that it does not create unmanaged data chaos.

SharePoint 2013 provides Enterprise Content Management tools that can help lower cost, decrease complexity, and increase user participation relating to content control. SharePoint 2013, combined with Microsoft Office 2013, takes this to a greater level by extending information control from the desktop environment to SharePoint 2013 sites and content.

Your aim in applying information architecture to the SharePoint solution being delivered is to reduce the manual user actions in setting metadata, to scale policies and processes across all types of content in an organization, and to increase compliance and transparency. You will need an understanding of the content lifecycle, which covers how users create, store, retain, process, and archive content. SharePoint 2013 provides tools to ensure that the content lifecycle can be designed and adhered to, by providing features such as Content Types, Document Sets, Information Management Policies, Metadata, Term Sets, and Content Organizers.

To set out the information architecture required, follow these practical techniques:

- Carry out an investigation and inventory of existing content.
- Classify the content.
- Look for definitions in structure, policy, and defaults.
- Identify organizational-level content by enterprise, department, and team.
- Define what is "general-use" content.
- Organize content into enterprise content types and document sets, as follows:
  - Content types are where there are definitions of structure, policy, and defaults.
  - Content types can inherit from other content types.
  - Document sets can be used to store collections of documents that are from the same project or work product.

Decide where information management policies apply.

- Consider access permissions, auditing, user restrictions (that is, not being allowed to print), retention, and deletion.
- Decide on applicable metadata.
- Define customized columns and associate them with documents and lists.
- Define any cases where the system or user may take different actions based on the characteristics of an item—the characteristics of the item are metadata.
- Find out what common things users will want to sort or filter items on.
- Find out what words or phrases that users are likely to tag items with.
- Use Choice and/or Lookup columns in SharePoint 2013 sites.
- Use the existing taxonomy, or create a taxonomy.
- Map the physical flow of the document.
- Decide where the content will be physically located throughout the lifecycle (that is, what lists, libraries, and sites will be involved).

**Tip** SharePoint 2013 architecture is a massive topic, and this chapter covers only the basics. I suggest that you learn as much as you can about information architecture because addressing it well leads to a successful SharePoint 2013 platform. To get a general perspective concerning planning and architecture, visit *http://technet.microsoft.com/en-us/library/cc262873.aspx*. (Even though this article is for SharePoint 2010, it is still applicable for SharePoint 2013.)

Site maps are a widely used information architecture tool. They show the overall structure and hierarchy of a website. To build a site map, lay out the information architecture and then provide the framework upon which to base the site navigation. The site map can then be reviewed by stakeholders to determine whether the structure of the site meets their requirements. Figure 6-4 shows a sample site map for a website, which includes the design elements for the site and navigation.

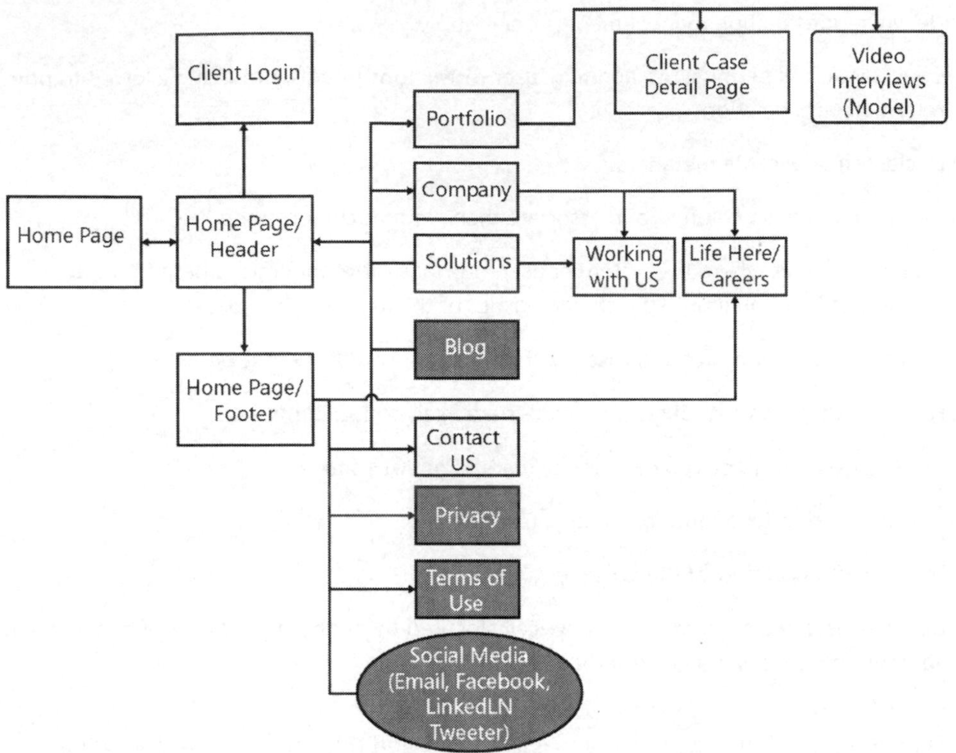


**FIGURE 6-4** A sample site map showing the structure of a website.

## Building your search strategy

These days, your users are aware of the many search engines available on the Internet, and they understand intuitively how to use these engines to find what they need. However, that experience often leads them to believe that Internet search (via Bing or Google, for example) is better than the Enterprise Search offered by SharePoint.

To put this into context, an Internet search engine derives its relevance from millions of people carrying out millions of searches. For example, I am a fan of Ridley Scott movies. So, when I use an Internet search engine to find out the actors and multiple versions of the movie *Blade Runner*, the people responsible for monitoring relevance for that Internet search engine would identify the following:

- What terms were used when searching for information about the film *Blade Runner*?
- What links were clicked?
- What is the metadata that builds up the searches pointing to the actor Harrison Ford in terms of how many versions of *Blade Runner* are available?

The answers to these questions produce a huge amount of information that can be used to improve Internet search engine relevance, because millions of people make Internet searches for *Blade Runner.* However, there are not millions of people in an organization. That makes determining the relevance of content to the organization that much more complex, particularly because resources to create relevance and metadata information are also at a premium. Organizations generally do not have teams focused on locating information and making it easy to access. And, if there is no Governance surrounding the classification of content, that makes the issue still more difficult. Understanding the importance of search is about as important as understanding the content itself (information architecture). However, many organizations see this as an afterthought.

Use the following checklist to build a good search strategy:

- **Provide focused results.** This means ensuring that a lot of thought and care is put into building good information architecture with good metadata. Train users to classify their content and understand the high-level principles that allow them to manage their content.
- **Explain the resources required.** If someone mentions to you that Google search is fantastic and wants the Google Search add-on to be applied to Enterprise Search, make sure to advise them of the extra resources required to deploy, test, and then support that feature going forward (including all the configuration management challenges). Remember that Google and Bing have significant people working with them, whose focus is to manage the search systems. There is no "best search system"—what makes a search system good is when the data has been optimized for search by being fully classified and categorized.
- **Ascertain the value of adding external search sources to SharePoint Search.** Consider this scenario: *Fabrikam wants to employ a product that will automatically scan documents and harvest that information in a database. It wants that database to be exposed to SharePoint search.* This means more resources in terms of people to support the product, a review of the UI in SharePoint, and additional costs. Work should be carried out to compare the value of doing that instead of classifying the content within SharePoint at the user level.
- **Keep content up to date.** If a user is locating information, the relevance of that information is critical. If the information is out of date, the user may have to navigate several pages to get the right information.
- **Limit the SharePoint delivery scope concerning search.** Identify what needs to be indexed (for example, SharePoint content, file shares, and/or external back-end Microsoft SQL Server databases). Doing this allows you to concentrate on primary areas of search and provide proper adoption channels to the users.
- **Use SharePoint tagging.** Allow users to tag their content. This enriches SharePoint search because the relevance of information is defined by both the users and the organizational metadata.
- **Ratify the content.** Check that content properties have been set. For example, if a Microsoft Word template has the original person who created the template as the author and is not

updated when the document is saved, that incorrect information will not help you determine who the real author is.

- **Continually monitor, tune, and measure the state of the SharePoint search technology.** Once your search system is operational, you must continually check that it is functioning and proactively look at methods to improve it (for example, send surveys to users to get their input).
- **Survey search usage.** Craft a survey asking users for their ideas on what would make a good search experience. Use SharePoint audit features to identify and monitor search requests and the results.

To provide a search strategy requires resources, an investment in people (content strategists and information architects), and an investment in content management (training of users and adoption). Ensure that SharePoint search is addressed before it gets fully and continually deployed, since User Adoption will be lost if individuals are unable to find information.

**More Info** For more information concerning planning a search system, visit *http://technet.microsoft.com/en-us/library/cc263400.aspx*. To find out about best practices in organizing SharePoint content and applying useful metadata read the article located at *http://technet.microsoft.com/en-us/library/jj683124.aspx*.

## Understanding geographical boundary implications

SharePoint 2013 includes collaborative tools that can help people stay connected across multiple organizational and geographic boundaries. This section describes how SharePoint should be provided when multiple locations are involved, which can change the way SharePoint solutions should be implemented. From a technical perspective, network connectivity in terms of bandwidth is important too. However, bandwidth is not the only variable determining which deployment solution to choose. The recommendations in this section are based on the following organizational scenarios:

- Government solution supporting multiple independent agencies
- Traveling workgroups (such as military units, cruise lines, dispatched research teams, oil drilling platforms, and so on)
- Central site supporting many branch offices
- Adoption of additional SharePoint solutions through company mergers or acquisitions

To help you understand how geographical locations affect SharePoint user actions, I will describe three different solutions that are based on how those actions will travel over a wide area network (WAN) to each regional location:

- All of the regional SharePoint 2013 user actions travel over the WAN.
- Most of the regional SharePoint 2013 user actions are local to the regional SharePoint 2013 server farm. Less than 20 percent of the SharePoint 2013 user actions travel over the WAN. These actions are related to using the enterprise-wide site hosted at the central site.
- Very little of the regional SharePoint 2013 user actions travel over the WAN. Because a regional site is hosted locally, less than 3 percent of the SharePoint 2013 user actions travel over the WAN.

From these descriptions, you can understand the implications of providing SharePoint for each of those solutions, as shown in Table 6-2. (Note that for brevity, I have not included the names of all the service applications that are provided with SharePoint 2013.)

**TABLE 6-2** Implications of SharePoint provision in geographical locations

| Solution | Central Site Hosts for Regional Site | Regional Site Hosts |
|---|---|---|
| Central SharePoint farm:<br>■ All SharePoint 2013 components and site farm services are hosted at the central site.<br>■ Users access all services across the WAN. | ■ Server farm running SharePoint 2013<br>■ Core Services<br>■ Crawling<br>■ Search (including scopes)<br>■ My Sites (SkyDrive and public views)<br>■ Alerts<br>■ Profiles<br>■ Audiences<br>■ SharePoint 2013 sites (team sites) | Nothing |
| Central SharePoint farm with regional team sites:<br>■ SharePoint 2013 sites are hosted at the regional site by a regional server farm. All SharePoint 2013 services are hosted at the central site.<br>■ Users collaborate with their local teams on the local SharePoint 2013 server farm.<br>■ Users access all central SharePoint 2013 service features across the WAN. | ■ Server farm running SharePoint 2013<br>■ Core Services<br>■ Crawling<br>■ Search (including scopes)<br>■ My Sites (personal and public views)<br>■ Alerts<br>■ Profiles<br>■ Audiences | Server farm for SharePoint 2013 sites (team sites) |
| Central SharePoint farm and regional SharePoint farm:<br>■ The regional site hosts its own SharePoint 2013 components and site and farm services. | Enterprise-wide search | ■ Server farm running SharePoint 2013<br>■ Core Services<br>■ Crawling<br>■ Search (including scopes)<br>■ My Sites (personal and public views)<br>■ Alerts<br>■ Profiles<br>■ Audiences<br>■ SharePoint 2013 sites (team sites)<br>■ Search scoped to the regional farm. |

Table 6-2 will help you determine the number of instances of SharePoint that would have to be implemented based on the three solutions. In addition, you can indicate the support requirements. For example, if there is a central SharePoint farm and one or more regional sites with SharePoint farms, that leads to an increase in support arrangements (particularly if the sites and the farm are in different time zones). Also, if there are multiple regional offices, but one SharePoint farm to support them all, that would require a clear investigation into disaster recovery and business continuity measures.

Now that you understand the implications of providing SharePoint for those three solutions, further investigation will reveal the positives and negatives of each approach. This will provide you with a measurement that you can then discuss further with SharePoint sponsors and stakeholders. To provide detail for each of the three solutions, you can use a table such as Table 6-3 to break down the solution against key areas of concern and offer suggestions.

**TABLE 6-3** Detailed analysis of SharePoint 2013 provision in geographical locations

| **Item** | **Solution 1: Central** | **Solution 2: Central SharePoint Farm with Regional Team Sites** | **Solution 3: Central SharePoint Farm and Regional SharePoint Farm** |
|---|---|---|---|
| Overall recommendations | This is the preferred solution if the available network bandwidth across the WAN provides a satisfactory experience for regional users. The advantages of this solution include:<br>■ No redundant hardware or services<br>■ Lowest level of overall administration<br>■ Consistent experience for regional users (search, My Sites, alerts, and profiles) | If the available network bandwidth does not provide a satisfactory experience for regional users, consider using this solution for the following types of usage:<br>■ Collaboration of teams within the regional site is mostly limited to the regional site. This solution is not intended for teams that collaborate across both the central and regional sites.<br>■ The use of centrally hosted services (search, My Sites, alerts, and profiles) is infrequent in comparison to the use of team sites. | Use this solution only if the available network bandwidth does not support the use of site services and features over the WAN or if the user experience is unacceptable for most SharePoint site use.<br>This solution does not provide collaboration for teams working across geographical sites. However, it greatly increases the performance of collaboration within the regional site. |
| Administration | Administration is centralized because all server hardware and server farm services are hosted at the central site. Administration includes ensuring that user-generated SharePoint 2013 traffic can enter and leave the regional site network securely. | Requires regional management of the server farm for SharePoint 2013 sites, including the following:<br>■ Hardware for the server farm<br>■ Hosting and management of databases<br>■ Security of the server farm and services<br>■ Back up and restore | Requires the greatest amount of administration because hardware and site services are duplicated at both the central and the regional sites. |

| Item | Solution 1: Central | Solution 2: Central SharePoint Farm with Regional Team Sites | Solution 3: Central SharePoint Farm and Regional SharePoint Farm |
|---|---|---|---|
| WAN bandwidth | All content must be transferred over the WAN. The user experience depends on the available bandwidth.<br>However, all SharePoint 2013 bandwidth usage is generated by the regional users. The central server farm search services do not crawl data at the regional site, greatly reducing bandwidth requirements. | ■ Collaborative operations most important to the regional user (such as document/ list management, SharePoint 2013 search capability provided by SQL Server full-text search) are performed on the regional network, not transferred over the WAN.<br>■ Content stored in My Sites with SkyDrive Pro synchronization features is transferred over the WAN.<br>■ If the region is included in enterprise-wide search, the central site search service uses a significant amount of network bandwidth to crawl the regional team sites. The search can consume all network resources on the WAN link when in operation over that link. | ■ Because all site services are hosted locally, this solution is not subject to the results of bandwidth limitations over the WAN.<br>■ However, the regional site can choose to use and be included in enterprise-wide search provided by the central site.<br>■ If the regional site chooses to use enterprise-wide search services, network bandwidth across the WAN is required to send and receive results to search queries and to download content associated with search queries.<br>■ In addition, if the regional site chooses to be included in enterprise-wide search scopes, the central site search service uses a significant amount bandwidth to crawl the regional content. The search can consume all network resources on the WAN link when in operation over that link. |
| Capacity planning | The greatest consideration when planning for capacity at the central site is the available network bandwidth to the regional site. | Capacity of the regional server farm for SharePoint 2013 can be calculated by using the standard SharePoint 2013 capacity planning guidelines. Accommodating user capacity for services hosted by the central site is identical to the central site scenario (Solution 1), but with fewer services being consumed over the WAN. | Capacity of the regional site server farm can be calculated by using the standard SharePoint 2013 capacity planning guidelines. |

| Item | Solution 1: Central | Solution 2: Central SharePoint Farm with Regional Team Sites | Solution 3: Central SharePoint Farm and Regional SharePoint Farm |
|---|---|---|---|
| Search | Search is hosted entirely by the central site. The central site provides enterprise-wide search and can also provide additional search scopes to the regional site based on the regional site's needs. | ■ SQL Server full-text search of documents, lists, and other local site content is performed locally.<br>■ All site search features are hosted by the central site. Regional users experience a slower response to site search queries.<br>■ The regional site can choose whether to be included in site search scopes. If included, the central search service requires bandwidth to the regional site to crawl the regional data. The amount of time required to crawl the content depends on the volume of content and the available bandwidth. | The regional site can potentially configure the use of any (or none) of the following search options:<br>■ Regional search hosted by the regional server farm running SharePoint 2013.<br>■ Enterprise-wide search hosted by the central site. This can be configured to include or omit content from the regional farm. If the enterprise-wide search includes content from the regional farm, WAN bandwidth is used to crawl the regional farm content.<br>■ Regional search scopes hosted by the central site (requires network bandwidth to crawl the regional content). |
| Crawling (content sources) | Add content sources as necessary. You should be aware of the effect on relevance when adding indexes. | Add a content source for each region. | Add a content source for each region. |
| Personal sites (My Site) | All personal sites are hosted on the central site. This does the following:<br>■ Ensures that users have only one My Site location<br>■ Simplifies navigation<br>■ Reduces the administrative overhead of hosting SkyDrive synchronization | Storing personal content on the Central SharePoint Farm and collaborative content on the regional team site results in an inconsistent user experience. | Users can create multiple personal sites depending on which site they are using. This results in an inconsistent regional user experience. To avoid duplication, you can configure security and scripting to redirect regional users automatically to their regional personal site. |

| Item | Solution 1: Central | Solution 2: Central SharePoint Farm with Regional Team Sites | Solution 3: Central SharePoint Farm and Regional SharePoint Farm |
|---|---|---|---|
| Globalization | This solution supports only one language for the server farm. | If you choose, you can configure the regional site to host a different language from the central site.<br>Example:<br>■ Central site is English.<br>■ Regional sites use local languages.<br>■ The central site can crawl all supported languages. | Each site can host a different language. Consequently, a regional site can host a different language from the central site. This deployment solution provides the most extensive support for multiple languages across geographic sites.<br>Example:<br>■ Central site portal uses English.<br>■ Regional site portal and team sites use the local languages.<br>■ The crawler at either the central site or the regional site can crawl all supported languages. |
| User profiles | User profiles are managed at the central site only. | User profiles are managed at the central site only. | User profiles are stored at the central level and at the regional level. Profile information does not synchronize automatically between the central and regional SharePoint farms or between multiple regional SharePoint farms. |
| Alerts | All user-created alerts are displayed in the My Alerts Web Part, in addition to being sent through email. | ■ Alerts created in the central site are displayed in the My Alerts Web Part, in addition to being sent through email.<br>■ Alerts created in the SharePoint 2013 regional sites are only received through email. These do not appear in the central site My Alerts Web Part. | ■ Alerts appear in the My Alerts Web Part on the personal site in the site in which the alert was created. There is no central location for all alerts on all sites, but alerts still work properly through email.<br>■ Regional users with personal sites located only in the regional SharePoint farm can view only alerts created in that regional site in their My Alerts Web Part. They receive alerts from all other sites through email. |

| Item | Solution 1: Central | Solution 2: Central SharePoint Farm with Regional Team Sites | Solution 3: Central SharePoint Farm and Regional SharePoint Farm |
|---|---|---|---|
| Backup and restore | All site and SharePoint 2013 site-level backup and restore procedures are completed at the central site. | ■ Backup and restore procedures for SharePoint 2013 sites must be completed at the regional site.<br>■ Performing backup and restore procedures across the WAN is not recommended. | ■ Backup and restore procedures for the site and the SharePoint 2013 sites must be completed at the regional site.<br>■ Performing backup and restore procedures across the WAN is not recommended. |

If you create a table like Table 6-3, you will be able to make decisions based on the risks outlined, as well as identifying the resources to provide the service to geographical locations (languages, backup, administration, and so on). Those are mostly technical. Now, a look at the business requirements based on the kind of scenarios related to the technical provision. You would construct another table like Table 6-4, which shows the three SharePoint provision scenarios again, and then for each, the organizational scenarios described at the start of this section.

**TABLE 6-4** SharePoint delivery provision showing types of organizational scenarios

| Item | Solution 1: Central | Solution 2: Central SharePoint Farm with Regional Team Sites | Solution 3: Central SharePoint Farm and Regional SharePoint Farm |
|---|---|---|---|
| State government supporting multiple independent state agencies | This is the recommended choice. This option works well for the following:<br>■ Agencies that do not want to host their own SharePoint sites<br>■ Agencies that are well connected by network links<br>*Note:* For agencies that require physical isolation of sensitive data, the central site can host a separate server farm running SharePoint 2013, or it could provide a separate and secure web application. | This option requires SharePoint support staff at the agency site to deploy and operate the server farm running SharePoint 2013. Consider this option for:<br>■ Agencies that insist on hosting their own data and have SharePoint support staff on hand<br>■ Agencies that are not well connected by network links | This option allows agencies to host their own site solution while providing the option to participate in enterprise-wide search. Consider this option for:<br>■ Agencies that require separate and partitioned search solutions and profile management to protect sensitive data<br>■ Agencies willing to take on the administrative responsibility of deploying and hosting their own site solutions<br>■ Agencies not well connected by network links but that require a well-performing site solution |

| Item | Solution 1: Central | Solution 2: Central SharePoint Farm with Regional Team Sites | Solution 3: Central SharePoint Farm and Regional SharePoint Farm |
|---|---|---|---|
| Traveling or dispatched workgroups (such as military units, cruise lines, dispatched research teams, or oil platforms not connected to a WAN) | Use this option only for either of the following situations:<br>■ Traveling workgroups can establish a reasonable connection to the central site (1–10 Mbps or greater).<br>■ Traveling workgroups do not require access to the central site while away from the corporate LAN. | This option works well for traveling workgroups that meet the following criteria:<br>■ Server hardware travels with the workgroup.<br>■ Traveling workgroups use mostly the SharePoint 2013 sites (rather than the central site).<br>■ The workgroup includes a team member who can maintain and operate the server farm running SharePoint 2013. | Consider this option only for large traveling workgroups that require a full site solution while traveling or dispatched. |
| Central site supporting many branch offices | This is the recommended choice. The investment in network bandwidth to support this solution outweighs the costs of hosting parts of the SharePoint 2013 solution at multiple branch offices for most organizations. | Consider this option if:<br>■ Branch offices are not well connected.<br>■ Content hosted by a branch office does not need to be available to other sites. | Not recommended. |
| Supporting sites with different language requirements | Not supported | This will result in a dual language experience for users at the regional site:<br>■ Content in the regional SharePoint 2013 sites appears in the regional language.<br>■ Content in the central site appears in the central site language.<br>This solution provides the least amount of administrative effort. Choose this option if users at the regional site primarily use the sites hosted in their own language and can tolerate an enterprise-wide site experience in a different language. | Use this option if the regional site requires a dedicated site experience in a regional language. |

| Item | Solution 1: Central | Solution 2: Central SharePoint Farm with Regional Team Sites | Solution 3: Central SharePoint Farm and Regional SharePoint Farm |
|---|---|---|---|
| Adoption of additional SharePoint 2013 solutions through mergers or acquisitions | Move to this solution as the final stage of migrating the merged or acquired unit to the central site, as follows:<br>■ Migrate the SharePoint 2013 sites and any remaining site content to the central site.<br>■ Configure crawling and search scopes at the central site to accommodate business requirements at the acquired site. | Use this option as the first or second stage in centralizing the SharePoint 2013 solution:<br>■ Provide the acquired site access to the central site and enterprise-wide search capabilities.<br>■ Maintain the SharePoint 2013 sites at the acquired site.<br>■ Migrate the site solution hosted at the acquired site to the central site. Or, simply remove the site at the acquired site if there is no loss of required functionality.<br>■ If you choose, crawl the content at the acquired site to include this content in enterprise-wide search scopes. | Use this option as a first stage in centralizing the SharePoint 2013 solution as follows:<br>■ Provide the acquired or merged site access to the central site and enterprise-wide search capabilities.<br>■ If you choose, crawl the content at the acquired or merged site to include this content in enterprise-wide search scopes. |

The key aspect of this section is to ensure that you have an understanding of the implications involved in providing a SharePoint platform in different geographical locations. In fact, even if you are going to provision a solution into a SharePoint farm with many geographical locations, this section will also give answers concerning how that solution will be used in multiple locations. For example, if the SharePoint farm was provisioned as a central farm in the organization's headquarters and then as a SharePoint farm for each geographical location, this not only increases the complexity of not just the delivery program, but configuration management and change management issues will surface as well. For example, the solution would have to be delivered to multiple locations, and if those locations are in different time zones, with their own support teams, that aspect has to be managed as part of the delivery team's responsibilities.

## Understanding why you need platform deployment documentation

In order to understand the capability of the SharePoint platform, and to aid your Governance committee so that they are clear on the premise of the SharePoint platform, you must create *platform deployment documentation* of the SharePoint platform. One of the reasons why a SharePoint platform fails to evolve is a lack of information concerning how the platform was built. Naturally in those situations, people would be overly cautious about modifying a platform that they do not understand. And deployment documentation is extremely important to providing a sufficient level of knowledge and capability in managing the platform. The deployment document is a working document used for any kind of SharePoint solution during the lifetime of the platform. The solution being delivered may be a SharePoint 2013 platform. Alternatively, the solution may be a product that is going to expand the capabilities of the platform. Either way, you must ensure that deployment documentation is available concerning the platform for the following reasons:

- Interfacing teams, such as your SQL Server team, Networking team, Active Directory team, and Exchange team may need access to infrastructure information.
- Your SharePoint support team uses this documentation as part of training and building their knowledge. User Adoption does not work without SharePoint support, and if SharePoint support is not available due to lack of documentation about the platform, then User Adoption of that platform will be poor to nonexistent.
- The deployment document directly relates to the original SharePoint delivery plan. It is required in order to complete the build section of the delivery plan.
- When requiring aid from external parties, you will need to provide information about your SharePoint deployment.
- When engaging future programs concerning the SharePoint 2013 platform, you will need to provide information about your SharePoint deployment.
- This specification should produce a clear, complete, and unambiguous set of documentation that describes the intended solution in terms of its function, performance, interfaces, and design constraints. This section will help you understand the purpose and how to build a SharePoint deployment document.

The key benefit that follows from the development of deployment documentation is the improved visibility and a better understanding of the technical aspects of the solution from the users to the interfacing support teams and the delivery team. Note that the deployment documentation is not restricted to SharePoint platforms. For example, delivering a SharePoint 2013 platform to an organization may be part of a program whose delivery is a complete technology refresh, which means that the organization may require not just SharePoint 2013, but also wishes to upgrade the client tools from Office 2010 to Office 2013 and include associated tools like Microsoft Lync 2013 (which is an extremely useful tool that allows messaging and shows presence information within SharePoint 2013). The requirement to include information about these products as part of the deployment document is particularly important in the case of Office 365, of which SharePoint is one element.

The deployment documentation must be laid out in a format that can be understood not just by the technical team, but also the client and anyone in the business concerned with the SharePoint 2013 platform. The format given next helps you to create several sections of documentation, each with specific details, which allows you to expand the sections easily without having to work on the complete document. There are other resources that you will need to help you record the configuration of the platform, relating to topics such as Backup, Managed Metadata, Upgrade, Records Management, Service Deployment, and so on.

**Tip** You should use planning worksheets so that you can consistently record information that you gather and decisions; doing this will help you build your deployment documentation. Such worksheets are available for download from *http://www.sharepointgeoff.com/planning-worksheets*. Download and complete the worksheets and then list them in the deployment document for the SharePoint platform. As you work, make sure that you reference the related SharePoint delivery plan so that people will see what the top-level requirement was. This is a helpful guide for your Governance committee, allowing them to be aware what program the platform relates to and therefore what business rules and policies should be applied. Also, the deployment document is useful when there are multiple SharePoint environments that have been created to meet specific requirements.

The "Building the platform deployment document" section, later in this chapter, describes what is required in the document. First, I will need to describe some concepts concerning SharePoint server infrastructure, topology, and migration considerations.

## Understanding the key SharePoint 2013 concepts

In a SharePoint farm, servers have roles such as Web, Query, Index, Calculation, Application, and Database. Farms have relationships such as Authoring, Publishing, Development, Test, Staging, and Production, as well as service applications covering Search, Profile, Microsoft Access, Business Data Catalog, Microsoft Excel, Managed Metadata, Secure Store, Usage/Health, and Microsoft Visio. In a SharePoint farm, SharePoint includes Servers, Web Applications, Databases, Site Collections, Sites, Lists, and Items (which appear in that order in the hierarchy).

**Tip** You should use as an example the topology design principle for SharePoint 2013, which is available from an article at *http://www.sharepointgeoff.com/topologies-for-sharepoint-2013-diagrams-available/*.

SharePoint 2013 can be deployed to a single server or many servers forming a SharePoint farm. There are three roles: Web Server, Application Server, and Database Server. In a small farm, these roles can be combined onto one or more servers. This is done to achieve redundancy, performance, and service resilience. For example, the organization may require that the SharePoint 2013 production environment has a high uptime (meaning that users are not immediately disrupted from loss of access to a SharePoint farm) and that the SharePoint farm needs to be robust. One method of achieving this is to add an additional Web Server and have both servers *load-balanced* so that they balance the requests between them and improve the response and reaction time on SharePoint. Adding other Web Servers increases robustness and resilience and reduces outages. If there is a situation where one of the Web Servers is not available, the other Web Server will take the load.

The Web Server provides the web interfaces for the users, hosting webpages, web services, and Web Parts that are used to process requests served by the farm. The Web Server is required for farms that include other SharePoint 2013 capabilities. In dedicated search service farms, this role is not required because Web Front End (WFE) servers at remote farms contact query servers directly. In small farms, this role can be shared with the Query role, which is a server role that responds to user search requests. The Query role can be placed on its own servers, and there is no hard limit to the number of servers in a SharePoint farm.

The Application Server is associated with services that can be deployed to a physical computer. Each service represents a separate application service that can reside on a dedicated application server, if required. Services with similar performance and usage properties are able to be grouped on a server, and then scaled out onto multiple services.

Client-related services can be combined into a service group. These service groups can be set dependent on the types and the level of SharePoint farms provided. For example, Query and Crawl are search roles and are cross-farm, meaning their services can be shared by another SharePoint 2013 farm. Others include User Profile, BDC, Web Analytics, Managed Metadata, and Secure Store. Services that are client-related are single-farm, meaning their services can only be used in one SharePoint farm. For example, Excel Calculation, Access, Word, PowerPoint, Visio, and Word services are single-farm client services; others include Usage and Health, Performance Point, State, and Foundation Subscription.

**Tip** After deployment, look for services that consume a lot of resources and consider placing these services on dedicated hardware.

The Database Server is where all SharePoint service and user-related content gets stored. Search, Content, and Service databases are located on the Database Server. Search databases could include Search Admin, Property, and Crawl; depending on the size of the farm, there could be more of these. The Content databases cover all SharePoint user content related to the site collections. There can be multiple Content databases, depending on the volume of the content and sizing goals for the environment. The Service databases include Access Services, App Management, Application Discovery and Load Balancer, Business Data Connectivity, Excel Services Web, Machine Translation, Managed Metadata, PerformancePoint, Search, Secure Store, Security Token, User Profile, Visio Graphics, Word Automation, Work Management, and Usage and Health Data Collection, including the Subscription Settings databases.

## Topology

SharePoint 2013 can start from a single-server environment and then expand to multiserver farms depending on requirements. Table 6-5 shows topologies that can be defined, as well as descriptions as to why you might want to use them.

**TABLE 6-5** SharePoint 2013 deployment types and descriptions

| Deployment | Basic Description |
|---|---|
| One-server farm—All roles on one server, including SQL Server or<br>Two-tier small farm—1 x Web Server and Application Server combination, and a database on a separate server | This deployment should be used only when evaluating SharePoint solutions, development, and testing. You can also use it for environments that have limited numbers of users and who do not require fault tolerance. This is supported for up to 10,000 users. |
| Three-tier small farm—Two Web Query Servers, one Application Server, and databases on a separate server running SQL Server | This provides high availability. Adding a dedicated application server for environments with moderate service usage. |
| Three-tier small farm optimized for search—Two Web Query Servers, one Application Server, one Search Database Server, and other databases on a separate server running SQL Server | With hardware dedicated to search databases, this topology is optimized for search to work well in environments with up to 10 million items. |

For medium-sized farms, scaling out (adding more servers, for example) depends on what services you want to make more resilient and available by pushing them onto their own servers. The strategy is to scale out all other servers based on the utilization of other services within the farm and the volume of content the farm will host. This would mean a potential expansion of the Web Server, Application Server, or the Database Server level.

**Tip** The number of users will affect the requirement for Web Servers. Factor in 10,000 users per Web Server as a starting point. Adjust the number based on how heavily the servers are being used. Heavy use of client services will increase the load on Web Servers. In addition, you should start with all application server roles installed on the one server (except search roles). Then, based on utilization, consider either adding servers with all the non-search roles installed, or add servers that dedicate resources to specific services. For example, if performance data indicates that Excel Services is using a disproportionate amount of resources, offload this service to a dedicated server.

For large farms, the strategy would be to group services or databases with similar performance characteristics onto dedicated servers and then scale out the servers as a group. For example, you could create multiple Web Server Groups—one group responsible for incoming requests, the other for crawling and administration. You could create multiple Application Server Groups, having each group covering specific areas like Crawl, Query, Sandboxed Code, and Services. Finally, Database Servers could be grouped into Search, Content, and other SharePoint databases.

**Tip** For more information about planning and architecture for SharePoint 2013, the solution architect should go to *http://technet.microsoft.com/en-us/library/ff829836.aspx* and read the article titled "Plan logical architectures for SharePoint 2013." This article provides information concerning service deployment and design, including links to architecture design.

Note that with each topology, the further you scale the SharePoint environment, the higher the cost, and those costs are not just connected to licensing. You will also need to factor in administration, testing, support, and maintenance costs. The key is to start with the essentials required to provide the initial service level, and then use benchmark testing, performance testing, and user requirements analysis to scale out the environment as required.

**Tip** To further understand what is technically required, read the article "Prepare for installation of SharePoint 2013," located at *http://technet.microsoft.com/en-us/library/ff608031.aspx*. This article describes the minimum hardware and software to install and run SharePoint 2013.

## Considering SharePoint 2010 migration

Although you could do a SharePoint in-place upgrade (which has been vastly improved in SharePoint 2013), consider the practical benefits of providing a parallel system, with one farm running SharePoint 2013 and the other running SharePoint 2010. This means that you would deploy SharePoint 2013 in its own clean server environment, and then attach your content databases from your SharePoint 2010 environment as per a schedule. Certainly, you would also have a test environment running SharePoint 2013, so that you can confirm whether all features from your SharePoint 2010 environment continue to work in SharePoint 2013. You do this also because there may be issues to overcome concerning branding and features. So as you work through these, you should schedule tests to ensure that both you and the client are satisfied that the SharePoint 2013 environment meets all requirements. Doing this strengthens your configuration management, delivery, user requirements, and User Adoption plans, giving the client confidence that the current SharePoint platform will not be affected as the switchover build gets under way.

**Tip** Microsoft has provided good deployment guides, including information about deployment scenarios, step-by-step installation instructions, and post-installation configuration steps. It also describes how to upgrade to SharePoint 2013 at *http://technet.microsoft.com/en-us/library/cc303420.aspx*. In addition, an upgrade process diagram for SharePoint 2013 is downloadable from *http://www.sharepointgeoff.com/topologies-for-sharepoint-2013-diagrams-available/*.

# Building the platform deployment document

Now that you understand the concepts of SharePoint 2013, you need to use a repeatable, concise, and standard mechanism for gathering all the related information concerning deployment documentation. There are several sections that make up the deployment documentation:

- Platform Overview
- Functional Requirements

- Performance Requirements
- Human Requirements
- System Management Requirements
- Availability, Reliability, and Maintenance
- Interface Requirements
- Test Requirements
- Design Constraints

Next, we will describe what each of those topics cover and what information is required.

## Platform Overview

You need to provide an overview of the detailed required characteristics of the platform.

Table 6-6 shows the contents of the Platform Overview section, which is a description of what program the platform relates to, the goals that the platform will meet, the stakeholders, and a brief description of any related User Adoption, Training, and Governance committees.

**TABLE 6-6** The Platform Overview section of the SharePoint 2013 platform deployment document

| Section | Description |
|---|---|
| SharePoint delivery plan title | You should state the related title of the delivery program. Also reference any associated documentation like technical infrastructure diagrams, wireframes and so on. |
| SharePoint goals | Describe the purpose of the SharePoint platform. For example, is it a Test, Stage, or a Production deployment? Briefly state the SharePoint sponsor high-level requirements, or, if they are already detailed in the SharePoint delivery plan, reference that plan here. State whether the deployment is on-premise SharePoint 2013, part of a hybrid connecting to Office 365, or an off-premise SharePoint 2013 online deployment. |
| Audiences | List the SharePoint sponsor, key stakeholders, and any other business units or business functions that would need to view this document. |
| Referenced | List any User Adoption plans, training plans, and Governance committee that relate to this platform and interdependent platforms. |

## Functional Requirements

The Functional Requirements define the format of the platform in terms of its structure and content. It includes the following:

- Sites and Site Collection
- Managed Metadata
- Records Management
- Document Management

You will need to describe at a high level the format of each key Web Applications and Site Collections. Describe the Metadata and Taxonomy, and state what Records Management features would be implemented.

## Performance Requirements

Recording performance (especially the performance of SharePoint) can be a problem because it is difficult to predict, and the cost of building extra performance quality into software or hardware designs can be prohibitive if estimates are not accurate or measured completely. This problem is exacerbated by the fact that accurate estimates of performance can be made only when the architectural design is completed. That said, it is vital that hardware and farm topology of SharePoint will deliver the required performance. Two areas that must be addressed are SharePoint capacity and SharePoint response.

SharePoint capacity can be divided into static and dynamic requirements as follows:

- Static requirements:
    - Maximum volumes of data to be stored
    - Number of users connected
    - Total number of messages input/output
    - Minimum allowance for storage
    - Minimum allowable RAM
- Dynamic requirements for normal and peak loading:
    - Number of transactions to be processed in a specified time
    - Maximum number of users to be connected at any given time
    - Access times and response times
    - Maximum percentage CPU utilization for WFE servers, Application Server, and SQL Server servers
    - Maximum percentage storage utilization

SharePoint response is concerned with the ability to express response times to hardware, to user, or specific events in a precise manner. Response times should be stated as overall system response times under specified conditions. For SharePoint, it is necessary to specify mission performance criteria and to express responses as absolute times or in terms of statistics. For example, the following statement could be used as a statistical response measure: "The WFE servers under peak operating load of 90 percent of responses shall be less than 0.5 second."

For each response, you should consider how performance will be measured and whether specific applications or tools will be required to carry out the measurement. Performance figures must be quantifiable and achievable in SharePoint.

SharePoint 2013 includes the following features to aid in performance management:

- An improved user interface helps administrators understand SharePoint 2013 faster. SharePoint 2013 Central Administration is laid out in a more logical way. Those using SharePoint 2010 Central Administration will be comfortable with the layout because the layout of SharePoint 2013 closely matches it.
- Health monitoring in SharePoint 2013 includes a health analyzer that reports using applied rules in a variety of categories, security, and performance. You can create your own rules, and more rules may be added to future SharePoint 2013 service packs.
- SharePoint 2013 includes large list throttling. You can now control how users can query and view data. You can set throttle controls on the number of items returned, which forces end users to create more efficient views, and set "happy hour" times when you expect heavier loads.
- SharePoint 2013 has a new request routing and throttling feature called Request Management. Request Management works by understanding the nature of incoming requests. The responses to each request can be customized and routed based on rules provided. This provides several benefits, such as the following:
  - Routing requests to WFEs with better health, minimizing disruption to low-health WFEs
  - Identifying harmful requests and denying them
  - Prioritizing requests to serve higher priority and throttling lower-priority requests
  - Routing requests to different machines; for example, routing SharePoint search requests to machines configured for SharePoint search services
- The Developer Dashboard in SharePoint 2013 can be used to identify components that are affecting performance. The Developer Dashboard in SharePoint 2013 provides tools to allow requests to be analyzed as "hits" to the SharePoint site.
- The Logging Database is now a central repository for usage and health information, allowing administrators to get more information, such as Slowest Pages, Top Active Users, and much more.

**Tip** There are many more technical features that are beyond the scope of this chapter. If you are interested in learning more about SharePoint technical features, you should read the article "Performance and capacity management (SharePoint Server 2013)" at *http://technet.microsoft.com/en-us/library/cc262971.aspx*. For even more technical information related to SharePoint administration and configuration, the Microsoft Press book *SharePoint 2013 Administration Inside Out* by Randy Williams is a good resource. For more information on the Developer Dashboard, see the video at *http://www.microsoft.com/resources/technet/en-us/office/media/video/video.html?cid=stc&from=mscomstc&VideoID=505bdd61-1fcc-4125-97fc-b5f0dda72cbc*.

## Human Requirements

User Adoption of a SharePoint platform does not just depend on the specific requirements from users. The SharePoint platform needs to meet user expectations, such as: How easy is it to use the SharePoint site? What are the components that make up the front page? Meeting human requirements and documenting those attempts to do so are very important areas as they relate to User Adoption and Governance.

To do this, you need to obtain the following information:

- **SharePoint user characteristics and style.** You should state the characteristics necessary to support proper operation of SharePoint from the user's perspective: the use of the ribbon, how to modify pages, perform administration, and so on.
- **Identification of each component of the user interface.** For example, you should state what the site layout is. Consider using *wireframing*, which is a drawing of a site marking the key areas of user interaction. For some sites, consider creating a number of wireframes, allowing the user to select the one that best matches his or her requirements.
- **Criteria for acceptance.** You should define the acceptance criteria under which SharePoint sites should be accepted by users. These would include the following:
  - **Learnability** The number of training hours needed to pass a standard SharePoint skill test
  - **Productivity** Percentage of error-free operations per day, logged automatically after one month's experience
  - **Likeability** Percentage of users who, after training, prefer the new system to the old one

## System Management Requirements

System management is concerned with how SharePoint is operated, administered, and controlled. Overall SharePoint operation requirements are expressed in terms of "normal" and "abnormal." These requirements are satisfied by mapping out all interfaced component connections to SharePoint 2013 and identifying who is responsible for each of these.

The management requirements for SQL Server if run by a SQL Server Database Administrator (DBA) team will not be the same as the management requirements for SharePoint administrators. SQL Server DBAs will have rules concerning how their environment will be configured, the rules for service accounts, database growth rates, and compression technologies. The SharePoint team in relation to SQL will have identified the level of access service that accounts should have, as well as the size of content databases and how these should be structured. Both teams will have connected rules concerning the procedure for restoration of a content database onto the same or other servers including of course disaster recovery procedures.

System management requirements should be summarized in the Statement of Operations (as detailed in the "Building the Statement of Operations" section of Chapter 5, "Planning SharePoint Governance") if they are enterprise-related (meaning that the system management requirement has an impact on the resiliency, availability, maintainability, or supportability). At the highest level, recording system management requirements in the deployment document means the Governance committee must have visibility of key system requirements. This leads to the next subject: availability, reliability, and maintenance.

## Availability, Reliability, and Maintenance

Other important components of nonfunctional requirements are availability, reliability, and maintainability. These factors are interrelated but independent. When implemented SharePoint 2013 may have a very high resilience but poor availability.

For example, let's assume that you have a SharePoint 2013 deployment with five sites, using multiple load-balanced servers, as well as a good disaster recovery process. In addition, there is a policy stating that the security applied to sites is to "speak to the Help desk and log a ticket for SharePoint Support to assign your site permissions." Your SharePoint support team, however, consists of only one person. Now suppose that you have scaled the example multiple site collections with hundreds of sites, but without scaling SharePoint support. You now have great resilience on your SharePoint platform, but poor availability to sites because of the bottleneck of issues caused by having only one staff member on SharePoint support. (Imagine how long you would have to wait in line to have a permission changed if all requests had to go through one person!)

For SharePoint, where the solution requires a full implementation of the software, you should define availability as part of your disaster recovery plan because disaster recovery is the process by which you resume business after a disruptive event. Once that aspect of the disaster recovery has been defined, Reliability, Availability, and Maintainability components can be defined as follows:

- *Reliability* is the probability of correct operation, and it depends on elapsed time and failure rate. The more practical measures are mean time between failures (MTBF) and its reciprocal failure rate. MTBF is usually expressed in hours, and the failure rate in failures per 1,000 hours.
- *Availability* is the proportion of time that SharePoint is available for operation. Therefore, it takes into account both the failure rate and the time taken to restore normal operation. For example, if you are running SharePoint backups and want to use a daily backup of a large site collection, you will need to be aware that if the site requires restoration in the future that the time taken to restore means impacts on Availability. In addition, if the failure rate is high and the time taken to restore is long, that is not a very good state of affairs for a disaster recovery plan on that site.
- *Maintainability* is both a measure of continuous improper service delivered and a measure of the time taken to restoration from the last experienced failure.

Resilience in SharePoint is a vital goal. It is measured by fault prevention, fault removal, and fault forecasting, as follows:

- Use the Health Analyzer and the logging function in SharePoint 2013 to help you identify and resolve issues before they become serious. Fault removal needs to be documented as part of a change control process under configuration management so that any SharePoint faults are traceable.

- For Availability, if there are high numbers coming back from the rate and time, then you may need to examine the resources assigned to the issue and address the configuration applied. For example, if an important service application like Excel Services is continually failing, the problem needs to be addressed either by looking at where the resources are being drained and/or increasing the available resources or by moving the service to its own server.

This section of the document should record the key SharePoint site collections, services, and components that need to be on a high level of availability, and describe what will be done to meet the Availability requirement. If the client is requiring a 99 percent uptime for all site collections, then there needs to be an agreement on what constitutes 99 percent operation and who is responsible for ensuring this level of operation. Considering the fact that most uptime guarantees are given on a monthly basis, if SharePoint were down 10 percent of the time, that means it was down for about three days. If this SharePoint instance was visited regularly, a 10 percent downtime costs the organization (in lost sales, productivity, or whatever) far more than the monthly cost of supporting SharePoint. Now let's take the most popular uptime guarantees and see what they really mean. A 99.5 percent uptime guarantee means that SharePoint can be down for as much as 216 minutes in a month; 99.8 percent uptime guarantee is 86.4 minutes of downtime; 99.9 percent uptime guarantee is 43.2 minutes of downtime; 99.99 percent uptime guarantee is 4.32 minutes of downtime; and 99.999 percent uptime guarantee is 0.432 minutes (or 26 seconds).

## Interface Requirements

SharePoint 2013 provides many templates to suit a particular site requirement. For example, a group of individuals may require a Group Work Team site because its "look and feel" is closer to the way they work than using a Projects Work Database site or a Blog site. Another may require a Community Site because the members need to manage a forum for knowledge building.

As you gather information through user requirements and make decisions through the planning of sites and site collections, you will be able to match what the user requires to the site templates that have been included in SharePoint. If the site templates are not available, or there is a template but branding through an editor is desired, this can be recorded and identified as a task. (Branding SharePoint requires detailed appraisal and could potentially create another project.)

**Note** The SharePoint 2013 interface is a massive topic area because it relates to accessibility, and consequently, the Web Content Accessibility Guidelines. For more information on what has been done to address SharePoint accessibility, visit *http://blogs.msdn.com/b/sharepoint/archive/2010/03/09/accessibility-and-sharepoint-2010.aspx.*

## Test Requirements

The primary requirement for testing is that the acceptance tests be designed to demonstrate that the system behaves in accordance with the requirements expressed in the Requirements or Deployment document.

Two types of tests can be applied to SharePoint: acceptance testing and integration testing. *Acceptance testing,* the most common type, comprises both user requirement and technical requirements testing. This kind of testing is designed to capture the supportability of any aspect of SharePoint under normal or abnormal operations.

When recording Test Requirements, make sure that you provide two sets. The first set is for the client, taking the visionary statements and listing the tests that will be performed to meet those requirements. The second set of tests cover the user requirements and the interfacing technical teams. The interfacing technical teams (for example, Active Directory teams, SQL Server teams, and Microsoft Exchange Server teams) in a disconnected and multidisciplined environment will need their connected platforms tested against the addition of SharePoint being integrated.

SharePoint acceptance tests must be based on the User Requirements specification. This means that it is possible to create tests for virtually every statement in the User Requirements section. User Requirements are helpful in determining some tests to confirm the requirements have been met. If, for example, you see a recurring theme of "Confirm that Excel Services can connect to a spreadsheet for Department X" in the User Requirements, then this means that the speed and performance of Excel Services should be tested.

SharePoint includes connectivity to systems that may or may not be under the control of the SharePoint support team. For example, Active Directory may be maintained by an Active Directory team, and SQL Servers may be managed by SQL DBAs. This causes the scope of testing to expand because it now includes not only tests of the hardware or software, but also tests of resiliency, robustness, support, and maintainability. Taking this further, if SharePoint is presented on three environments—such as Test, Stage, and Production—providing performance tests may be different depending on the type of infrastructure, network connectivity, and other configuration.

Therefore, the Test Requirements would need to cover user experience, software, hardware, connectivity, and performance. The last type of test, performance, needs to be defined clearly in terms of the user requirements. Make sure that when these are collated, they can be set against known criteria in SharePoint. For example, if you are testing the speed of upload from a client desktop, then in the Applications section of the User Requirements section, you should state what needs to be tested.

**Tip** It is very important to test the Database layer of SharePoint (SQL) because this represents a significant portion of SharePoint performance and is likely to present latency issues if left unchecked.

Use the Health Analyzer in SharePoint 2013 to provide more tests, and make adjustments to see the thresholds of your SharePoint environment. The Health Analyzer in SharePoint 2013 Central Administration allows administrators to confirm that levels of operation of SharePoint are adequate. This component also allows the setting of customized alerts, meaning that, for example, it is possible to create SharePoint administrative tests by setting the alerts at various values of tolerance.

If SharePoint development is included in the Test Requirements section, you should ensure that the test schedule is documented against whatever product is being applied to SharePoint. In other words, developer testing of a product being "customized" in SharePoint could be a significant project; for example, branding of a SharePoint My Site would require a number of tests on usability, accessibility, and other functions.

Table 6-7 indicates the kind of testing that should be considered. One way of using this table would be to create a table of the test headings, and then, for each one, specify what would be tested and what requirement (whether user or technical) it would relate to.

**TABLE 6-7** Tests to apply to the SharePoint solution

| Test | Description |
|---|---|
| Correct Function Tests | List tests that you expect users to carry out. Do not worry about how basic the tests should be. Remember, the business user perception of a SharePoint site is not the same as someone who is a technical user. For example, a test could be based on a user accessing a site who is a contributor, expecting to be able to upload a file into a document library. People may say, "This test is far too basic," but I have had clients who insist on proof that SharePoint can perform basic operations. |
| Incorrect, Abnormal, or Error Path Tests | List some tests where the operation will fail, but state what the outcome will be and what message the user will receive then. |
| Performance | List any timing tests that verify that specified SharePoint actions are performed within specified times. |
| Capacity and Volume | List tests that seek to load SharePoint with the maximum allowable values for any storage or loading values. There are tools available that allow you to populate with test data, though testing may be difficult if you don't have a significant amount of space capacity. |
| Endurance | List tests that will investigate the ability of SharePoint to perform continuously over a period of time. These kinds of tests should always be done if the system is to be available 24 hours a day. |
| Operability | Using available user documentation, list tests to prove that users can do particular operations based on the current documentation available. |
| Graceful Degradation | List tests where SharePoint operations can be brought to a stop without major disruption. |
| Security | List tests involving site access, web application access, and the testing of relevant permissions assigned. For example, where customized permissions are applied to specific SharePoint sites, test whether users can access those sites who don't have permission to do so. |
| Recovery | List tests to confirm that backups can be carried out at the farm and the site, and a granular backup can be done. Ensure that recovery is being tested, and that the tests are timed. |

| Test | Description |
|---|---|
| Availability, Reliability, and Maintainability | List tests to confirm the robustness of SharePoint and failovers. For example, test load balancing on the SharePoint WFEs; test the availability of service applications; and test how much work it takes to maintain all the enabled service applications. |
| Service Applications | Test the configuration of SharePoint service applications. For example, you should test the User Profile Service, Search Service, Metadata Service, and other applications. |

## Design Constraints

The technical authority may impose design constraints on hardware and software, which fall into four categories:

- Software constraints, which include requirements for compatibility and interoperability.
- Hardware where a specific vendor must be chosen.
- Human constraints, which include the skill levels expected of team members such as SharePoint administrators.
- Development process aspects, which cover the use of recommended methods and tools in the development process. For example, the client may not allow the use of SharePoint Designer 2010, which would require modifications to training.

**Tip** Human constraints should be listed in the Human Requirements section.

The design constraints that you will face are based on the areas that are described in Table 6-8. Not all these design constraints will get entered in your SharePoint project plan. However, it's important that you understand the distinction and ensure that the relevant constraints are documented against the relevant area in the deployment document.

**TABLE 6-8** Software design constraints document headers

| Heading | Description |
|---|---|
| Standards | List the standards concerning the implementation of service accounts, giving format, management, password placement, and how information is to be recorded. |
| Packages | List any specific packages that may be required, including a justification statement for each package. |
| Database | List any external system that SharePoint may need to integrate with, including a short description of the reason. |
| Operating System | List the client operating systems used by the users to connect to SharePoint. If on-premise, list the server environment that SharePoint will be installed on. If off-premise, list the Office products available to the users from the Office 365 tenant. |

| Heading | Description |
|---|---|
| Installation Guide | For on-premise, list references to the SharePoint installation guide that details the process of the installation from the prerequisites through to the creation of site collections and associated services configurations. For off-premise, list the references to the SharePoint guide used to record all updates to the relevant Administration section of Office 365. |

## Documentation, installation, and integration testing

Once the SharePoint deployment document is complete, test its validity by checking each section. Those who prepared the documentation should be able to present their findings in such a way that it is understandable to the relevant audiences. Also, consider running tests against the documentation (especially if they also concern installation documentation) in a test environment, and then do it again in a User Acceptance Test (UAT) environment before deploying to a production environment.

**Tip** For most of these tests, you could apply them first to the Test environment, and then run the same tests again on the Stage environment. This makes it easier to deploy the features in the Production environment. At least then you and the client would be comfortable that not only have you met the agreed-upon goals, but you have coordinated it all without any detrimental effect to the Production environment. For Office 365 testing, consider using a separated developer Office 365 tenant where installation and uninstallation tests can be carried out without unduly disrupting the production environment. Remember to use platform governance to protect the integrity of the production environment.

## Integration and hardware testing

If your SharePoint implementation is in a small-farm topology, your integrated tests will be a lot smaller than if SharePoint sits in a multi-farm topology and a disconnected environment.

It is important that you have integration tests so that at the hardware level, you will be able to iron out any network connectivity or security or bandwidth issues. At the software level, for example, you will be able to ascertain which services enabled in SharePoint are taking up valuable resources. You will also be able to test how client applications such as Excel, Word, Visio, PowerPoint, and Microsoft Outlook interact with SharePoint. These applications in particular are integrated with SharePoint—for example, Visio Services in SharePoint allows the display of a fully functional Visio diagram that includes external database connectivity. Therefore, your integrated test for this would not only be Visio, it would be the diagram and the network connectivity to whatever back-end database was connected. Table 6-9 describes integration testing options that you should consider including in the SharePoint deployment document.

**TABLE 6-9** Types of integration testing

| Test | Description |
|---|---|
| Subsystems level | SharePoint Services configuration tests, Search Tests, User Profile Tests, and so on. |
| Hardware and software components in SharePoint | Site-level components, web parts enabled on major portals, enabled features. SQL Server, DNS Server, and SharePoint farm servers (for example, WFE, Application, and Load Balancing). |
| Equipment external to the system | This could be any hardware component that is connected to the SharePoint platform to provide a service. For example, this could be an internal server connected to a camera passing real-time information into a SharePoint site through a Business Data Connection (BDC). |
| Any of the above, where one or more components are supplied via a third party | What you are testing is not just the configuration of the equipment, it's the response of the support arrangements in place with the third party, including other tests in line with Acceptance Testing. |

To identify hardware constraints, prepare a statement concerning any standards for the building of servers and the preparation of the operating system installation and any monitoring equipment, including network connectivity, load balance connectivity, and environmental factors (for example, communication rooms and/or data center configuration).

## Summary

As described in this chapter, a deployment document should produce a clear, complete, and unambiguous set of documentation that describes the SharePoint platform in terms of its function, performance, interfaces, and design constraints. Once completed, the SharePoint sponsor and stakeholders can collectively sign off the user requirements, technical requirements, and all the planning and decisions captured in the relevant services that warranted further investigation.

The deployment document is a working document that reflects the technical user requirements; it is also a key resource for governance and support. The deployment document lists the design of the SharePoint platform and the build of the platform reflects that design. Change management will affect this document. For example, if there is a requirement to include Visio 2013 diagrams in the SharePoint 2013 platform at a later stage, then this must be factored into the Performance, Availability, and Testing Requirements sections of the deployment document.

Building a deployment document is a significant task. You will need several resources to help investigate and accomplish this. This chapter mentioned some of those resources, such as the solution architect, content strategist, information architect, and business analyst, and they are further discussed in Chapter 7.

CHAPTER 7

# Organizing SharePoint delivery resources

In this chapter:



All Microsoft SharePoint delivery programs are significant undertakings that will require skilled human and material resources to be a success. The kind of solution that you are going to deliver will invariably dictate the kind of resources that you need. This chapter describes those resources and their roles, so that you can associate them to your delivery program.

## Organizing the delivery team

Table 7-1 shows the roles being discussed, with a basic description of each.

**TABLE 7-1** Delivery team roles and responsibilities

| Role | Responsibility |
|---|---|
| Business analyst | Responsible for gathering user requirements and helping map them to SharePoint solutions |
| Communications | Responsible for managing the communications plan and coordinating messages |
| Content strategist | Responsible for creating strategies to audit existing content and applying content management strategies that improve how users manage content |
| Information architect | Responsible for organizing and labeling content and building classification strategies to manage that content |
| Infrastructure specialist | Responsible for managing technical products supporting the SharePoint platform |

| Role | Responsibility |
|---|---|
| Quality assurance | Responsible for carrying out acceptance tests |
| SharePoint administrator | Responsible for supporting customers and managing SharePoint platform(s) |
| SharePoint delivery manager | Responsible for delivering the SharePoint solution to the business |
| SharePoint developer | Responsible for creating custom solutions using code |
| Solution architect | Responsible for providing the technical solution that addresses user requirements |
| Trainers | Responsible for building and delivering training plans, schedules, and events |
| User interface designer | Responsible for ensuring that navigation, appearance, and interaction of the SharePoint solution is acceptable to a wide range of users |
| Web developer | Responsible for building custom solutions |
| Web graphic designer | Responsible for designing and building the look and feel (branding) of a SharePoint solution |

In terms of business requirements, SharePoint delivery programs are limited only by the customer's creativity. Hence, the kinds of resources required to deliver solutions can vary dramatically. Every SharePoint solution must be delivered in a consistent fashion, and it must be supported. Each SharePoint delivery team must include a delivery manager, a business analyst, and a solution architect, at the very least. Do not underestimate the resources you need, as the success of the SharePoint delivery program depends on the application of the relevant roles of the delivery team, combined with the skills of the team members.

## Creating the terms of reference

You should provide terms of reference (TORs) for each member of the delivery team before bringing them on board. By doing this, you will structure the team based on the members' capabilities and skill sets.

Other benefits include:

- The team will have the foundation to build trust in each other.
- The team will be able to express disagreements with each other in a constructive way.
- The team will put the team first, accepting and supporting collective decision making.
- The team will define success as the success of the team, not of the individuals in it.
- The SharePoint sponsor will be able to identify value based on roles in the team.
- The delivery manager will be able to assign tasks to teams based on their TORs.

The TORs are created by the SharePoint delivery manager based on the requirements in the Delivery Plan. A TOR contains information about the role and responsibilities of each delivery team member, so that it is easy to associate the various tasks in the delivery plan. These items should always be reviewed to ensure that they reflect the size and scope of the SharePoint delivery program. As previously mentioned, each TOR is written before any members of the team are recruited. You should not create the TOR until you are clear on the tasks required.

You need to ensure that there is a recruitment process in place, even if the members come from the organization. What you don't want is a situation where the SharePoint sponsor has simply given you resources under the assumption that you need an IT team without questioning the process. If the SharePoint sponsor thinks of SharePoint 2013 as just another software product and that installing it simply involves a few clicks, then that is not a SharePoint delivery program, and you do not have a SharePoint delivery team.

So, as a delivery manager, you need to create TORs, get approval from the SharePoint sponsor, and then recruit the relevant members into the team. When you're building the TORs for your SharePoint delivery team, make sure that you write each one in a standardized way. Table 7-2 provides a sample TOR for SharePoint delivery managers. (The entries given in the Definition column need to be altered to suit your delivery program.)

**TABLE 7-2** TOR for the SharePoint delivery manager role

| Term | Definition |
|---|---|
| Job title | Enter the title of the SharePoint delivery program. |
| Line of business (LOB) | Enter the LOB that the solution is going to be delivered to. |
| Job holder | Enter the name of the SharePoint delivery manager. |
| Commencement date | Enter the date when the SharePoint delivery manager will start the program. |
| Reporting to | Enter the name of the SharePoint sponsor, including the business unit, department, and function in the organization. |
| Purpose | Enter the purpose of the role. For example: *The SharePoint delivery manager of the XYZ SharePoint solution is to ensure that the delivery team achieves the contracted deliverables to the satisfaction of the SharePoint sponsor in the time frame required and within the approved budgets.* |

Create TORs for other members of the delivery team using the same format as described in Table 7-2. When reading about each of the different roles of the delivery team in this chapter, refer back to this table so that you can create a TOR for that role.

## Building the delivery team

As each TOR is completed, make sure that each team member is clear on the purpose of his or her role, and record all TORs into the SharePoint delivery site.

The key to ensuring that the delivery team focuses on succeeding is get all team members to commitment to the objectives stated in the delivery detail plan and provide a solution that meets the vision provided by the SharePoint sponsor. The SharePoint delivery manager's leadership skills are very important. He or she will need to have the ability to present the SharePoint sponsor's vision so that the delivery team will want to achieve that vision. The SharePoint delivery manager will require the ability to build relationships with the delivery team and organize resources effectively.

> *"As team leader one of your most important roles is to steer your team towards decisions so that they can then commit to them."*
>
> *Floyd Woodrow and Simon Acland, from their book* Elite!

Sessions will have to be defined so that they investigate the objectives and lead to decisions concerning the build of the SharePoint solution. There are four types of sessions that you will need to include as part of the program:

- Strategy Brief
- Architectural Design Session (ADS)
- Engagement Summary
- Demonstrations and Presentation

The purpose of each of these sessions is discussed in the following sections. The descriptions have been expanded from the detail plan as listed in the "Building the SharePoint delivery plan" section of Chapter 3, "Planning SharePoint solution delivery." It is important that these sessions are given priority and that you include every one of them. You may need to repeat demonstrations and presentations sessions as the program unfolds. For example, you may find that you would like to demonstrate the test environment to a technical team or an intranet site to a team, or describe the features of SharePoint 2013.

## Strategy Brief

Creating a high-quality SharePoint solution requires detailed plans and skilled implementation of those plans.

SharePoint includes a vast number of building blocks (tactics) that can be employed to maximize return on investment (ROI). To use these tactics effectively, it's important to develop a blueprint in advance that will do the following:

- Create specific goals
- Establish a baseline
- Outline specific tactics
- Outline budget allocation
- Outline measurements and milestones

Therefore, your Strategy Brief to the SharePoint sponsor must be documented and will include input from the solutions architect and business analyst.

- Description of the business goals
- Description of the relevant SharePoint 2013 features and benefits
- Description of the infrastructure and other resources required

This then feeds into the second session, which covers the design of the solution, and that is where other roles are applied, such as the information architect, content strategist, and business analyst.

## ADS

The ADS will enable business goals to be translated into design goals. Be aware that this session should be repeated to ensure that each area of the solution delivery is covered. For example, if the solution includes branding, a number of wireframes of the solution will be produced, showing the design options that will be applied. For example, building wireframes for branding solutions, or even designing the SharePoint site layout, will help guide the selection, deployment, operations, and adoption of SharePoint.

The ADS comprises three outputs: discovery, envisioning, and planning. All team members have a part to play in this section, depending on the user requirements.

- **Discovery** This is a description of the business key requirements and their context.
- **Envisioning** This is an extraction and description of business scenarios against the business key requirements, followed by a list of the SharePoint technologies and approach to be used to meet those scenarios.
- **Planning** This involves investigating user requirements, and then mapping them to alternative methods of delivering the solution.

The ADS then provides outputs that are the design decisions based on the following topics (dependent on the solution being delivered):

- Enterprise content management
- Enterprise search
- Social collaboration
- Portal collaboration
- Taxonomy metadata
- Work processes' business intelligence
- Infrastructure design
- Capacity design

- Governance
- Risk discussions
- Tools and resources
- Deployment
- Cost model

**Tip** You should use the Value Management process described in the "Value Management and Value Engineering" section of Chapter 4, "Preparing SharePoint solution User Adoption," and the article concerning building user requirements at *http://www.sharepointgeoff.com/welcome-to-sharepointgeoff-home-of-stationcomputing/user-requirements/* to help you build user requirements and test your alternatives to identify the best value.

## Engagement Summary

The third area, Engagement Summary, is a program milestone that allows you to review the solution based on design outputs from the ADS stage. These meetings with the SharePoint sponsor and stakeholders can be held repeatedly during the project to ensure that the design alternatives have been addressed and to suggest the best recommendations. An output of engagement is the production of the full delivery plan.

## Presentations and demo sites

You should hold awareness sessions, carry out communication exercises, and prepare training sessions during the next phase. You might also want to provide SharePoint test site areas and allow users and stakeholders access to those areas. Demo sites are useful while user requirements are being collected by the business analyst. By showing SharePoint sites in a workshop designed to capture user requirements, the attendees could be shown areas relevant to the SharePoint solution and then asked questions. This enables the attendees to become further engaged with the product and learn more about its features and benefits.

**Note** You must ensure that users know that no backup or retention plans are available to test sites. Users need to be made aware of this so that if, for example, they want to use the sites in real life, the relevant sites can be migrated to the stage for full testing and then moved on to production as soon as the testing has been approved.

**More Info** There is more information concerning running workshops, which can be used to help you work through the sessions. For more information, see Chapter 11, "Managing workshops and closing the delivery program", section "Managing workshops".

## Understanding the delivery team roles

When the delivery team is performs well, you will find that every team member has his or her own distinct responsibilities and contributes something unique to the project. To have a high-performing team, you need to understand and set clear roles, accountabilities, and responsibilities for each member. Once roles are set, everyone in the team has an understanding of the role that each person is playing. This section describes the various roles associated with SharePoint delivery.

### Business analysts

When delivering a SharePoint solution, two levels of research are required: technical and business. For the technical research, the solutions architect (as well as interfacing teams, if applicable) gets an understanding of what technical resources will be required that would physically house the SharePoint solution.

For the business research task, business analysts step in. These people have the task of guiding and documenting the SharePoint sponsor's requirements in detail, and they communicate that information to the solutions architect and technical authorities (through the SharePoint delivery manager).

Interestingly, the business analyst role is often downplayed or eliminated by those who want to push out SharePoint quickly and those who are more focused on the technology instead of the information and collaboration challenges faced by the organization, which determines how the technology can be placed to meet those challenges.

Without an understanding of the organization's current use of technology and its user requirements, you cannot possibly ensure that whatever is provided will meet expectations, be resilient, perform, and be supportable in the SharePoint sponsor's environment.

The business analyst role in a SharePoint delivery program is extremely important. The output of this person is brought back to the SharePoint delivery manager, who then echoes the requirements to the solutions architect and business stakeholders.

In some cases, people might argue that the business analyst and solutions architect should be the same person. This might be a good idea when the business analyst, who needs to interface with the business and record user requirements, is also the person who has a deep understanding of SharePoint. Combining these roles ensures that the information captured is valid and the goals outlined are achievable.

While this is a possible approach, there are some drawbacks that make this arrangement inappropriate for certain types of delivery. The only information captured in the analysis is what is going to be achieved according to the guidance of a solutions architect, with not enough emphasis on whether value can be achieved (whether or not it can be achieved in SharePoint). In addition, in a large implementation, you'll wind up with an overcommitted solutions architect who will be attempting to investigate, design, and help implement the wishes of both the technical and business sides of the SharePoint 2013 program.

There is also an argument that, with an eye to keeping the team small and compact, the roles of business analyst and solutions architect can be rolled into one. However, this assumes that the solutions architect is interfacing directly with the business and is not responsible (even indirectly) for defining the raw SharePoint implementation requirements (such as additional technical information like server specification, capacity plans, and network security), which the SharePoint sponsor might not have the sufficient knowledge to quantify or detail.

Therefore, if you are implementing a large program, the business analyst must be separate from the solutions architect because the business analyst has a single responsibility: to gather the user (business) information requirements and seek an accord between the technology and the business within the guidelines of the program scope. Adding any other responsibilities to the mix would be too distracting.

**Note** Business analysts who stay with the organization after the completion of a SharePoint delivery program tend to become a combination of SharePoint administrator and SharePoint champion (a SharePoint champion is an individual in the organization who is not a member of the SharePoint support team, but is seen by peers to have a good working knowledge of SharePoint). This is in part because of the champion's knowledge of SharePoint and how it has been implemented in the organization. If this takes place, the business analysts/champions would be wise to impart information to other people in the business to create more SharePoint champions.

The business analyst skill set should feature the following program tasks:

- Help build business and functional requirements by describing what the SharePoint feature, process, product, or service must do to fulfill the business requirements, working closely with the solutions architect, information architects, content strategists, and others in the delivery team.
- Help build user requirements that will be reflected in a SharePoint solution, thus allowing that solution to be designed and developed, and defining how user test cases must be formulated.
- Help build Quality-of-Service (QoS) requirements that do not perform a specific function for the business requirement but are needed to support the functionality (for example, SharePoint performance, scalability, security, and usability). These are often included within the system requirements (where applicable) and through working with the solutions architect.

## Content strategist

Good content management in SharePoint is crucial. To achieve this, work needs to be done in terms of content structure and presentation. Key considerations include publishing, workflow, and the content life cycle. Content strategists work closely with information architects and business analysts to provide content Governance planning and define retention policies and distribution strategies. They also develop a metadata strategy. Content strategists combine the content that needs to be viewed and think in a holistic way about what users should see when they visit a SharePoint site. Benefits of having a content strategist on the delivery team are as follows:

- A content strategist has a passion for content, not only in terms of written documents but also art, photos, film, and video.
- A content strategist can distinguish meaningful content from dead weight. They can cut, tweak, and trim to emphasize meaningful content. This is particularly useful when providing solutions based on refactoring content on a large site (for example, an intranet that has more than 100,000 items of content, and yet more than 70 percent of that content is out of date).
- A content strategist is comfortable and can define the principles of content management, and has experience with databases.
- A content strategist can carry out critical analysis and pattern recognition and can aid in the creation of a content strategy.

The content strategist skill set should include the following program tasks:

- Understand the core business objectives of the organization and define the achievable goals to be attained from online content activity.
- Ensure consistent and timely publishing of content, syndicating to push high volumes of traffic to key conversion points.
- Use personalization and behavioral content targeting techniques to ensure a transactional content flow and maximum ROI.
- Create bespoke content concepts, taking into consideration goals, brand, products, audience, emerging technologies, resources, and budgets.
- Devise long-term, flexible editorial schedules that mirror business messages within a set of content guidelines, encouraging users to instill a "think of content first" philosophy within the organization.
- Create internal and external audits by establishing the quality and quantity of existing content inventories.

## Web graphic designer

Depending on the solution being delivered, you may need a web graphic designer. The solution may contain a branding of the intranet or a branding of a public, off-premise SharePoint site. A web graphic designer is the person that generally comes up with the layout and look of a SharePoint site. This person doesn't necessarily have to create the artwork and graphical content for the website, but he or she generally codes it and styles its template. Whether the delivery of the solution is for an internal SharePoint site or a public SharePoint site, two key factors must be considered:

- The web graphic designer needs to have an understanding SharePoint styling and themes. There is very little point in a site being designed in a graphics package by a web graphic designer and then finding that the person(s) involved in that design cannot apply it to SharePoint.

- User Adoption is as vital as the content. The user interface must meet user expectations and match usability requirements, and you must make sure that the users can be trained on how to use the site.

So, even if you as a delivery manager have the services of a web graphic designer, ensure that this person has worked on programs where the business has dictated the design, and understands SharePoint branding in terms of limitation and issues. By doing this, the output will be one that is supportable and that the users can adopt. If you must use a web graphic designer who has not worked directly with businesses in the past, check the output periodically.

The web graphic designer skill set should include the following program tasks:

- Design and create graphics that meet the specific guidelines relevant to user requirements that can be applied to the SharePoint solution.
- Meet stakeholders to discuss needs, objectives, and requirements (working with the business analyst and others).
- Interpret the user requirements and develop concepts.

## Information architect

Information architects create plans for how data in the organization is created, stored, archived, and retained. In essence, they define and manage the nature of metadata management in the SharePoint sponsor's organization.

In large organizations, you might see an entire team responsible for this task. If you do, your SharePoint delivery program needs to bring in this team as quickly as possible. If you don't, depending on the nature and size of the SharePoint delivery program, you might wish to use your business analyst or solutions architect instead of using a separate information architect.

*Information architecture is the study of information, organizational structure, and information flow. This topic is discussed further in the "Understanding the importance of information architecture" section of Chapter 6, "SharePoint program delivery considerations."*

Information architects are used in the Plan phase of SharePoint solution implementation. They provide information about document metadata, organizational structure, and information flows between business units. This data is invaluable for the design of sites in terms of their document libraries, data hierarchy in SharePoint 2013 (content type mapping), and SharePoint 2013 site inheritance. This information also leads to business workflow provisions and links to the work of the business analyst.

The information architect works with technical material and translates the material into layperson's terms. Information architects examine the process of document management in that platform and document for the users how document management should be applied in the context of their work.

This means that while users need not have complete knowledge of SharePoint 2013, they need to understand how the user interface works (for example, how to upload and download material, create content, assign keywords, and work with metadata).

In terms of SharePoint 2013 content management features, the information architect may be working with one or more of the following:

- Social personal classifications
- Taxonomy and metadata to improve navigation and browsing
- Taxonomy and metadata to improve search and discovery
- Shared content types across site collections
- Life-cycle content management
- Centralized taxonomy administration and import metadata functionality
- Content enrichment through controlled vocabulary

The outputs of the information architect provide taxonomy design, standard processes, and (if it's implemented properly) well-trained users. This means that even after the SharePoint implementation is completed, the processes related to taxonomy, metadata, and the implemented architecture continues. Separate resources need to be applied to these areas outside the program, and the SharePoint sponsor needs to understand this from the outset—right at the point of defining the SharePoint 2013 Quality Plan.

Information architects categorize data so that it is easy to locate. SharePoint 2013 metadata management includes working with terms, managed terms, and managed keywords.

The information architect skill set should feature the following program tasks:

- Support the solutions architect and business analyst by providing blueprints of data flows in the organization, including taxonomy and metadata structures
- Organize and label communities to support usability and findability
- Design and construct the structure of the information in the organization, or if it has already been done, helping to refine this for SharePoint 2013

## Infrastructure specialist

An infrastructure specialist is a person in a mixed IT environment who works with the hardware and back-end systems that provide the base for SharePoint (and other technologies and components). Infrastructure specialists will work with other interfacing teams and will address infrastructure support issues, maintaining and managing the overall performance and availability of SharePoint and other technologies in their remit. They will also be called upon to provide support outside the SharePoint delivery program to face other technology products (for example, printers and telephony). In terms of SharePoint delivery, infrastructure specialists would be called upon to aid in topics such as network connectivity (for example, geographical boundaries) and consumerization (for example, "bring your own device," or BYOD). Careful decisions concerning the infrastructure specialist need to be made. Some organizations may decide to combine the infrastructure specialist and SharePoint administrator roles. This may work in small organizations, but not in larger ones. User Adoption requires support to work, and merging these roles will not satisfy users who need to have clear and well-understood lines of support available. For SharePoint delivery programs where there is a new provision of SharePoint, having someone available for infrastructure design and support will be needed. This includes platform Governance, where that person could represent interfacing teams.

The infrastructure specialist skill set should span the following possible program tasks:

- Troubleshoot and remediate infrastructure related to the provision of the SharePoint platform
- Administer the SharePoint platform production environment and other server infrastructure
- Install and support of hardware (including servers, PCs, network hardware, printers, telephones, and so on)
- Install and support of software (including desktop and server applications)
- Support Microsoft Exchange Server, Active Directory, SharePoint, and many other server-based platforms
- Relate with other support teams and third parties to ensure that incidents are escalated and resolved within the service-level agreements
- Execute business continuity activities, including backup and restore functions
- Maintain system documentation
- Process incidents and problems escalated from the help desk within clearly defined processes aligned to best practices

## SharePoint administrator

The SharePoint administrator is responsible for the initial configuration of the SharePoint platform and follows the rules stated by the solutions architect and the infrastructure specialist. You will need to have in place a SharePoint administrator in the early days of the SharePoint delivery program because the administrator is key to providing support and aspects of platform Governance for the SharePoint solution.

The SharePoint administrator is responsible for planning, operating, maintaining, and optimizing the SharePoint 2013 environment. On a day-to-day basis, this person is expected to work with other internal teams to define services, host, and maintain security authentication and data mirroring. This person also works through Central Administration to monitor quotas, throttle, report, and carry out system maintenance. In addition, SharePoint administrators are key to providing training to IT support and help-desk members.

**Note** There are a number of excellent tools within the central administrator function in SharePoint 2013, including a SharePoint Best Practices Analyzer and Health monitor, which will help administrators solve problems. In addition, the ability to manage the SharePoint 2013 environment—in terms of disaster recovery, backups, and reporting—is much improved. The SharePoint 2013 administrative features are covered in more detail in the "Building the platform deployment document" section of Chapter 6.

## SharePoint delivery manager

The SharePoint delivery manager has a single, overarching responsibility: to complete the program successfully within the guidelines of the budget, resourcing, and scope requirements. The delivery effort requires planning, control, and technical judgment, and the SharePoint delivery manager's responsibilities are primarily related to planning and control.

For the SharePoint delivery manager to carry out his or her responsibilities, the full support of the SharePoint sponsor's business group is required; therefore, the authority to plan and implement the SharePoint program is granted by the SharePoint sponsor through the TOR for the SharePoint delivery manager role. The SharePoint delivery manager, then, has the ability to recruit the team and set the terms of reference for each team member. It is absolutely critical that the SharePoint delivery manager has final say on this, and any alterations to any individual's TOR must be agreed to by the SharePoint delivery manager and, if necessary, the SharePoint sponsor.

**Note** To support the SharePoint delivery manager in larger SharePoint implementations, additional human resources are needed to help coordinate the program and gather and organize delivery plan documentation. Essentially, in larger programs, the SharePoint delivery manager requests support from the coordinator for things such as document and data control. This support role is useful in SharePoint 2013 because the coordinator can manage a delivery program SharePoint site that is used to house delivery program content.

The SharePoint delivery manager skill set should feature the following program tasks:

- Plan and control the activities of the SharePoint 2013 program by maintaining an up-to-date program and cost-to-completion tracking, monitoring program progress, and initiating corrective action where required.
- Ensure that all staff allocated to the program are gainfully employed, minimizing contract effort.
- Interact with other managers in the business group and LOB when planning staff allocations to ensure that the program's requirements for staff are met; that vacancies are identified in good time where they exist; and staff, whose allocation to the SharePoint 2013 program is ending, are reassigned as quickly as possible after each assignment is complete.

- Ensure that current and planned expenditures are contained within approved budgets, and to ensure that no work is undertaken without authorized financial cover.
- Ensure that the team adheres to the SharePoint 2013 Quality Plan.
- Provide technical guidance to program staff, or to delegate such guidance to a nominated member of the team.
- Delegate the management of tasks and subtasks where appropriate.
- Manage program risks using, where appropriate, a formal risk register within the SharePoint 2013 Delivery Plan.
- Ensure that technical reviews are held and recorded and that follow-up actions are discharged and closed down.
- Provide monthly reports or, as otherwise directed, record the status of and outlook for the program.
- Check that team members allocated to the program have sufficient qualifications and experience to do the work they are being tasked to undertake.
- Contribute to staff performance reviews as part of the appraisal process.
- Manage the equipment and facilities under your control in accordance with company policies and procedures.
- Communicate matters of company, divisional, and local issues to the team, and to represent their concerns to the SharePoint sponsor.

The SharePoint delivery manager has the following responsibilities:

- Tasking of staff assigned to the program
- Authorization of all formal program documentation
- Financial authority, within the limits set
- Authorization of time sheets for program team members

## Solutions architect

The solutions architect is a key resource for SharePoint solution implementation. This person is knowledgeable about the platform from the operating system through dependent technologies such as Domain Naming System/Windows Internet Naming Service (DNS/WINS), firewalls, infrastructure design, capacity, growth, performance, and resiliency. This person also must have a strong understanding of what it takes to fulfill a SharePoint 2013 business requirement and how to apply SharePoint technology to solving those business requirements.

Because this role is pivotal to the provision of a SharePoint delivery program, the SharePoint delivery manager and the SharePoint sponsor must work together to recruit the person who will fill it. This person will interface with the SharePoint delivery team, the organization's technical teams, and the business on a daily basis. The solution architect provides the design, the specifications of that design, and the delivery of technical support, and changes management processes to protect the integrity of the solution.

The solutions architect skill set should include the following program tasks:

- Advise on the design and analysis techniques, as well as on procedures that should be used in the SharePoint program
- Detail disaster-recovery specifications
- Detail capacity plans
- Detail network security
- Provide support to the SharePoint delivery manager in reviewing the customer requirement; help to produce the requirement specification
- Endorse the verification and validation of the SharePoint delivery program, including the following tasks:
  - The number, level, and timing of technical reviews
  - The approval of the technical review records produced
  - Approval of all technical documentation produced
  - Signing of design certificates (particularly if third-party products are assigned to the SharePoint implementation)

## SharePoint and web developer

Some organizations faced with wanting to implement SharePoint have done so by recruiting a SharePoint developer contractor who then installs SharePoint, carries out customization, and then leaves the organization. This approach, as you can imagine, leaves the SharePoint sponsor with a virtually unsupported platform, resulting in it being completely rebuilt at some point because it either becomes impossible to upgrade or because configuration management information is not available. Other companies find that they are locked into attempting to keep the SharePoint developer, who then becomes a kind of SharePoint administrator and developer (but remember, no one is a SharePoint superhero). As you'll see from reading this chapter, a SharePoint program team is much more than someone getting a copy of SharePoint 2013, dropping it into a server DVD drive, and after a couple of clicks, telling the customer, "Here's SharePoint! Have fun!"

SharePoint developers are not planners; neither are they architects, business-focused analysts, or information architects. Their task is to customize SharePoint to add functionality to specific SharePoint sponsor requirements. SharePoint 2013 provides users with more ability to customize the software than SharePoint 2007 did; hence, the requirement for customization is reduced (to a degree) in SharePoint 2013. However, in a program that requires a SharePoint platform to be delivered, you do not need a developer because there would not be a specific SharePoint sponsor that requires customizing SharePoint 2013. Development in SharePoint 2013 is a completely separate program because it includes its own quality planning, delivery, configuration, and deployment phases.

I've seen and implemented environments where there have been heavy customization requirements, and where there have been absolutely no requirement to modify SharePoint out of the box. In neither case is a developer required from the outset because the SharePoint sponsor wants SharePoint. It's what needs to be done with SharePoint post-implementation that warrants further development.

So let me be clear here: Development means programming, which requires separate tools, processes, and management. It is not the same as implementing SharePoint in a SharePoint sponsor's infrastructure. I am not saying that developers are not required—they are, definitely. But their involvement in the configuration of a SharePoint solution that features a SharePoint platform is minimal unless the user requirements are such that a SharePoint developer is needed to build in the extra functionality needed.

The role of the SharePoint developer is to create solutions to meet user requirements that cannot be provided from built-in SharePoint features. A SharePoint developer is comfortable in Microsoft Visual Studio. Yes, the developer could just use Microsoft SharePoint Designer and do a lot of custom development without ever using Visual Studio or .NET code. They have knowledge of SharePoint Designer, JavaScript, jQuery, and Collaborative Application Markup Language (CAML), which is the XML-based language used to build and customize websites based on SharePoint. After investigating and analyzing the business requirements, good SharePoint developers design the solution. The design elements could include anything from diagrams to formal design documents to proofs of concept to complete working prototypes, or any combination of those, depending on the complexity of the need and the audience.

The developer's skill set should include the following program tasks:

- Customize functionality of specific web parts
- Assemble workflows
- Implement branding and style—for example, master pages, styles for web parts, and so on
- Develop web parts
- Develop features (including list definitions, site definitions, and so on)
- Develop list event handlers
- Develop a workflow

**More Info** Deciding when you should and should not customize SharePoint is very important in understanding whether there is a requirement for a SharePoint Developer. For more information, see Chapter 10, "SharePoint customization impacting User Adoption".

## The SharePoint 2013 One-Stop Shop

SharePoint 2013 is a great tool for program management document control and planning. It provides all the relevant features and benefits, allowing you to build a successful and duplicable program management office that will become the SharePoint One-Stop Shop for the organization, providing a crucial resource. Figure 7-1 shows a SharePoint 2013 site developed as a One-Stop Shop site.

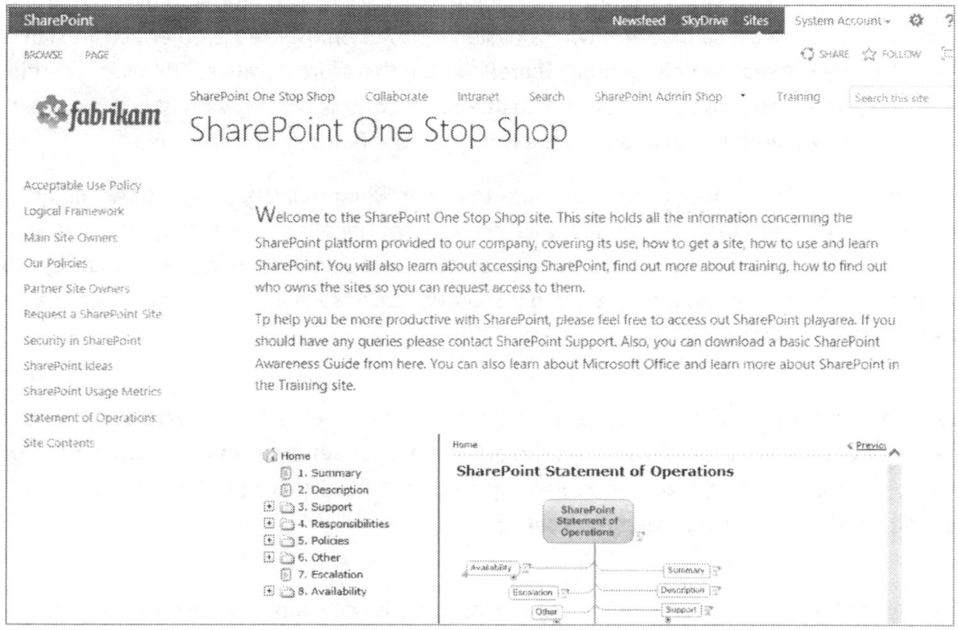


**FIGURE 7-1** An example SharePoint 2013 One-Stop Shop site.

This SharePoint 2013 site will house everything related to the SharePoint delivery program. This includes policies, statement of operations, FAQs, "How Do I" files, performance and resiliency information, backup information, requests for sites, keywords, and even an Admin section for SharePoint 2013 administrators to use.

There are many excellent reasons to have a SharePoint One-Stop Shop site. Think of the learning needs of the delivery team and the organization as a whole. For example, a business manager once said to me, "I have a whole bunch of people who want to learn SharePoint in a week." I said, "OK, what aspect of SharePoint?" He said, "What do you mean? All of it, of course. It can't be that hard!"

I had to explain to the business manager why learning everything related to SharePoint would be impractical, would be difficult in the extreme in only a week's time, and would not solve any user information challenges. Here are the key reasons:

- **No one person can be a SharePoint superhero.** No one (except maybe a few people on the planet) knows absolutely everything about SharePoint.
- **Not everything in SharePoint can be taught.** Therefore, one person can't gain complete knowledge (unless that person is a savant). Some things in SharePoint take time to learn and

require experience using it before it all sinks in. That's why there are different skill sets and roles, such as SharePoint administrator, developer, and architect.

- **Everyone has different needs.** Not every member of the organization does exactly the same thing every day with SharePoint, so not everyone needs to know every little thing about the technology.
- **SharePoint is not a silver bullet.** This point goes back to planning and user requirements. SharePoint is a scalable platform whose design is based on user requirements. The Plan, Build, and Deploy phases of implementing SharePoint are therefore iterative. The user is continually learning based on those changes, and SharePoint is continually evolving. It will not meet every single user requirement, now and in the future, on the first day of deployment.

A SharePoint One-Stop Shop is very important to a SharePoint delivery program. As the program takes shape, you will be gathering requirements, creating specifications, collecting information from meetings, and more. This information will have to be centralized and made available to those who need to collaborate; storing this information in a SharePoint site such as a One-Stop Shop is a perfect way to ensure that this happens.

**Note** The SharePoint 2010 One-Stop Shop can initially be created on a separate machine made available for the project team. As the environments get created and information gets moved onto the platform, the One-Stop Shop can be shifted to a home accessible to all (after the production environment is created).

Naturally, the function of the SharePoint One-Stop Shop is not simply to hold information concerning the delivery plan; it also exists to educate users about the project. Having access to this information will cause users to become engaged with SharePoint, learn what the product is, understand how it has been deployed, and know what services and roles are implemented in managing the platform. It also exists to store items such as FAQs, policies, guidelines, rules, and policies that come from decisions made by the Governance committee.

**Tip** A SharePoint One-Stop Shop is very useful for providing Governance-related information concerning business rules and policies. An output of Governance is the Statement of Operations, a guidance document that outlines the maintenance, administration, and support of the organization's SharePoint environment. Lines of ownership for both business and technical teams are detailed in the Statement of Operations. You could create a page dedicated to this and have it accessible from the SharePoint One-Stop Shop. More information concerning the Statement of Operations is in Chapter 5, "Planning SharePoint Governance."

You could, therefore, have a SharePoint site that is dedicated to "everything SharePoint" in the company. Such a site might enable users to learn SharePoint from the inside out. And because they can access a SharePoint site to get information about the product, you can easily provide many mechanisms to educate and inspire them to come to grips with all types of SharePoint features. For example, you might create blogs with articles describing how to carry out certain functions in SharePoint.

The One-Stop Shop should contain all topics concerning the use of SharePoint in the organization. This can include technical information for the support teams through the use of SharePoint blogs and Really Simple Syndication (RSS) feeds to external sites such as MSDN, Microsoft TechNet, and subject matter expert (SME) blogs and websites. This information can be made accessible to technical staff so that they can learn how SharePoint has been configured, refer to relevant service account settings, and store information about the installation of features and products.

**Tip** You might want to make it easier for users to get to the One-Stop Shop. For example, if the One-Stop Shop had a site named SharePoint and you wanted users to be able to type **SharePoint** in the browser and go directly to the site, the quickest and easiest way is to create a DNS entry called SharePoint and create a web application with a new site collection associated with it. If your SharePoint One-Stop Shop is a site within a site collection, you can use a vanity URL (a web application that redirects users to the location of the site), but note that you should not store this in a SharePoint content database, and it will require manual maintenance on each web front-end server in the farm.

For more information on redirection using a vanity URL in SharePoint, read the article "Redirection options in SharePoint," at *http://www.toddklindt.com/blog/Lists/Posts/Post.aspx?ID=48*.

Also, you should update organizational promoted results to target specific blogs, wiki pages, or published portal pages as guidance documentation to solve common tasks that users face in SharePoint. For example, let's say that you have a blog about how users get access to SharePoint content. Many organizations having SharePoint will have distributed ownership on their sites, meaning the procedure is to request access from the owners, who then set the permissions on the user sites.

On this site, if users complain that they see an "Access denied" message when they want to access particular content and want to know how to solve the issue, the description of this process should state whom users should contact to request access to the content instead of having directives such as "Click Site Actions, go to Site Permissions," and so on. So users can then type in a keyword to search; assuming that the best possible keyword has been assigned to the content, users will then find the blog instructing them how to access the content. By providing guidance such as this, you educate the user base, as well as use less time and cost to get the issue sorted out than if the users had had to go to the Help Desk for assistance.

A member of an organization who works in the accounting department has different requirements and needs than a member of the organization who is on the communications team. These users' needs are different; therefore, some elements of their training and education will be different (and if necessary, customized to meet their requirements). The One-Stop Shop should ideally be designed to suit all generic requirements. For example, members of an organization might want to know any or all of the following:

- How to modify navigation on their site
- How to create a survey
- What the policies are regarding setting site permissions

The solutions for all these user needs could be found in the One-Stop Shop if you successfully understood the client's needs. These needs are encapsulated in the user requirements. The user requirements documentation details what users want from their sites, the content in the site, the features required, how users will work with those features, and (critically) what users want to do with SharePoint. As you gain understanding of the user requirements, you will see a common trend in the problems that users face. For example, a majority of users are likely to want to use Microsoft Project 2010 with SharePoint. Therefore, you need to focus on providing information about key tasks that people might perform in Project 2010 and SharePoint.

So, let's recap. To provide a source of education for users concerning SharePoint, your implementation of the new platform needs to include a central point where users can go to find information about it. In time, as the business grows with SharePoint and SharePoint champions emerge, roles can be expanded so that the business takes more control of the One-Stop Shop, and therefore is even closer to managing SharePoint users.

The One-Stop Shop can easily be started from a Blank Site template or a Team Site template. In any case, this central location should at a minimum have the following areas:

- **A Landing page** Create a "welcome" Landing page. The Landing page displays up-to-date information concerning key aspects of the SharePoint instance status, web application and site collection lists, site owner lists, and a framework of the service (how the sites are set in terms of taxonomy). It should also provide procedures and policies, a statement of operations, new site requests, new keyword best bet requests, and key Governance statements.
- **A How Do I? area** Create a community subsite. This site should include FAQs, training information, and question-and-answer discussion areas for the SharePoint administrators to review. In particular, this holds a list of blogs answering popular user queries and detailing step-by-step instructions to help users solve issues as well as to provide ideas to users.
- **A Training and Education area** Create a subsite to provide a SharePoint Training and Education area. This could include the training strategy, classes, courses available, requirements, and so on. The subsite also can provide access to online classes for users. The user learns how to use SharePoint by using online classes, webcasts, podcasts, online videos, and interactive workshops. Activity can be tracked by users subscribing to the service so that they are aware of their progress and can match their requirements to the training modules provided.

**More Info** The SharePoint Training site (*http://www.microsoft.com/learning/en/us/training/sharepoint.aspx#2010sec3*) provides training materials concerning core and advanced solutions. Courses also prepare you for certification on SharePoint.

- **Admin** This is a subsite of the One-Stop Shop that is accessible only by SharePoint administrators, interfacing teams, and affiliated technical staff. The SharePoint 2013 Central Administration site provides most of this data, but the Admin page provides more of a "human" face and expands on Central Administration by providing information to educate and inform the IT support staff. Also, the Admin subsite provides a central base of operations for SharePoint administrators and ensures that they also control the One-Stop Shop. The following items can be provided in the Admin area:
  - **Admin blogs** An up-to-date account of any software or hardware issues or information that would be useful concerning the administration of SharePoint.
  - **Task list** A list holding jobs for administrators to perform. For instance, this can be a task list stating the monitoring jobs to be carried out on a daily basis and then linked back to the Admin blogs. So a blog appearing in Admin blogs could be related back to a task.
- **Logs** Create a page displaying Monitoring logs from SharePoint servers. You can monitor which are the slowest pages and most active users against sites and services and then return statistics such as the following:
  - Average duration (seconds)
  - Minimum duration (seconds)
  - Maximum duration (seconds)
  - Average database queries (count)
  - Minimum database queries (count)
  - Maximum database queries (count)
  - Number of requests

**Tip** You can monitor and report on all timer jobs, search reports, and many other elements and have this information displayed in the Admin site. In addition, consider that if there are existing help-desk systems, they may be able to include information that can also be displayed on a webpage in SharePoint.

- **Growth rates** Create a webpage to display a continually updated content growth rate dashboard. This enables you to see the size trends of the content databases. Who better to provide this information to than the Microsoft SQL Server teams?

- **Site lists and dynamic analysis trends** Create a webpage to display SharePoint sites analytics. Help desk staff can then use this area to identify what site owner is responsible for what site and how that owner can be reached.

> **Tip** Several automated tools have been created to aid you in providing reports that would normally be time consuming to get by using SharePoint. An example of this is GELISTALLSITES, which allows you to list not only all or some sites of a site collection, but also shows who has specific rights on those sites. For example, it helps you to know who owns what site. This information is output to a text file, which then can be fed into a SharePoint site. For more information, check out *http://gelistallsites.codeplex.com*. In addition, tools such as the following are available from more established development firms: Dell [who owns Quest (*http://www.quest.com*) provides tools a site administrator can use to manage SharePoint farms, including migration, recovery, reporting, and security tools. AvePoint (*http://avepoint.com*) provides backup, recovery, migration, and archiving tools. Axceler (*http://axceler.com*) provides management tools to automate, provide Governance and auditing for SharePoint site content. There are quite a few more firms that provide software solutions in specific or multiple areas of SharePoint. When selecting an additional product, ensure that it is fully tested and vetted for use before committing to it and the organization that's responsible for creating and supporting the product.

- **Delivery program site** Create a subsite to be the home of the SharePoint delivery program. This site could be based on the Projects Web Database that houses all the information relevant to SharePoint 2010 implementation planning, or utilizing the Project Web App web parts.

A SharePoint One-Stop Shop provides a central base of operations for your SharePoint technical team to operate from, a place for users to visit to find out anything related to SharePoint or the SharePoint delivery program. By building this site with users, you will help them to learn about the product and provide the organization with a point of presence for the SharePoint implementation.

In organizations where I have implemented the One-Stop Shop, user productivity has increased to a major degree, and the support desk has seen far fewer calls. Prior to implementing the One-Stop Shop, many calls for support were being made to an already-busy SharePoint team. A few key concepts to keep in mind are that the One-Stop Shop is on a continual life cycle of updating and reviewing, and anything that happens in SharePoint where users need to know needs to be reflected on it.

The SharePoint One-Stop Shop does the following:

- Serves as the central repository for all program-related material related to the implementation of SharePoint 2013
- Provisions collaborative features that allow information to be shared among program members and program visitors
- Provides a home for any organizational SharePoint 2013–related topics

## Interfaces: Teams in the organization

A significant number of components and platform technologies are connected to any installation of SharePoint 2013. What makes SharePoint 2013 really special is that you can add further components to it with ease. Of course, you would never connect all of this yourself because you are not a SharePoint superhero. You need various teams to work with you. Also, by bringing in these teams, you increase their knowledge of the platform and ensure that they have an understanding of it from a technical and support perspective.

Here are a few of the technologies required to enable SharePoint 2013 to operate:

- Active Directory
- Exchange Server
- SQL Server
- Windows Server

Some people might argue that they can easily install SharePoint by themselves in a single-server environment. While this is achievable, it's not really advisable. If you install SharePoint, Active Directory, Exchange Server, and SQL Server on a single server, you'll end up not having an easily scaled solution or a supportable platform. Some SharePoint programs start that way and then run into trouble because the person installing SharePoint has not taken into account where the SharePoint sponsor wants to go with the technology. In addition, that person has not identified what the user requirements are or worked out how SharePoint will grow with the organization.

To make this a little clearer, consider this analogy. If you purchase a Cadillac, but you really want a high-powered sports car like a Lamborghini, you will be disappointed when the Cadillac can't make the tight corners at the Indianapolis Speedway. Or maybe the reverse is true—you've bought the Lamborghini, but all you want to do is go to the grocery store; you don't need all the high-powered sports car features of the Lamborghini.

SharePoint 2013 can be delivered to a single-server platform. That means having Active Directory, Exchange Server, and SQL Server all installed alongside SharePoint 2013. But in a multi-support–driven organization with disconnected and managed support services, having all services installed on one server would be unwise and difficult to manage. In a single-server SharePoint environment connected to a local SQL Server instance, having a support environment where a SQL Server team is already managing a SQL cluster for the organization does not guarantee consistent support. Surely, SharePoint would be pushed into the SQL cluster environment so that it can be supported and controlled as part of the organization's data storage policies. The same goes for Exchange Server and Active Directory. Imagine that you decide to connect SharePoint to a locally installed Active Directory on the server in a multi-supported environment where there is an Active Directory team in place. Doing that creates support issues for the Active Directory team. Finally, imagine the performance and support issues that arise from running all technologies on one server.

If there is no multi-supported environment and all support is provided by one person, you still do not necessarily have to install all the technologies on one machine. Remember that you need to be able to validate the installation and provide an effective support service. If you are that person and are reading this book, I strongly recommend that you speak to the SharePoint sponsor and identify the shortfalls of taking on SharePoint with limited human resources to support the technology.

Most often, you should assume that Active Directory, Exchange Server, and SQL Server should be run by separate teams. You need to have a list of these teams in your SharePoint 2013 Quality Plan. The SharePoint delivery manager and technical authority should negotiate which members of those teams will tie into the SharePoint 2013 program, and they need to draw up TORs for those teams so that each team member understands what will be required of him or her and when.

**Note** You, as the SharePoint delivery manager, can work with your solutions architect and infrastructure specialist to organize workshops to gather more information about how the current infrastructure operates.

There are many roles relevant to teams that SharePoint consumes services from and, as mentioned previously, the key teams are Active Directory, SQL Services, and Exchange Server. Making sure that you get the information needed to provide an on-premise installation of SharePoint 2013 is important. Here are some of the types of information you need:

- **Active Directory** Service account creation procedures; the format of the accounts
- **SQL Services** Database-creation procedures; account-creation procedures
- **Exchange** SMTP connectivity information; domain connectivity; email creation procedures; security issues

You might have noticed that I added "security issues" to the list of information needed by the Exchange Server team. Providing the Exchange Server team with security information is extremely important for any SharePoint installation. All teams have procedures concerning the provision of their services to SharePoint. Each will have security procedures detailing how relevant services will be provided. For example, let's consider service accounts.

In SharePoint, you have to install Exchange Server using a number of service accounts. You could easily make up these service accounts and then ask your Active Directory team to create them for you. However, the Active Directory team might have some security procedures concerning the creation of these accounts. The accounts might have to be formatted in a certain way (for example, to have *as_* in front of each service account), for the password to be complex, and for the accounts to sit in a certain organizational unit in Active Directory. All of this is acceptable for SharePoint 2013, of course, but the key element is to ensure that you and the team are both aware of these security procedures up front, and that they are all enforced on your SharePoint 2013 installation. However, it should also be pointed out here that the Active Directory team would like for certain things to be defined for SharePoint service accounts concerning account expiration, failed logon attempts, group policies, and so on—some of which might cause support and operational issues for SharePoint. For example, employing account expiration settings results in the service settings for SharePoint to be reconfigured for new passwords every so often, meaning that services can get disrupted sometimes.

Remember, it is not your place as either the SharePoint delivery manager or the solutions architect to question the procedures that the SharePoint sponsor teams have. However, it is your responsibility to adhere to their procedures and ensure that they adhere to yours. And you'll find some organizations where none of these procedures exist. It is a best practice, therefore, that you form the SharePoint 2013 configuration management procedures for your environment quickly.

Let's take SQL Server as an example. A significant portion of a SharePoint delivery program is SQL Server–centric. Therefore, it is absolutely critical that the security provision between SQL Server and SharePoint is agreed to by the solutions architect working with the infrastructure specialist and the SQL Server team.

SharePoint interfacing teams aid the delivery programs by doing the following:

- **Providing best practice Governance and procedures** Include service accounts, naming conventions, monitoring plans, escalation paths, and service-level agreements (SLAs)
- **Providing technical aid** Includes provisioning of Active Directory, Exchange Server, SQL Server, and so on
- **Providing support for knowledge transfer** Includes keeping teams abreast of information concerning SharePoint 2013, such as information related to monitoring, troubleshooting, and so on

## Interfaces: Consultants from outside the organization

Put yourself in the mind of the SharePoint sponsor, who wants to implement SharePoint but does not have any SharePoint delivery managers available. If you do not have any in-house SharePoint expertise available, but you still want to use SharePoint, what can you do? In this circumstance, it is possible for SharePoint to be implemented by an external company (for example, a subcontracted consultancy like a Microsoft Gold Partner with SharePoint expertise). Microsoft provides a directory for the Microsoft Partner Network, where you can locate trusted experts who are supported by Microsoft. For more information, visit *http://www.microsoft.com/en-gb/business/how-to-buy/Microsoft-Partner-Network.aspx.*

Now, imagine that you want to add some third-party functionality to SharePoint and you need some advice on doing that. Tools, resources, and advice can be provided by an external consultancy (examples include backup tools, document management tools, building strategy, training, and so on). The relevant functionality could be delivered as part of a SharePoint delivery program.

One benefit of using an external consultancy is that knowledge transfer to the organization occurs. When an external consultancy is brought in to implement a SharePoint solution, it most likely will have its own delivery manager, who will report to you. A delivery manager hired as a consultant—that is, one who is not part of the SharePoint sponsor organization—will require more time to prepare than an internal SharePoint delivery manager because the internal SharePoint delivery manager will already be in tune with the relevant program management procedures and policies. However, it is distinctly possible that a delivery manager from an external SharePoint consultancy will have more experience and not be tied to any political issues; however, they may have to take longer to gain the full cooperation of the staff in the organization.

While they do cost money, external consultancies can provide excellent service if they are knowledgeable about the product, have dealt with delivering SharePoint solutions in the past, and follow repeatable processes and procedures (such as the ones that I am covering in this book). Keep in mind, though, that at the end of the process, the external consultants should not just step away and leave you to your own devices. This is because your business must have the ability to provide some kind of support to your users, even if the consultancy is supporting the delivery of the solution.

**Note** The SharePoint sponsor might request the use of an outside organization to provide SharePoint, especially if this person believes that the outside consultants will not be hampered by the internal politics of the organization; or if there is no skill set in the organization that meets the solution requirements. (The latter would have to be proven to the SharePoint sponsor; the SharePoint sponsor usually won't just assume this.) Also, the SharePoint sponsor might regard the use of an internal program management office as being too closely aligned with one portion of the business or another, or they might conclude that the processes of the organization concerning technology releases are not mature enough.

**More Info** The article "Harmony in Delivery," at *http://www.sharepointgeoff.com/articles-2/service-delivery—working-in-harmony-with-external-sharepoint-agencies,* will help you understand what kind of information is required to build a TOR using external organizations. Remember that the key requirements when choosing an external consultant are service, trust, and the capability to deliver against that TOR.

## Communications

The communications team is responsible for updating staff on the developments of the SharePoint delivery program. During a SharePoint implementation, there will be lots of news for staff concerning training, support, demonstrations, question-and-answer sessions, and opportunities to engage with the program team. Utilizing this role is vital because it helps staff properly engage with SharePoint and helps them feel as if they are part of the implementation.

## Quality Assurance

During the gathering of user requirements, individuals will be assigned as a tester of a particular feature or service that has been requested, or as a Quality Assurance resource to confirm that the feature or service works effectively. These individuals are assigned those roles in the context of what is to be tested, with the agreement of the SharePoint delivery manager. For example, if there is a requirement for a SharePoint site, then the process of gathering user requirements for that site will reveal those people who will act as testers. These resources carry out acceptance testing of SharePoint solutions to ensure that there is documented proof that the solutions have met the requirements set out by the users.

**More Info** "Verify and Validate SharePoint solutions," an article that describes a Verification and Validation strategy (known as V & V), is located at *http://www.sharepointgeoff.com/verification-and-validation-of-sharepoint-implementation/*. This article describes the procedures that can help you provide V & V activities, which will confirm that the logical planning, design, and build of the solution operates in the organization's physical SharePoint environment.

## SharePoint trainers

Through collaboration and coordination with internal stakeholders, the SharePoint delivery program will identify the needs for training and require a training model, which comprises of strategy, planning, and schedules. SharePoint trainers help build the SharePoint training model, which is described in the "Creating a SharePoint training program" section of Chapter 5. SharePoint trainers help carry out training needs analysis, which is done by taking outputs from the business analyst, holding sessions with users to identify their training requirements, and gauging user skills and knowledge of SharePoint. SharePoint trainers are used to providing presentations using Microsoft PowerPoint and other presentation applications.

The SharePoint trainer skill set should include the following program tasks:

- Develop and recommend strategies to educate users on new and enhanced SharePoint capabilities.
- Identify, develop, and coordinate with stakeholders the appropriate educational materials and delivery methodologies needed.
- Solicit and review training requirements across the organization to obtain user input into all training designs, impacts, and decisions.
- Be able to conduct live and online training for users.
- Help maintain the central training repository and/or knowledge base and update training materials.

*Making sure that a sustainable training delivery plan after the SharePoint solution has been delivered is in place is vital. For more information on this whole process, read the "Confirming that training delivery has been completed" section of Chapter 11, "Managing workshops and closing the delivery program."*

## User interface designer

SharePoint 2013 now gives rise to *commoditization,* where the user can select SharePoint apps from the Office Marketplace or custom solutions made available in an app catalog. These apps and solutions can then be applied to the SharePoint site. Because of the many different apps available from many different suppliers, this may introduce issues concerning variations in interface design among these apps. So, in order to meet web design standards, you need to review the apps to see whether they adhere to those standards. To do this, you may need a special resource to help you meet that challenge.

Carrying out web design standard reviews is useful because you are ensuring that user design Governance for SharePoint apps is available. This is a form of platform Governance where the app is defined as valid for use based on the fact that it meets the defined standards. In addition, this aids User Adoption and training.

User interface designers have skills in interface design navigation, appearance, and interaction. They are able to manage the user's experience of SharePoint webpages by designing familiar structures and processes for them. The user interface designer can create forms that enable the user interface to be friendlier and more acceptable to a wider range of users. This enables all users to be more productive and satisfied with the app in terms of its look and feel.

**More Info** User interface design is a huge topic, particularly due to the nature of SharePoint app design. So you should consider learning more about web design standards. The World Wide Web Consortium (W3C) is an international community where member organizations, a full-time staff, and the public work together to develop web standards. It publishes information concerning website quality and accessibility, as well as about what web standards are available and why they should be used. For more information about W3C, visit *http://www.w3.org/standards/about.html.*

# Summary

A SharePoint delivery program is not just a technical effort. A SharePoint delivery program requires a team with business skills, technical skills, program skills, information analysis skills, training skills, and many other areas of expertise. Under no circumstances should someone be randomly elected "the SharePoint techie" and be made entirely responsible for a SharePoint delivery program. Making your Windows Server administrator the solutions architect and SharePoint administrator, for example, is courting disaster.

To have a successful delivery team requires clear TORs, unambiguous objectives, and a skilled mix of team members. While it is possible that individuals from the organization can be drafted into the delivery program team, it is vital that a sufficient budget is available to outsource any expertise that it is not available in the organization. The resources that you choose to apply depend on the solution that is being delivered. Consider drafting aid from external courses, such as Microsoft Gold Partners.

Good examples of roles that you may have to get from external sources are the solutions architect, SharePoint web developer, business analyst, and SharePoint administrator.

Also, consider that training of users adds value to the program and aids your delivery team, particularly in the creation of SharePoint champions, and devolved business administration of SharePoint sites ensures that self-governance of SharePoint owned by the business is in place. This will help the delivery of any SharePoint solution and provide a good basis for user acceptance testing.

Don't be afraid to ask for the resources you need, and get them, or your SharePoint delivery program will not be successful.

CHAPTER 8

# Building a SharePoint service delivery model

In this chapter:



The key concept for sustained User Adoption and Governance is based on customer experience in a Microsoft SharePoint environment where customer engagement is rapidly shifting. To sustain a good customer experience in using SharePoint solutions, you need to implement an agile customer service strategy that meets the needs of customers on their own terms across all channels. Those channels could be On-Premise SharePoint or SharePoint through Microsoft Office 365. Good customer service is delivered in two ways: on a reactive basis, by solving user problems with provisioned SharePoint solutions; or on a proactive basis, by identifying better ways to improve the customer experience. This chapter describes the importance of service delivery, how to create a SharePoint support service, and the impacts on service delivery from compliance, legal, and cloud issues. The chapter also describes the importance of resiliency and availability of SharePoint solutions and their impacts on service delivery.

## Understanding SharePoint service delivery

As we begin, I want to explain why I'm focusing on SharePoint service delivery. I have worked in so many organizations where the delivery of a SharePoint solution has an overarching imperative, which is simply to provide customer satisfaction and good customer experience in using that solution—even beyond where the solution has been implemented. This is so they can ensure that they are getting the best value from the available tools and making a satisfactory return on investment (ROI).

SharePoint is a business platform. Therefore, service delivery is required to guarantee that SharePoint solutions can be delivered using practical techniques and in a logical fashion. You will not be able to provide adequate services without taking into consideration issue, change, service-level, and operational requirements. Here is my definition of SharePoint service delivery: *SharePoint service delivery is about delivering services effectively which exceed customer expectation, aligned directly to customer requirements and is fully supportable.* SharePoint service delivery combines what is being offered with how that service will be delivered. Service delivery is about ensuring that service always meets customer expectations.

The most important aspect of sustaining User Adoption is ensuring that you are capable of managing the SharePoint solution, understanding the customer, and providing a customer-driven, measurable SharePoint service. SharePoint service delivery is about capability, availability, customers, and service. What you will need to understand is why these elements are important.

*Why is SharePoint service delivery about capability?*

- Because SharePoint support services must be capable of supporting the delivered solution in line with customer expectations.
- Because the SharePoint delivery teams must be capable on delivering on the promises that were made about time and quality.
- Because associated SharePoint support services must be capable of standing over any key performance indicators (KPIs) or service-level agreements (SLAs).
- Because the people must be capable of using the delivered SharePoint solution.
- Because processes and procedures created through the delivery of the solution must be capable in enabling and enhancing business productivity, knowledge, and solving information and management collaboration challenges.

*Why is SharePoint service delivery about customers?*

- Because customers need to appreciate what is being delivered through User Adoption.
- Because customers are the ones who will give you feedback concerning the SharePoint service failures and successes.
- Because customers are the people who have the power to accept or reject the financial costs of SharePoint service. These costs could include the licenses for a SharePoint app or charges made to external customers to provide support services.
- Because without customer satisfaction aligned to SharePoint support excellence, User Adoption will fail.
- Because customers will measure the excellence of SharePoint support services.

*Why is SharePoint service delivery about service?*

- Because SharePoint service delivery implies that something is going to be delivered in a sequenced and logical approach that the customer will understand.

- Because SharePoint service delivery implies a degree of excellence.

*Why is SharePoint service delivery about availability?*

- Because customers are among the organization's key resources. A disruption of this resource due to non-availability of SharePoint solutions will result in customers not being able to perform their tasks.
- Because the availability of SharePoint solutions is based on the risk tolerance of the customers or the organization's culture.
- Because customers need to understand the impact of an outage or disruption of SharePoint services.
- Because understanding the resources available to support the service is key to understanding its availability.

While there are factors that will define the level of service, there is nothing to stop you from delivering that service excellently. You do this by creating a SharePoint support service, and to do that, you need to understand the capabilities that the customer will require support for, related to internal and external considerations. Cloud, compliancy, legal issues, availability, and resiliency are some of these considerations, and all are discussed in this chapter. The point of understanding these considerations means that you will be able to create a well-implemented SharePoint service whose performance can be measured by the customer.

## Creating a SharePoint support service

SharePoint means websites for everyone; the ability for people to create and manage content in websites. When the Internet was new, information was exploding and search was coming into its own, Microsoft created a platform that allows individuals to create and manage their own content online—and without the use of developers or website designers.

SharePoint 2013 is not a minor release. SharePoint is now fully part of the Microsoft Office suite, and fully integrated into Office 365. Microsoft is focused on providing a streamlined customer experience across Office Suite. This customer experience now extends into service delivery, and therefore, the importance of customer experience with SharePoint needs to be examined. Good SharePoint support has to be reactive, on demand, specific, and proactive.

SharePoint support success needs to be achieved because if support succeeds, that will create sustained User Adoption and Governance. To guarantee that this happens, you need to build a support service model that includes the customer and provides satisfaction and good service that is repeatable and meets all expectations.

Any SharePoint customer perception is based on the premise that SharePoint support service is a single point of contact for all information challenges, with *transparent escalation,* and be readily available to solve their problems. While that may be true, it creates a reactive support service. Any

SharePoint support service needs to expand to proactive support, where SharePoint support staff intuitively know how to improve their services in anticipation of customer expectations.

So you will need to create a SharePoint support services model, and to do that, there are several tasks, each requiring significant work. This is because creating a support service for SharePoint is a complex process. SharePoint is a business platform, and the number of services that need to be supported is based on what is provided to the business. Those services could include Enterprise Products, Business Intelligence, Search, Information Publishing, and Social Features, among others. Each requires support. Therefore, you need to ensure that a support model is in place to support those services to customer expectation.

My definition of SharePoint support is as follows:

> *SharePoint support is a specialist function that retains, on behalf of the organization's user population, technical knowledge about SharePoint and the way that the organization uses it. SharePoint support does this in order to deliver that knowledge in a focused form to solve specific technical and business problems on both a reactive and proactive basis. This enables user productivity to be maintained and enhanced, and helps the user contribute to the organization's business goals.*

The support effectiveness of the SharePoint platform is directly related to the resources that are available and needed. For example, the support arrangements for a single-server environment with only search services enabled is nowhere near the same as a multihomed SharePoint environment utilizing a myriad of application services. You need to judge the kind of resources needed to manage and support the necessary services.

To create a SharePoint support service, you will need to know your product as well as your customers. There are more tasks to consider, and with each of these, it is important to understand what the task is, why it is needed, and when it should take place. I devised a 10-part approach, which will provide you with practical techniques to create a first-class SharePoint support service. The SharePoint support service needs to be *strategic* and *measurable*. Being strategic is vital because whatever the SharePoint support service does needs to dovetail into IT support and corporate strategy. And the service must be measurable because the SharePoint support service provided to customers needs to prove to stakeholders that it is satisfactory, and you cannot do that without having some way to gauge success.

This chapter describes 10 tasks that need to be completed in order for you to create a first-class SharePoint support service. Collectively, these 10 tasks make up a SharePoint support model, as shown in Figure 8-1. Each of these tasks is described in the subsections that follow.

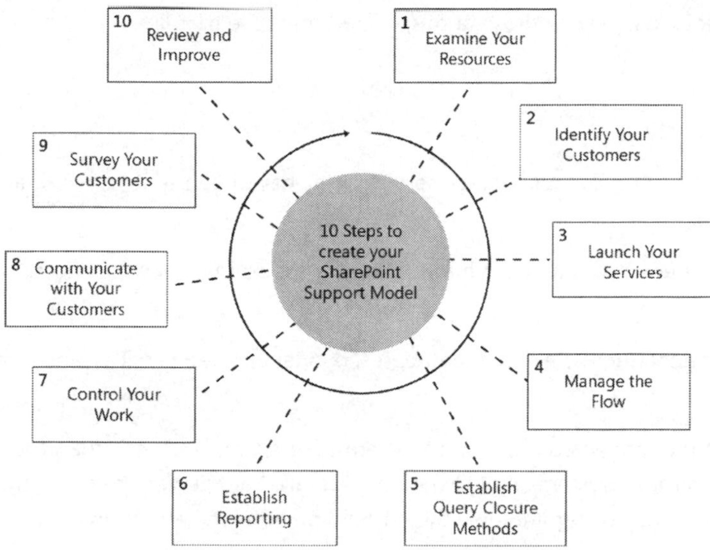


**FIGURE 8-1** The 10 tasks to create a SharePoint support model.

## Task 1: Examine your resources

As explained earlier in this chapter, you cannot create a SharePoint support service unless you know exactly what you can support and who is available to provide support. To complete the task of *examining your resources*, you need to build inventories of contacts and equipment, create infrastructure diagrams of the SharePoint platforms, to review support team capabilities, and build an inventory of contacts responsible for the connected infrastructure. These subtasks are relevant to those organizations that have split up support teams based on specific areas of technology. For example, your organization might have a network team responsible for platform engineering, storage engineering, and so on. There might be a separate Microsoft SQL Server database team, a separate email team, or even a separate disk storage team. All of these are crucial for SharePoint because SharePoint will be directly dependent on those components.

Consider the following practical techniques to complete this task:

- Build an inventory of contacts concerning any third-party applications directly connected on the SharePoint platform. Include user account information needed to access any of their online help-desk systems.
- List each of the servers for all SharePoint farm(s), such as production, preproduction (stage or User Acceptance Test, or UAT), development, test, engineering (lab), and so on. Consider creating a diagram showing the connectivity of the servers, IP addresses, purpose, and so on. Include any references to build documentation that will include service accounts, passwords, key configuration information, and so on.

- List solutions and services assigned to those farm(s), including those that are
  - Supplied internally
  - Supplied by a third party
  - Included with the farms (for example, search services may have been split into several servers in the farms)
  - Ensured that where there is user account information for the solutions and services, that it is recorded.
- List connected components (such as external databases, connected web services, and custom SharePoint apps).
- List in detail the externally connected monitoring systems. For example, if the organization is using any service monitoring systems that also monitor SharePoint servers, describe them, including any documentation concerning how they should be accessed and used.
- List client applications that are being used with SharePoint by information workers. For productivity suites, such as Office, include the version and list all the products of that suite that are in use, as well as those that are available but not provided.
- List any plans to procure, produce, and/or implement any additional component that has the capability of being implemented with SharePoint.
- Describe geographical locations. Be aware of the regional splits in your SharePoint environment, and if you have multiple implementations of SharePoint in different regions, record SharePoint infrastructure information relevant to those locations and who is responsible for those.
- Understand the capability the support team has, including the technical skills in managing SharePoint infrastructure and the technical skills in supporting the users. Compare the technical skills available to what the customer is using. Be pragmatic. Development skills, for example, is not likely to be a high priority when helping users with Office and SharePoint. Consider also that business skills, as well as communication and people skills, are very important.
- Consider drawing infrastructure diagrams of the SharePoint environment, which should be classed as working documents and regularly updated with any changes to the environment in any of the abovementioned areas. Use knowledge from associated technical teams to help build infrastructure diagrams. Infrastructure diagrams are extremely useful in SharePoint support for the following reasons:
  - They show the true nature of the SharePoint environment.
  - They educate the evolving SharePoint team.
  - They show everyone that SharePoint is a service that includes equipment, components, and resources.

## Task 2: Identify your customers

You will need to understand who your customers are and what services they use. Note that I used the word *customer*, not *user*. This is because *user* reminds me more of a technocratic term applied to corporate IT, whereas *customer* has a less technical connotation. A *customer* is a person who uses the SharePoint support services, while a *user* is a person who uses the SharePoint solutions. The following definition, which I apply to SharePoint support services, shows why this is the case:

> *A SharePoint customer is anyone who consumes anything he or she perceives that you have produced. That is whether or not the perception is correct, whether or not you intended to produce it, and whether or not you knew you had created it.*

The reason for that definition is that it reminds me of what customer satisfaction truly is all about. As part of delivering SharePoint support services, I could increase my services, increase service levels, keep solving problems, and so on. But that applies only to the services that I know I have produced or am producing. If the customer measures me on that alone, then that's great. But they do not. A customer measures my SharePoint support services on anything that enters their imagination or stimulates an opinion. I could say to customers that I have achieved a higher success rate of solving problems than the industry standard, but that would be meaningless to them because to them, customer satisfaction based on their own experience in getting their problem solved—that is of paramount importance. Conversely, I could say that I have achieved a success rate to a satisfactory standard, but, if the customer says that is not good enough, then it is not good enough.

Here is an example of a customer perceiving something as part of SharePoint, but the IT department assumed that the issue was not its responsibility.

*Scenario 1: A customer accesses a purchasing product called XYZ, which is a non-SharePoint, web-based, third-party product. She accesses this product by going to a SharePoint site, and then clicking a link that displays the logon page in a page in SharePoint. One day, this customer starts calling the help desk to complain, "I cannot access the SharePoint XYZ product."*

The vital part of this statement is that it reveals customer perception. Customers will not care that the XYZ product is not part of SharePoint. To them, it is part of SharePoint because they access a SharePoint site to get to the product. There would be no sense and no value in IT explaining to the user that's not a SharePoint problem, when the customer thinks it is. What you need to do in this scenario is not only solve the problem, but also educate customers concerning the use of product XYZ.

Identifying existing customers should be easy enough. From User Adoption, communication, and training plans, you will have a good idea of who the customers are because they are recorded as part of the delivery program. However, you will need to consider those who are not your customers yet. It is precisely the fact that they do not use your support services that you should be concerned about, especially if you're not sure why. Here are some possible reasons:

- The support services provided do not appear to match their needs.
- The support services are misunderstood or have not been adequately communicated.
- The support services are not trusted.
- The support services have not left customers feeling satisfied with the service.

Whatever the reason, you need to know what it is so that you can market and match support services to potential customer expectations. These potential customers may be harmless and ignorant of SharePoint support, or they may feel negative and be badly informed about the software. Treat both as an opportunity to ensure that support services meet customer expectations. Set priorities when identifying your customer groups. You will find that some customer groups hold more power than others and you will need to adjust priority levels accordingly. For example, you will treat the SharePoint sponsor with respect because a SharePoint sponsor can influence budgets, income, staffing level, resources, and so on, just by using SharePoint support. Build your service based on your customer base. Do not assume that charging out SharePoint support services provides excellent service. If you fail to attract customers, you will lose a purpose for having SharePoint support in the first place. When that happens, those who would otherwise finance SharePoint support will likely become less disposed to do so.

Another consideration is that customers are not the prime organizational directive—money is. Customers are merely one of several resources that produce the organization's final product. The final product is the organization's continued existence. This means that as a SharePoint support manager, you need to know what the goals are and strive toward those goals by keeping an eye on the money. Money is the main reason why the organization exists, and SharePoint support is there to contribute to that, no matter how obscure that contribution is.

*Scenario 2: Charlie Herb is a SharePoint support manager for Fabrikam, a manufacturer of communications switching equipment. Fabrikam had a wide market, and because of the specialization, as well as looking after internal customers, Charlie and his team had to take the occasional call from external customers. Charlie took his job seriously. He adopted the prevailing organizational culture and took it upon himself to believe in the company slogan: "Our Customers, Our Priority." One Friday afternoon, in the weekly report session with his manager, Charlie was having a hard time explaining why the team performance was lower than usual. Charlie described how the SharePoint support team had been busy looking after a particularly troublesome customer, and that he did not want that customer to see him as not committed to service quality. Charlie was shocked to hear his line manager say "Oh, that account? Forget it—they are not a target this year." For days after, Charlie pondered that. Clearly, priorities were operating here, but what the advertising person told him and what his line manager had said seemed to conflict. Customers were clearly less important than target business. Armed with that conclusion, he reviewed the SharePoint support services to offer new and improved services to targeted customers. Also, he ensured that all future meetings with his line manager included reviewing changes to business targets.*

When identifying the goals of the organization, also be mindful of the political power of your customers. For example, a SharePoint sponsor would have more political power than a SharePoint information worker or a member of an external technical support team.

*Scenario 3: The SharePoint sponsor is the CEO of the company and a former staffer at the help desk. His secretary appears to get top priority when calling into SharePoint support, and she uses that to her advantage to ensure that her requests are dealt with first. Following discussions, it was found that she knew about the SharePoint sponsor's power and used it as a method of ensuring that her issues were dealt with first.*

The point of this scenario is that as the leader of SharePoint support services, you must address customer priorities. If you do not, customer experience will not be consistent and customer perception will be that issues are based on rules outside of the control of the SharePoint support services. For example, a customer who requires a major solution in SharePoint was important at the time the solution was implemented. If the organizational goal changes, and the importance of that SharePoint solution reduces, so does the importance of that customer.

Here are some practical techniques you can use to identify your customers:

- Identify both users and non-users of your services.
- List them in order of priority. Be pragmatic and clear-eyed. Their priority may come from their importance to the organization, or it may come from the power they wield.
- Identify your delegation and escalation channels. This is particularly related to internal technical teams which SharePoint consumes services from. For example, if there is a query concerning email-enabled document libraries not functioning, you may need to escalate to the Exchange Server team. If a customer requires access to a SharePoint site, you may wish to delegate this to the business owner responsible for the site.

One method of identifying key customers and their level of importance (which shows their priority) is to build a SharePoint support customer map. Figure 8-2 shows an example of this type of map. It is developed by placing SharePoint support in the center and then listing all customers by function or department inside and outside the organization that requires your services. Then, for each of those customers, indicate how each customer would accept the support service; is this person a decision maker, an influencer, or a user who requires consent? Also indicate what their attitude is likely to be concerning SharePoint support services. This you can gauge by surveying and the communication tactics described in Communications planning. Initially, you should focus your efforts on those who have a negative attitude because that will enable you to improve services before they are launched. For example, if you wish to alter your services, you may need a particular customer's consent.

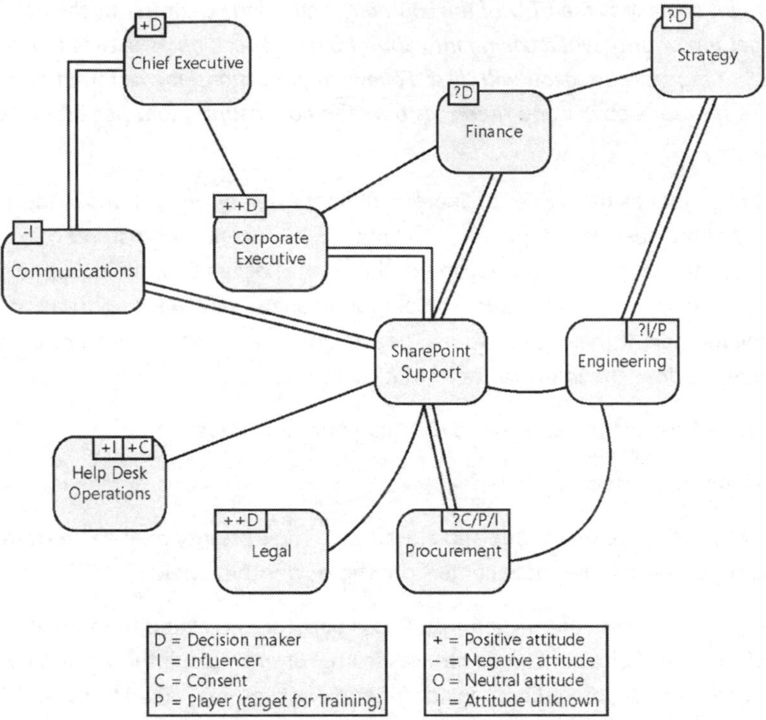


**FIGURE 8-2** An example of a SharePoint support services customer map.

## Task 3: Launch your services

Once you have examined the resources and identified the customers, you are ready to launch your support service. Launching the SharePoint support service means that you are at the point where you are ready to handle requests and issues relevant to the SharePoint service. Generally, your key customers will know about the service before you are ready to bring support services online. This is because if you're following the steps in this book, there would have been User Adoption, communication, and training plans executed for key customers. But those are not the only customers of those services. Your support services need to meet the majority of customer needs.

Marketing the support desk is a great way of informing potential customers that new support services are available. This is because by marketing the support desk, you are informing the customers about the following:

- That the support service has a face
- When the support service can be contacted
- What services they can contact you about
- How to contact the support service

You need to establish call procedures so that customers are aware of the various methods of contacting the support services. Typical methods include using the phone to call a centralized number, creating a ticket by going to a particular page on a website, and emailing a specific support service email address. Always provide more than one method, and always provide a backup method. For example, if the primary method of contacting the support desk is by telephone, you must have a secondary method in place in case the telephone network fails. The call procedures should also include information about how you will contact the customer. This is very important, and is further discussed in Tasks 4 and 5.

The top-level SharePoint support service is documented in the SharePoint Statement of Operations, which describes the fundamentals of your SharePoint support offering. You will find that as SharePoint solutions are added, there will be solutions that are customized, or that the customer needs a different arrangement concerning the levels of support services provided. Examples of this are the back-end offices, like finance. Others include key back-end systems that have different levels of support because they are covered by third parties. For small organizations to medium-sized organizations, if SharePoint services have the same types of customers or the same kinds of solutions, the Statement of Operations will suffice. There may be a situation where you will need to develop an SLA, which is referred to in the Statement of Operations. Creating an SLA means that a particular service being provided by SharePoint support services is to be handled differently from the majority of the others. The decision to create an SLA for the service should not be taken lightly, and it should be approved by the SharePoint sponsor. Bear in mind that the creation of an SLA must be associated with a review of the available resources to manage the normal support services as dictated by both the Statement of Operations and the SLA. The SharePoint SLA layout is shown in Figure 8-3.

**More Info** For more information concerning the creation of a SharePoint SLA, read the article at *http://sharepointsla.geoffevelyn.com*.

Practical techniques to launch your SharePoint support service are:

- Market the SharePoint support service as part of the User Adoption plan.
- Use your SharePoint champions to promote using the call procedures to contact SharePoint support.
- Regularly maintain a central bank of training materials and FAQs so that customers can use those (this is described further in Task 4).
- Build the Statement of Operations to include information about the services provided.
- Launch the Statement of Operations as a base to provide support services to the majority of your customers.
- Establish call procedures so that customers know how to contact the support services, and when they are available.
- Encourage any customers who find the services inappropriate to create a SharePoint SLA and fine-tune your support services to meet their expectations.

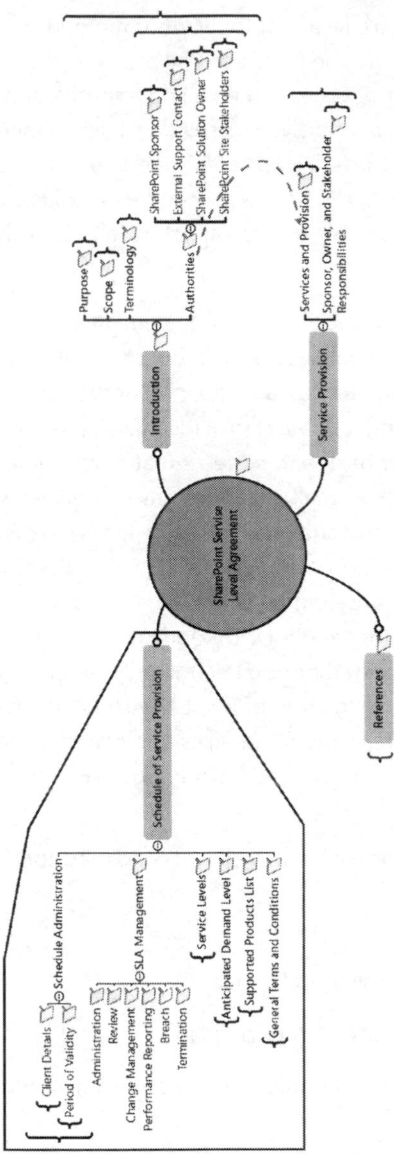


**FIGURE 8-3** SharePoint SLA layout.

## Task 4: Manage the flow

Once you start receiving calls to your SharePoint support service, you will need to manage how the calls are dealt with. Remember the priority and importance of the customer, and the services that are applied to those customers to decide how the call should be prioritized. You will need help providing support to your customers because the sheer number of solutions to support cannot be completely covered, and because no one is a SharePoint superhero. The organization requires ROI on SharePoint, which will include ensuring that the productivity of the customer is not impaired. Surely a great method to improve ROI, and at the same time provide aid to the SharePoint support service, is to add resources to help that support arrangement, but this should not be done at the cost of harming customer productivity by making customers act as SharePoint support members.

Business rules can help form your support services. For example, a key business rule that I always advocate is that the business is responsible for managing its own content. Managing that content includes maintaining its security at a basic level. So, if a SharePoint site is provided, I ensure that there are at least two owners of that site. The business rule that governs them having the site is that they own the site and therefore are responsible for the security access to that site. Of course, they get trained on that before they incorporate the site as part of that delivery. By advertising to those site customers that there are owners of that site who can guide them on basic operations in the site, and by setting the security access to the content through requests from those customers, I have received help with my support service, which allows me to manage the flow.

In SharePoint support services, you should have three levels of support: first-line, second-line, and third-line. The first line is the customer who simply uses a SharePoint site; the second is the customer who owns the site; and the third is SharePoint support. There is no fourth line, but there is escalation or delegation, which is managed by SharePoint support (the third line). The reason for the three-line division is to create business rules at each level. Business rules in the first line are managed by the second line, and business rules in the second line are managed by the third. The business rules in the third line are set by the Governance committee.

Table 8-1 describes the lines of support based on the most fundamental of SharePoint solutions: sites on a SharePoint platform. You should consider using these lines of support as a way to manage the flow of calls into SharePoint support and as part of the call procedure.

**TABLE 8-1** Lines of support associated with a SharePoint support services model

| Line of Support | Responsibilities |
|---|---|
| First | To provide devolved administration in a SharePoint site, the site owner (a member of the second line of support) may assign owner rights to specific repositories on that site to specific users. For example, specific users may be given the ability to manage a specific announcement, document library, picture library, or lists. Therefore, those who require access or request to modify those repositories would seek aid from those users instead of requesting it from the site owner. Of course, the site owner still retains control of the entire site in case the relevant repository owner is not available, and the site owner is responsible for managing those specific users who have repository-based owner rights. |
| Second | Site owners are responsible for managing the site and all subsites of that site. This means that they manage the structure and security of that site. There are generally at least two owners. If there is a sitewide issue that requires support intervention, they raise that as a request to the third line of support. Here are some of the area that a site owner would be responsible for:<br>■ Site administration<br>■ Management of user security<br>■ Management of sites<br>■ Site configuration<br>■ Basic branding (site title, description, theme, and web part layout)<br>■ Cascade training of users and ensuring access to training information relevant to the site |

| Line of Support | Responsibilities |
|---|---|
| Third | Members of the third line of support are part of the SharePoint support services team. They are the point of contact with all targeted customers. They are responsible for assisting with Governance to provide a consistent, resilient, and available SharePoint platform. Here are some of the tasks that a third-level support person might perform:<br>■ Set storage quotas on site collections to encourage storage management.<br>■ Define management of disk space and search relevancy.<br>■ Help define usage, data retention, customization, and deployment policies.<br>■ Manage organizational metadata (technical).<br>■ Monitor the SharePoint platform.<br>■ Manage Operational and Service SLAs.<br>■ Manage Backup and Restore/Recovery and Business Continuance SLAs.<br>■ Produce reports concerning uptime, downtime, and performance against SLAs.<br>■ Manage technical architecture.<br>■ Manage SharePoint solutions and back-end components.<br>■ Manage the infrastructure of all SharePoint environments. |

Use training materials and centrally stored FAQs to help manage the flow of calls into the support service. By guiding customers to use these resources, you are creating a standard way of answering frequent questions, which will encourage other customers to do the same.

Practical techniques to manage the flow of requests for aid from SharePoint support services are:

- Create business workflows for different types of customer requests. Establish effective workflow management for SharePoint support services. Figure 8-6 shows an example workflow for managing customer queries.
- Create support levels. Define *call management, job allocation,* and *devolved business administration* of SharePoint solutions.
- Set up query prioritization. Using the identified resources and customers, set out priorities based on the services offered.
- Define *problem escalation.* SharePoint support is the third line, and is responsible for escalation, which consists of interfacing with either technical teams or third-party companies for customized or integrated products. Ensure that the routes of escalation are set and understood.

**Note** You can manage the flow only after you have launched your services because you will not be exactly sure how to manage the workload until you know what it looks like.

## Task 5: Establish query closure methods

A query closure method is a tool used by SharePoint support to ensure customer satisfaction once a query has been resolved. I have seen instances where a customer is informed that their issue was resolved with a one-word email message: "FIXED." I have also seen instances where the customer is not informed that their query has been resolved at all, and when he or she calls to find out the status of the query, the support person says something like this: "I fixed that already. Didn't you know?"

Neither of those methods of dealing with queries is going to increase customer satisfaction—quite the contrary, in fact. The query resolution in a case like the one just described was simply a reaction, and the technician involved in resolving that query was only interested in the issue, not the customer. This will result in the customer looking elsewhere, and if that happens, the importance of the SharePoint support service fails for that customer and will have a negative impact on User Adoption. That dissatisfied customer will talk about his or her experience, and any other customer who hears about it will refrain from using the service.

So, establishing a process of closing a query is important and must be attached to any call-taking procedure put in place. Practical techniques to establish query closure methods are:

- Use feedback mechanisms (call-back, auto email notification) to confirm that the issue has been resolved to satisfaction.
- Use UAT to confirm success without disrupting production sites. Make sure that tests to confirm resolution that may disrupt production services are carried out in a UAT environment. Document the changes and release as change control procedures. (Chapter 5, "Planning SharePoint Governance," has more information about change control policies and procedures.)
- Create a SharePoint site as a help desk (if you do not already use a help-desk system). SharePoint sites can be configured to act as a help desk where tickets can be logged. A help-desk site template for SharePoint 2013 is available, which includes repositories to record requests, track status, manage frequently asked questions, etc. For more information, visit *http://www.sharepointgeoff.com/sharepoint-2013-helpdesk-site-available/.* Figure 8-4 shows a SharePoint 2013 site acting as a help desk, providing access to several subpages for service representatives, knowledge managers, and service report managers. The ability for customers to create service requests is also available.

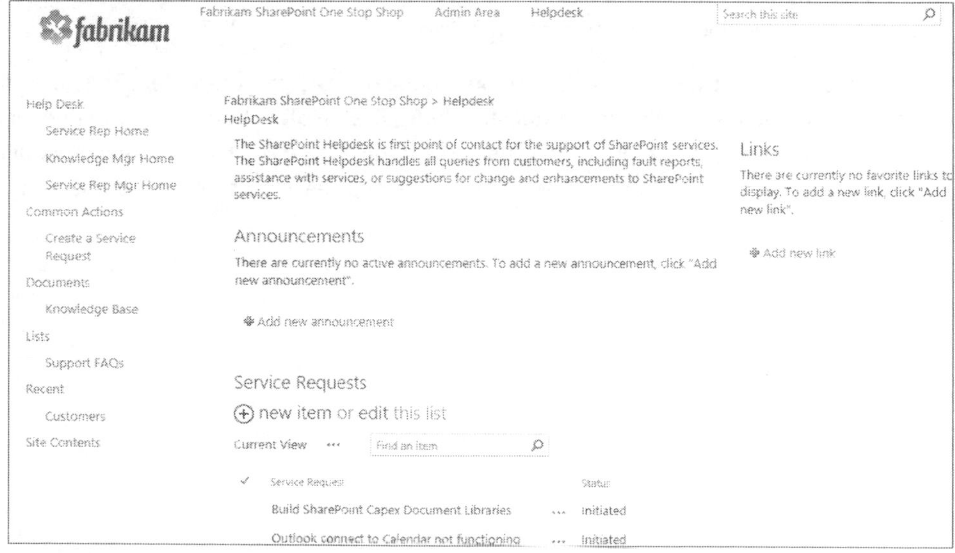


**FIGURE 8-4** A sample screenshot of a SharePoint 2013 help-desk site.

You will learn more about managing customer queries in "Task 7: Control your work." This section provides more information on creating call-taking workflows.

## Task 6: Establish reporting

In order to extract or offer the most appropriate reports about the SharePoint support service, first you need to know why reporting is necessary. If you do not understand the need for reporting, then there is a strong possibility that the reports that you create or use will not have their intended effect. The essential purpose of reporting is to communicate results to those who need to make decisions about those results (regardless of whether the recipient is your SharePoint sponsor, a delivery manager, a stakeholder, or even yourself). However, often this is not the actual purpose of reporting. You must determine the true purpose of any report before designing or submitting it.

Like any other action performed in SharePoint support service, creating reports requires resources. You will need to take this into account. Never produce a report that has no eventual payoff for you—if the payoff is only for other people, then it is their responsibility to produce the report, not yours. Check that the reports you send out are used. If they are not, discontinue them to stop wasting time and effort (both yours and your recipients'). Be prepared to negotiate with anybody who complains about the loss of the report. If people are not using it, then why should you produce it?

In addition to being a means of communication, reports, in all their forms, are a service to your customers. This fact implies that you should always be looking for new possible recipients of this service. This increases the range of SharePoint support services to customers, and along with it, the number of people in the organization who benefit from the SharePoint support service.

First, find out whom you are reporting to and whether that person or persons need a report. Consider the needs of the support service staff. Ensure that you create reports that show them how they are doing. You must do this to provide feedback so they can help improve the support service; this is key to motivating your staff to be proactive.

An effective report will contain conclusions about any statistics presented. This saves the reader the trouble of trying to work out the statistics themselves. It also shows the awareness of the fact that the support service staff are specialists in the trade. Figure 8-5 shows an example of the type of format you might use to produce a report about the high-level calls taken and the conclusions made as a result.

| SharePoint Support Services | | | | |
|---|---|---|---|---|
| Weekly Report #125 | | 7th February 2013 | | |
| From: | David Jaffe | SharePoint Services Support Manager | | |
| To: | Malvin Seale | Corporate SharePoint Program Manager | | |
| Cc: | All IT Helpdesk and Support Staff; SharePoint Organization IT Services Library | | | |

| Key Statistics | | This Week | Last Week | Same week last year |
|---|---|---|---|---|
| | Calls taken | 434 | 365 | 429 |
| | Spot Rate | 82% | 83% | 74% |
| | Fixed same day | 12% | 12% | 7% |
| | Fixed in two days | 4% | 3% | 15% |
| | Over two days | 2% | 2% | 4% |
| | Fixes/resolver/day | 5.2% | 4.1% | 4.5% |

Conclusions

The number of calls made came back up to normal levels Is following last week's big drop due to the network being down for a day. We are still making more or less the same number of calls this time last year, even though there are more users. No cause for action as I am examining the calls to try to assess whether the users have got more sophisticated.

The key figures are more or less constant now. But this is with two fewer staff compared with last year. This means the users are getting at least as good as service, but for less money. I intend to find out if they agree with that conclusion by running a survey around Easter.

Key events

Charlie Keen, one of our SharePoint Administrators, has completed his training and is now able to apply that training to solving specific user problems. We will have a contractor as he will be on holiday at the end of the month. I am expecting the figures to get worse over the next few weeks.

The SharePoint site for Accounts seems to be giving more problems due to the failure of a key SharePoint solution applied to that site. We hope to have that under control, but I will have to take their site offline next Friday to run diagnostics.

**FIGURE 8-5** A sample weekly SharePoint support services report.

Practical techniques to establish reporting mechanisms in SharePoint support services are:

- Provide snapshots of the workload by creating reports to specific audiences on a regular basis.
- Ensure that reporting includes resource requirements, particularly staff-related ones.
- Centralize the reports so that is easy for the relevant report audiences to get them.
- Establish Dashboards based on calls received, resolved, and so on.
- Record resolutions in a centralized knowledge base and update training materials as necessary.

## Task 7: Control your work

To control the work in a SharePoint support service, the support service must be proactive. Proactivity takes many forms. One of the most common is the study of user problems encountered, with a view to preventing them in the future. Another is the creation of an inventory of SharePoint solutions to help with diagnosing and solving problems with those solutions that the user may have. What these forms of proactivity have in common, however, is that they are all actions to be carried out now in order to influence the future.

Therefore, logically it could be said that extreme reactivity is the result of denial, or at least ignorance, of the future. However, in business, and certainly in SharePoint, the future is inevitable; often, it is so close as to be blinding. Change is happening all the time. And if the users, the technology, and the problems change, so should your SharePoint support service. I always ask SharePoint support managers two questions to get them to understand proactivity: "Do your SharePoint services look different now than they did when you started?" and "Are your customers as happy with your SharePoint support service as they were at the beginning?" The typical answer I get to the first question is yes. For the second question, the answers I get depend on whether and how the SharePoint support service was organized.

To design a proactive SharePoint support service, you need to ask yourself what else your support service could be doing that would deliver a real additional benefit to the customers. Then, compare the potential value of that benefit to the actual value of the benefits that you are currently delivering. Where the potential value of the new activity exceeds the value of the current one, stop delivering that current service and start delivering the new one in its stead. You can justify this by saying that all you have done is adjust your priorities. If you find that your customers wish you to carry on with the old service, then that is the one that would need to be justified, not the new one.

Real productivity comes from changing the reasons why customers need you now. If customers have problems with a SharePoint solution, what can you do to fix those problems? If you have customers who do not use your SharePoint support services, what can you do to encourage them to use the service? Conversely, if there are customers who are using your service in the wrong way, or for the wrong reasons, what can you do to change that?

A major reason why, as a SharePoint support manager, you may wish to shy away from proactivity is because it changes things. In the past versions of SharePoint, particularly SharePoint 2003 and SharePoint 2007, the perception of SharePoint support from the people who run it was that SharePoint is a technical solution provided by technical people, and therefore support is reactive. Support is there to wait for a problem to happen, and then to fix it. Technical people back then were conservative (and some are still that way). Many of them did not like change. It's better to simply wait for the telephone to ring. SharePoint 2013 is a business platform, so customer experience is vital to aiding User Adoption of it. SharePoint support, therefore, must be an enabler to sustained User Adoption, providing and seeking better ways to improve services for customers. Proactivity must be enshrined in SharePoint support. Use the following ideas to generate proactivity in the SharePoint support service:

- Produce a formal analysis of the last two weeks' help-desk queries, identifying customers who seem to have the same type of query. Contact those users and design mutually acceptable solution to plug knowledge gaps.
- Produce reports on changes made to the SharePoint environment, how the organization has benefited from those changes, and how users can employ them.
- Compile and maintain a directory of regular reports concerning SharePoint usage. Break this down by business unit. Provide those reports to specific business unit owners to show where their SharePoint investment is being used well, and perhaps also where it is being wasted.
- Maintain a register of SharePoint solutions in use, so you can identify what users are using which, and which solutions are becoming obsolete. This will enable you to advise users when solutions should be replaced, and what should replace them.
- Keep a central catalog of SharePoint solutions, scripts (for example JQuery, JavaScript), and other elements in use by site location, and offer that catalog to users so they can share those solutions.
- Produce a monthly newsletter of hints, tips, and goings-on relevant to SharePoint, including any related information so that users are kept up to date with SharePoint in general.
- Monitor the performance and learning rate of users working with SharePoint, and offer reports to the users. Doing this could allow you to recommend changes to the organization's induction process concerning the information that new users get before using SharePoint, for example.
- Analyze new products that integrate with SharePoint as they arrive on the market, and offer reports to the users. Topics could include how the organization could implement a new product, and what benefits could be gained. You should ensure that any new product becomes part of a SharePoint delivery program. Doing that, then, will show how useful the product is in practice, how the product differs from others, and what support queries is the product likely to raise.

Each of these suggestions will add value to the SharePoint support service. In almost every proactive service, you have to look at what your users could employ and create a service to satisfy demand.

Another part of reporting in a SharePoint support service is to produce reports concerning the support staff and structure. You must have and retain motivated members of the support team who do not shy away from managing user requests. If you do not do this, then all you will have is a support team whose members write documentation and do not engage with the users. Support staff is only part of the problem. If your support service is divided into only a first-line group and a resolution group, then that is not going to encourage proactivity. You have to dedicate resources to cater for a non-reactive function.

*Scenario 4: Miles Reid runs a SharePoint support service for The Phone Company, a large telecom equipment provider. The support team consists of five SharePoint administrators, and it has 15,000 customers and several external partners as well. Their SharePoint platform includes 10 third-party solutions, all of which are supported by external help desks, which his team keeps in close contact with. Miles has come to realize slowly that his teams' reactivity was hurting both him and their customers. This happened when he recognized that the last three solutions that had been installed were being supported by external help desks. He had not thought much of it before now, as those SharePoint solutions were all specialized and not directly in his teams' area of expertise. One of the solutions was for accounting, one for running a production line, and the other for monitoring the delivery fleet. But, now that he thought about it, all those solutions could have been provided by SharePoint features. He had missed out on the SharePoint delivery programs for those (being too busy solving customer problems), which meant that he could have influenced the purchasing decision. The organization had three departments now rebelling against the corporate IT strategy, and had four different standards of user support, and this was having a negative impact on the team. The SharePoint administrators' motivation was ebbing. Even though they had kept up with new SharePoint technologies, their hearts did not seem into being proactive. The trouble was, there was nowhere to promote support staff.*

*Miles needed to keep the team together and motivated. He described the situation to his line manager, who was also concerned with the fragmentation of the corporate IT strategy. He convinced his line manager to increase the salaries of the SharePoint administrators and to include in the Terms of Reference for the administrators to learn as much as they could about the way users worked with SharePoint and gain an understanding for the problems they were facing. This allowed the SharePoint administrators to use their technical knowledge to make adjustments to SharePoint to make it more usable and attractive. As a result, the SharePoint administrators would examine the market to see what SharePoint products would suit the users. After all this was implemented, users got better support and assistance in obtaining SharePoint solutions and apps. The IT department got control over what the users were buying, and the SharePoint support service got a chance to prepare for the new products that were being introduced.*

Procedures and standards are also important in controlling the work of the SharePoint support service. There are already formal procedures and standards in place for technical help desks, and they are well known. Most of these are included in a set of manuals called the Information Technology Infrastructure Library (ITIL). ITIL is not fully applicable to the creation of a SharePoint support services model because it does not show support and IT managers how to do their jobs; rather, it describes the techniques and methods that they use. For SharePoint support, the library is not applicable because it is inward looking and not customer oriented. It is far too focused on technical issues and therefore could not act as an operational guide for SharePoint support. SharePoint support is all about customer expectation, communication, and motivation. Therefore, the best procedures for you and your customers are ones that you design yourself. Use the designs as shown in ITIL, but modify them to suit your particular situation, so that they are easy to comply with and sell to your support team and customers.

**More Info** I recommend that you find out more information about ITIL because the procedures and standards are useful if you have never created a support service. For more information, visit *http://www.itil-officialsite.com/*.

As already stated, ITIL is a good standard to understand, and there are some useful procedures that you can adopt, modify, and apply to your situation. However, never lock your support services into any management methodology unless you can categorically prove that it is doing some good to your support service and customers. If there are procedures worth writing, write them. The key procedures you should look at stem from the flow of work through the SharePoint support service. Start from a generic perspective, and then modify the details to suit the customer experience. Flowcharts are extremely useful because often they are easier to follow than textual descriptions. Provide these graphically on the SharePoint One-Stop Shop for customers to view, so customers and support staff can see what is expected and what will happen, and this can also clarify for you whether procedures are being followed.

Figure 8-6 is an example of the sort of flowchart you could use to document part of the work in a SharePoint support service. It shows the workflow as seen from a member of the SharePoint support services team's point of view. A number of queries have arrived, and, with answers readily available, the team member can resolve the query. The team member examines the resulting queue of outstanding queries, and this flowchart illustrates the way that this team member handles them. As the team member is solving the query, new ones are being delivered, and the state of those queries already outstanding is also being changed by the arrival of new resources or information. The team member claims the query from the list of outstanding ones. This act of claiming means that the team member has to notify the support team that the query has been marked for their attention. The customer is also notified that the query has been assigned. Some further prediagnosis may have to be done (including examining the central knowledge base to find out if the query has been answered before), and it must be determined whether any further information is needed from the customer. If the team member needs to talk to the customer, the customer must be available. If the customer is not available, a notification is sent to this person explaining that the team member needs to contact him or her. The team member can then claim another query. If the customer is there, the team member can then obtain the information required. If there is not enough resources or information available to solve the query immediately (for example, the query needs to be put to another help desk), then the query is put in abeyance until resources are available, and the team member claims another query. If resources or information is available but the resource needs to be quickly obtained, then the priority is altered. The "Diagnose," "Test," and "Resolution?" boxes are in a cycle that continues until the query has been resolved. The customer is then advised of the solution to the query. If new information has been obtained concerning the query, that data is added to a central knowledge base. The team member then closes the query and checks whether the resources used can also be retained to help similar queries in the future.

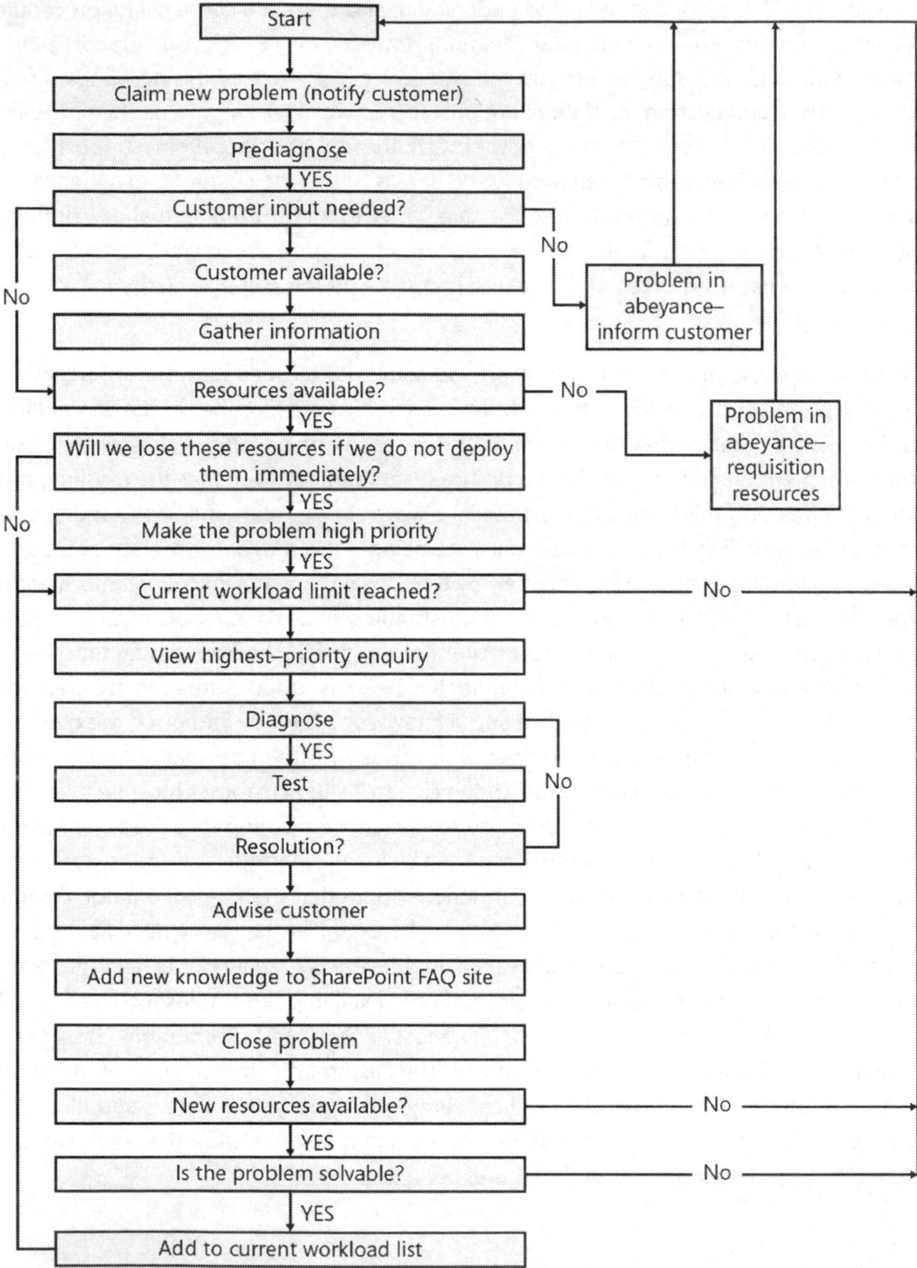


**FIGURE 8-6** A sample flowchart for managing customer queries to SharePoint support services.

Practical techniques to control the work in SharePoint support services include the following:

- Be proactive and always review new and improved methods of controlling work.
- Build business rules and policies. Make sure that they are standard and clearly understood by the team and customers.
- Use workflow to chart the work and communicate this to supporting teams and customers (as necessary).

## Task 8: Communicate with your customers

SharePoint support services need to be involved in setting customer expectations. By doing that, their performance can be measured against benchmarks that are not unreasonable or irrational. SharePoint support services must keep in touch with its customers. The principle of this is to increase understanding between SharePoint support and customers. The reason why this is so important is that there is a natural gulf between SharePoint technical specialists and the business user. This comes from the early history of computing, where the only people who understood computers were scientists. Then, in the 1970s and 1980s, some of the larger computer companies contributed to this by marketing their systems as instruments of corporate control rather than tools of user enablement. They also advocated huge IT departments to run these machines, speaking in a language which by its nature would be confusing to anyone outside the IT realm.

SharePoint (and in fact, the emergence of Content Management Systems) has changed the support model. The support model requires a direct connection with users and, speaking in their language, at a level that provides measurable customer satisfaction.

SharePoint support is the customer face of IT. Customers will not get a mental picture of the concepts of the IT department and the SharePoint support service. To customers, the IT department and the SharePoint support service are one and the same. If the IT department fails, so does SharePoint support. SharePoint support must therefore talk to its customers in business terms—the complete opposite of the way things have been done. Nowadays, many support professionals are self-taught and come from a user background rather than a technical one. Even so, these support professionals are then advised to sit behind a computer screen and wait for a customer to call them. This is reactive. It is the duty of SharePoint support to engage with the customers.

To understand how to communicate with your customers, you will need to know the various routes of communication. Each of these routes has a purpose, each with its own potential advantages and disadvantages. To illustrate this, Figure 8-7 shows a general impression of communications traffic affecting a SharePoint support service. The inner circle is the technical function within the SharePoint support service, combining the areas of a help desk, the resolvers, and a knowledge base library. The solution to any customer query to SharePoint support will come from the technical function. This must be established as a resolution, particularly if the query requires aid from the support administration (these are interfacing technical teams or external help desks) and/or from the users. The commercial pressures imposed from the outside world will affect both the users and the support administrations. In addition, users are part of the outside world because they are representatives of the business and the organization.

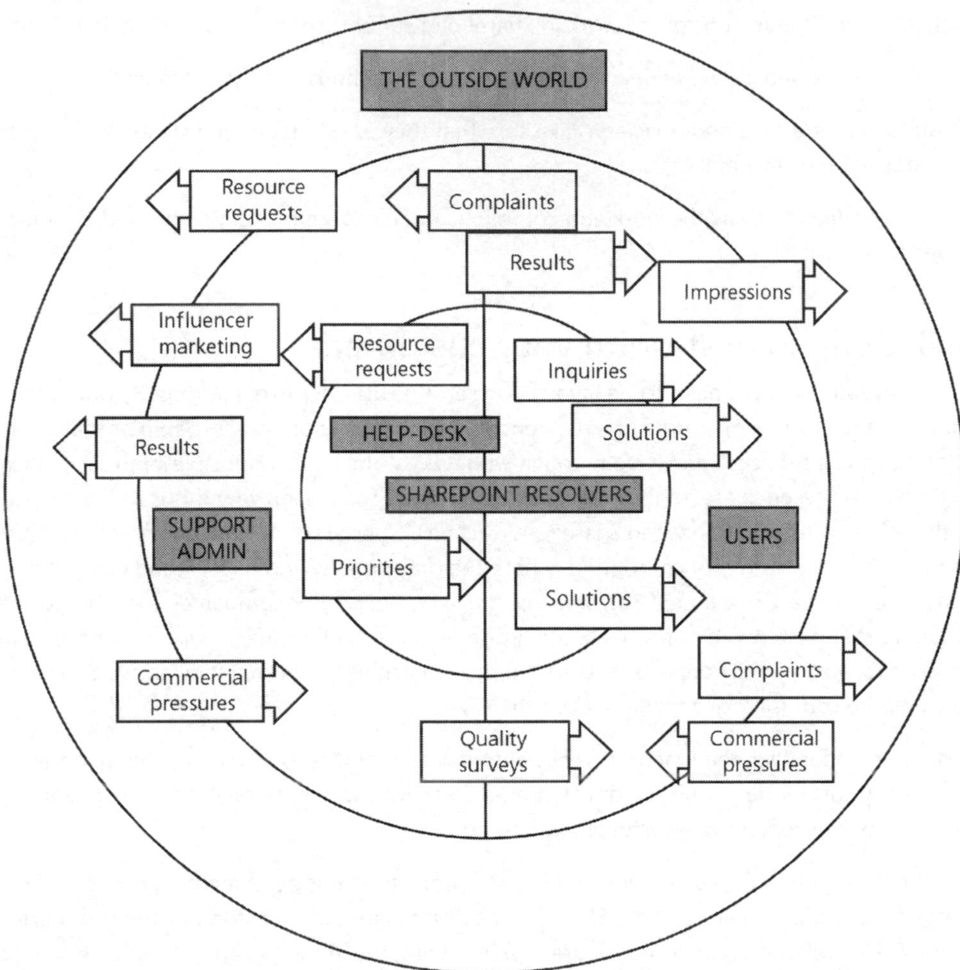


**FIGURE 8-7** Communication routes around a SharePoint support service.

Therefore, it is very important for SharePoint support to find out what the users are being measured on and to whom they report. This is so the support staff can be clear where they should be concentrating their limited resources.

As discussed in "Task 7: Control your work," customers will see the SharePoint support service as having two flaws: it is reactive, and it has limited resources. When a customer contacts the support service, it is usually because there is a problem; therefore, you will find that medium difficult to exploit in terms of communication and get a positive outcome. However, that medium can be used to express professionalism and job-ownership if the support service team members taking on the problem will notify the customer that the job has been taken, they are responding, and that the problem has been resolved.

For communication to be truly effective, it must be proactive. You must investigate and exploit channels of communication. Use the communication plan of the SharePoint delivery programs to show you what they are. The following list describes the various sources of communication. Note that each has its advantages and disadvantages. Be mindful of the organization's culture and resources related to the sources of communication. Obtain agreement on which methods of communication should be used with the stakeholders and the communications team (if there is one available in the organization):

- The SharePoint support help desk or the IT help desk
- Visits by the SharePoint support service staff to users
- Usage reports compiled by SharePoint support services
- Customer solution focuses forums and SharePoint community sites
- User newsletter
- Service review meetings
- The Intranet News page
- The User Booklet

Practical techniques to communicate with your customers using SharePoint support services are as follows:

- Identify the channels of communication and use them to engage with customers.
- Ensure that the language used in that communication can be understood by the various audiences.
- Market support services using the channels of communication. Personal contact is vital.
- Use SharePoint champions to help pass on information about SharePoint support service benefits.

**Tip** In addition, if you have a SharePoint site acting as a help desk, you could use information from that site as part of communicating to users. This is particularly useful in compiling usage reports. More information concerning using a SharePoint site as a help desk is described in the "Task 5: Establish query closure methods" section earlier in this chapter.

## Task 9: Survey your customers

You will need to know what your customers think about the SharePoint support service. By visiting customers, you will find out a great deal. But that measure is not scientific and will not give you any way to measure in concrete terms the effects that your services are having. To best measure customer opinion, you should consider surveying your customers.

In doing so, you must realize that customers will have neither the time nor the inclination to fill out a freestyle survey. Not only that the more freestyle the replies, the harder they are to measure, thereby defeating the point of taking a survey. On the other hand, if the survey questions are set with a majority of multiple-choice replies, then you are setting the agenda, which is limiting.

Before polling your customers on what they think of the support service, ask yourself these questions: Is the organization the sort of place where a customer survey can be conducted safely? Is the SharePoint solution conducive to objectivity, criticism, and examination?

As a SharePoint support services manager, an alternative to the multiple-choice-type survey is the random client poll. Generate a random five call-log tickets from the support services help desk, and then ask the relevant customers a series of questions. Compile the responses into a report and provide this information as part of the weekly report. Doing this has several benefits over a multiple-choice survey:

- It shows the customers and your support team that you care about quality.
- You get a measure of quality that can then be showcased.
- It forces you to keep in regular contact with customers.
- It exposes you to the way the customers are really treated.

Practical techniques to survey your customers using SharePoint support services are as follows:

- Establish methods of surveying.
- Make improvements to the support service based on results.
- Consider carrying out regularly scheduled random phone polling.
- Consider participation rewards for those completing surveys.

## Task 10: Review and improve

A good SharePoint support service is based on the art of giving customers precisely what they want, with a professionalism and flair that they would not expect. That professionalism comes from the SharePoint support service understanding their own job, the services they provide, and customer needs.

Believe in your SharePoint support team and make sure that SharePoint support services are the best in the organization. Establish an identity for the SharePoint support service. I have even seen organizations create a badge to signify membership and excellence. Create a mission statement that clarifies the importance of SharePoint support, and have goals that the team can strive toward. Give the team objectives to achieve so they can fill in their personal histories with professional success.

Finally, incentivize the work that the SharePoint support service needs to do, and review the entire setup of the SharePoint support service every six months. Once you make a review, use any of the techniques described in the previous nine tasks to enhance and improve relevant aspects of the service.

## Understanding compliance, legal, availability, and resiliency implications

As discussed in this chapter, service delivery is about capability, the customer, and the ability to improve services. Because of this, you need SharePoint services to provide data features that ensure the integrity of the content, and is resilient and available. This section will help you understand a number of compliance and legal implications, which will need to be understood.

Organizations will face challenges concerning the management of content, and not from the features provided by SharePoint that allow tagging, classification, and records management. These challenges come from User Adoption of those tools through training and communication, because the approach needs to suit the organization's culture and be adaptable.

If users do not understand the importance of classifying content, compliance is not the only thing that suffers. Search suffers because it will take longer to find content which should have been classified. There is a financial cost to the organization because content would have to be re-classified (because the content was never classified in the first place, or was incorrectly classified).

*Scenario 5: Tailspin Toys has a number of business units, each of which stores content in its SharePoint site. All the business units had migrated to SharePoint two months ago, and as part of the migration, copied content from their file servers into SharePoint. The business units did not carry out a review of the content on their file servers, and no one suggested that they do so. All the content in their SharePoint sites used a naming convention created by the relevant department. Last week, Tailspin Toys was sued for a breach of privacy concerning a merger. As part of that, they were audited for data compliancy as part of building a case to produce the last six years of financial documents. Chaos ensued, as people did not know whether to use SharePoint, whether to use the file servers, or even whether the contents were structured or classified. As a result, Tailspin Toys hired consultants to sort out the classification of content and froze SharePoint use to protect the integrity of non–file server content.*

In addition, the security of content must be addressed fully—again, not by using SharePoint features, but by understanding the risks that come with not linking security policies to content. The following scenario shows how important that in today's climate of allowing access to SharePoint over the Internet has security implications, and can then lead to compliancy issues.

*Scenario 6: A university in England allowed confidential information, including bank account details on 20,000 students and staff, to be accessible from its SharePoint site, which had anonymous access set to that site over the Internet. This situation was reported by a student in the university. Following an investigation, it was found that SharePoint support services failed to address SharePoint platform security completely. In addition, the university failed to run any checks to quantify the risk. The university was not only reported on widely, both nationally and internationally, for this failure, but it was found in breach of the UK Data Protection Act of 1998 because it failed to provide adequate security measures. Not surprisingly, this incident had a major negative effect on User Adoption. Students and staff felt uncomfortable about the SharePoint platform being secure and they also blamed SharePoint support services for the failure.*

Compliance and legal implications for SharePoint service delivery starts with users. Getting users to understand the security implications of SharePoint is important. Without that, the integrity of any content on a SharePoint site is at risk. For more information about this topic, visit *http://www.sharepointgeoff.com/sharepoint-security-and-helping-users-become-more-aware/*.

Also, content classification and understanding the document lifecycle (which is particularly relevant to records management) are vital. Again, users need to be aware of this. You will need to configure the capabilities of SharePoint 2013 to allow the categorization of enterprise content in the organization.

**More Info** Records management is a huge topic, and the full details of it are well beyond the scope of this book. But there are many sources of information concerning SharePoint 2013 on-premise and SharePoint 2013 off-premise through Office 365. For an overview of records management, visit *http://technet.microsoft.com/en-us/library/cc261982.aspx*.

If there is a requirement to deliver Office 365, you should ensure that the SharePoint sponsor understands the compliance and legal issues. To help with this, the Cloud Security Alliance published the Cloud Control Matrix to help consumers evaluate cloud services and identify questions that should be answered before moving to cloud services. Microsoft created a document to outline how you can meet the suggested principles and mapped them to the International Standards Organization (ISO) 27001:2005 and ISO 27002. You can download this document from *http://www.sharepointgeoff.com/security-in-office-365-whitepaper-available/*.

Business Continuity Management (BCM) is a process that provides a framework to ensure the resilience of your business in response to any eventuality, to help ensure continuity of service to your key customers, and to protect your brand and reputation. Defining a SharePoint BCM provides a basis for planning to ensure the long-term survivability of your systems following a disruptive event (that is, any event where SharePoint becomes unavailable). This could be due to the loss of a data center, the loss of Internet access (for off-premise), and even more serious occurrences. By understanding and then implementing a business continuity plan for SharePoint, you are providing customers with the assurance that operations will continue in a form that is acceptable to them.

**More Info** Many improvements in SharePoint 2013 support business continuity management. For information on how to plan for disaster recovery from a technical standpoint, visit *http://technet.microsoft.com/en-us/library/cc263031.aspx*. To understand the processes of business continuity and disaster recovery and how to apply the principles involved, visit *http://www.sharepointgeoff.com/sharepoint-business-continuity-introduction* and *http://www.sharepointgeoff.com/developing-drp/*.

Availability of SharePoint to the organization is vital. Considerable publicity has been given in recent years to the lack of security definitions and policies concerning the security of assets relevant to Content Management Systems (CMSs). Because of the centralization of content into these CMSs, it has become more and more apparent that the risks to organizations concerning data availability have grown. To start looking at the availability of the platform, you should do the following:

1. Get a list of all assets in your SharePoint platform (as described in the "Task 1: Examine your resources" section, earlier in this chapter.).
2. Create a capacity risk analysis. Examine any points where there could be a failure. Examine the SharePoint servers, as well as the back-end tools and technologies that support SharePoint: ISA, Active Directory, Domain Name Systems (DNS), Microsoft Exchange Server, and SQL Server. Examine your firewall and proxy. Examine third-party connections; for example, web applications that have their own functionality that may affect SharePoint.
3. Once the risk analysis has been carried out, review all known possible failure points. Review issues concerning connectivity to these services. Examine the logs concerning a failure to connect and document them. Audit all backups and schedules and identify a priority backup path.
4. Examine the sites, list those that contain critical and/or confidential content, contact the owners, and get a business SLA recovery identification. Define your site topology to ensure that high-impact content can be provided in the event of a disaster. Review the server provision of your SharePoint environment and plan to scale as necessary.
5. Create a risk management plan that lists countermeasures. Now that you have identified known threats (and note the list may well not be exhaustive), it's time to select countermeasures for each issue.
6. Implement, review, review, and review again. Your SharePoint instance will grow, and you must ensure that your SharePoint availability plan grows with it.

**More Info** For more information about planning for high availability and disaster recovery in SharePoint 2013, visit *http://technet.microsoft.com/en-us/library/cc263031.aspx* and *http://www.sharepointgeoff.com/sharepoint-platform-availability-mitigating-the-risks/.*

## Cloud versus on-premise

In terms of providing a SharePoint service, you will need to understand how an effective support model can be provided for SharePoint cloud-based solutions (through Office 365), as opposed to on-premise solutions (through SharePoint on company premises).

The price of bandwidth and storage continues to fall. Office 365 is becoming more and more attractive to small and medium-sized organizations. These organizations are committed to reduce licensing costs, not IT staff. However, you should be aware of this and not assume that the cloud solution is always best. In SharePoint delivery, no solution is exactly the same in terms of service provision. You should always investigate how benefits can be maximized in the existing setup and compare those to a cloud-based service. Note that by using a hybrid model (a combination of on-premise and off-premise SharePoint), organizations can have the best of both worlds, without long-term commitments.

Off-premise SharePoint through Office 365 is an attractive option to small and medium-sized organizations that need to use technology at lower risk and cost. They do not have to invest in hardware or software, and licensing and renewal costs are lower. Total cost of ownership is based on only what is used. Table 8-2 lists a few of the advantages concerning on-premise versus off-premise provision, and Table 8-3 lists a few of the disadvantages of this approach.

**TABLE 8-2** Advantages of on-premise and off-premise SharePoint

| On-Premise | Off-Premise |
|---|---|
| Configuration management is under the complete control of the organization. | You can quickly create a website presence. |
| The organization owns the infrastructure. | There is no cost for infrastructure. |
| Customization development can be defined in specific and full SharePoint environments. | The latest version of SharePoint is available. |
| Performance is easier to monitor. | Office products are packaged and at the same version of SharePoint. |
| Integration is easier to manage and define. | 99 percent availability and clear status display of services, showing both scheduled uptime and downtime |
| Data management is easier—you can control what site collections go to what content databases, what service applications are associated, and so on. | Available so long as you have access to the Internet |
| | Configuration management is taken care of by the host provider, which is Microsoft. |

**TABLE 8-3** Disadvantages of on-premise and off-premise SharePoint

| On-Premise | Off-Premise |
|---|---|
| License, hardware, and software costs are higher. | Migration from on-premises to Office 365 is difficult and will require a third-party product. |
| Infrastructure support is required, meaning that more costs and technical skills need to be maintained. | No server-side development is available. |
| | Data management is not under the control of the organization; compliance, security, and privacy are subject to the country where the data resides. |

You must carry out a full investigation before taking making a decision to use off-premise, on-premise, or a hybrid of the two. To understand whether there is a business case to take on the cloud provision, you should do the following:

1. Create a business case identifying the services available from a business agility, cost savings, and service quality perspective.

2. Identify what SharePoint solutions can migrate, and carry out a risk analysis to identify whether an off-premises provision is suitable.

3. Take into consideration the SharePoint roadmap, particularly if you already have SharePoint on-premises.
4. Measure the capability and maturity of your organization and contrast that against what may be expected for SharePoint support services.
5. Measure the capability of the SharePoint support services versus the available off-premises support services (especially if you are thinking of adopting a hybrid approach).
6. Examine the development model for the off-premises provider; ensure that it is manageable and can dovetail with your current processes.

## Summary

SharePoint support services are a vital requirement to guarantee sustainable User Adoption of SharePoint. It connects with Governance and provides policies and rules under which SharePoint will be supported. This chapter described the tasks required to create a SharePoint support service. Additional concerns about supporting SharePoint come from the implications of its compliancy, legality, availability, and resiliency. The SharePoint platform provides features to cover all of these considerations, and the process of putting them in place needs to be understood.

Finally, this chapter briefly addresses the implications of moving to off-premises services, also called *cloud-based services*. This also has implications on the provision of service support and affects compliance, legality, availability, and resiliency.

This chapter has been devoted to service delivery, which encompasses all of these topics and describes from a practical perspective the work required to put the customer first and simultaneously provide a fully measurable SharePoint service. That is the essence of sustained User Adoption and Governance.

CHAPTER 9

# Controlling the delivery program

In this chapter:



As a Microsoft SharePoint delivery manager, you need to have an extremely good understanding of planning, control, and SharePoint technical judgment. Controlling the delivery program requires good communications, both within the delivery team and across the organization. This chapter describes key areas of schedule planning, including report delivery and managing costs. In addition, the chapter describes risk and issue management, which is crucial to mitigating impact.

*This chapter builds on the description concerning the creation of the SharePoint delivery plan presented in Chapter 3, "Planning SharePoint solution delivery." If you have not already done so, ensure that you read Chapter 3 to get an understanding of the SharePoint delivery plan.*

## Creating a delivery schedule

The delivery schedule is a supporting document of the SharePoint delivery detail plan. The management of the delivery schedule is one of the most important and fundamental project management techniques—so much so, in fact, that many people (incorrectly) think that building a schedule is all that is needed. In fact, there are a number of documents that support the SharePoint delivery detail plan. At a simple level, the delivery schedule tells how long it will take to deliver the program or any part of that program. In addition to giving time scales, a well-produced delivery schedule also tells you the following:

- Who is accountable for every aspect of the program
- The approach being undertaken

- The major deliverables from the program
- The timing of key review and approval points

The schedule is also the basis on which cost and resource plans are constructed. However, unlike costs and resources, which are seen by only a few people observing a program, key dates are visible to everyone connected with the program. A well-publicized delivery date, when missed, is very hard to hide. While *time* may not be the most important aspect for you on some of your programs, observers may develop their own perception of success or failure purely from the performance of your program against the publicized target dates.

The ability to build and manage the delivery schedule is one of the prerequisite skills that all delivery managers should have. Managing the delivery schedule is far too important for you to delegate to team members, particularly in the early stages of the program when the overall strategy and approach is being developed. The delivery schedule sets the course for the remainder of the program. Once fully authorized, it is very difficult to change or improve, as all decisions that have the most influence on time, costs, and benefits have already been made.

Carried out effectively, the delivery schedule will benefit you and the delivery team by providing all of the following:

- A baseline against which to measure progress (without a delivery schedule, words such as *early* and *late* have no meaning)
- A common understanding of the approach that you are taking to achieve your objectives
- A breakdown of the program workload into manageable pieces (called *work packages*) based on the deliverables/outputs wherever possible
- A clear way of showing interdependencies between activities and work packages with the program and to/from other external parties
- A listing of accountabilities for different activities and work packages
- A tool for evaluating when corrective action is needed

The activity in creating the schedule and involving the delivery team serves to forge team spirit and a high level of common understanding and commitment. All delivery programs are undertaken in an environment of risk, and good planning is done with the full knowledge and acknowledgment of those risks. Where possible, you should avoid risk by undertaking the program in a different way and plan contingencies to deal with the unavoidable risks. Figure 9-1 depicts the steps required to prepare a SharePoint detail plan.

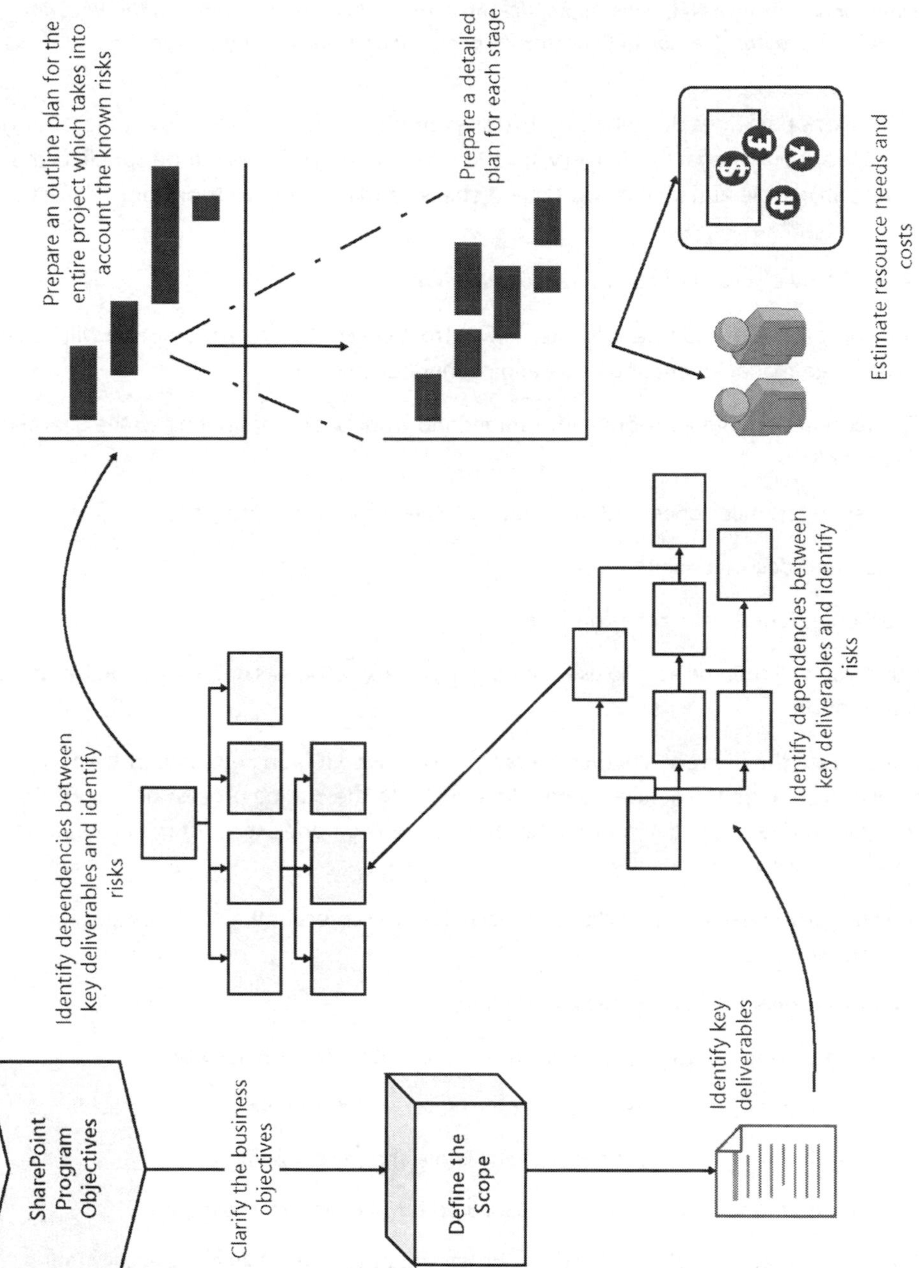


**FIGURE 9-1** Steps to create an outline delivery plan and delivery schedule.

You will need to consider your plan on two levels, both of which are in the SharePoint delivery detail plan. The outline delivery plan is used as a management summary to present overall progress. The delivery schedule shows the detail for each stage listed in the outline delivery plan constituted as discrete work packages.

*For more information concerning the makeup of the SharePoint delivery detail plan, read the "Preparing a SharePoint delivery program" section of Chapter 3, "Planning SharePoint solution delivery."*

**Note** For work packages done by others (for example, under contract), the person or group doing the work will prepare a delivery schedule. However, you need to be satisfied that this schedule is workable and includes sufficient checkpoints for you to monitor progress.

The outline delivery plan will comprise the following:

- The approach to be adopted (or alternatives from which the preferred option will be chosen using value management and value engineering techniques)
- The segregation of the program into stages and work packages relating to the SharePoint deliverable
- The key dates, milestones, and time constraints relating to the program
- Review and decision points
- Interdependencies with other projects

From this, you will then be able to estimate the necessary resources and cost of delivering the SharePoint solution.

You must create the delivery schedule before you start working on any stage of the program. The approach to creating the detailed schedule is similar to the outline process described previously, except that you will be working in more detail, perhaps only on one aspect of the program at a time. This includes the following:

- Breaking down each work package into activities to represent the work content for each deliverable
- Identifying dependencies between activities
- Agreeing with those accountable on completion dates for each activity
- Checking that key milestones and the program completion date can still be achieved
- Ensuring that there are appropriate checkpoints and review points
- Ensuring that time and resources are allocated for planning the next stage
- Confirming that the tasks assigned can be carried out by those who are accountable

The last point of this bullet list is key. It means that as a delivery manager, you must work closely with the delivery team and continually communicate. Here is a scenario I witnessed:

*Scenario 1: Peter Waxman is a SharePoint delivery manager heading a team of five people at Fabrikam. He has been asked to deliver a solution for the existing SharePoint platform. Because there are two other company projects with higher priority, his staff is limited. The SharePoint sponsor, Seth Grossman, assigns Peter five business analysts, three rookies and two veterans. Peter assigns them to take on project tasks. The two veteran business analysts are primarily working on other projects. After a significant amount of time, only one team member has completed any of their tasks accurately or on time. The two who are involved in other projects have not completed any tasks. One of the remaining team members has done work, but not accurately, and the final member is working very slowly. Peter's project appears to have grown stagnant. Seth asked Peter to a meeting to ask why the project has problems with delivering. Seth then suggests that one approach to avoid problems like this is through effective team communication, and there are many ways to do this. Peter starts to hold daily meetings and asks all team members to submit weekly status reports. Peter also starts to use Microsoft Project 2013 and SharePoint 2013 task lists to report progress regularly to Seth.*

**Tip** The more obvious way to avoid the above-mentioned scenario is by building an effective team. Factors to keep in mind while team building include employee skill, experience, participation ability, the projects that employees are already working on (to avoid overallocation), and morale. Newer resources should be paired with mentors.

## Tracking and communicating progress

Tracking progress toward your objective is essential. The control cycle is shown in Figure 9-2. Once a plan has been agreed to, it is necessary to measure progress against the plan, reforecast to the end, note any variances, and take steps to bring the program back on schedule.

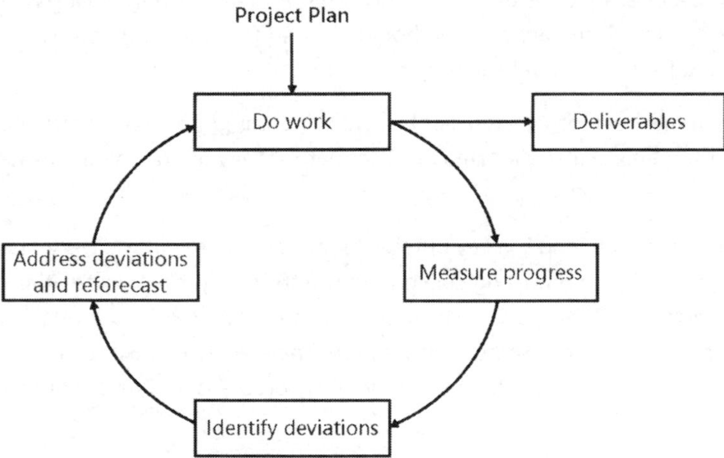


**FIGURE 9-2** Schedule control cycle.

There are many ways to measure progress, the most common being the following:

- Assessing % completion
- Assessing the time remaining for an activity
- Estimating the date when an activity will be completed

In traditional project management, many people use the *% complete* method. However, this method has potential problems if a realistic estimate of % complete cannot be determined (such as measuring hours worked). It is not unusual to find an activity is 90 percent complete for 90 percent of its duration. A simpler and more easily verifiable method for SharePoint delivery is to estimate the date when an activity will be completed.

**Tip** Split activities down to bite-sized chunks and avoid having long durations for each one. This will enable you to track progress and avoid surprises.

Your schedule comprises a number of tasks, each one called an *activity*. Each activity has a duration that has a start date and an end date. The progress made completing each activity is indicated as a percentage out of 100. Therefore, in terms of progress, an activity is one of the following:

- Complete (that is, 100 percent complete)
- Not started (that is, 0 percent complete)
- Started but not complete

Activities that are started but not finished are assumed to be 0 percent complete, but a current best estimate of the expected finish date is made.

The schedule should be updated at least monthly, but for faster-moving projects, weekly or biweekly would be more appropriate. This update cycle should tie in with the regular progress or highlight reporting on the project because it is the most concise method of showing what has been achieved and what is to happen next. Summary reports should be used for reporting upward, and detailed reports should be used for reporting to the project team.

Do not concentrate on what has been completed. Look at what is coming up next. Consider, based on your experiences, whether the time scales allocated are adequate. If they are not, you may need to take preemptive action.

You should ensure that program reporting is a key output during the SharePoint delivery plan lifecycle. It is important that you maintain reporting concerning progress on program activities reflected in the schedule. Reports should be made by all members of the SharePoint delivery team who are responsible for delivering part of the SharePoint solution. These reports must focus on progress achieved, costs incurred, difficulties encountered, and likely progress in the next reporting period.

Each SharePoint delivery team member will own part of the schedule, and the purpose of this person's report is to show progress, problems, solutions, and plans. The report is used to form an overall picture of progress across the team, and then across the program. The report is useful as a means of tracking progress, controlling resources, and spotting problems early and solving them. Recipients of reports can include team member(s), the delivery manager, and the SharePoint sponsor.

Although the level of detail in the reports will differ for different report types, you should apply common principles to standardize what will be in them. Consider these practical techniques:

- Highlight tasks started and/or completed during the reporting period.
- Summarize the progress made on each task and state what work remains to complete the task.
- Summarize problems encountered and whether they have been resolved or are yet to be solved. Be prepared to show these to team members because they may be able to apply a proven solution if the problem has not been solved. If the problem has been solved, be prepared to have the solution verified.
- State the time taken on tasks and an estimate of the effort required to complete the task.
- Estimate any amount of rework to be undertaken for each task, if any.
- Identify any items relevant to the task, either internally or externally which will affect the ability to complete the task.

## Understanding the content of delivery program reports

Reporting will vary according to the size of the program and the size of the delivery team involved. The following examples reflect a large program, with several layers of participants below the delivery manager.

### Team member reports

Reports will be produced weekly by every delivery team member for the delivery manager. The delivery managers' *line manager* (if one exists) should decide whether the delivery manager needs to also produce one of these reports. The team member report may be the basis for any weekly team meeting. The report must contain the following information:

- A record of progress, in terms of both achievements and problems
- Time spent on each task in person-days, and effort required to complete the task
- Day-to-day problems
- A description of any rework, including time spent (for example, machine crashes, misinterpretation of the specification, and so on)
- Resource problems (staff, machines, and so on)
- Next week's targets, including replanning if required
- Suggestions, including ideas to prevent waste and rework

## Delivery manager reports

Reports should be produced weekly by each delivery manager in the program. They should be based on the content of the team member reports and the delivery managers' own knowledge of events that might affect the team. Reporting should be done against the current, authorized plan. The report should contain the following information:

- Effort spent on all tasks in the period
- Effort to complete all tasks on which work has started
- Nontrivial problems that have affected team progress, both those that have been solved and those that still must be solved
- Progress against the plan
- Targets for the next two weeks
- Summary of rework undertaken by the team, and the reasons for the rework
- Resource profile for the team, including planned absences (for example, holidays, vacations, courses, and so on)
- Suggestions and progress on any related programs that may affect team resources
- What risk management actions have been undertaken and any changes to identified risks associated with that team's work area

## SharePoint sponsor reports

Reports for the SharePoint sponsor should be produced at the end of each financial month by the delivery manager. They will be produced from the delivery manager's weekly reports. Reporting should be done against the approved plan. The report should contain the following information:

- Progress against the plan, with any slipping tasks highlighted
- Financial issues including spend (both actual and forecast)
- Significant problems encountered or overcome by the program
- Summary of rework and implications, particularly with respect to milestones
- What risk management actions have been undertaken, and any change to the risks
- Project resource profile for the team, including any planned absences (for example, holidays, vacations, courses, and so on)

## Subcontractor reports

If you have subcontractors on the delivery team, they are expected to submit reports on a similar schedule as the SharePoint sponsor reports. They should contain a status report against their deliverables.

## Understanding the bar chart

As delivery manager, you must ensure that the schedule is visible in a central location available to the entire delivery team. There are several types of reports to consider, all of which are extremely important and add to the kind of delivery program reports. Each report type listed in this chapter will describe the purpose of the report, when you should use the report, and how to complete each report.

*The "Building the SharePoint delivery plan" section in Chapter 3 shows examples of using the Deliverables App in SharePoint 2013.*

The bar chart (also called a *Gantt chart*) is a representation of the schedule in graphical form. It shows the duration of activities against a time scale, and it defines who is accountable for each activity and work package and the place of each activity in the work breakdown. Project 2013 shows dependencies between activities, using arrows to link them. You must use bar charts because they are the most effective way of communicating a schedule. For this reason, you must include them when you wish to communicate plans.

Bar charts can be produced manually; however, a better method is by using SharePoint 2013 and/or Project 2013. Figure 9-3 shows a bar chart created using Project 2013. Bar charts are produced from a list of activities once the start and end dates of each activity have been calculated. The left portion contains a reference number, description, duration, the name of the person accountable, and the start and finish dates. The right part shows a bar against a time scale that spans from the start to the finish of the activity. Milestones (dates for key events) are shown as diamonds, and dependencies from outside the project are shown as down arrows.

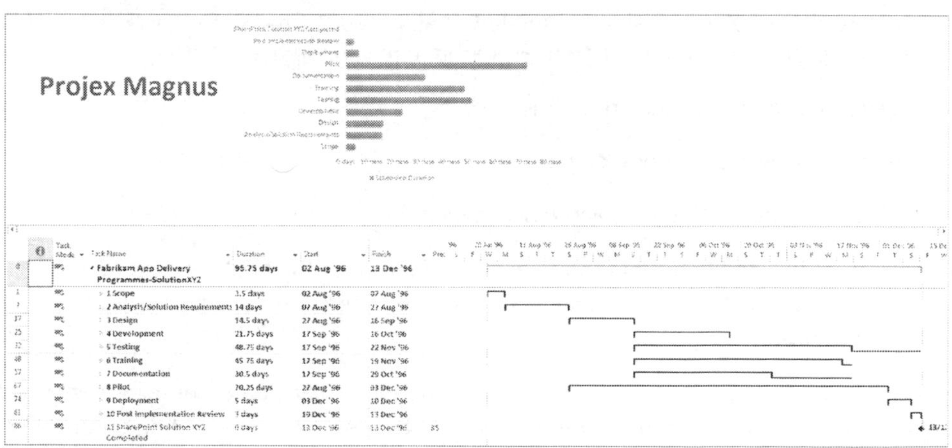


**FIGURE 9-3** A bar chart example of a SharePoint solution outline plan from Project 2013.

Project 2013 can synchronize the project to a SharePoint 2013 task list. This is useful when the delivery team wants to maintain the project schedules in Project 2013 but also wants to share updates in a SharePoint site. Figure 9-4 shows what happens after the bar chart shown in Figure 9-3 is synchronized with a SharePoint 2013 task list.

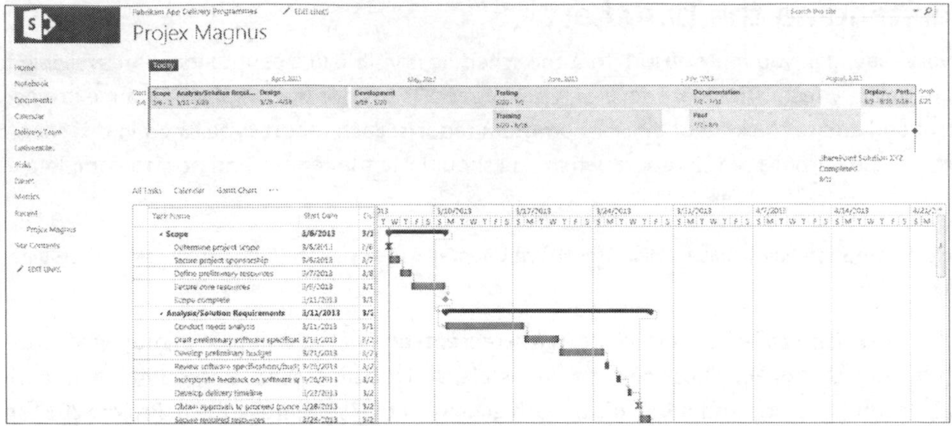


**FIGURE 9-4** A Project 2013 plan synchronized into a task list in a SharePoint 2013 site.

Another type of bar chart is the progress bar chart. This shows the current forecast dates for each activity and milestone compared with the baseline plan. The dates given are the actual, or current, forecast dates. Comments about progress may be included against any item. These are identical in structure to the bar chart; however, plan dates are shown as a line below the current forecast, so that a visual appreciation of slippage is readily apparent. A progress bar chart also includes features to show the float available for each activity, including other specialized information.

## Creating management summaries

The management summary is a concise presentation of the progress bar chart that is aimed at providing a high-level report on the progress. From this, one can see the following:

- The key stages and associated responsibilities
- Important review and approval points
- Progress compared with the agreed baseline plan

You should use this format for reporting to the SharePoint sponsor, or SharePoint delivery manager (if you are accountable to providing a management summary to him or her), and any other stakeholder to the progress report.

The report contains only the specific lines of information (summary, detail, or milestone) that the user wants to present. The report should be kept as short as possible, concentrating on the life cycle stages, key work packages, and milestones.

## Creating the deliverables log

The deliverables log lists all the key deliverables from the plan, including who is accountable for preparing them, reviewing them, and finally signing off on them. These items should be specifically mentioned in the SharePoint delivery plan. This format is used when the SharePoint delivery manager wants to focus on the deliverables and be explicit about who is accountable for the quality aspects of each one. Unless you know who is to review a deliverable and approve it, you cannot be certain that what is being produced is really fit for its purpose. The report is an extract from the schedule, with those activities and milestones relating to deliverables filtered to produce a listing.

You can use Project 2013 to generate a deliverables log by simply choosing the columns, and then using the synchronization tool from Project 2013 to generate the columns in the task list. Conversely, this is achievable using SharePoint 2013 by modifying the task list to suit. Figure 9-5 shows a SharePoint 2013 task list, which is synchronized with Project 2013. A new view called Deliverable Log is created, showing just the relevant columns for that report.

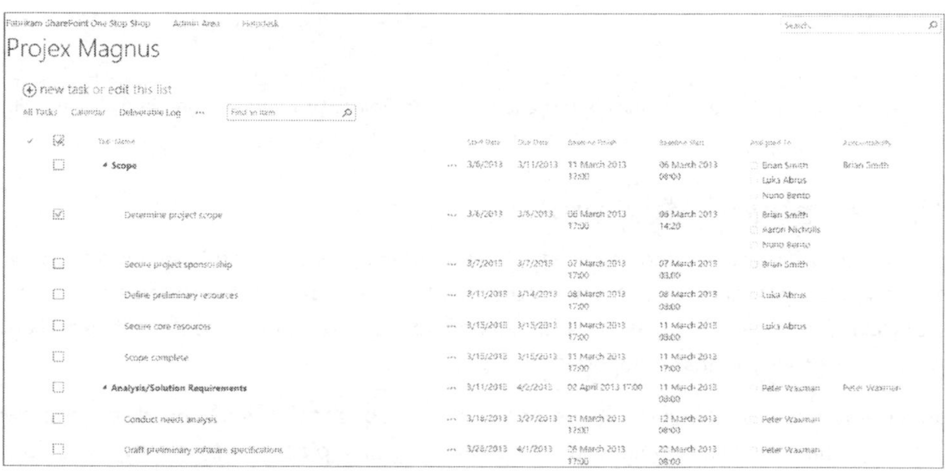

**FIGURE 9-5** A deliverables log produced by using SharePoint 2013 task list synchronized with Project 2013.

## Creating a late activities report

A late activities report is used to focus attention on activities that are likely to be late. This enables the delivery manager to assess the likely impact and take whatever action is necessary to bring the delivery back on schedule. The objective is not to use the report as a tool to punish those accountable for late activities, but rather to focus attention on putting things right. With this in mind, the late activities report lists only incomplete activities.

This report is useful for helping the delivery manager to identify those activities that are expected to be late, and hence focus his/her attention on remedying the situation. The report is compiled by extracting the late and unfinished activities from the progress bar chart of the deliverables chart. This can be achieved using Project 2013; however, SharePoint 2013 is extremely useful for building such a chart. By creating calculated columns to subtract the due date from the baseline date and linking that to % Completed tasks as a filter, a view can be constructed. Figure 9-6 shows a screenshot of the task list that has the filter applied, and which I have titled "Late Activities in SharePoint 2013." Note the column called *DaysLate* in the screenshot. This shows the number of days late the relevant work package and tasks are. In addition, only those tasks that are not completed are displayed.

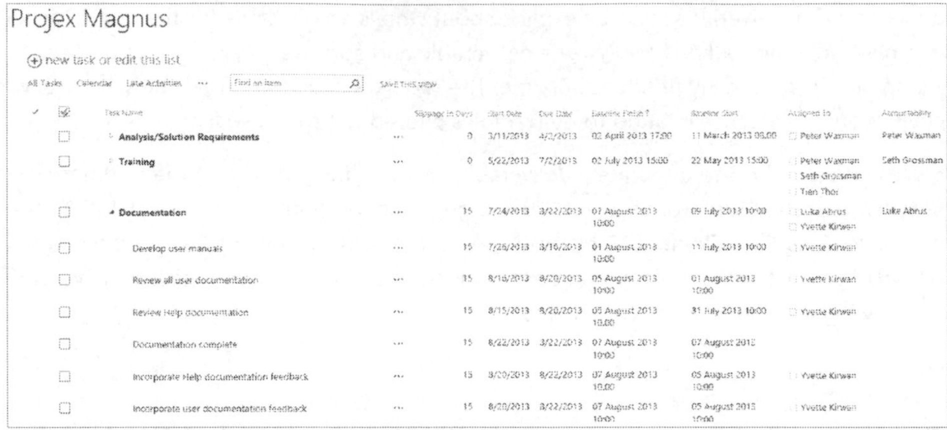


**FIGURE 9-6** A screenshot of a late activities report against a SharePoint 2013 task list compiled by using filters.

## Creating a network diagram

The network diagram is used to show the logical relationships (dependencies) among different activities, work packages, and plans. It is needed only when the logic is complicated enough to require special attention. It can be used for identifying natural checkpoints, as the network diagram will show where various strands come together.

You should use the network diagram whenever a complex sequence of events needs to be shown clearly. This is particularly handy when you are first drawing up a plan, as it is not always obvious what logical dependencies are. It is also a useful format to use at planning workshops for determining dependencies between activities, before any idea of time scale/duration has been gained.

The plan is developed by mapping out those activities that can be performed in parallel and those that must be carried out sequentially. Activities or milestones are represented in boxes, and their relationships with preceding and succeeding activities are shown with arrows. An activity may not start until its predecessor has been finished. This is called a *precedence network* and is the most versatile method for depicting the logical sequence of the schedule.

Network diagrams are great for developing activities, milestones, and deliverables in a planning workshop. Consider using sticky notes or mind-mapping software such as Mindjet MindManager. You should start by setting out the deliverable with a question:

*What would I need to have in place in order to deliver the SharePoint solution?*

For example, in order to develop a business case for a SharePoint delivery program, you would need to carry out an initial investigation, which is associated with a plan of action based on the initial requirements from the SharePoint sponsor. Figure 9-7 shows a simple network diagram showing the development of activities to create a business case.

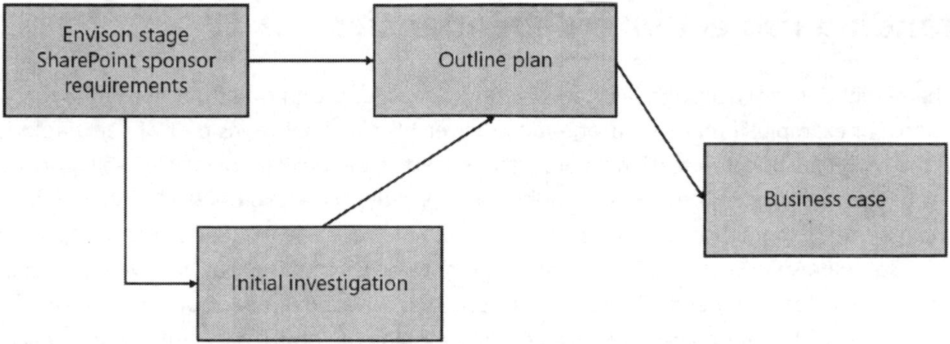


**FIGURE 9-7** A sample network diagram whose objective is to create a business case.

## Creating a milestone report

The milestone report shows progress against the key targets for the schedule. These are items that should be specifically mentioned in the delivery plan. You should use this report because it is an excellent, nongraphical way of communicating progress and expectations. The milestone report shows the timing of key milestones, such as key delivery dates and approval and review points, including interdependencies with other projects.

The milestone report is presented in tabular format, showing the target description, the planned end date, the current forecast of the end date, and the actual date that the target is achieved. The Slippage in Days column indicates how late the milestone is compared to the baseline finish date. The report consists of all the activities of zero duration that the delivery manager wants to highlight. Figure 9-8 shows an example milestone report in SharePoint 2013 using the task list. This task list is synchronized with Project 2013; however, the construction of the milestone report has been customized to provide the relevant filtering of milestone activities.

Projex Magnus

⊕ new task or edit this list

All Tasks  Calendar  Milestone Report  ...

| Task Name | Baseline Finish | Due Date | Actual Finish | Slippage in Days | Notes |
|---|---|---|---|---|---|
| **Scope** | 11 March 2013 17:00 | 3/11/2013 | | 0 | Design may be delayed |
| Scope complete | 11 March 2013 17:00 | 3/15/2013 | | 4 | |
| **Analysis/Solution Requirements** | 02 April 2013 17:00 | 4/2/2013 | | 0 | |
| Analysis complete | 04 April 2013 11:00 | 4/10/2013 | | 6 | |
| **Design** | 25 April 2013 12:00 | 5/10/2013 | | 15 | |
| Design complete | 24 April 2013 16:00 | 5/2/2013 | | 8 | |
| **Development** | 27 May 2013 10:00 | 6/11/2013 | | 15 | |
| Development complete | 27 May 2013 10:00 | 6/11/2013 | | 15 | |
| **Testing** | 09 July 2013 10:00 | 7/24/2013 | | 15 | |
| **Unit Testing** | 21 June 2013 10:00 | 7/8/2013 | | 17 | |
| Unit testing complete | 21 June 2013 10:00 | 7/8/2013 | | 17 | |
| **Integration Testing** | 09 July 2013 10:00 | 7/24/2013 | | 15 | |
| Integration testing complete | 09 July 2013 10:00 | 7/24/2013 | | 15 | |
| **Training** | 02 July 2013 15:00 | 7/2/2013 | | 0 | Training document needs to include MS Office 2010 |

**FIGURE 9-8** A sample milestone report in a SharePoint 2013 task list.

## Understanding project interdependencies

Many SharePoint delivery plans require deliverables from other programs as a prerequisite to completion. For example, if there is a program to deliver Microsoft Office as part of a technology refresh to an organization, there will be a program related to the delivery of Office itself. Conversely, if there is to be a delivery of Office 365 in addition to upgrading SharePoint 2010 to SharePoint 2013, there could be two programs in operation. Another example could be that the implementation of a SharePoint software solution requires another program to deliver a particular hardware configuration before it can be tested. You need to ensure, therefore, that the scope of each program is well defined, particularly when different departments in an organization are involved. If the full scope of each program is not clear, accountability for delivery becomes vague, which will threaten success.

The breakdown of a program into discreet work packages related to specific deliverables is essential to avoid confusion. The plan for a program should show only those activities for which the delivery manager is accountable. Activities done by others, in other programs, should not be shown in detail. Such linkages should be explicit, however, and the example progress bar chart report shown in this chapter needs to be designed with this in mind.

When considering dependencies between programs, the following question should be asked:

> *What do I (in Program A) require from other programs to complete the defined scope of work?*

This may result in a list of one or more specific deliverables that should be identified in the other program plans. The delivery manager(s) of the other program(s) should be aware of what you require and when you need it. Two projects cannot be accountable for delivering the same deliverable.

## Managing the finances

After managing time, management of the finances is the next most important and fundamental aspect of a SharePoint delivery program. Without a good schedule, it is impossible to have a reliable financial plan. However, while the schedule is the most visible aspect of a program to outsiders, cost is often the most visible to insiders, such as your SharePoint sponsor. Sometimes it is the only aspect that they want to review.

Figure 9-9 shows an example of the costs over the life of a SharePoint delivery program. Use this to help you understand the importance of having a financial plan. At a simple level, a financial plan will tell you each of the following:

- What each stage and work package in the schedule costs
- Who is accountable for stage and work package costs
- The financial benefits of the program
- The financial commitments
- What the cast flow looks like
- The financial authorization (sanction) given

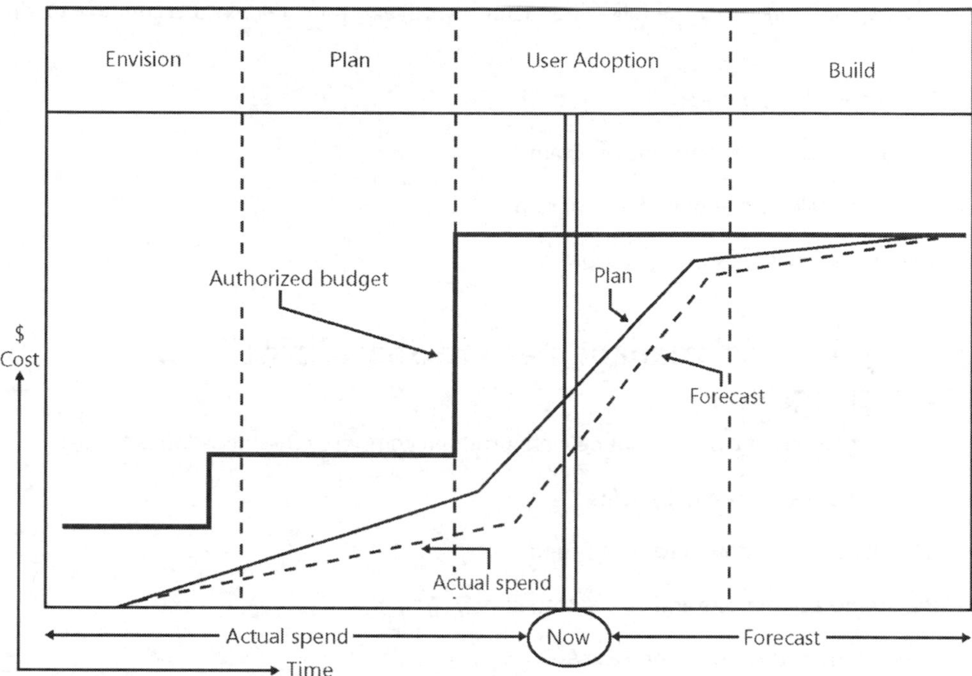


**FIGURE 9-9** A sample of SharePoint delivery program costs over the life of the program.

Just as a schedule is used as the baseline for measuring progress in terms of time, the financial plan is the basis for measuring costs and financial benefits. Many of the principles that have been explained in terms of schedule management in this chapter (for example, milestone reporting, bar charts, progress bar charts, and management summaries) are also applicable to the management of finances. Schedule and cost plans share the same work breakdown structure (WBS). In terms of recording the information, they can be stored easily in Project 2013 plans as well as SharePoint task lists. By recording costs with schedules, you ensure that:

- Accountability for both the activities and costs resides with the same person.
- There is no overlap (that is, no double-counting of costs).
- There is no gap (that is, no missing costs).

In practice, you will develop the financial plan to a lesser level of work breakdown than you would the schedule.

The financial plan, like the schedule, is developed in outline for the full program and in detail for each stage. There is little point in developing an accurate and detailed financial plan based on an unstable schedule. No matter what granularity you take the calculations to, they will be fundamentally inaccurate. You should take the level of accuracy and confidence forward, with the schedule and related costs matching.

The costs are influenced by the following factors, which you must take into account when drawing up your plan:

- The scope of the program
- The approach you take to the program
- The time scale to complete the program
- The risks associated with the program

## Applying financial management to SharePoint delivery programs

Financial management of a SharePoint delivery program comprises the following activities:

- Estimating the costs and benefits
- Obtaining authorization to spend funds
- Recording actual costs and committed costs
- Forecasting future costs and cash flow
- Reporting actual and forecast actions versus what the plan and budget say

Financial management is carried out in the context of the schedule control cycle (as depicted in Figure 9-2) and operates in the same way. You will need to do this because tracking progress toward your objective is essential. If you do not do this, you simply will not know how much the program will cost. Once a financial plan has been agreed, you will need to measure actual expenditure against the plan, reforecast to the end, and note any variances and take steps to bring the program back within budget if needed.

You also must estimate the costs and benefits of preparing a financial plan. Cost estimates should be based on the work scope and outline plan defined in the business case of the SharePoint delivery plan. Use the same WBS as for the schedule, and then estimate to the same level of accuracy (outline versus detail).

The estimate should consist of the cost of using the SharePoint delivery team and the cost of external purchases made as a result of the program. The overall cost plan/forecast should be built from three elements. These three elements are the base estimate, scope reserve, and contingency.

The *base estimate* is the total of the costs of all the activities you have identified, including the SharePoint delivery team time and all external purchases. The *scope reserve* is an estimate of what else your experience and common sense tells you, in terms of what needs to be done, but has not yet been explicitly identified. Scope reserve can be as high as 50 percent of the base estimate, or it may be zero. The authority to use scope reserve is often delegated to the SharePoint delivery manager. *Contingency* is the estimate to take account of the unexpected (that is, risks). The purpose of contingency is not to compensate for poor estimating. If a risk does not occur, the money for contingency is put aside and not spent. For this reason, the authorization for spending contingency may rest with the SharePoint sponsor. Formal change management should be used to move the costs from contingency to base estimate. Unspent contingency should be returned to the business.

The proportion of your estimate divided between base estimate, scope reserve, and contingency will alter as the program moves through its life cycle stages. You should expect a higher proportion of scope reserve and contingency in the early stages than in the later stages. The accuracy of estimates also alters depending on the lifecycle of the program. Figure 9-10 shows that in the earlier stages, you expect the bulk of the cost to be *soft,* except for the next stage. The next stage should be a *hard* estimate. This matches the principle of outline and detail planning. Outline plans tend to be soft; detail plans hard. A soft estimate is one to which a low level of confidence can be placed, whereas a hard estimate is one in which you have a high level of confidence.

**Tip** Regardless of whether your estimates are soft or hard, it is important that you state any assumptions, constraints, or qualifications you have in the business case of the SharePoint delivery plan.

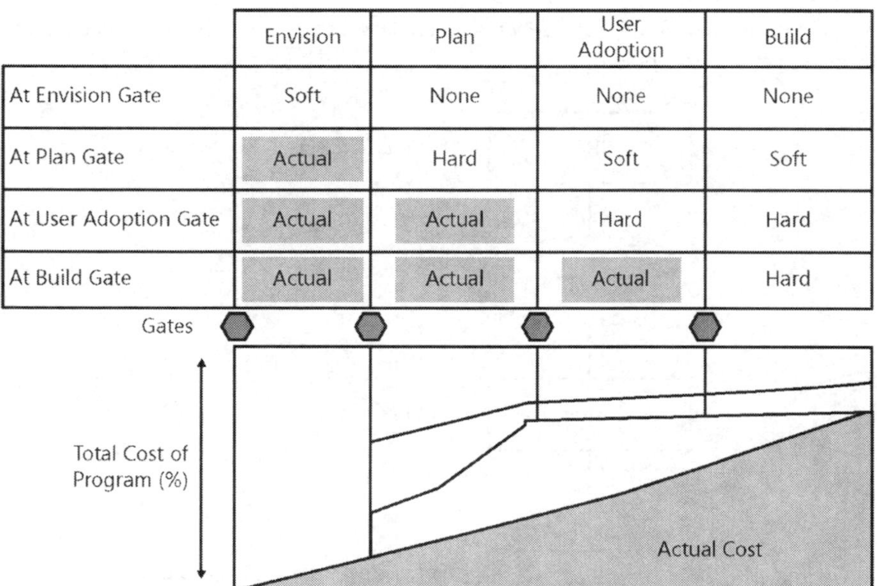


**FIGURE 9-10** Estimation of the soft and hard costs of a SharePoint delivery program.

## Recording actual costs and committed costs

If you are to have the ability to monitor the cost of the SharePoint delivery program, you need to use a system for capturing the costs, from wherever they originate in the organization, and then allocating them to the delivery program.

From this information, you will be able to identify the following:

- The internal use of resources (for example, cost of labor)
- Purchases (paid to contractors, suppliers, consultants)
- Costs for any part of the program (stages, work breakdown elements) that you wish to define.

In addition, it is essential to have the costs captured for each framework stage of the program so that you can confidently manage actual spend against authorized budget on a stage-by-stage basis.

## Managing risks and issues

Managing risks and issues is a key aspect to controlling the delivery program. Risks and issues are inextricably linked. A risk will become an issue if it occurs. Issues can be resolved either within the scope of the program as currently defined or via a change to the program. Figure 9-11 gives a visual representation of the flow of risk to issue to change. This section looks at risks and issues in terms of controlling the delivery program.

*Change will affect your ability to deliver the SharePoint solution. This topic is discussed further in Chapter 6, "SharePoint delivery program considerations."*

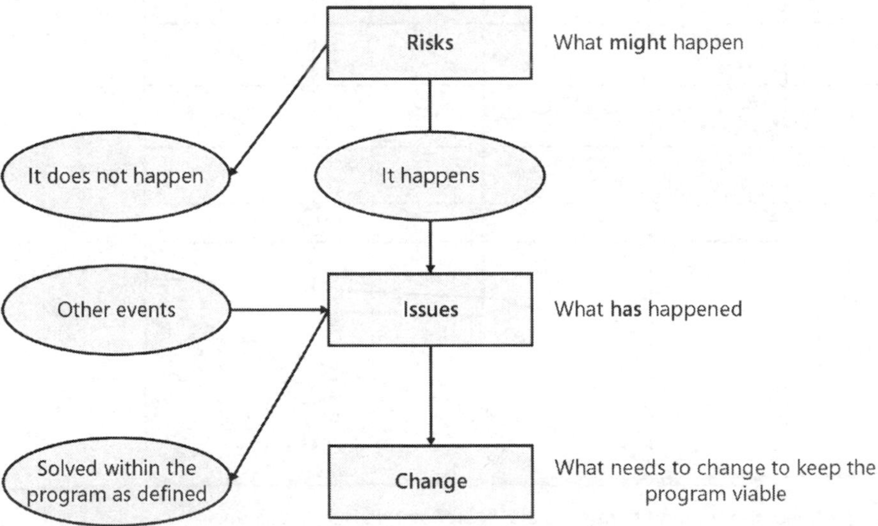


**FIGURE 9-11** The connection between risks, issues, and change in delivery programs.

## Managing risk

*Risk* is any uncertainty, potential threat, or occurrence that may keep you from achieving the objectives set in the SharePoint delivery program. It may affect time scale, cost, quality, or benefits. All programs are exposed to risk in some form, but the extent of this will vary considerably.

The purpose of risk management is to ensure that when creating the SharePoint delivery program, risks are identified and evaluated in a consistent way, and recognized risks to program success are addressed. You cannot use risk management to eliminate risk altogether, but it will enable you to avoid it in some instances or minimize the disruption in the event of it happening in other programs.

You should first address risk when the program is being created in the Initial Investigation stage of the Envisioning section of the SharePoint delivery detail plan. You should also address risk when creating the outline plan and the delivery schedule. Risk is an important section within the business case. When the SharePoint sponsor approves the program, he/she does so with full knowledge of the stated risks and agrees to accept the consequences should things go wrong.

The steps you should follow are as follows:

1. Identify the risk. Log all risks that may potentially jeopardize the success of the program. Remember to include those under the control of the delivery team (for example, completeness of program scope, quality of technical solutions, and competence of the delivery team), as well as those that are largely outside its control (for example, legislative changes or economic climate). Figure 9-12 shows a sample risk log.

2. Estimate the risk. Review each risk in turn to assess the likelihood of the risk occurring and the severity of the impact on the program if it occurs.

3. Evaluate the risk. Use a risk matrix to determine the risk category (High, Medium, or Low) and assess how acceptable the risk is. Consider using Microsoft Excel 2013 to create a risk matrix following the example in Table 9-1 to identify how severe the impact of the risk already identified and listed in the risk log.

**Tip** You can easily construct the same list in a SharePoint 2013 site, or simply create the risk log using Excel, and then import it into SharePoint 2013.

| | | | | | Risk Management | | | |
|---|---|---|---|---|---|---|---|---|
| Ref No. | Description of Risk and Impact | Date Raised | Probability of Occurrence | Severity (1–10) | Risk Category | Action | By | When |
| 1 | Tailspin Toys may launch a new product for the same target market. This will reduce revenue by up to 30% | 03/02/13 | Unlikely | 7 | Medium | Monitor Tailspin Toys market activity. **Accept** | | Seth Grossman |
| 3 | The contractor for the program is unable to deliver on time due to lack of resources and other commercial commitments. This may delay the program by up to 2 months | 06/20/13 | Likely | 3 | Medium | Build relationship with contractor. Find alternative supplier. Build contingency time into schedule. **Contingency plan** | 01/08/2013 | Aaron Nicholls |
| 4 | The SharePoint warehouse management app will be delayed beyond the planned start of testing. Contingency action nulifies this risk | 06/29/13 | Almost certain | 5 | High | Provide Excel based system and write up procedures during initial testing (see issue log). **Reduction** | | Seth Grossman |
| 5 | The credit control system that needs to be integrated will be delayed beyond the planned start of testing the SharePoint solution being delivered. This will delay the Ready For Services (RFS) date and benefit realization | 06/29/13 | Likely | 8 | High | Build 3 months contingency into the schedule. **Reduction** | 01/08/2013 | Luka Abrus |

**FIGURE 9-12** An example of a risk log.

**TABLE 9-1** Example of a risk matrix

| Severity of Impact | Very Unlikely (<10%) | Unlikely (20–50%) | Likely (50–90%) | Almost Certain (100%) |
|---|---|---|---|---|
| Low (Score 1–2). Minor impact on schedule, scope, and cost. No impact on benefits. | Low | Low | Low | High |
| Medium (Score 3–5). Major impact on schedule, scope, and cost. Some impact on benefits. | Low | Medium | Medium | High |
| High (Score 6–10). Major impact on schedule, scope, and cost. Program likely to become unviable. | Low | Medium | High | High |

Depending on the risk category, you can use the following techniques as follows:

- **High risk** Take definitive action to prevent or reduce risk. Reconsider the viability of the program before proceeding further.
- **Medium risk** Take action to prevent or reduce risk where appropriate. Prepare a contingency plan if risk cannot be reduced. Manage and implement the contingency plan where necessary.
- **Low risk** Take action or reduce risk if cost effective to do so. Monitor risk, as it may become more significant later.

Taking positive steps to reduce the possible effects of risks is not indicative of pessimism; rather, it is a positive indication of good program management. Many possible options exist for reducing risk, including the following:

- **Prevention** Where countermeasures are put in place either stop the threat or problem from occurring or prevent it having any impact
- **Reduction** Where the actions either reduce the likelihood of the risk developing or limit the impact on the project to acceptable levels even if the risk occurs
- **Transference** Where the impact of the risk is passed to a third party; a special form of risk reduction
- **Contingency** Where actions are planned or organized to come into force when the risk occurs
- **Acceptance** Where the company decides to go ahead and accept the possibility that the risk might occur and are willing to take the consequences

Consider the following suggestions as well:

- Bring risky activities forward in the schedule to reduce the impact on the program outcome if they are delayed.
- Modify the program requirement to reduce aspects with inherently high risks (for example, new, leading-edge SharePoint solutions).
- Allow appropriate time and cost contingencies.
- Use prototypes and pilots to test the viability of new approaches.

You must address risks once the program has started. You should do the following:

- Maintain a log of the risks, similar to the one shown in Figure 9-12.
- Monitor the risks regularly with the delivery team and reassess their likelihood of occurrence and seriousness of impact.
- Log, categorize, and assign accountability for new risks, along with the action being taken to deal with them.
- Report new, high risks in the delivery manager's report.

During the course of a project, either of the following can happen:

- A risk event occurs. This should be noted in the Action column, and a corresponding entry made in the issue log, ready for escalation and/or resolution.
- A risk event has passed (that is, the program proceeds and the event does not occur). The risk category should be recorded as *None*.

In both cases, the risk is closed, and the line in the log should be marked as dealt with so the event no longer requires risk management.

Here are some tips concerning the use of the risk log:

- Phrase each risk to complete the sentence "There is a risk on this program that . . ."
- Only have one risk per line. Grouping risks can make managing them difficult.
- Do not add to existing risks. Cross-reference to the issue log when a risk occurs.
- Keep all risks visible, even those that have passed or taken place.

## Managing issues

*Issue management* is the process of recording and handling any event, query, or problem that either threatens the success of the program or represents an opportunity to be exploited. Examples of issues are the following:

- A late delivery of a critical deliverable
- A reported lack of confidence by the users
- A lack of resources to carry out the work
- The late sign-off of a critical document or deliverable
- A reported deviation of a deliverable from its specifications
- A requirement for additional functionality
- A recognized omission from the program scope

An issue is something that has happened and either threatens or enhances the success of the program. Compare this to a risk or opportunity, which is something that *might* happen.

When an issue is identified, you must do the following:

1. Record the issue in an issue log. An example of an issue log is given in Table 9-2. When recording, you must note the issue, who raised the issue, the date, and the priority and impact of the issue.
2. Agree who will be accountable for managing the issue resolution. If the issue cannot be dealt with by the delivery team, you should escalate it to a person who has the necessary level of knowledge and/or authority to deal with it (for example, the SharePoint sponsor). In doing this, you should record in the issue log the name of the person accountable for managing the resolution of the issue and the date by when it is expected that the issue will be resolved.
3. Agree and take action to resolve the issue (for example, implement the associated risk management plan). Note the proposed action in the issue log.
4. Update the progress commentary regularly in the issue log.
5. Once the issue has been resolved, record the method and date of resolution in the issue log. The line can then be shaded to show that the issue no longer requires attention. If the issue resolution requires an amendment to the program scope (deliverable), cost, time scales, or benefits, it should be handled through the change process.
6. Report new, significant issues in the delivery manager's report.

**TABLE 9-2** Issue log

| Ref | Description of Issue | Date Raised | Raised By | Issue Owner | Date Resolved | Priority | Comments |
|---|---|---|---|---|---|---|---|
| 1 | The warehouse management system release has been delayed and will not be ready for the start of testing. How can we ensure that the testing program is on time? | 1/4/2013 | Adrian Dumitrascu | Nuno Bento | 3/5/2013 | 2 | From Risk 4. Use the prototype system. |
| 2 | No time has been allocated for the staff training. How can we ensure that the solution is delivered and there are sufficient resources to provide training? | 5/4/2013 | Yvette Kirwan | Nuno Bento | 3/5/2013 | 1 | |
| 3 | There is a general lack of awareness of what this program will do for the organization. How can we address this? | 5/4/2013 | Yvette Kirwan | Nuno Bento | 3/5/2013 | 3 | Provide and update in the team briefing. |

**Tip** Office 365 includes the Project Web App feature, which will create an issue log and a risks log automatically. You can easily use those logs or construct your own from a custom list. Note that you could add another column to the issue log list that connects that list to the risk log (or vice versa).

In the Priority column in Table 9-2, I have entered a number that signifies the priority of the issue. The priorities I have used are in the range 1–5, as follows:

- Priority 1: Critical—needs escalation
- Priority 2: Major impact—can be handled by the delivery team
- Priority 3: Medium impact
- Priority 4: Minor impact
- Priority 5: No importance

You should expect a large number of issues to be raised at the start of the program or at the start of a new stage in the schedule. These will mainly be queries from people seeking clarification that aspects of the program that they are concerned with have been covered. The issue log is a rich source of feedback on stakeholder concerns, as well as a check on the completeness of the program scope.

Make sure that you record issues, even if you have no time to address them or cannot yet find a person to manage their resolution. Just making them visible is sometimes enough to start the process of resolving them. Also, many issues cannot be resolved on their own, simply because they do not reach the core problem—they are merely symptoms. Once other symptoms appear as issues, it is possible to start making connections that can help identify the core problem. When this happens, a number of issues can be taken care of all at once.

## Summary

This chapter concentrates on the practical techniques required to control the SharePoint delivery plan, and suggests methods of using Project 2013 and SharePoint 2013 to build schedules. This chapter also describes the kinds of reports needed and the importance of building a financial plan as part of the schedule. Risk and issue management are also described, the aim being to give the delivery manager some standards to use when controlling the delivery program.

CHAPTER 10

# SharePoint customization impacting User Adoption

In this chapter:



Delivery of Microsoft SharePoint solutions includes the understanding of the levels of customization. Technology commoditization is the rule of today's provision of apps to SharePoint 2013. This is the ability for third-party products to be packaged in such a way that allows users to easily deploy these apps, which are now available with functionality in SharePoint that is ready-made, without needing developer or administrator interaction. You should not take a stance that curtails the ability for customization and app provision; rather, you should just be ready for whatever kind of customization requests you will receive. This chapter does not focus on what it takes to create, customize, or modify SharePoint functionality. Many other technical books have covered those topics. Rather, we are focusing on the best practices surrounding the processes concerning the delivery of apps, when to decide customization is required, the various developer options, User Adoption impact, Governance impact, and the key to sustaining SharePoint support, training, and documentation for any customizations.

## Deciding when you should and should not customize SharePoint

You will need to be able to judge when the requirement to customize SharePoint functionality is really valid. Coding enhancements in SharePoint are a major plus because they show the level of modifications that can be applied to this technology, but they can also bring countless disadvantages if they are not carefully controlled and prioritized.

The rich development features for SharePoint 2013 provide the ability for developers and users to customize the software. This can include third-party additions, modifications to existing apps, and enhancements through the development of additional apps and services. For many organizations, customization is related to writing code. However, for SharePoint, the level of customization is such that even configuring a document library through SharePoint Designer constitutes customization. Customization in SharePoint provides a rich environment of customization abilities that can be provisioned by a business user or SharePoint/web developer.

However, this leaves the door wide open for bad choices, including knee-jerk reactions when it comes to making decisions concerning whether customization is required. Making wrong decisions and not taking enough time to investigate values and alternatives led to User Adoption problems, inflated costs, and support and Governance issues. Examples of this can be seen all the time; they stem from either a misunderstanding of the features in SharePoint or a misunderstanding of the roles required to provide a SharePoint solution. Both of these flaws can result in you overengineering a solution or having difficulty supporting and scaling the solution provisioned. In any case, there needs to be a standard by which you can consistently provide value, meet return on investment (ROI) goals, and be able to forge User Adoption and Governance strategies. The following scenario describes a situation where customization that is just being implemented as an attempt to impress new SharePoint users is not going to guarantee the success of delivery and, consequently, of User Adoption.

*Scenario 1: Fabrikam is an energy company that wants to use SharePoint. The users have never used SharePoint before. The client engages a consultant, and instructs her that the company's objective is to implement SharePoint as quickly as possible. The consultant meets with the SharePoint sponsor, who tells her that he wants to present a "wow" factor when users visit SharePoint and to create an intranet. The SharePoint sponsor, eager to broadcast his background in graphics, has already engaged several graphic designers and presented his own design for branding SharePoint. The consultant suggests bringing in web developers to apply the design to SharePoint, and the SharePoint sponsor agrees. The consultant hires four web developers at a cost of $40,000 over two weeks. SharePoint is installed by the IT help desk and the web developers. The sponsor tells users to get on the intranet and start putting content on the site. Meanwhile, the developers brand the new intranet, despite the fact that users are trying to work on it. At the end of two weeks, the sponsor requests more changes to the intranet, and the consultant suggests that four more weeks of work are needed. The sponsor agrees. This costs Fabrikam an additional $80,000. At the end of four weeks, the users are angry because they do not understand the design of the intranet and they have not been shown how to use it. The IT help desk is about to release an update but has been advised that branding changes will cause the intranet to break because they are incompatible with the new release. Eventually, as costs spiral out of control, the content on the intranet is backed up. The consultant is fired, along with the four web developers. The SharePoint install is deleted and reinstalled. The result of bringing SharePoint to Fabrikam was seen as a disaster because the users were not trained in the basics, there were countless performance issues, and the cost of just branding the intranet was more than $120,000, with no success.*

Another point about this scenario is that the consultant did not simply focus on the business requirement. If she had done that, she would have realized that creating a delivery program that included connecting SharePoint built-in features to user requirements was the best way to get the users on board. The consultant should have advised as much to the sponsor.

Therefore, you need to know about some practical techniques that you can use to identify whether SharePoint should be customized. Before that, I will first describe a SharePoint development decision flowchart that will help you make the right decisions. You can apply this flowchart to any engagement of SharePoint delivery that may require building a SharePoint solution. Figure 10-1 shows the SharePoint development decision flowchart, which you should follow before deciding at what level a solution can be best provisioned. Then I will discuss each of the areas, along with a description on how to use the flowchart.

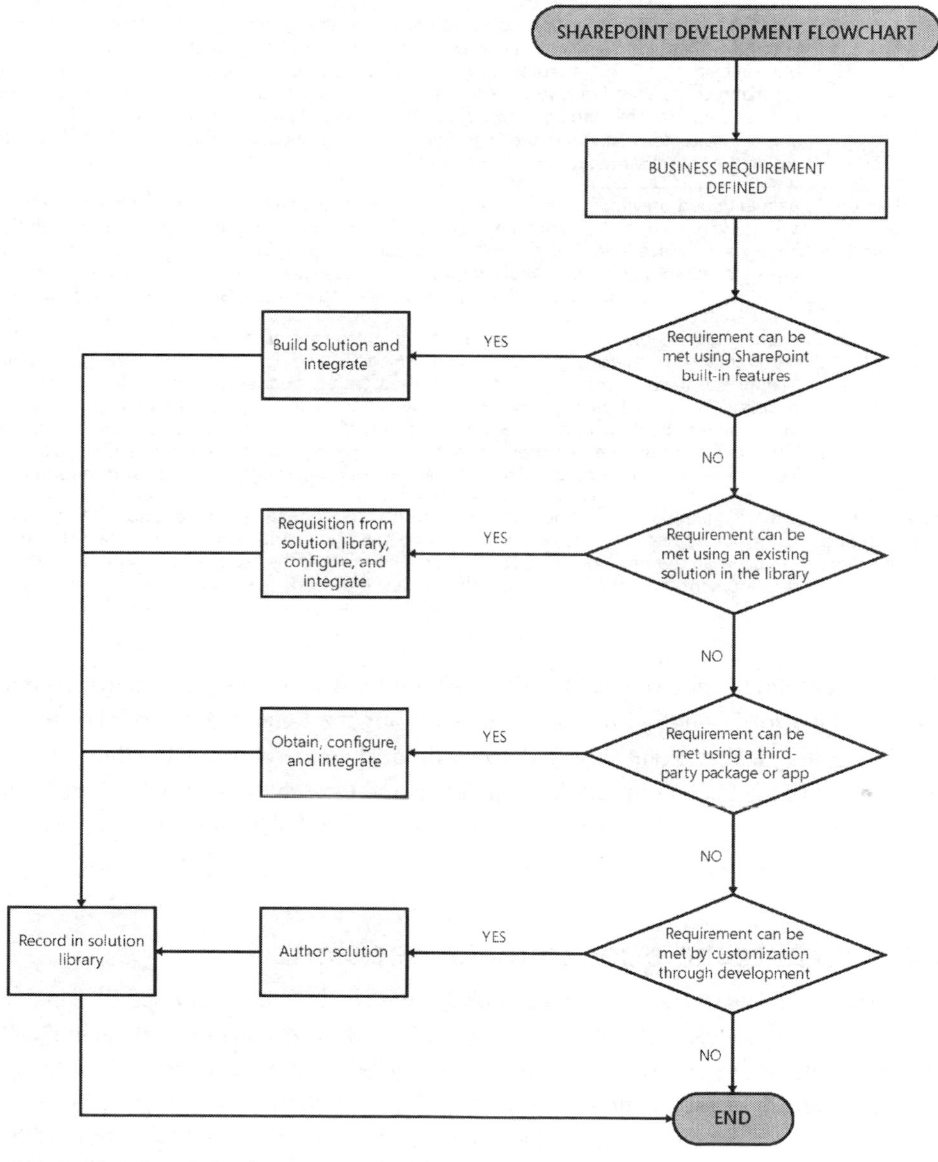


**FIGURE 10-1** SharePoint development decision flowchart.

The flowchart shows four decision points, which are described in Table 10-1.

**TABLE 10-1** Explanation of SharePoint customization decision points

| Decision Point | Description |
|---|---|
| Requirement can be met using SharePoint built-in features | More often than not, SharePoint business collaborative requirements can be solved by crafting the solution using the built-in features of SharePoint 2013. If the solution is a site, there are already a significant number of templates available. And document library and list types (known as *apps*) are already available in SharePoint 2013. In addition, if the requirement comes from users who are new to SharePoint, then providing a simple start through tools that are already available is far better than using coding. That is because training and communication, so important to User Adoption, come into play. Therefore, investigation of the built-in features comes first. If built-in features of SharePoint fulfill the business requirement, then those built-in features can be provisioned, and listed in the solution library. The solution library is a list that records SharePoint solutions. The aim is that this solution library becomes a reuseable bank of solutions that can be drawn upon. The solution library can be constructed from a SharePoint custom list within the SharePoint One-Stop Shop, and then it can be referred to within the SharePoint Statement of Operations. |
| Requirement can be met using an existing solution in the library | As mentioned previously, any business requirement successfully fulfilled by the provision of a SharePoint solution becomes a named item in the solution library. Therefore, the solution library is the place to look to see if there is a solution listed in the library that can fulfill the business requirement. This is vitally important because this is the key to sustained User Adoption (training and communication), and easier-to-manage Governance and support. |
| Requirement can be met using a third-party package or app | Numerous third-party applications have been written solely to meet one or more requirements. Numerous apps could be downloaded and applied to the solution as required. Making this decision means you have identified, tested, budgeted, and agreed with the business that a third-party package or app would fulfill the business requirement. And, once agreed, the third-party package or app would be recorded in the solution library. It is important to note here that support for the third-party package or app needs to be addressed because the support arrangements for the third-party package or app must be adequate. |
| Requirement can be met by customization through development | If the requirement cannot be provisioned using built-in features, there is no existing solution in the library, and the requirement cannot be met by the addition of a third-party package or app, then the only course of action is development. If the requirement cannot be met by development, then the SharePoint solution delivery needs to be reviewed. |

**Tip** Create a SharePoint solutions list, to record all solutions that have been delivered into the SharePoint platform, whether they are active or dormant. Refer to the model given in Chapter 8, "Building a SharePoint service delivery model," concerning the building of an inventory covering the SharePoint platform. Refer also to Chapter 5, "Planning SharePoint Governance," concerning the SharePoint One-Stop Shop and the Statement of Operations.

## Using practical techniques to make decisions

You should carry out an investigation to ascertain what route you will go down when thinking of customizing SharePoint 2013. SharePoint 2013 has the ability for developers to create SharePoint apps. Features to help do this include Web Parts, Content Types, Controls, and Lists, which can be combined to create ready-made solutions, which are reusable. To do this, SharePoint 2013 has a new Apps model that enables you to deploy these solutions from a corporate catalog or the Office Marketplace. Licenses can be managed specifically, and these apps can be made available on a permission basis.

An example of when you would use SharePoint apps is SharePoint 2013 on-premise line-of-business (LOB) systems that are hosted in external systems, such as travel booking, travel expenses, and human resources systems. Other examples include the integration of existing applications with SharePoint 2013.

SharePoint app customizations can be made available from the Office Marketplace to be downloaded by users. Alternatively, SharePoint app customizations can be done internally and then made available centrally in a SharePoint 2013 Store. From that store, apps can be extracted to be used by the business on its SharePoint 2013 site. The following steps describe the process of provisioning an app from an app store so that the app is available to users:

1. The developer creates a SharePoint 2013 app.
2. The developer submits the app to the Office AppHub for validation for use with SharePoint 2013. This is done to confirm that the app will not cause any harm to the SharePoint 2013 environment.
3. Once validated, the app is made available within the Office Marketplace (*http://office.com*).
4. From the Office Marketplace, users of SharePoint 2013 sites can then use the SharePoint 2013 Store, a feature that allows users to select apps from the Office Marketplace and apply them to their SharePoint 2013 sites. Note that the ability for this to take place needs to be configured and enabled by request.

**Tip** Although SharePoint apps are the preferred option standard for developing any customization for SharePoint 2013, other types of customization may still be required. For example, if the development requirement is to build a SharePoint 2013 timer that carries out back-end tasks on a SharePoint site, then it is an on-premise solution developed for a SharePoint 2013 environment. For more information, watch the video titled "SharePoint 2013 App Model and Customization Options," at *http://www.microsoft.com/resources/technet/en-us/office/media/video/video.html?cid=stc&from=mscomstc&VideoID=f67456e3-513c-4ca0-ac35-608b90ec145b*.

Even though the kind of customization required will define the resources and the process by which the solution is delivered, ensure that you prioritize the objective. Map the customer requirement and match it to the available SharePoint 2013 resources, which means ascertaining whether the customer requirement includes development for Office 365 or SharePoint On-Premise. Use the following checkpoints to help define the correct course of action:

- **Apply Value Management techniques.** To help you make the correct decision as to whether customization of SharePoint functionality is required, you should apply Value Engineering and Value Management techniques, as described in the "Value Management and Value Engineering" section of Chapter 4, "Preparing SharePoint solution User Adoption." By following this method, you will be able to create a common understanding that covers the design problem, identifies the design objectives, and gets a group consensus about various courses of action.

- **Get agreement on meeting the basic objective.** Virtually all SharePoint requirements will be based on the fundamental user requirement, which is to collaborate with others. SharePoint 2013 has been designed to have a mass of collaborative features designed to solve basic collaborative needs. Office 365 has been designed in the same way, except that customizing it to add more features could be costly and complex. Therefore, start with the built-in features first to get the user to adopt it, and then approach the specific requirement stages in the delivery program. Advise the sponsor of the pitfalls of doing heavily customized branding just because he or she believes it will make users flock to the site. They might at the start, but that platform sustainability is going to be severely affected when solutions need to be upgraded, which could not take place because of that customization. Add to that the cost of provision and support implications, and you may conclude that it isn't worth it.
- **Create discreet schedules for SharePoint development work.** If development work is going to take place, ensure that the plans for delivering a solution require that development is packaged correctly into a discrete block of work. Reasons for this include the fact that there could be a number of solutions being created simultaneously, by multiple assignments. This needs to be controlled, so the best way of doing this is to provide a schedule of work. More information concerning creating schedules of work is located in Chapter 9, "Controlling the delivery program."
- **Get the right people on board.** To build a SharePoint solution that uses built-in features may not be as complex as developing a web service. In fact, the two tasks require two distinct skills. Skills required to craft a solution with built-in features could be those of SharePoint information workers, or SharePoint champions, aided by a business analyst, or even members of the SharePoint support team. However, to build a web service requires a web developer. To create a web part using the SharePoint application programming interface (API) requires a SharePoint developer. Organizations that need a solution provider to look after the SharePoint platform sometimes mistakenly advertise for a SharePoint developer, or they hire a SharePoint developer to brand the organization's intranet. These types of errors get made when an organization has not yet properly engaged with SharePoint through any kind of delivery program. A SharePoint developer will not be much use to an organization that requires training on SharePoint basics. Getting the right people to develop and focus on building and supporting solutions is important. Read Chapter 7, "Organizing SharePoint delivery resources," for more information concerning roles.
- **Build business rules and policies.** To protect the integrity of the SharePoint platform, sites, and content with respect to customizing SharePoint, you should create some simple business rules and policies. Some of these will be platform related, meaning that they are there to protect the platform. Others just protect the content. But no matter what their purpose, they all have a bearing on customization.

## Creating customization policies to protect the SharePoint platform

You need to create a policy that ensures that developed software will be documented and tested adequately before it is used, and that designated owners and server custodians for the critical information being accessed are aware of the product. Chapter 5 mentioned a customization policy, which is an overarching policy designed to inform users what customization is available and the process by which that will be applied. The following is an example of the main points used in a policy statement applied to customization, based on a solution that will be installed on a SharePoint platform. The SharePoint platform has a production (live), a stage (user acceptance), and a test environment. The customization was developed in-house.

- Any requests to install internally developed products on the test, staging, or production will be prefaced by a help-desk request. SharePoint support is responsible for deploying products to SharePoint servers and is defined as the installer and administrator.
- Documentation must detail relevant accounts to be used, where and how those accounts are to be installed, and what permissions need to be set.
- The location of the completed Microsoft Windows Installer file (MSI), along with full installation documentation detailing how and where it is to be installed and what post-configuration needs to be managed by SharePoint support.
- Any other information concerning the location of the logging information must be documented.
- Any tests that the installer needs to do to ensure the product works must be documented.
- The relevant help-desk request must be updated to reflect the signoff of any products deployed in this fashion.

When a decision has been made, the people involved have to agree to it. The resources used for development in SharePoint 2013 depend on a number of factors concerning infrastructure. The following section describes the various options.

# Choosing the correct resources

In order to develop customized SharePoint 2013 solutions, you need a development environment. The kind of development environment required depends on the kind of SharePoint 2013 customization being implemented. Reasons for customizing SharePoint could include the following:

- That you want to build solutions that use the server-side object model exclusively
- That you want to create and publish apps for Off-Premise SharePoint in Office 365
- That you want to develop apps for SharePoint for a corporate catalog

SharePoint developers will know they can build server-side farm solutions that extend core SharePoint capabilities. That has always been an option when developing SharePoint solutions. SharePoint 2013 takes another step forward; it offers a new flexible development model. In SharePoint 2013, developers can now create apps for SharePoint that take advantage of standard web technologies, such as JavaScript, OAuth, and OData. SharePoint 2013 provides functionality to interact with SharePoint resources and a wide range of hosting options. The new app for the SharePoint development model gives the ability to build apps that take advantage of SharePoint capabilities and that run in the cloud instead of on an on-premises SharePoint platform.

The new development model for SharePoint is a significant step. Website component development and mobile development have reached the app, widget, and plug-in era. Wordpress sites have a huge base of widgets, plug-ins, and components, all of which can be called "apps" because they add functionality to a base site. Facebook, Amazon, and Bing all use the same functionality. Mobile devices provide functionality for virtually every known app. These apps have been developed by large corporations, the mobile providers, and developers working for organizations and for themselves. This has changed the face of software development, which is reaching commoditization, the age of literally taking a product of the shelf and applying it to the platform. SharePoint 2013 on- and off-premises has built-in features allowing the business to access a centralized catalog of apps and apply it to their sites without IT involvement. This opens the doors for SharePoint developers because they have an additional avenue to bring their products to the masses. If you want to start coding in SharePoint to develop an app and need help doing so, there are huge resources available.

In the context of a SharePoint delivery program where there is a requirement to provide a SharePoint solution, whether it be an app or a server-side product, the important thing is to understand what the resource requirement is. As a SharePoint delivery manager, you need to understand and agree with the developers of the delivery team what resources they need to build a solution.

## SharePoint 2013 development environment options

For SharePoint 2007, development environments were restricted because the developer needs an increased level of resources to build components. SharePoint 2007 could be installed only in a Windows Server environment, not to the desktop. Developers were given either virtual environments (using Microsoft Virtual PC or VMware, for example) or a separate desktop to build SharePoint tools on. This arrangement was difficult to manage and control because, generally, it was considered time consuming and problematic to connect local resources to the SharePoint virtual instance (for example, mapping local drives, USB drivers, external CDs, and shared drives). This changed with SharePoint 2010, which had the ability to install SharePoint directly to the client operating system, whether it was Windows 7 or Windows Vista SP2.

SharePoint 2013 provides more opportunities, as well as some changes. The key development environment setup considerations for SharePoint 2013 are as follows:

- SharePoint installations directly to the client operating systems are not supported by Microsoft.
- Windows 8 can be used to host clients in Hyper-V or VMware technologies, meaning that the development environment could be run in a virtual environment.
- There are cloud-hosting companies offering Infrastructure as a Service (IaaS), which allows developers to create development platforms in the cloud. This interesting proposition is useful because organizations have little or no need to provision local development environments. A good example of a cloud-hosting company offering this service is CloudShare (*http://www.cloudshare.com*).
- SharePoint 2013 has additional functionality and applications, such as Office Web Applications and Windows Azure Workflow. These can be added to the development environment as required.

**Tip** Windows Azure is the best method to develop either SharePoint autohosted apps or provider-hosted apps, which are the two new types of cloud-hosted apps for SharePoint 2013 Off-Premise. Windows Azure can be used to develop apps in environments such as Office 365. Consider this when you are required to provide the additional functionality that is normally only available in Sharepoint 2013 On-Premise. More information concerning how to create a development environment using Windows Azure and Office 365 is located at *http://blogs.msdn.com/b/steve_fox/archive/2013/02/03/setting-up-your-development-environment-for-o365-amp-azure-development.aspx.*

A development environment is a sandbox environment. The term *sandbox* is commonly used in web services development to refer to a mirrored production environment for use by external developers. Typically, a developer creates an application that uses a web service from the sandbox, which enables developers to validate their code before migrating it to a staging environment so it can be tested by users before being published to the production environment. Sandboxing is used by Microsoft, Google, Amazon, PayPal, eBay, and Yahoo!, among others.

To help you understand this better and decide what kind of development environment is required, three types of development environments are illustrated in this section. Refer to Table 10-2 to see what the various abbreviations used in the illustrations mean.

**TABLE 10-2** Abbreviations used in development environment illustrations

| Abbreviation | Description |
|---|---|
| DEV CLIENT | This is the laptop or computer that the developer uses. |
| DEV ENVIRONMENT | This is the virtualized HYPERV or VMWARE development environment that is hosted by the DEV CLIENT. |

| Abbreviation | Description |
|---|---|
| TFS SERVER | This is the Team Foundation Server responsible for centralizing the development (needed if there are multiple developers). |
| TEST ENVIRONMENT | Accessible to the DEV ENVIRONMENT, a SharePoint environment set so that the developers can test apps in the UAT or PRODUCTION ENVIRONMENT without disruption. Change control is under the management of developers, not the business. |
| UAT ENVIRONMENT | Belongs to the SharePoint sponsor's organization. SharePoint support manages this, not the developers. Used to provide a test area for the customers to test created apps from the developers, which has been provided to SharePoint support, installed by SharePoint support and made available to customers. |
| PRODUCTION ENVIRONMENT | Belongs to the SharePoint sponsor's organization. SharePoint support manages this environment. Configuration management is described in the "Creating platform Governance" section in Chapter 5. |

The first development environment, shown in Figure 10-2, is a SharePoint 2013 individually hosted environment.

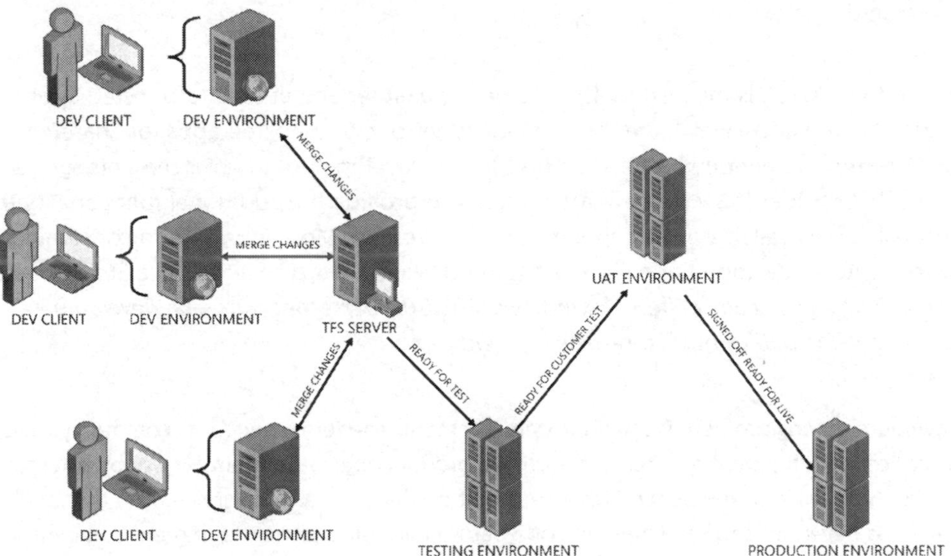


**FIGURE 10-2** A SharePoint 2013 individually hosted development environment.

The centrally hosted development environment shows individual developers carrying their own development environment with them. Their own development would be a virtualized environment, carrying SharePoint 2013, Microsoft Visual Studio, and relevant tools and applications. There are implications with this approach, since the DEV CLIENT will require resources (sufficient memory, processing power, and storage) to ensure that it can run the DEV ENVIRONMENT on the machine. The DEV ENVIRONMENT is a standardized virtual environment that would be copied to other members of the SharePoint delivery team's clients. When development is done as a team, there would a centralized location to save and have changes merged (TFS SERVER). The DEV ENVIRONMENTS would be connected to that TFS SERVER. Before any SharePoint customizations are provisioned for the customer to test, they need to be packed and then tested in the TEST ENVIRONMENT. Once the testing has been completed and the app deemed functional, the app is then repacked and deployed into the UAT environment. This is where the customer can confirm the requirements have been met. Once that testing is completed, the package can be deployed into PRODUCTION under Change Control.

If there is a requirement not to have the developer environments provided individually, then the next option is to enable the developer environments to be hosted centrally. Figure 10-3 shows an example of this setup. The centralized location could be a virtualized platform that can host multiple virtual environments. That environment could also host the standardized developer environment, which would then be copied to provide other developers with the same developer environment. This means that the developer machine (DEV CLIENT) does not have to be powerful because the only purpose of that is to connect to the centralized virtual host to access the developer environments. The other advantages include that the developer can move from machine to machine to access the developer environment without any impact. Through the use of the developer environment, the developer can have their changes merged in the TFS SERVER. From there, the same process applies as per the centrally hosted developer environment shown in Figure 10-2. Packages are made available to the TEST ENVIRONMENT, then to the UAT ENVIRONMENT, then finally to the PRODUCTION ENVIRONMENT.

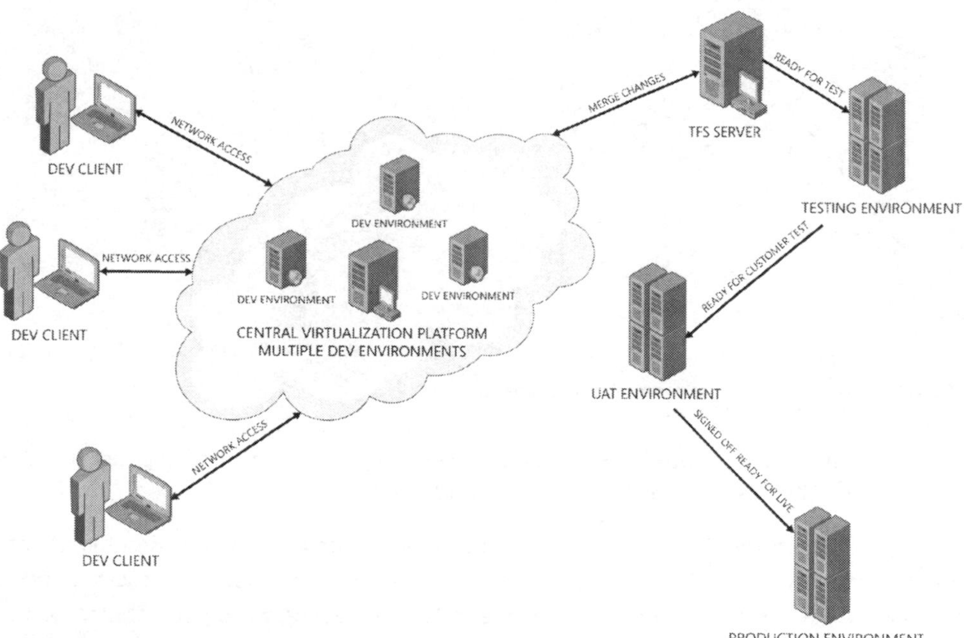


**FIGURE 10-3** A centrally hosted development environment.

Another development environment takes place in the cloud. This is depicted in Figure 10-4. IaaS providers are now available that can provide developer environments hosted in the cloud. This uses the same model as the centrally hosted developer environments shown in Figure 10-3; however, the developer environments are not hosted on-premises. This frees up the reliance on internal IT provision; however, the rules concerning the control of releasing solutions to UAT and PRODUCTION

ENVIRONMENT need to be fully investigated and agreed upon by the SharePoint delivery manager. Note that with some IaaS providers, they are already providing the same developer environment model (that is, TFS SERVER) to allow developer teams to work together. However, that is generally provided as a Platform as a Service (PaaS). All the developer needs is Internet access to the IaaS provider. The IaaS provider could have templates for several types of developer environments. Also, with IaaS, the developer environments are provided on demand, meaning that they are available only when the developer is using the developer environment.

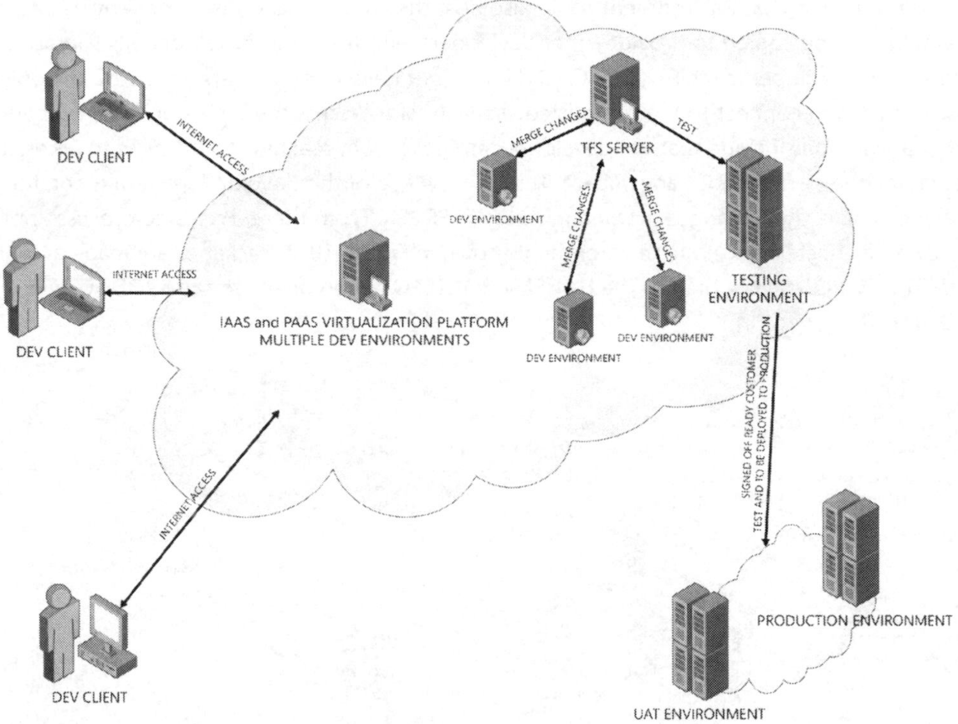


**FIGURE 10-4** A cloud-hosted development environment.

*IaaS, PaaS, and Software as a Service (SaaS) cloud provisions are described in the "Knowing your SharePoint features" section of Chapter 2, "Defining the SharePoint solution scope."*

Deciding the kind of development environment and the resources on that environment for the purpose of customizing SharePoint is very important. Those decisions affect the process under which the solutions are developed, the cost, and the time scale of the delivery program. This section only touched on the areas of selecting the development environment.

**Tip** There is a lot of related documentation and great books available that go into depth concerning SharePoint development, which can be found at the following links:

SharePoint 2013 development books: *http://search.oreilly.com/?q=sharepoint+2013+development&x=0&y=0*

SharePoint 2013 development overview: *http://msdn.microsoft.com/en-gb/library/jj164084.aspx*

SharePoint 2013 app model and customization options: *http://www.microsoft.com/resources/technet/en-us/office/media/video/video.html?cid=stc&from=mscomstc&VideoID=f67456e3-513c-4ca0-ac35-608b90ec145b*

SharePoint 2013 app infrastructure configuration and isolation: *http://www.microsoft.com/resources/technet/en-us/office/media/video/video.html?cid=stc&from=mscomstc&VideoID=5b491c7b-43f9-411d-8974-0cf86cc6c3b0*

"How to: Set up an on-premises development environment for apps for SharePoint": *http://msdn.microsoft.com/en-gb/library/fp179923.aspx*. This article will show you how to set up an on-premise SharePoint 2013 development environment that comprises SharePoint 2013 and Visual Studio 2012.

## Understanding the User Adoption impact

Generally, users see SharePoint development as a black art. Generally, user perception of software development is that the "developers write the code, but they do not speak to users," and that they themselves do not need to understand what it takes to build a solution. Therefore, developers will have to change the way they work with users, and the emergence of SharePoint apps in SharePoint 2013 compels that change. Developers will have to prove that they can support their products (particularly if they are provided through the Office Marketplace), and that they follow a change management process, such as the Agile Requirements Change Management process. They will need to get closer to the configuration management process and understand the nature of change control and how products are released to organizations. They will need to embrace systems analysis, and they will need to understand how to create system specifications, which is key to best practice software development.

This is simply because of the emergence of the SharePoint app, combined with the user perception of software development. Users can access Office Marketplace apps or the central catalog of apps, and deploy those apps to their sites. Figure 10-5 shows the Office Marketplace in a SharePoint 2013 site.

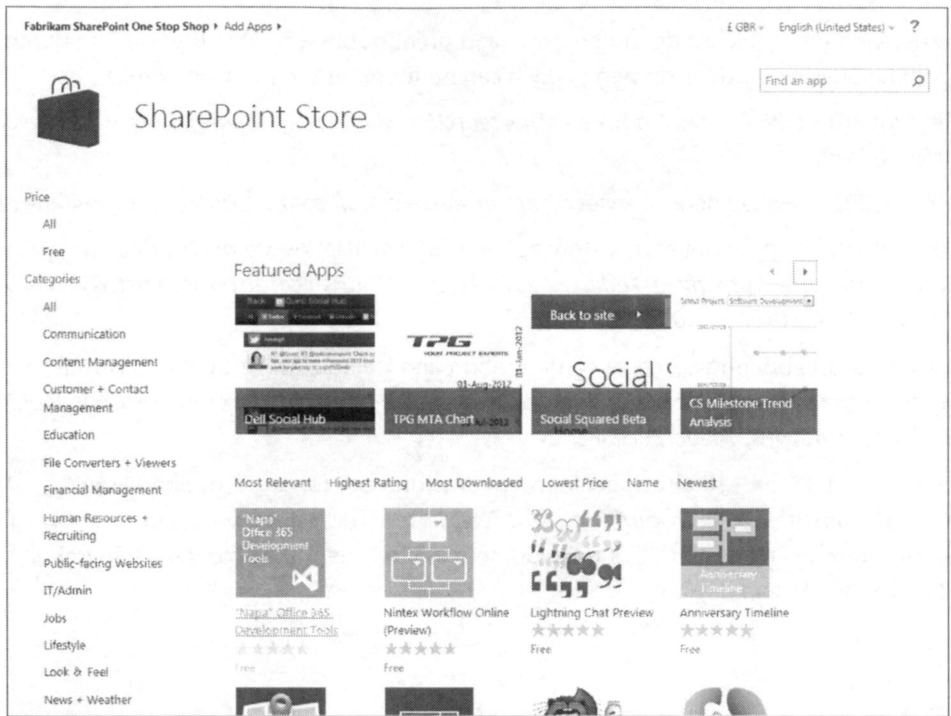


**FIGURE 10-5** The SharePoint Store in SharePoint 2013.

One of the User Adoption impacts concerning the provision of customized SharePoint apps, while making the lives of the users easier in choosing reusable functionality that can be planted into their sites, brings forth some User Adoption challenges. The following scenario illustrates the issues involved here.

*Scenario 2: A developer writes a free app that provides functionality to a SharePoint 2013 site. The app is noted as being required by a business unit in the organization. The product is deployed to the business unit's SharePoint site from the Office Marketplace. Support for the app is limited, however, because the app is freeware. The business unit is informed about this, but the communication does not reach everyone. Calls increase to the support team due to requests for aid concerning the app. The support team tries to contact the developer for further information, and the developer says that he can provide only limited support, but he helps out when he can. The problems continue. Meanwhile, the developer's app gets picked up by a lot more organizations. The developer has a lot less time to respond to requests for aid, so he stops. Users blame SharePoint support for failing to help them resolve issues with the app.*

As you can see from this scenario, SharePoint support takes the blame for an app that was not developed internally, which was free and had only limited support from the developer. The User Adoption challenge here is not how to get the users to use the solution; it is getting the business users to understand the limited level of support available for that app and to accept the consequences of that. The level of support provided is associated with the level of control required to update the SharePoint app. In addition, changes to the infrastructure must take into account potential impacts on SharePoint apps. Investigate any risks associated with SharePoint app upgrade, and ensure that users are aware of any implications. Ensure that your support level includes references to any potential procedures that will need to be adopted concerning the maintenance of SharePoint apps.

Software development affects User Adoption because of the hidden requirements needed to provide adequate support. This is true regardless of whether On-Premise or Off-Premise SharePoint is involved. Also, it does not matter whether the app was developed internally or by a third-party company.

## Understanding the Governance impact

To manage a SharePoint development environment properly, it is important to have SharePoint 2013 software development best practices. The purpose of these best practices is to manage the process for developing new products in the SharePoint 2013 environment and implement them in a production environment. SharePoint app development brings with it a wealth of new opportunities to users, but also a new set of challenges concerning security, risk, and change management.

SharePoint apps (both free and for purchase) are available through the Office Marketplace. If users have permission to deploy any app to their sites, they need to be aware of the security implications. Some apps require access to basic information about the site and the users. For example, Figure 10-6 shows what happens when a free SharePoint app is deployed to an Office 365 site. (The black boxes in the screenshot cover the name of the app, including its logo.)

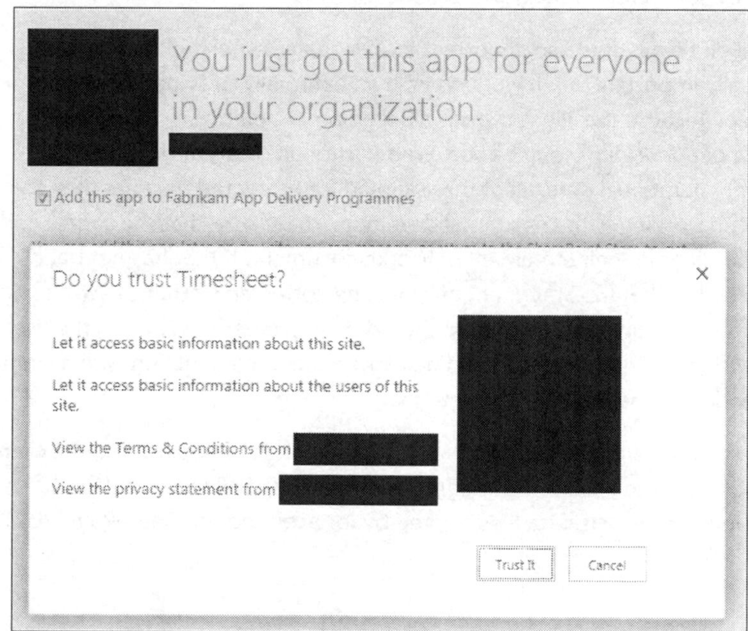


**FIGURE 10-6** Apps have to be trusted.

Of course, the users applying the app to the site can see the privacy statement and terms and conditions, but they must be made aware of why doing this is necessary from a security standpoint. The risks of inappropriate site and user access from this app are unknown until the privacy statement and terms and conditions statements have been understood; at that point, risks sometimes can be mitigated. As a SharePoint developer, it is important to stress this fact to the organization because all apps will need to be given trust from the site before being deployed to it. In terms of change management, you should ensure that any SharePoint app that gets developed is fully tested before being provisioned into a site.

**Tip** Generally, the terms and conditions come from the Office Store Standard Application License Terms, located at *http://office.microsoft.com/en-us/office-store-standard-application-license-terms-HA102821243.aspx*. But you should also ensure that a privacy statement is provided or supplied from the developer.

## Ensuring developer environment separation and ownership

There should be separations among the SharePoint 2013 production, user acceptance, development, and test environments. Where these distinctions have been established, developers should not be permitted to have access to SharePoint 2013 production or user-acceptance platforms. Likewise, all production software testing must use sanitized information on the SharePoint 2013 user-acceptance platform. All application-program-based access paths other than the formal user access paths should be deleted or disabled before software is moved into production.

When developing SharePoint tools, it is also important to designate ownership and control of those tools; this is especially important when working with an externally provided developer who has been subcontracted. Because the client owns the development platform, SharePoint 2013 applications, Web Part or application source code, Web Part or application object code, documentation, and general operational data, all of these should be protected because they are all the client's property. When working with an external developer, make sure that the source code will be made available to the client in their Statement of Works document. If that has not been done, it is strongly recommended that the Statement of Works be corrected or that the work not be undertaken. The only time that non-source software should be implemented is when the user base requests third-party software. This request should be carried out in conjunction with a support agreement, keeping the vendor on the hook for corrections.

As for the ownership of requests and authorization for a SharePoint 2013 application, the client needs to take the appropriate steps to ensure the integrity and security of all SharePoint 2013 Web Parts and application logic, as well as data files created by (or acquired for) SharePoint 2013 applications.

## Provisioning SharePoint 2013 Designer to developers

Using SharePoint Designer, advanced users and developers alike can create SharePoint solutions rapidly in response to business needs. Advanced users can compose no-code solutions that encompass a variety of common scenarios, from collaborative sites and web publishing to LOB data integration, business intelligence (BI) solutions, and human workflows, using the building blocks available in SharePoint in an easy-to-use environment. In addition, developers can use SharePoint Designer 2013 to get a quick start on SharePoint development projects, through creating data-rich webpages, building powerful workflow-enabled solutions, or designing the look and feel of a SharePoint site. From a Governance perspective, you should select users who can use SharePoint Designer and ensure that specific sites have it enabled, although this should be ratified as part of the SharePoint Governance plan. Will some users have access to SharePoint Designer 2013? In my experience, SharePoint Designer should be provided only to those who are qualified developers in the organization; it should not be made available to users who are not sufficiently trained in the product because damage to sites and content can occur if users do not understand the purposes of the tool.

**Tip** Ensure that anyone who is about to use SharePoint 2013 Designer is aware of what is required to develop workflows in SharePoint 2013. For more information concerning SharePoint 2013 Designer, visit *http://msdn.microsoft.com/en-us/sharepoint/hh850380.aspx*.

## Ensuring that a system development life cycle is followed

Once there is a SharePoint development environment in the company, the developer should be made fully aware that he or she is fully responsible for developing, maintaining, and participating in a system development life cycle (SDLC) for any SharePoint 2013 development programs.

**More Info** For more information about SDLCs, see *http://en.wikipedia.org/wiki/Systems_Development_Life_Cycle*.

All SharePoint 2013 software developed that will operate in SharePoint 2013 production, particularly for On-Premise SharePoint, should be developed according to the SDLC. At a minimum, any design documentation should include a User System Specification document and a User Manual. You should ensure that only copies of nonrestrictive and nonconfidential production data content are available to developers, and that you provide only segments of data, not an entire production content database. Check that once the site is provisioned, there are no links back to the production environment (where it's possible for users visiting the user acceptance testing environment to inadvertently alter information in production).

The developer's realm of control is the development environment and its companion test environment. The developer does not have the ability to manipulate user acceptance or the production environment directly. The developer must interface with SharePoint administrators to ensure that adequate documentation and communication regarding the installation of the package are available.

I cannot stress enough the importance of creating work packages for SharePoint development rather than just diving in, writing some code, and pushing it directly onto the SharePoint production servers. Make sure that the SharePoint sponsor understands what technical and human resources are required to customize SharePoint. Acquiring the right amount of equipment and the correct personnel to carry out the relevant tasks is absolutely vital for success.

Also, SharePoint 2013 administrators must perform periodic risk assessments of SharePoint production servers to determine whether the controls employed are adequate. All SharePoint production and user acceptance platforms should have an access control system to restrict who can access the system and the privileges available to these users.

## Creating documentation for customized SharePoint solutions

The fundamental belief is that the dominant factor that distinguishes a successful customization of SharePoint from an unsuccessful customization of SharePoint is the effective dissemination of key information. I've seen other customizations fail because the stakeholders, SharePoint support, the IT help desk, and others did not understand or agree to the reasons for customization. Other examples of failure include when objectives weren't clearly defined, the delivery team did not agree on the requirements, or the delivery team had different perceptions of what the final product would look like. SharePoint developers, therefore, need to provide documentation that includes:

- A User Solution Specifications document with the following:
  - List of key requirements and features
  - Solution flowchart
  - Interface specifications
  - Design, dependency and data flow diagrams
  - Detailed specifications for each component
  - Implementation, validation, and testing plans
- A User Manual
- An Operations Manual

The remainder of this chapter describes how to construct this relevant documentation, including the format and why each document is required.

## Creating the User Solution Specification document

Users need to be comfortable with using the new solution. SharePoint support needs to understand the basics of resolving any requests from users when they use the solution. The Governance committee needs access to detailed information concerning the solution. When any customization is carried out, the developer, with help from members of the delivery team (for example, the business analyst, solutions architect, and others), must create a document that details the solution in such a way that allows users to understand the solution.

Once the service delivery manager has authorized the start of the design and development of the SharePoint solution, it is necessary to provide the SharePoint stakeholders with information about the main features of the solution. This information is contained in the User System Specification document, which should form the basis for any final agreement with those who are expected to use the solution. The specification should not have to be updated once the contents are agreed upon. However, you should consider producing the User Manual from the User System Specification document. The specification also plays an important part in user education and may be used for staff familiarization before the User Manual becomes available. In addition, it could be presented as a training aid rather than a reference manual.

The contents checklist provided in Table 10-3 shows the structure of the User Solution Specification document. Note that this does not include any working documents whose audience is a developer. Working documents should be used only when you know that these will be acceptable and understandable to the user. The User Solution Specification needs to be able to present data and procedures in language that the stakeholders understand.

**TABLE 10-3** User Solution Specification document headings and descriptions

| Section | Contents |
|---|---|
| Introduction | Provides a brief introduction to the solution, reasons for introducing changes, a statement of the problems that will be resolved, objectives, and expected benefits (linked to the delivery program plan). |
| Procedure summary | Provides a one-page summary of the major changes and explains the principles of the solution. Includes a solution outline and a flowchart of its operation. |
| Procedure specifications | Describes the clerical and interactive procedures within the solution. Identifies the key points of the flowchart user interaction and solution input and output. Describes in nontechnical language the objectives of the solution input and outputs. |
| Data | Lists samples of mock-ups of input and output documents, displays, and specifications of any clerical files (for example, output logs, output screenshots). Summarizes any related files showing their connection to the solution. |
| Supporting information | Depicts an organization chart showing the lines of responsibility in terms of the solution. For example, if the solution is a SharePoint site, show an organization chart listing the owner, contributor, and reader. |
| Changeover | Describes any plans for changing to the new solution. Includes any time scales, critical activities, and workloads. |
| Operations | Lists anticipated schedules (linked to the program schedule where the solution is listed). Lists any deadlines and critical points. |

**Note** Stakeholders will ultimately have full responsibility for executing the solution. The User Solution Specification document is often the stakeholder's last opportunity to request changes when the design fails to meet their requirements. Once they have accepted the User Specification document, you as SharePoint delivery manager should declare that the specification can be changed only through Change Control.

*For more information about how change affects the ability to deliver the SharePoint solution, refer to Chapter 6, "SharePoint delivery program considerations."*

## Creating the User Manual

The User Manual is a form of communication that is permanent (as distinct from the User Solution Specification document and changeover instructions, which be archived when they have served their purpose) and must be available to users before the SharePoint solution goes live. Its purpose is to instruct the users how to operate the solution successfully and to inform them of the facilities offered by the solution. The User Manual also informs SharePoint support staff of the constraints to the solution's operations and actions that should be taken in the event of failure or errors. The User Manual must always be accessible for reference purposes throughout the operational life of the solution. Therefore, it should reflect the solution's current state and be updated whenever changes are made.

The User Manual is created by the developer in conjunction with members of the delivery team (for example, the business analyst). Even if the developer writes the User Manual, the stakeholders all must read and agree to it, with the understanding that it is written for the user. The User Manual should only contain information that is directly relevant to and easily understood by the user. For example, if the solution outputs a number of files (user audit information, log information, and so on), then the User Manual should contain only information that is specific for the users, and not system information unless absolutely necessary. The manual should be particularly explicit in those areas where user staff has little or no previous experience. Users who have had no previous experience in using the solution are not usually aware of the importance of formal and strict adherence to instructions (and hence the care that is needed to avoid problems). Therefore, the User Manual needs to reflect that reality, the training schedule relevant to the solution needs to stress the importance of the User Manual as the key reference document users should look to, and the User Manual needs to be placed in a centralized location. SharePoint support should take into account key questions and answers from the User Manual and record resolutions in a centralized knowledge base.

*The User Manual has an impact on training and support. To find out the role of the User Manual in a training schedule, see the "Creating a SharePoint training program" section of Chapter 5. For more information about how the User Manual is important to SharePoint support services, see the "Task 3: Launch your services" section of Chapter 8.*

The contents checklist provided in Table 10-4 shows the common structure of the User Manual. Feel free to use the same structure or modify it to suit your solution and user requirements.

**TABLE 10-4** User Manual structure

| Section | Contents |
|---|---|
| Title page | Details the title, author, month and year of publication, and the name and contact information of the point person in the event of problems during the operation of the solution and for general inquiries on use of the solution. |
| Contents list | Gives a table of contents. |
| Solution summary | As briefly as possible, and in nontechnical language, explain the solution. The summary should not be longer than one page. |
| Clerical and input procedures | Depicts a solution flowchart and describes the whole solution, explaining exactly what the solution does, and, if necessary, provide a procedure flowchart for any subprocesses. |
| Solution input documentation | Provides and annotates screenshots of the solution. |
| Solution output documentation | Provides a sample of each output and explains the contents of each output. Describes how the output is provided and includes any reports on errors and the handling of those errors. |
| Glossary of terms | Explain any technical terms that the user may have to understand. |

## Creating the Operations Manual

An Operations Manual is a permanent reference document that informs SharePoint support about the solution, the work carried out in its operation, and any special features. It is the formal vehicle to communicate solution details to SharePoint support, but is not the only one. The IT help desk, SharePoint support, and technical interfacing teams play an important part of solution development. They are a sounding board and the source of technical expertise, particularly prior to the design of the solution and to the production of Operations Manual. Such material will be produced progressively as the solution is developed (for example, SharePoint Server names, Web Application names, Service Application names, and other integrated systems). It is essential that provisional details of the solution be supplied to the IT help desk team and SharePoint support to afford them the opportunity to prepare preliminary schedules and training in and familiarization with the SharePoint solution within those teams.

*Interfacing teams are described in the "Interfaces: Teams in the organization" section of Chapter 7.*

The contents of the Operations Manual should be clear and factual. It may be necessary for the manual to be partitioned to the requirements of the IT help desk, SharePoint support, and interfacing teams (for example, data capture, data control). The structure of the Operations Manual should be determined in conjunction with the service delivery manager, and it should be designed to enable operation problems to be solved without needing to go back to the developer. The contents checklist provided in Table 10-5 shows the common structure of the Operations Manual. Feel free to use the same structure or modify it to suit the solution and user requirements.

**Tip** You should store the Operations Manual in the Admin section of the SharePoint One Stop-Shop because that is where the IT help desk, SharePoint support, and interfacing teams can access that document. The Admin section of the SharePoint One-Stop Shop is described in "The SharePoint 2013 One-Stop Shop" section of Chapter 7.

**TABLE 10-5** Operations Manual structure

| Section | Description |
|---|---|
| Title page | Details the title, author, month and year of publication, and the name and contact details of the point person in the event of problems during the operation of the solution and for general inquiries on use of the solution. |
| Contents list | Gives a table of contents. |
| Solution details | Gives a brief description of the solution, including options, alternatives, and exceptions to normal SharePoint operations. |
| Solution location | Describe the deployed location of the solution (for example, what servers it is on in a SharePoint farm). |
| Summary of operations | Give a solution outline, a solution flowchart, and wireframes (if required). |
| Timetable | Gives the frequency of all timer jobs (including duration), or relationships to any calendar periods. |
| Solution requirements | Describes the technical components required to build the solution. |
| Input data | Describes the sources of input data, samples, minimum/maximum/average quantities or load, and other data details. |
| Files | Describes the purpose of each file, site, or repository used in the solution. |
| Output data | Shows samples of output, including screenshots. |
| Applications used to construct solution | Details the packages and software used to develop the solution, including any integrated components used and any authors. |
| Operating procedures (normal) | Lists the sequence of events the solution goes through, any actions required by the users, and monitoring reports and samples. |
| Operating procedures (abnormal) | Lists any failure reports and the actions that should be taken, as well as the contact details for anyone who should be told if there is a failure. |
| Operating procedures (restart) | Lists any actions to be taken if the solution requires restart after failure, and references to any connected solution that may need also to be restarted. |

## Summary

This chapter focused on SharePoint customization. It touched on the technical and human resources required, the reasons why customization should be deemed a separate program, and, in particular, what needs to be addressed.

Although customization is available in SharePoint 2013, you should carry out a Value Management exercise to decide whether it is really necessary. Particularly when you are providing new SharePoint platforms to users who have never seen SharePoint, it is definitely not a priority. Microsoft has designed SharePoint 2013 to be clean, simple, and fast, and work with a significant number of built-in features. Modifying SharePoint could add complexity and introduce performance and upgradeability issues. In particular, User Adoption could be affected because more energy would have to be focused on working with user and groups if SharePoint has been customized. Conversely, customization can add value, if you first ensure that users understand how to use SharePoint 2013 to improve their productivity, enhance collaboration, and identify and promote best practices.

Having the right SharePoint developer is important to any customization process. If you need to customize, do not hesitate to ask for help, and make sure that help is qualified. For example, do not allow developers who have few skills in SharePoint development to customize a production platform. Even if there is the need to customize SharePoint, do not think that simply putting in a SharePoint development platform will solve the problem. Be sure to assess the human resources required to carry out the customization, and make sure the personnel selected are up to the job.

As for developer environments, think carefully about the kind of environments needed and when they are needed. For example, customization is not a priority for a program designed to provide a new SharePoint platform. Developer environments are created after the SharePoint production and UAT environments go live, and in fact, they can even be created after resiliency and disaster recovery platforms are in place.

CHAPTER 11

# Managing workshops and closing the delivery program

In this chapter:



Workshops are extremely useful to any Microsoft SharePoint delivery program. They act as an instructive process to guarantee SharePoint services. You need to have workshops to find out what the SharePoint sponsor and stakeholders need and to understand the nature of the business where the solution will be delivered. In addition, you need to be able to finalize program delivery. All programs have a beginning and an end. If you do not have a formal closure process, delivery teams can fail to recognize the end, and then the program can drag on, sometimes at great expense. By having a formal closure process in place, you will be able to know that the outcomes match the stated goals of the program, the stakeholders are satisfied with the results, and that lessons can be learned from successes and failures.

This chapter will help you to understand what needs to be done to prepare, create, format, and manage those workshops effectively. This chapter will also help you learn what you need to do to measure quality and to close the program.

## Managing workshops

The purpose of SharePoint workshops is to provide a plan, roadmap, and agreement to provide a SharePoint solution. This takes place following the Envision and Initial Investigation stages.

The output of SharePoint workshops will help answer the following questions:

- **Timeline** How long will it take to deliver the required solutions?
- **Responsibilities** Who will be responsible for delivering the program and associated solutions?
- **Budget** What is the budget, and what are the review dates?
- **Technology** What technology will be used in developing the solution, what platform will be used to house the solution, and what infrastructure will be made available?
- **Resources** What people and technical resources are required?
- **Business agreement** Who are the stakeholders, and which of those stakeholders will you require consent or agreement from concerning the solution delivery ownership?
- **Sponsorship** Who will own the solution, including all top-level decisions concerning requirements?
- **Training** What is the training model, and who will be responsible for delivering training?

The SharePoint workshops also guide you toward defining the SharePoint sponsor and establishing that the SharePoint delivery program is managed by the business and that the budget provided will achieve the priorities that have been agreed to. By having SharePoint workshops, you will be able to ensure that the SharePoint sponsor has no illusions concerning the work required to deliver a program that will address service delivery, licensing, User Adoption, and Governance considerations as described in this book.

As a service delivery manager, you must guide the SharePoint sponsor, which is another reason that workshops are extremely useful. If you do not provide Workshops to help guide the SharePoint sponsor, there will be no plan, budget, or business involvement from the outset. For example, do not assume that if an ad-hoc service is provided, that the budget will be increased and that will lead to organic growth automatically. Use SharePoint workshops to extract all the requirements and associate value with each one.

**Note** As an indication of how important it is to hold SharePoint workshops, an article from eWeek reported: "Just 33.8 percent said their SharePoint plans directly connect with their business goals, with 60.5 percent stating their plans ranged from being neutral to not at all linked to business objectives." If you want to read the entire article, go to *http://www.eweek.com/it-management/collaboration-tools-hampered-by-governance-challenges/?utm_source=twitterfeed&utm_medium=linkedin&utm_campaign=Feed%3A+RSS%2Feweekwebservices+%28eWEEK+Web+Services%29.*

While the delivery program is underway, you will begin workshops to discuss the working group issues that have been raised. These workshops begin during the Envision section of the SharePoint delivery detail plan, and continues into the Initial Investigation, which builds the business case, determines milestones, and confirms success criteria. You can use the sessions as a group to look at what the SharePoint solution needs to have. From there, you can draw up a priority list of aspirations that can be satisfied in SharePoint, which will bring early wins for the relevant stakeholders.

These workshop sessions are with the business. The example sessions described in Table 11-1 are based on the provision of an off-premise SharePoint 2013 via Microsoft Office 365 to an organization.

**TABLE 11-1** Sample SharePoint workshop sessions

| Workshop Session | Description |
|---|---|
| Analysis | The delivery team examines the business documents created in a particular timeframe and look for common issues and threads that pave the way for quick wins. It also looks at any specific issues raised at that time to see how they may be resolved in off-premise SharePoint 2013. The output of this session is a briefing document. |
| Solution Objectives | This workshop concentrates on gathering the aspirations, strategy, and key deliverables that the Office 365 site will offer. It is the starting and key workshop to realizing exactly what the current position is in terms of the business current delivery structure, and where the business wants to aim in in the context of website presence in off-premise SharePoint 2013. The answers in this workshop are free-form. That means that once this workshop is completed, any alteration may lead to revisiting other areas to ensure that changes in objectives are kept in sync with changes in the off-premise SharePoint 2013 site design. The workshop will consider the primary goals of the business; for example, does the business need to provide current or potential customers with information? |
| Content | This workshop will begin to explore the content that the business manages. This section is iterative for the off-premise SharePoint 2013 site. Some example questions are: What specific services will you be offering? What key services that will be provided, and what is the priority? How do you see the process flow from providing information to your viewer? Can you list the services offered within the relevant business unit(s) that will be using Office 365? What source of information is in electronic form and where is it stored, and how many people contribute to or are responsible for the content? This workshop must be guided by the business analyst, who may already know some of the answers to the questions in advance, but the details still require clarification. |
| Applications, Audience, and Search | This workshop discusses what applications are normally used to create content. For example, does the business use Microsoft Word more than Microsoft Excel? Is Microsoft PowerPoint a critical application? How is Microsoft Outlook currently used? Also examined are the recipients of the created content, how the business currently accesses the created content, and what should be in place to enhance that experience. |
| Advanced | This workshop looks at considering reporting methods and to whom information is reported. The aim is to see how reporting can be best achieved using off-premise SharePoint 2013. For example, the workshop would consider Key Performance Indicators (KPIs), dashboards, and how other parties may want real-time access to reporting statistics. |

One other type of session is the Pre-workshop session. This has not been listed in Table 11-1 because it is a precursor to workshops that are within the delivery program. A Pre-workshop session with customers called "The Art of the Possible" should be held before Envisioning, where you can help business users understand the capabilities of the platform from a business, not technical, standpoint. This is because business people will be unaware of what they do not know about the platform, or will have bad previous experiences from failed deployments of likewise platforms (or, for example, where SharePoint was used as a glorified network file share). You have a Pre-workshop session to ensure that the business definitely wants a SharePoint solution, so you will not waste time holding the forthcoming sessions. The following scenario indicates why having a Pre-workshop is extremely useful.

*Scenario 1: A SharePoint consulting firm was approached by Fabrikam, a construction company, which was by then leading the purchasing department of a family-owned real estate construction company. The consultants were told that Fabrikam had been having internal discussions about SharePoint. Fabrikam also described to the consultants its daily struggle for information and the endless duration of internal process, document management via email, businesses processes based half on paper, and half on digital material. Fabrikam asked the consultants if SharePoint could help, and they responded by asking Fabrikam for details and requirements, and setting a date for demonstrations. The demonstration date was not confirmed, but Fabrikam maintained that all stakeholders were in favor of SharePoint, saying that it views using SharePoint as a good way to speed up the business. The consultants were asked to provide a SharePoint platform for Fabrikam stakeholders to try, and they installed SharePoint on the Fabrikam premises. No demonstration was provided because Fabrikam said that it did not want the stakeholders to be subjected to technical discussions or workshops. After four weeks, the consultants met with Fabrikam about SharePoint and found that Fabrikam was not clear at all on how its business could relate to the platform. From further discussion, it also transpired that Fabrikam had no real vision of what it wanted to do with SharePoint as a complete business solution, and that the use of SharePoint by the purchasing department was determined to be nice, but not top priority. Then, Fabrikam informed the consultants that it might consider a mid-sized document management solution for the finance department first, and then think more about the general strategy and requirements after that. Fabrikam also informed the consultants that it wanted more time to think about its business IT needs and what it wants from SharePoint.*

Once the delivery program is under way, and you are engaged in the sessions described in Table 11-1, your aim is to create a consistent representative group and have the members discuss their aspirations with SharePoint from a business perspective. You will have discussed how the business handles files, information, and content, and what it is aiming for with the new off-premise SharePoint 2013 environment. You will have considered how the company currently works and what tools it uses. You will have created an understanding of how it wants to use other SharePoint services.

From these sessions, you can then present a summary document that will detail exactly what has been discussed and agreed to during any initial investigations. The summary can then be used to build the outline and schedule plans to provide the solution.

## Conducting the workshops

So, now that you have an understanding of the kind of workshops required, you need to understand how to hold them. The key thing to remember is that when people come to these workshops, they are not doing their "real" jobs. If doing workshops ends up wasting time, this will lead to a detrimental impact on User Adoption. You must not waste management time and effort (yours and theirs), and you must ensure that there is a disciplined approach to conducting workshops.

### Before the workshop

The person calling the workshop should do the following:

- Set a venue, date, time, and who will attend well in advance.

- Keep the number of workshop participants to a minimum.
- Ensure that all parties are represented and have the authority and knowledge to make decisions and make a valid contribution.
- Set accountability and time limits for each agenda item.
- Issue the agenda and written submissions in time to allow for preparation.

## At the workshop

The person managing the workshop should do the following:

- Start and finish the workshop on time.
- Stick to the agenda and timetable.
- Ensure that there is an agreed-upon process for getting through each agenda item.
- Keep the meeting focused.
- Ensure that full, participatory discussion takes place.
- Shelve knotty issues for resolution outside of the workshop.
- Summarize each agenda item at the end of the workshop, and ensure that agreements and actions are recorded.
- Agree and fix a date for the next workshop, if needed.
- Seek participants' feedback on the workshop's effectiveness.

**Tip** You need to record a lot of information during workshops, so you should designate someone to take notes. The person managing the workshop cannot also be the note taker. In my experience, you need at least two people to run each workshop effectively. If you cannot assign a particular person to do this, consider extending the workshop time so that there are adequate breaks to record decisions and actions against each agenda item.

The participants of the workshop should do the following:

- Keep to the point and be brief.
- Listen to others and do not hold private meetings within the session.
- Be constructive, adopting a can-do approach.
- Agree to realistic targets, which should be attained with a realistic amount of effort.
- Make a note of their own actions.

## After the workshop

The person managing the workshop should review the effectiveness of the meeting and note improvement points for the next workshop. The note taker (if any) should publish and send summary documents to the participants and those who need them within two days. You should also ask the participants to assess the workshop's effectiveness, note areas for improvement, and pass these comments to the person managing the workshop.

## The importance of listening to and knowing your audience in SharePoint workshops

The workshop is an important aspect of being able to record aspirations and ideas and then using them to design SharePoint solutions. You must ensure that you listen closely to all points made by attendees. A method of making sure that you have all the relevant details is to tape-record the session. If you want to do this, ensure that you get the consent of all attendees beforehand.

In addition, knowing your audience is important. You should look at the attendees of the workshops beforehand so that you are clear on what is likely to be said, and you are sure that their presence will help deliver the solution. Here is an example of what happens when you do not know your audience:

*Scenario 2. With hundreds of employees in the audience, the CEO began speaking about dealing with information challenges and describing how the organization will back SharePoint. Suddenly, he noticed a man in the corner of the room, leaning against the wall, not paying attention to the presentation. Furthermore, the man wasn't dressed like the rest of the audience; he was in jeans and a ragged T-shirt, with a baseball cap on sideways. Here was the perfect example, the CEO thought, to show employees that such laxity was no longer going to be permitted. "You in the corner," the CEO yelled. "How much do you make in a week?" Looking up in surprise, the guy replied that he made about $400 a week. With a smirk, the CEO reached into his pocket and pulled out $1,000 in cash. "You're fired!" he said. As the man in the baseball cap took the money, the CEO noticed a funny grin on his face, but he ignored it. After the speech, the CEO called one of his lieutenants over. "So, how do you think I did?" he asked "I sure made an example of that guy. By the way, who was he?" The lieutenant replied, "That was Johnny, the pizza delivery guy."*

The moral of that story, and the cardinal rule in communicating, is *Before you speak, know your audience.* Before you are about to invite attendees to SharePoint workshops, develop and use the customer map to identify where the attendees can and cannot add value in attending. Carry out some investigations using the User Adoption techniques described in the "Building SharePoint User Adoption strategies" section of Chapter 4, "Preparing SharePoint solution User Adoption."

## Brainstorming

Brainstorming is a popular technique for generating ideas in a group and is a recommended approach when carrying out SharePoint delivery workshops. In my experience, you should use the following practical brainstorming techniques:

- **Defer judgment.** Do not criticize any ideas generated as part of a brainstorming session. If each idea is analyzed as it is created, few ideas will actually surface, and many will be suppressed. This will be either because you will run out of time or because the proposer of an idea may not want to look *silly*. But an idea that seems silly may trigger unique and creative solutions.
- **Quantity breeds quality.** By deferring judgment, you will increase the quantity of ideas. This in turn leads to an increase in the probability of delivering more creative solutions.
- **The wilder the idea, the better.** Divergent thinking requires a certain amount of risk taking. Breakthrough ideas are hardly likely to come from safe propositions. In SharePoint workshops, an attendee calling out something that may make him or her look foolish is not taking a risk. The bigger risk is that your attendees are quiet, and their ideas (which could turn out to be a brilliant solution) never see the light of day.
- **Combine and improve ideas.** Build on what is in place; the aim is improving productivity, gauging the benefits impact on return on investment (ROI), and much more.
- **Take a break from the problem.** Idea generation is tiring, and tired people do not perform well. Keep the idea generation sessions to about 10 to 15 minutes, then stop for a little bit and then begin again.

To manage a brainstorming workshop, follow these four practical techniques:

1. **Define the subject.** Write the subject on a flip chart. Make sure that all attendees can see the flip chart and understand what is recorded there.
2. **Choose a facilitator.** This person will not take part in the idea generation session. Rather, he or she will ensure that the founding principles of the meeting are upheld and act as the scribe, adding ideas only if the flow has stopped in order to get the group started. The facilitator should start by reminding everyone of the principles of brainstorming and the topic of the workshop.
3. **Generate ideas.** Ask the group to contribute ideas by calling them out. The facilitator should write them on sticky notes and display them prominently, where all attendees can see them.
4. **Evaluate the ideas.** Organize the ideas into groups to aid the selection and the analysis of ideas.

**Tip** I have attended SharePoint Solution delivery workshops where an electronic whiteboard was used with mind mapping software. This was a great way of gathering ideas and then immediately posting the workshop record as a mind map on a SharePoint site.

## Carrying out a quality review

Quality review is a method of checking that aspects of the SharePoint solution (such as a deliverable) or the complete SharePoint solution meets requirements. It is normally undertaken by all interested parties, including the prospective users of the SharePoint solution. You should carry out quality reviews as part of meeting particular milestones in the delivery schedule, or against any key aspect of the solution being delivered, as part of closing the delivery program. For example, run a quality review against a customized SharePoint app, against SharePoint search, or against an implementation of SharePoint.

More often than not, the perception is that when a SharePoint solution has been created, there is no need for a quality review. Excuses include "We do not have the time to do a quality review," or "The solution speaks for itself." However, there is no basis for such pretexts. A quality review provides real measurements for ROI. A quality review provides comfort to the users and is a driver for change. A quality review provides a basis for training and training materials.

The quality review must be approached constructively. It is in everyone's best interests to identify defects so that they can corrected. The reviewers are helping the SharePoint delivery manager to improve the SharePoint solution. Personal criticism should be avoided.

A review has three parts, as described in Table 11-2. You can carry out this review informally or formally. An informal review can be held by circulating a document for comments. However, if the SharePoint solution is significant, it is prudent to hold a formal review meeting.

**TABLE 11-2** Parts of a quality review

| Part | Actions |
|---|---|
| Prepare | Circulate information concerning the deliverable (whether it be a model, a test, a prototype, or the finished product) to participants in advance of the review.<br>You should provide a sign-off form that can be used to make it clear that participants are taking part in the review and approval of a deliverable.<br>Participants should prepare by assessing the deliverable against its requirements (as specified in the delivery program detail plan).<br>Each participant should send a list of errors or omissions to the person who circulated the information concerning the deliverable.<br>The person coordinating the review should collate all the errors and omissions and decide if a formal review is required. |
| Review | You should ensure that all errors and omissions be discussed and clarified during the review.<br>You should ensure that the focus is to understand the errors and omissions, not to find a solution immediately.<br>You should clarified subsequent actions (including a follow-up meeting if necessary), including the process for sign-off, responsibilities, and timescales. |
| After the review | The person(s) accountable for the deliverable should consider all the comments.<br>All participants should be advised of any action taken. |

## Signing off on SharePoint solution delivery

It is good practice to have each deliverable approved as it is produced. Examples of this include sign-off of a completed SharePoint app, a configured SharePoint Search implementation, the list of user attributes against a SharePoint 2013 user profile, or the implementation of a SharePoint support model.

Of course, the choice of what to sign off on depends on the solution being provided. You must confer with the SharePoint sponsor and stakeholders as to exactly what needs to be signed off on and why. The point of sign-off is having official confirmation that deliverables meet user requirements and auditable documentation that can be stored with the business case and other related documents for the delivery program.

Sign-off is rarely done for SharePoint, simply because there is a wrong perception that getting the SharePoint sponsor to indicate concretely that they agree that the deliverable has been met is overkill. The purpose of sign-off is to ensure that the user perception of the solution is the same as yours, and that you both agree about understanding the solution functionality. Also, it is a good indicator in terms of spotting relevant SharePoint champions, who may well be part of the sign-off.

Therefore, you will need to have a SharePoint deliverable sign-off form. An example of such a form is given in Figure 11-1. Use this form when you need to get confirmation that a deliverable meets user requirements; use it only at key stages in the program.

Quality reviews mean that the user requirements can be confirmed and delivered. Key points of this task are:

- Do not leave it to the Quality Assurance department to determine quality. Quality is defined as fitness for purpose, and many people in many areas are in a good position to gauge this.
- Plan quality from the start, carry out quality reviews regularly, and definitely do so when the SharePoint delivery program is about to close.
- Take responsibility for the quality of your deliverables. Users must be comfortable using the SharePoint solution. All deliverables that make up the solution get you closer to ensuring that your users can use the solution and understand its makeup. Make sure that you take responsibility for making quality reviews take place, and assign those quality reviews to the right people.
- Test all deliverables to ensure that they meet quality requirements. When deliverables have been completed, they should always be checked against the original requirements using testing techniques.

**SharePoint Deliverable Sign-off Form**

Program Name: ______________________________

**Part 1 – Request (to be completed by the originator)**

**Reviewer:** ______________ **Originator:** ______________

**Issued to (date):** ______________ **To be returned by (date):** ______________

| Deliverable: |
|---|
| Review criteria: |

**Part 2 – Response (to be completed by the reviewer)**

I have reviewed the above deliverable on behalf of:

__________ (function)

- ☐ The deliverable is accepted
- ☐ The deliverable is accepted subject to inclusion of the comments noted below
- ☐ The deliverable is rejected for the reasons noted below

Comments:

Name: ______________ Function: ______________

Signature: ______________ Date: ______________

**FIGURE 11-1** An example of a SharePoint deliverable sign-off form.

## Confirming that training has been completed

Training is a key aspect of User Adoption. You will need to confirm that training has been achieved throughout the delivery program. The following indicates who should be trained and when they would have been trained. Use a checklist to confirm that training was delivered.

Based on a scenario where delivering a SharePoint solution could take up to two years, you can ensure that checkpoints are in place to show the SharePoint sponsor and the delivery team that a training schedule is operating. These checkpoints take place at the following times:

- 6 to 18 months before the solution is live
- 4 to 8 months before the solution is live
- 1 month before the solution is live
- When the solution is live

Table 11-3 shows the training checklist, organized by who is doing the training and what the training consists of, based on these checkpoints.

**TABLE 11-3** Training checklist

| When | Who | What |
|---|---|---|
| 6 to 8 months before the solution is live | Information architects and business analysts | SharePoint functionality<br>SharePoint limitations |
| | SharePoint administrators and developers | Infrastructure planning<br>Custom development |
| | SharePoint champions | SharePoint functionality<br>SharePoint limitations |
| | Web designers | Branding and publishing |
| 4 to 8 months before the solution is live | SharePoint champions | SharePoint functionality<br>SharePoint security<br>Third-party tools |
| | Users | Basic introduction of the SharePoint solution |
| | Selected users (stakeholders) | SharePoint functionality and usability |
| 1 month before solution is live | Users | Workshops<br>Basic functionality<br>Introduction to the SharePoint solution |
| | Selected users (stakeholders) | Detailed solution functionality that meets the relevant business requirements |

**Note** When the solution is live, training must be sustained. Use the training checklist row "1 month before solution is live" to continue training. Use the training model to manage and schedule that training accordingly. This is further discussed in the "Sustaining User Adoption" section of Chapter 12, "Maintaining the solution."

*Training schedules are discussed in the "Creating a SharePoint training program" section of Chapter 5, "Planning SharePoint Governance."*

## Creating a closure checklist

The objective of SharePoint program closure is to ensure that the process of closing the program is carried out in a structured manner, and that the program is closed down in a controlled and organized way. Program closure also ensures that all accountabilities have been discharged or transferred to other related programs.

A program can be closed either when it has completed or when it has been terminated. Termination may occur because the program is no longer viable, the driving need no longer exist, or the risks associated with it have become unacceptably high. The closure review should do all the following:

- Review the efficiency of the program in terms of meeting the original time, cost, and resource targets.
- Confirm that any benefits that have been delivered have been built into the business forecast.
- Record and communicate any lessons that can be beneficial to future programs.

As far as the SharePoint sponsor is concerned, either the program has been completed, and he or she can expect to benefit from it, or the program has been terminated. In the latter case, this may be because the original business need no longer exists, but if the program has been terminated because it did not meet the need, the SharePoint sponsor will need to take action to address the unresolved business need that initiated the program in the first place.

There are four key steps to closing a program:

1. Create a closure checklist.
2. Prepare and agree the closure report with the delivery team.
3. Close the program formally.
4. Carry out closure actions and communicate them to the SharePoint sponsor and necessary parties.

It is either the SharePoint sponsor or the business program board's role to approve the closure of a program. However, if the program is to be terminated partway through and other programs are affected (the business case will define any program interdependencies), approval may need to be sought from a higher authority or agreed with other affected parties. For this reason, termination should be treated as a change and managed using the change process.

*For more information concerning change, see the "Managing risks and issues" section of Chapter 9, "Controlling the delivery program."*

When the SharePoint solution is deemed operational, the relevant work required to deliver that SharePoint solution into the live environment has completed and needs to be closed. This does not include User Adoption or Governance; those continue past the point of the SharePoint delivery program itself and will not conclude until the SharePoint solution itself is terminated.

To consider closing the SharePoint delivery program, answer these questions:

- Has the objectives stated in the business case been met?
- Has the delivery schedule concerning the SharePoint solution been marked as completed?
- Has the training plan been defined and operational?
- Has the User Adoption plan been defined and operational?
- Is there a Governance committee in place?
- Have the relevant stakeholders completed testing the solution?
- Have user acceptance tests been completed?
- Has testing of the SharePoint solution been signed off on?
- Has a support model been set up to manage the solution and to handle customer requests?

Closing a SharePoint delivery program requires that you confirm with the SharePoint sponsor that the SharePoint solution meets their requirements. At the same time, you are getting the clients to understand their responsibilities to the system that has been implemented. You do this because the SharePoint solution passes from being part of a delivery program to being part of the business (called Business As Usual, or BAU), and part of the organization's IT framework.

Table 11-4 shows the SharePoint delivery program closure checklist. Feel free to modify it to include anything else you want to ensure gets completed.

**TABLE 11-4** SharePoint delivery program closure checklist

| Considerations | Y | N | N/A | Reference |
|---|---|---|---|---|
| **Deliverables** | | | | |
| Do SharePoint program files record the issue of program deliverables? | | | | |
| Have all internal copies of the deliverables been distributed? | | | | |
| Do the program files record the clients' acceptance of the deliverables? | | | | |
| **File Management** | | | | |
| Is the filing complete, with all references to all program material? | | | | |

| Considerations | Y | N | N/A | Reference |
|---|---|---|---|---|
| Has all temporary material, including disks and files, been removed? | | | | |
| Has the software used on the program, including soft copies of the deliverable documents, been backed up and referenced in the files? | | | | |
| **Archiving** | | | | |
| Have the master copies of the program deliverables been archived to the SharePoint One-Stop Shop? | | | | |
| Have the program files been archived? | | | | |
| **Loan Items** | | | | |
| Have all client/subcontractor loan items been collected/returned? | | | | |
| Has the client/subcontractor returned all loaned items? | | | | |
| Have leased items been returned? | | | | |
| **Subcontractors** | | | | |
| Has all subcontractor work been completed? | | | | |
| Have all subcontractor invoices been received, authorized, and sent to Finance? | | | | |
| Has a subcontractor performance report been completed? | | | | |
| **On-Site Work** | | | | |
| Have all program material been returned from the client's office? | | | | |
| Have all passes returned to site reception? | | | | |
| **Finance** | | | | |
| Has the final invoice been issued to the client? | | | | |
| Have all invoices to subcontractors been finalized? | | | | |
| Have all program-related contract commitments been met? | | | | |
| **Commercial** | | | | |
| Has the client agreed to the closure of outstanding teaming/confidentiality agreements? | | | | |
| **Program Closure** | | | | |
| Have any support or warranty arrangements been established? | | | | |
| Where appropriate, have staff résumés been updated? | | | | |
| Has the potential for follow-up work been explored with the client? | | | | |
| Has a Client Questionnaire been sent to the client? | | | | |
| Have all Quality Assurance non-conformances been closed? | | | | |
| Has a Program Experience Questionnaire form been completed? | | | | |
| Has this completed form been copied to the central program management office (PMO) or to the client? | | | | |

| SharePoint Delivery Name: | Date: |
|---|---|

## Creating the closure report

The purpose of the closure report is to record accurately the reason for the closure, the benefits the program achieved, and any outstanding accountabilities that need to be handed over. It also documents any lessons to be learned regarding how the program was conducted and the efficacy of the supporting process. You can use the closure checklist to create the closure report. When a program is to be closed, the SharePoint delivery manager should do the following:

- Check the status and completeness of the business case, the change, risk, and issues logs, the most recent progress report, and any papers referring to early termination of the program.
- Prepare a draft program closure report with the delivery team, including the terms of reference for the business review.

The program closure report should include the following topics and be formatted using the organization's template:

- Business objective
- Closure statement
- Benefits measurement
- Outstanding risks, issues, and deliverables
- Program efficiency
- Lessons learned
- Acknowledgments

To help you create a closure report, examine the checkpoints in Table 11-4. For each one, evaluate whether it has been completed or not, and if not, document why. Use any points gathered from Table 11-4, and then create a report based on the checklist given in Table 11-5.

**TABLE 11-5** SharePoint closure report checklist

| Area | Description |
|---|---|
| Deliverables | Have all program deliverables been signed off and handed over to ongoing owners?<br>Has accountability for outstanding deliverables been agreed? |
| Risks and Issues | Have all issues been resolved?<br>Has ownership for outstanding issues been accepted by a named person or people?<br>Have any outstanding risks been handed over for ongoing management? |
| Business Forecast | For the business units and functions where the solution has been delivered, update their plans to take into account the operational resources, costs, and benefits.<br>Has a person accepted accountability for monitoring the benefits?<br>Have review points been defined for monitoring the benefits? |
| Team and Stakeholders | Have all people who need to know about the closure of the program been informed?<br>Have all team members been reassigned to other activities?<br>Have any appraisals relating to the delivery team been completed?<br>Have those who deserve special credit been acknowledged? |

| Area | Description |
|---|---|
| Program Accounting and Other Systems | Has the program account been close such that no further expenditure can be attributed?<br>Have relevant cost tracking systems been updated? |
| Program Documentation/ Facilities/Contacts | Has all documentation pertaining to the program been filed and referenced?<br>Have all program facilities been released (for example, desks, office space, IT resources, and so on)?<br>Are there any contractual implications resulting from closure? |

## Formal closure of SharePoint delivery programs

You should invite key individuals to a meeting at which the program is formally approved for closure by the SharePoint sponsor. By bringing this group together, the SharePoint delivery manager has an opportunity to do the following:

- Acknowledge the efforts of everyone on the team.
- Confirm that all program deliverables have been handed over.
- Assign accountabilities for outstanding issues.
- Ensure that any feedback that has been received reflects the differing viewpoints of those involved.

The quality and sharing of feedback is always greater when done in a group than when conducted in isolation. A suggested agenda for the closure meeting is given in Table 11-6.

**TABLE 11-6** Suggested agenda for a SharePoint delivery program closure meeting

| Agenda | Description |
|---|---|
| Deliverables | Confirm that all deliverables have been signed off and accepted by the business. |
| Outstanding Risks and Issues | Review outstanding risks and issues and, for each one, obtain agreement from a specific person who will be accountable for its management or resolution in the future. |
| Benefits, User Adoption Plan, Training, Governance, and Communication | Confirm that the benefits have already been built into the User Adoption plan. Confirm that the training plan has been modeled and the schedules are defined. Ensure that communications plans are operational. Ensure that accountabilities for managing User Adoption, training, and communications are in place. Confirm that Governance has been defined concerning the SharePoint solution. |
| Acknowledgments | Providing a SharePoint solution requires a lot of hard work from the delivery team, which comprises of business and technical staff. The SharePoint delivery manager should acknowledge all contributions to the team, listing key successes. |
| Formal Closure | Assuming all the preceding business has been conducted, SharePoint delivery manager and SharePoint sponsor signs-off the program. |
| Lessons Learned | The SharePoint delivery manager should describe what worked well in the program, and what did not. Also, describe what processes of the program can be reused, and what should be done differently next time. In addition, all the controls put in place for the program should be discussed. |
| Suggested Attendees | SharePoint sponsor<br>SharePoint delivery manager<br>Delivery team<br>Persons accountable for signing off key deliverables<br>Persons who will accept accountability for outstanding issues<br>Persons who will accept accountability for sustained User Adoption, training, and communications plans |

A draft program closure report should be circulated prior to the closure meeting. This provides the briefing for the attendees. You should have this amended based on the discussions and feedback received at the meeting.

Not all SharePoint delivery programs require formal closure meetings. If the SharePoint delivery program is simple, or if the SharePoint sponsor and SharePoint delivery manager do not believe a closure meeting will add value, formal closure should be agreed upon by the SharePoint sponsor after a review of the closure report by the relevant individuals.

Conversely, large SharePoint delivery programs may require more than one closure meeting. The first closure meeting could be held to cover learning, and the second to cover formal closure. This is particularly valuable when you know that the program can contribute greatly to the organization's corporate experience, and you want to ensure that the lessons are captured prior to the delivery team being dissolved.

### Closure actions and communication

Following approval to close the program from the SharePoint sponsor, the SharePoint delivery manager should do the following:

- Finalize the program closure report.
- Prepare a communication that includes the approved program closure report, and send it to the SharePoint sponsor, delivery team, and stakeholders.
- Obtain agreement to close the program.
- Communicate any suggested process improvements to any relevant business process group.

## Summary

The objective of SharePoint program closure is to ensure that the process of closing the program is carried out in a structured manner, that accountabilities have been set (particularly for User Adoption, Governance, and training because they will continue), and that the organization gets to understand successes, failures, and methods to improve future SharePoint delivery programs. As a SharePoint delivery manager, you should follow these basic guidelines:

- Check interdependencies to other programs and/or projects before terminating your SharePoint delivery program.
- Make the program closure explicit.
- Communicate closure to all stakeholders.
- Make sure all related documentation is been signed off by the customer.

- Get a final signoff on implementation/solution acceptance; do not assume that the sponsor will agree based on your having a great relationship with him or her.
- Conduct a "Lessons Learned" session with the SharePoint sponsor and the delivery team. The information you get from this is invaluable for you, the SharePoint sponsor, and any service delivery initiatives (for example, support).
- Hold a proper handover to SharePoint support. Make sure that SharePoint support has the necessary information to support the SharePoint solution properly.
- Keep in touch with the SharePoint sponsor. You may have a 30-day or a 90-day agreement for you to remain available to the SharePoint sponsor, and for your team to remain available while handover to SharePoint support is taking place. Keep checking back with the SharePoint sponsor after that point as well.

CHAPTER 12

# Maintaining the solution

In this chapter:



The focus of this book has been on providing methods and techniques for developing and implementing User Adoption, Governance, and support strategies. You must ensure that actions are taken to drive and sustain those strategies, which will continue over the lifetime of the Microsoft SharePoint solution. User Adoption is about changing user behavior, Governance is about enforcing business policies and rules, and support is about ensuring excellent service delivery.

Therefore, the skills and methods used are not wholly technical or wholly business. They require a combination of skills and knowledge of how best to apply methods and use the practical techniques described. This chapter will help you understand how to sustain User Adoption, Governance, and support for SharePoint solutions.

## Sustaining SharePoint support

Your SharePoint support model needs to ensure that those responsible for providing support (IT help desk and SharePoint support) are capable of supporting the new SharePoint solution, know who the customers are, and are aware of the kinds of issues and requests that they may get and the processes by which they can resolve them. SharePoint support covers not just the things that are strictly labeled "SharePoint"; it extends to anything that the customer thinks is accessible using SharePoint. Figure 12-1 is an example of just some of the products for which SharePoint support will be expected to provide service to its customers.

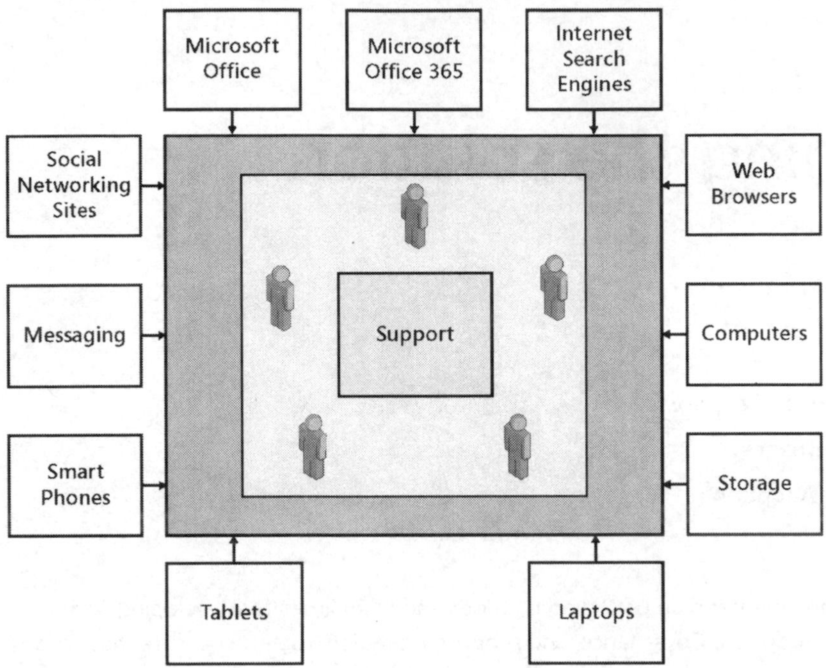


**FIGURE 12-1** SharePoint support does not just cover SharePoint; it includes a wide variety of areas.

There is no possible way in which SharePoint support can provide support for all the products shown in Figure 12-1. As we've said many times in this book, no one can be expected to be a SharePoint "superhero," or an expert in all products. To set realistic expectations and provide a measurable support service, here are several practical techniques that you can use:

- A process needs to be created identifying how the customer can contact SharePoint support.
- An induction guide should be available in a centralized SharePoint location and its location communicated.
- A specific help guide for specific areas of the SharePoint solution and relevant products should be placed in strategic locations in SharePoint.
- User Adoption videos, which show scenarios depicting common information and collaborative challenges and how SharePoint has been used to solve them, should be created. A centralized knowledge base, which houses learning materials, procedural documentation, and FAQs for all software technological products used in the organization, is also helpful.

These points are tools to provide training and communication to information workers. However, people are required to staff SharePoint support. This is very important because the level of user satisfaction with support is directly related to this. If you have a low level of SharePoint support, users will find this out very quickly, especially if, for example, they are trying to get answers from a very busy SharePoint support person looking after four separate SharePoint server environments and handling requests from 10,000 users.

Business rules concerning the level of support provided must be documented in the Statement of Operations. This is not a one-time event. Monitor the growth of SharePoint continually against the resources you have to support the platform. Why is it important to ensure that you have the correct level of support for SharePoint?

*Scenario 1: SharePoint has been delivered to a large organization, where three server environments were created (Production, User Acceptance Test, and Test Environments). A Windows Server administrator was promoted to be a SharePoint master to look after these SharePoint environments. The rules of site ownership are not set, and therefore, users assumed that permissions are set by IT (in other words, by the SharePoint administrator).*

Based on this scenario, we would see a SharePoint administrator whose responsibilities have been "stretched" changing the security level of certain content simply because a user requests it. And because of the administrator's preconceived ideas about setting permissions (using experiences from Windows), that situation escalates out of control. For example, suppose that a user wants full access to something and says to the administrator, "Give me access rights." So the SharePoint administrator, in the absence of any stated policies, and using his experience, gives Full Control to this person. The equivalent of the Wild West ensues.

Does this sound a bit extreme? It really isn't. In my experience, personnel in quite a few organizations assume that anything that has the word "Admin" attached to it means technical administration, not business administration. I have seen organizations that have SharePoint, but all staff have been granted Full Control permissions. Ensuring that the SharePoint support team members have the necessary skills is one way to fix this. However, User Adoption and Governance are more important. Enforcing business rules and policies that ensure data ownership is set and understood.

*For more information about creating a support model, see Chapter 8, "Building a SharePoint service delivery model," which includes a checklist to create a SharePoint support model.*

## Sustaining Governance

In Chapter 5, "Planning SharePoint Governance," I described how you can address crucial areas of Governance (by examining platform Governance) and the practical techniques that you can use to bring Governance to the SharePoint solution delivery program. However, going forward, you need to sustain a Governance model that ensures the integrity of the solution, and describes best practices in terms of how the solution should be used from a business, IT, and organizational perspective.

Although there are many books, ebooks, articles, and videos concerning Governance, the key point that needs repeating is that Governance is not a hardware, software, or human resource solution. Governance is the art of enforcement, which is in itself a journey. This starts with the policies in the organization, combined with meeting information and collaborative challenges that users face. These policies will be organizational-, business-, and IT-specific, and will affect how users employ the SharePoint solution. Policies will then be prioritized and investigated by your Governance committee (including resources assigned to sustaining User Adoption). The output of those investigations then provide the rules under which the SharePoint solution is used.

Rules are enforced through the service delivery model in place, which also includes the resources to convey those rules to users. Those resources would include the relevant communications channels and training. Those resources also include materials to describe those policies (for example, the Statement of Operations, the centralized knowledge base, New Starter Induction documents, and so on). Finally, those resources could include third-party software to help enforce some of those policies.

Enforcement requires a sustained cycle of policy, investigation, agreement, rules, and enforcement review, which completes when SharePoint ceases to exist in the organization. Figure 12-2 shows the cycle, which I have called "Sustaining Governance." Use this model as a method of describing the work required and resources required putting the model in place and assigning relevant resources.

Sustaining Governance is about achieving and sustaining business and IT agility. You need to ensure that the right individuals involved in the Governance committee are empowered with decision rights and management activities. This can be achieved through applying SharePoint service delivery, which concerns itself with the capability of SharePoint services and resources.

**More Info** Several articles describe in detail the guiding principles of SharePoint service delivery and give you some ideas about how to prioritize the policy areas. These are "Some Guiding Principles for SharePoint Service Delivery," located at *http://www.sharepointgeoff.com/some-guiding-principles-for-sharepoint-service-delivery/,* and "What is SharePoint Service Delivery?" located at *http://www.sharepointgeoff.com/what-is-sharepoint-service-delivery/.*

Establishing and maintaining SharePoint Governance involves establishing rules and managing, scoping, and structuring the platform to ensure that SharePoint continually meets user requirements. The people who do this are part of the SharePoint Governance Committee. To maintain Governance, set regular meetings that provide input on the current state of business policies against SharePoint, and output decisions and business rules to manage SharePoint.

Meetings and administrative activities that should take place include the following:

- Weekly operations meetings, so that there can be reports on the current week's SharePoint activities, infrastructure issues, changes, modifications, and enhancements and to describe the following week's highlights.
- A monthly business review, in which committee members review user trends, issues, pain points, success stories, and key policies (for example, policies related to acceptable use, operations, the logical framework, and training guides).
- A biweekly technical or infrastructure review meeting (with administrator attendance mandatory), so that interfacing teams that work with SharePoint administrators, architects, business analysts, and developers review the network infrastructure, confirm network connectivity, and discuss security, disk space, memory, performance, and so forth.

*For more information about defining a Governance plan for SharePoint, read Chapter 5.*

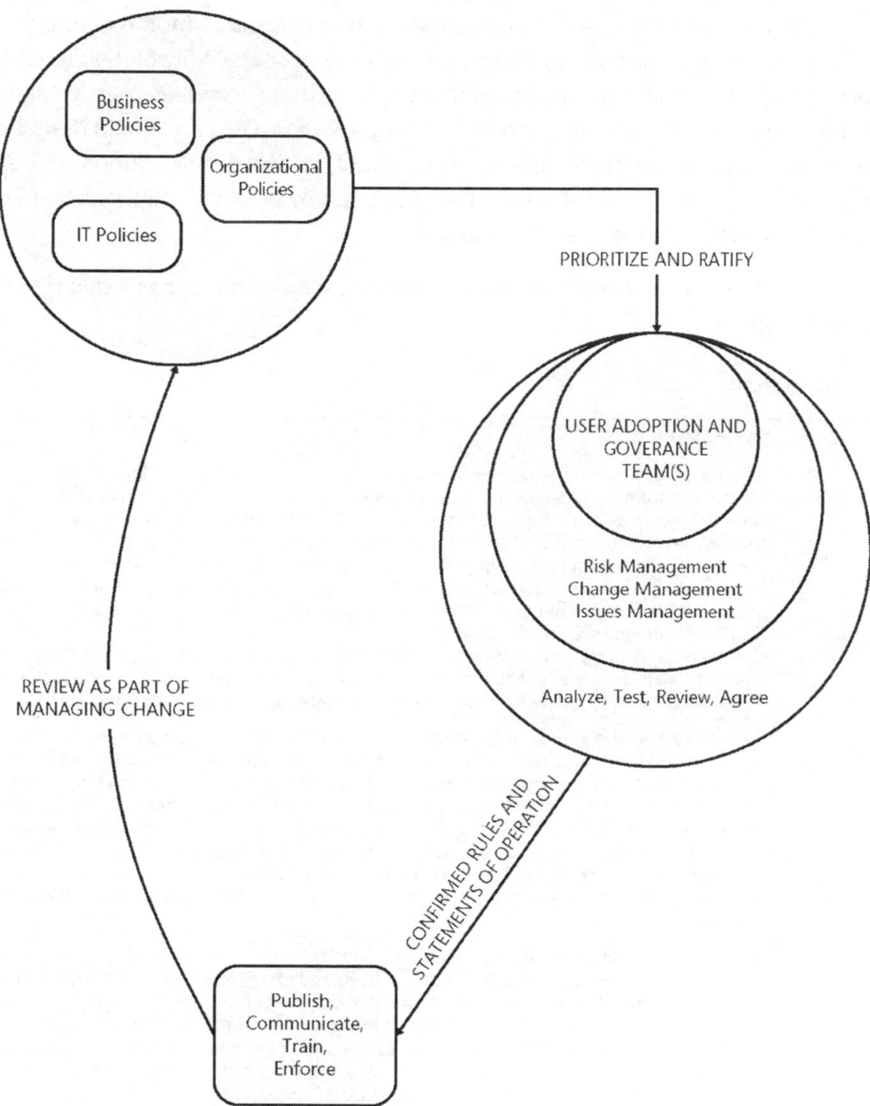


**FIGURE 12-2** Sustaining Governance.

# Sustaining User Adoption

Now that the SharePoint solution is provided, this does not mean the end of User Adoption or Governance. Both are a journey without an end. Training and communication are both important and are needed to ensure that users remain on the path of using the solution in the way that it was intended, and remain productive.

In the "Confirming that training has been completed" section of Chapter 11, "Managing workshops and closing the delivery program," I provided a checkpoint list to prove that training has been included in the delivery of the SharePoint solution. As shown in that checklist, 1 month before the solution is live, users are attending workshops and being trained in basic SharePoint solution functionality. This is an important step in introducing users to the SharePoint solution. However, users change; they move to another function, or even leave to go to another organization. Even if your old users did not change, you will always have new users who need to learn about the SharePoint solution. Therefore, after going live with the solution, you must sustain User Adoption by providing methods that enable users to be productive when using the SharePoint solution.

Table 12-1 describes the various training methods, which you should consider associating with the solutions being provided.

**TABLE 12-1** Training methods

| Method | Description |
|---|---|
| Classroom | Use classroom training to deliver focused and practical SharePoint solution training. Classroom training allows you to teach people in a safe, quiet, and clean environment, away from the noise and pressures of the work area. Training groups can be large or small. The classroom environment provides the important "human touch," which is often missing in technology-based training. Group interaction enhances learning. Employees learn from one another, as well as from the trainer. The group setting also teaches employees how to interact with one another in a professional, productive, and cooperative way, which other forms of training often don't provide.<br>Disadvantages of classroom training include that you have to pull people off the job, which cuts into work time and production schedules. If your employees work in specified shifts, it's often hard to schedule this kind of training, especially for night-shift workers. |
| Online | Use online training when it is beneficial to the organization to keep people constantly updated and knowledgeable. Online training provides flexibility that allows people to schedule their learning time themselves. Online training is available wherever there is Internet connectivity and can be accessed at any time (assuming that the online training materials are available). Online training is cost effective because the organization saves money on traveling and accommodation expenses often related to classroom training. Online training material can be easily revisited many times.<br>Disadvantages include a lack of the human touch and a certain lack of real-world scenario training. |
| On-demand | On-demand training consists of modules provided through a portal allowing users to take online courses. They include video tutorials, downloadable product manuals, FAQs, and so on. Like online training, the benefits are that users can train anywhere, anytime. They are able to learn at their own pace. The disadvantages of on-demand include lack of control from those providing the training, particularly concerning time scales for completion. On-demand training modules can be provided as a customizable product from the training provider, or they can take place online or through an e-learning provider. |
| Computer-based training (CBT) | CBT allows users to train by using products directly. For example, a SharePoint solution could include CBT that is customized so that the user learns to use that product without having to sit in a classroom. It differs from on-demand and online training because of the flexibility in the training modules of the relevant CBT. |

| Method | Description |
|---|---|
| Workshops | Having workshops is very useful in learning user requirements, confirming decisions, and agreeing the way forward to provide a SharePoint solution. These are also useful for brainstorming sessions, where new ideas are required to solve collaborative and information challenges. A workshop, therefore, is not necessarily a training medium; however, you can use them to impart information about SharePoint features and tools. More information concerning workshops is detailed in the "Managing workshops" section of Chapter 11. |
| E-learning | E-learning allows users to learn anywhere, usually at any time, but the user must be preconfigured to access the e-learning service. E-learning can be CD-based, network-based, Internet-based, or intranet-based. Typically, at the end of an e-learning course, there is a test to confirm the learner's knowledge of the subject. |
| Certification programs | Microsoft certification is an industry standard that is recognized worldwide. Those who earn Microsoft certification have access to a number of benefits. Several certifications are available, including Microsoft Certified Professional (MCP), Microsoft Certified Trainer (MCT), Microsoft Office Specialist (MOS), Microsoft Certified Solutions Expert (MCSE), Microsoft Certified Solutions Master (MCSM), Microsoft Certified Technology Specialist (MCTS), Microsoft Certified IT Professional (MCITP), Microsoft Certified Professional Developer (MCPD), and Microsoft Certified Master (MCM). For more information concerning these certifications, visit *http://www.microsoft.com/learning/en/us/sharepoint-certification.aspx#fbid=qME-HIWAPQQ.* |

*Each of the training methods needs to be considered before it becomes part of the training model. For more information on how to create a training model, see the "Creating a SharePoint training model" section of Chapter 5.*

The training method provided will influence how learners absorb information on how to use the SharePoint solution. Keep in mind that you do not necessarily have to decide between, for example, e-learning and classroom, classroom and online, or on-demand and e-learning. A blended option may be an ideal solution. For example, e-learning can provide the foundational knowledge about a SharePoint topic, and follow-up classroom sessions can enable learners to get more in-depth information and allow for practice and application of skills. To help you decide, there are several factors to consider:

- **Is the audience in various geographical locations?** If the audience is dispersed geographically, then you may consider online training because that will enable you to train them more efficiently than in-person training, which requires coordinating travel arrangements, increasing costs for accommodation, and other costs.
- **Will the SharePoint solution change frequently, and/or is the impact of SharePoint solution changes going to be significant on the users?** It is typically more difficult to make content updates to e-learning than to instructor materials. So if the SharePoint solution is likely to change frequently, or the change in the SharePoint solution will require a steep learning curve (in the change from SharePoint 2007 and Microsoft Office 2007 to SharePoint 2013 and Office 2013, for instance), you may wish to consider face-to-face classroom training.
- **Do your users need to focus on their SharePoint skills?** If you need a method of testing knowledge of the SharePoint solution, then on-demand e-learning courses can be quite effective. However, consider that a classroom environment provides more opportunities for practice and discussions.

- **Can you get groups of learners into a classroom?** If there is going to be difficulty in getting groups of learners into classroom sessions, consider e-learning as a way for learners to complete training.
- **Do you have training resources available, such as training rooms with computer equipment?** If there are limited training resources, consider e-learning because instructor-led training requires enough room to accommodate all your learners and a facilitator.

**Tip** An article describing more about the training impact covering support and information worker roles can be found at *http://www.sharepointgeoff.com/articles-2/training/*.

Users will pose support queries related to Office products, particularly because virtually all interaction with content in SharePoint will come from the use of Microsoft products such as Microsoft Word, Excel, PowerPoint, Outlook, and even more specialized software such as Microsoft Project, Visio, and OneNote, among many others. Another aid to sustainable User Adoption is to focus on training workers on key Office tools (as mentioned in the "Sustaining SharePoint support" section earlier in this chapter). This is an excellent method in ensuring information workers remain productive with Office, to make them more empowered, and to give them a sense of achievement. You should advise information workers of the MOS certification, of which SharePoint is part.

**More Info** For more information about the MOS certification, visit *http://www.certiport.com/Portal/desktopdefault.aspx?page=common/pagelibrary/mos2010.html*.

By workers taking such a course, benefits include helping SharePoint service delivery. This occurs because the worker has become more capable, and this capability extends to his or her peers. This aids SharePoint support because then you have a line of defense in terms of resolving Office queries. SharePoint is part of the Microsoft Office certification, meaning that information workers can become Microsoft Office Specialist SharePoint certified. This means that they have the ability not only to learn the product, but to add it to their skillset as valid proof that they can use and pass on their SharePoint skills.

A rich User Adoption strategy is required to sustain and boost adoption. You will need to take actions to sustain and drive the User Adoption strategy over the life of the SharePoint solution. The term "Go live" (a project-centric approach) does mean that User Adoption has been sustained. Changing user behavior is the key to sustaining User Adoption.

Here are a number of practical techniques that you can use to ensure that User Adoption is sustainable:

- **Get the right people to lead the User Adoption program.** Delivery of the SharePoint solution is carried out by a delivery team, but they are not necessarily the right people to drive the User Adoption program. You should build your bank of SharePoint champions, identify the relevant customers who can influence other users, and run a communications exercise using the techniques described in creating the communications plan. This is further described in the "Developing Communication Plans" section of Chapter 4, "Preparing SharePoint Solution User Adoption." While training and communication are important, they alone do not provide User Adoption unless there is action. That requires human resources. Engage with a consultant or outside User Adoption experts to provide support.

- **Appoint an owner for SharePoint Solution User Adoption.** Your SharePoint sponsor, who has the authority, accountability, and the right resources, can help sustain User Adoption of the SharePoint solution. They need to be motivated. They need to support SharePoint champions and key customers, and they need to be able to help provide resources, such as aid to training and support.

- **Create measures of success.** Set measurements in terms of value, return on investment (ROI), and specific SharePoint success. Use SharePoint surveys, brown-bag sessions, and other communication channels to measure success. Create dashboards showing analytical data (for example, visits to SharePoint sites). Set goals; for example, set competitions for SharePoint champions and be prepared to reward them for their achievements. Showcase success stories, again by using any available communication channels.

- **Continue to analyze the organization.** Set up review points to examine policies, processes, communication activities, and changes in user attitudes. Good options to investigate the analysis and make decisions include the Governance committee, SharePoint champions, and the SharePoint sponsor. Modify and re-execute the User Adoption strategy based on key changes.

- **Examine user adopter types and remove barriers from laggards continually.** Laggards are users who do not like change. As the SharePoint solution evolves, so do changes in them.

- **User Adoption is not the end; it is personal and a constant process.** Training and communications are simply a part of User Adoption. You need to drive excitement, facilitate change, and empower, monitor, and assist users continually.

- **Identify SharePoint champions.** These come from the business, and have the objective of helping to develop SharePoint solutions and then evangelizing them.

- **Examine collaboration scenarios.** Look at structured and ad-hoc collaboration; examine what Microsoft tools are being used and how they are used.

- **Get users to change.** Start small. Keep things simple. Focus on the key elements of the SharePoint solution. Create methods that allow people to want to embrace the solution. Evangelize key SharePoint features, and engage with SharePoint features such as Newsfeed, Community Site, Search, and Alerts. Note that you must ensure that you understand the customer culture. Inject fun into using SharePoint: create competitions and other events and give rewards based on SharePoint usage and creativity.

- **Create and sustain a training model.** This must meet the users' requirements, so that you can ensure that they are comfortable with the solution being provided.

- **Create and sustain a communications plan.** Manage key messages and use brown-bag sessions, workshops, newsletters, and announcements to keep the users up to date with SharePoint as it evolves.
- **Ensure that SharePoint support is ready.** Without SharePoint support, there is no User Adoption and no Governance. You must ensure that SharePoint support is adequately prepared and resourced. The "Sustaining SharePoint support" section earlier in this chapter lists practical techniques for achieving those goals.
- **Listen for feedback, monitor the situation, and showcase results.** Create measures to understand the effectiveness of your User Adoption strategy. Use analytics to prove buy-in from users. Showcase the feedback from surveys.

*User Adoption strategy techniques are described in the "Building User Adoption strategies" section of Chapter 4, Chapter 5, and the "Managing change in the SharePoint delivery program" section of Chapter 6, "SharePoint delivery program considerations."*

*A SharePoint sponsor is crucial in any SharePoint delivery program. For more information on how to define your SharePoint sponsor, see the "Engaging your sponsor and stakeholders" section in Chapter 3, "Planning SharePoint solution delivery."*

The thread throughout the book concerning User Adoption and Governance is *communication* and *delivery*. To do this, you must listen to your users and empathize with them, because it is their vision that you must strive to achieve. This starts the very first time you meet a potential customer who requires a SharePoint solution. You must really get to know your customers first, instead of simply delivering SharePoint and then attempting to "glue" User Adoption to that delivery. A good example of understanding the audience is the following scenario.

*Scenario 2: I attended a meeting whose purpose was to decide the price of delivering SharePoint to a large organization. The meeting was held in a spectacular, luxurious hotel, and yet the SharePoint sponsor arrived in a pair of jeans and a T-shirt. Wearing my formal suit and tie, I felt rather jealous of his comfortable clothes. When I heard his negotiating starting point, my discomfort increased. His position was so extreme that it threatened to derail the negotiations before they had even begun. He wanted a price at least three times lower than the very best price I could offer. Fortunately, I had discussed this eventuality with my colleagues before the meeting. We had performed extensive research about the SharePoint sponsor we were meeting with and had also made a point of talking with a number of people who had dealt with him in the past. This was invaluable because those people had given us a blow-by-blow account of their initial meetings and how the relationship developed over time. So from what we knew of the SharePoint sponsor, we had anticipated the possibility of a completely unreasonable opening position. Therefore, we were ready with all the information necessary to demonstrate that his starting point was commercially unviable for us without him losing face. Because we were honest about our commercial position, we established a position of trust in response to his opening gambit. We knew that this would strengthen the relationship because he was actually very astute commercially, and he actually expected us to rebuff his offer. The ultimate benefit was that we struck a very fair deal that enabled both groups to walk away feeling that they had achieved success in the negotiation. This has also resulted in a strong relationship based on trust and respect, whereby other projects have been brought to the table as a result of this initial meeting.*

## Summary

User Adoption is accomplished through a delivery program and requires a continued delivery team covering platform Governance, business engagement, User Adoption, and SharePoint service delivery (support and maintenance). Like this entire book, this chapter has detailed techniques that can be used to sustain User Adoption and Governance.

To finish, here are some key messages concerning SharePoint delivery and why you need to use a structured method of delivery that is defined, measured, planned, and executed.

- SharePoint solution delivery is not about technology, but about business processes.

  Many people believe that a new, shiny SharePoint solution is a magic potion that will fix whatever glitches there are in the way people work in the organization. They assume that after installation, profits will be up, downtime will be decreased, and productivity will go through the roof. However, this is often not the case. If the current process for tracking an invoice or managing customer relations is inefficient, simply putting a SharePoint solution in place will merely speed up a bad process. For example, customers will still wind up getting duplicate mailings, but they'll be delivered in two days rather than three. The first step in any SharePoint solution delivery is to find out how things are really being done in a department, not just what the training manual describes as the process. When you've assured that you have done that, changes can be made to design the optimal process to achieve success using the new technology.

- SharePoint solution acquisition is more about people than technology.

  SharePoint adoption requires that users alter the way that they have always done things. So users must leave their comfort zone. Because people don't usually like change, they tend to resist and complain, and sometimes they even leave the organization. Unless the users are involved in the planning from the beginning, they see a new SharePoint solution as something done to them, and they feel powerless. The people in an organization who are doing the most work with the current system are invaluable assets in the task of making their job more efficient. Make sure that you define SharePoint Governance, engage with your users using User Adoption strategies (both from the business and technical sides of the organization), and look critically at user requirements from both camps.

- Wisely choose and train a cross-organizational team to set goals and priorities.

  The best and the brightest from each department make good working partners with senior management when choosing new systems. That way, no one gets surprised by the costs in terms of money or effort when implementation time comes around. Creating a cooperative atmosphere, of course, is a key to making this work. Buy-in doesn't happen automatically. Often, the attitudes of people lower in the organizational hierarchy are that they are considered merely window dressing and that the senior managers will make the final decisions regardless of their input. A skilled facilitator is necessary to get past this distrust. You need an evangelistic SharePoint delivery manager to make this happen. Or, depending on the scale of the technology release (that is, if SharePoint and other new technologies are involved), you might need a third-party consultant to enhance client understanding and help create a vision.

- Establish good protocols for interviewing the client and users.

  It's easy for the user or client to be overwhelmed by slick SharePoint presentations, particularly when they are talking about things that most people don't completely understand. Showmanship can get in the way of demonstrating real capabilities. Unless the review team is judging each vendor against the same list of needs, with the same understanding of the significance of each rating, likeability can prevail over capability. Make sure that you use people who can interact with users. Business analysts are very important in helping you elicit responses from the client and users. The purpose of interviewing is to enable both sides to learn—the client and users learn about the platform, and the interviewers learn about what the client and users do and what they need from SharePoint. Generating a list of requirements is hard work. If the team hasn't bonded before these discussions, a power struggle may well ensue, with each faction holding out for its own "essential" specifications. An outsider with no ties to any internal group is usually better able to bring about consensus than someone from the inside. The overarching goal is to produce a list of standards that support the mission of the enterprise. The more immediate goal is to create unity that transcends the narrowness of each participant's vision of that mission. The team meeting that follows each presentation must reinforce the common purpose while giving everyone a chance to voice their understanding (or lack of it), as well as their concerns.

- Obtain real agreement on user and client requirements.

  Meeting SharePoint user requirements relies on finding multiple solutions to multi-criteria problems. Every business wants a high-quality, easy-to-use SharePoint implementation that happens instantly and costs next to nothing! Of course, that doesn't exist. It's the actual frontline users who will be responsible for making the new system add value to the enterprise. Even if the management team does not provide their requirements, the project will proceed faster, more efficiently, and with a better result if the frontline people have a real voice in the selection of features and other specifics about the platform. Getting their buy-in at the start seems like a delay, but it results in a shorter, better project in the long run.

- Identify system requirements without alienating users.

  Getting agreement on system and user requirements is an art as well as a science. It involves establishing productive communication between people who encounter many obstacles to achieving clarity. It is a frustrating process, but when done right, it is the foundation for success. When the people who will be most affected by the change are motivated to help the project succeed and see the project's value to them as well as to the organization, meeting their requirements will be an exciting design adventure, not a boring and confusing chore. The key is training the parties in terms of communication and team effort. With both your knowledge and practical exercises, you can build a team that will succeed.

- Work with users and the SharePoint sponsor during delivery.

  Success means that everyone succeeds. The users, SharePoint sponsor, stakeholders, implementation partners, and hardware vendors must all achieve common success—if they don't, all will fail. When there is agreement on vendors and implementation partners, the road is much smoother. When the vendors, implementation partners, and organization teams are adversaries, the road leads to disaster. Everyone must believe that success requires everyone to succeed.

- Prepare the users to adapt to the changes required by the new system.

  Change management is a process, not an event. It should occur continuously throughout the course of the procurement and implementation. Your SharePoint sponsor should not assume that everyone is going to accept the new system without a great deal of preparation. The selection and implementation teams will be consumed for a significant amount of time with the task of bringing the project to completion. However, their efforts won't even appear on the mental radar screen of most users unless there is a deliberate effort to raise awareness of the coming change. Because people don't like change in general, it's hard to introduce a particular change without changing the initial attitudes that people have about the concept. This is the first and most essential level of change management. After that has been addressed, people are more apt to be open to the detailed changes that will be required. Define Governance and User Adoption strategies to ensure that users will engage with SharePoint continually. As SharePoint grows and becomes more of an enterprise platform, the more users will feel comfortable with it, become more productive, and feel that they have a stake in the future of SharePoint in the organization.

# Index

## A

## B

# C

## D

## E

# H



# I

## J



## K



## L

## M



## N



## O

# P

# Q



# R

## S

## T

## U

## V



## W

# About the author

**GEOFF EVELYN** is a Microsoft SharePoint Most Valuable Professional (MVP) with over 25 years of experience in information systems technology. He has worked in the education, service delivery, IT support, government, military, banking, oil, and gas industries, and has been focusing his efforts on SharePoint since 2003. Geoff is a member of the IAP Software Development Practice Journal Editorial Board, a fellow of the Institute of Analysts and Programmers, a fellow of the Institute of Computer Technology, a member of the Institute of Management Information Systems and Engineering Technology, and a Prince 2 practitioner.

He also is certified as a Microsoft Certified Desktop Support Technician (MCDST), a Microsoft Certified Solutions Developer (MCSD), a Microsoft Certified Technology Specialist (MCTS), a Microsoft Certified IT Professional (MCITP), and a Microsoft Office Specialist (MOS). Geoff is the author of *Managing and Implementing SharePoint 2010 Projects,* the *MOS 2010 Study Guide for Microsoft Office SharePoint,* the *MOS 2013 Study Guide,* and co-author of the *MOS 2010 Study Guide for Microsoft Word Expert, Excel, Access, and SharePoint,* all titles published by Microsoft Press.

Lightning Source UK Ltd.
Milton Keynes UK
UKOW01f2300091013

218758UK00004B/26/P

9 780735 671645